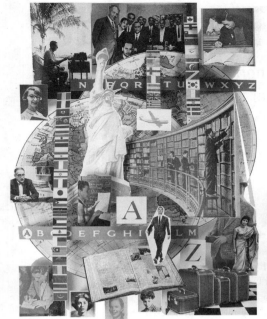

GH00937970

SEVENTH EDITION

ELT GUIDE

ISBN 0 951 4576 67

Published by
EFL Ltd., 9 Hope Street, Douglas, Isle of Man
IM1 1AQ, British Isles

Printed by
Mannin Printing, 28-30 Spring Valley
Industrial Estate, Braddan,
IOM, British Isles.

Editor Paul Lakin

Marketing Shaun Collins

Advertising And Distribution Julie Garner, Kirsten Wilson

Desk Top Publishing Sheldon Pink

Publishers John Gorner and Daniel Ward

Contributors Melanie Butler, Rupert Cocke, Chris Graham, Antony Hughes, Paul Lakin, Norman Renshaw, Barry Tomalin, Mathew Hancock, Dan Ward.

Cover Illustration Richard Caldicott

Acknowledgements We would like to thank the following for their invaluable help: Anglo-Mexican Cultural Institute, ARELS, Sally Avens, Bluefeather School of Languages, British Institute Indonesia, The British Council, Dickens Institute Uruguay, ELICOS, ELTA Cologne, Nigel de Gruchy, Finnish-British Society, Tom Heap, IATEFL, International House, JALT, The JET Scheme, Samantha Khandker, Richard Johnson, Roy Kingsbury, Sarah Lampert, Linguarama Nederland, Helen Mattacott Cousins, NZEIL, Lynette Murphy O'Dwyer, Poobie Naidoo, Helen Panzarino, Clare Parry, Martin Prendergast, Carol Read, RELSA, Salisbury School of Languages, Saxoncourt Recruitment, Shane English School in Taiwan, Geoff Smith, TESOL, Jane Spilsbury, Trailfinders, Trinity College, UCLES.

Acronyms Used In The Guide

One thing the English Language Teaching world is not short of is acronyms. The following are the most common which you will encounter in this Guide.

ACELS: Advisory Council on English Language Schools

AAIEP: American Association of Intensive English Programs

ARELS: Association of Recognised English Language Services

ACTDEC: Accreditation Council for TESOL Distance Education Courses

ATT: Association for Teacher Training

BALT: British Association of Language Teachers

BASELT: British Association of State English Language Teaching

BATQ1: British Association of Tesol Qualifying Institutions

BC: British Council

BTEC: Business and Technical Education Council

CALL: Computer Assisted Language Learning

CEELT: Cambridge Examination in English for Language Teachers
An UCLES/RSA exam for non-native teachers of English.

CILT: Centre for Information on Language Teaching and Research

CIS: British Council Central Information Service

COTE: Certificate for Overseas Teachers of English
Initial qualification for English teachers who are non-native speakers.

CTEFLA: Certificate in the Teaching of English as a Foreign Language to Adults
One of the many names for the UCLES/RSA teacher training course/exam.

DOS: Director of Studies

DOTE: Diploma for Overseas Teachers of English
Advanced teacher training course for non-native speakers of English.

DTEFLA: Diploma in the Teaching of English as a Foreign Language to Adults
One of the many names for the advanced UCLES/RSA teacher training course/exam.

EAP: English for Academic Purposes
The study, or teaching, of English with specific reference to an academic course.

E2L: English as a Second Language

ECIS: European Council of International Schools

EEP: East European Partnership

EFL: English as a Foreign Language
The general UK term, although in the US and Australia it is used to refer to teaching abroad only.

ELICOS: English Language Intensive Courses to Overseas Students
The general Australian term.

ELT: English Language Teaching or Training
A general international term used widely by publishers.

ESL: English as a Second Language
The general US term for any English language teaching within the country, but in the UK and Australia it refers to teaching English for immigrants.

ESOL: English for Speakers of Other Languages
Another general US term.

ESP: English for Specific Purposes
Teaching or studying the English necessary for a specific task.

IATEFL: International Association of Teachers of English as a Foreign Language

IELTS: International English Language Testing System
Exam for non-native speakers of English developed by UCLES and the British Council.

JALT: Japanese Association for Language Teaching

JET: Japanese Exchange and Teaching Programme

LCCIEB: London Chamber of Commerce and Industry Examinations Board

NATESOL: National Association of Teachers of English for Speakers of Other Languages
US teachers association.

NATECLA: National Association for the Teaching of English and Community Languages to Adults

NEAS: National ELICOS Accreditation Scheme

OSB: Overseas Service Bureau

PGCE: Post Graduate Certificate in Education
The main UK teaching qualification - essential for work in the state sector.

QTS: Qualified Teacher Status
State teaching qualification awarded to a teacher who has qualified and gained one year's experience.

RELSA: Recognised English Language Schools Associations
Irish organisation of independent language schools.

RSA: Royal Society of Arts
Examination body which, in conjunction with UCLES, has developed some of the key TEFL teacher training exams.

SIETAR: Society of International English Cultural Training and Research

TEC: Training and Enterprise Council

TEFL, TESL, TESOL
The prefix (T) simply stands for Teaching. TESOL is also the name of an American association of English Language teachers.

TOEFL: Test of English as a Foreign Language
Key US exam for students of English.

UCLES: University of Cambridge Local Examinations Syndicate
Examination body which, in conjunction with the RSA, has developed some of the key TEFL teacher training courses and exams.

UNV: United Nations Volunteers

VSO: Voluntary Services Overseas

Introduction

Writing this introduction brings back many happy memories of my own time as a teacher of English as a foreign language, firstly in Spain in the mid 1960's where I worked at the Berlitz School, Santander. Following that, I then spent two years in Paris, teaching English but also taking the opportunity to improve my French by enrolling on courses at The Sorbonne. I have no doubt that the experience broadened my outlook, enhanced my teaching skills, deepened my understanding of English and hopefully was of some benefit to my students!

The best way to learn a language is to teach it. That is one reason why I encourage people picking up this guide to take the plunge and train to teach English to students of other nations, if you are not already working in this field. If you then choose to work abroad you will find the experience of living and working in another country an enriching one. As well as learning the language of your host country, you will learn more than you imagine about your own language, and how to communicate more effectively.

English is the primary international language. It is the major international means of communication for trade, finance, industry and commerce. Teachers of English as a foreign language are doing their country a service as well as teaching the students who benefit from their effort. In so many sectors of employment, especially trade and finance, the concept of the global village is becoming more of a reality. For students across the world a command of the English language will be vital in their careers.

I am pleased to recommend the ELT Guide to people involved in or considering teaching English as a foreign language. The guide is wide ranging and informative and will be of assistance to anyone interested in this area. I wish the Guide and its readers every success.

Nigel de Gruchy,
The UK's General Secretary of The National Association of School Masters and Union of Women Teachers

How to use the guide

The Guide is for anyone considering, or already involved in, English Language Training; prospective teachers; training and personnel managers; publishers; consultants as well as suppliers needing to know about the profession but different sections will naturally be more relevant to some groups than others.

PROSPECTIVE TEACHERS

Turn straight to **Section One – Becoming a Teacher** – for anyone considering EFL/ESL teaching as a career, or as a short-term means of working while you travel, this section maps out a route by providing clear advice and information on basic teaching courses and qualifications. Once you have read this, go to **Section Four – World English** to find out what opportunities there are for you in the countries of your choice. If you are relatively sure that EFL is the career for you, **Section Three** shows how to go about getting a job and **Section Two** will help you plan a long-term career strategy with advice on further qualifications and training.

TRAINING/PERSONNEL MANAGERS OR CONSULTANTS

Start with **Section Five – Business English**, which examines the commercial benefits of language training and English in particular. It is especially relevant for the training manager of a small to medium-sized company, which is considering investing in language training but wants to ensure the company gets value for money. Turn to **Section Three** for information on Homestay courses. Check the listings in **Section Four** for local training providers.
To get a real understanding of what you can expect from teachers, read through **Sections One and Two** which show what teaching qualifications actually mean and assists you in specifying your training requirements.

TEACHERS/EFL PROFESSIONALS

If you do not have a qualification, go to **Section One.** If you want to improve your career prospects, **Section Two** explains how further qualifications will help. For ideas about teaching and associated jobs turn to **Section Three.**
Section Five will give you an insight into the hugely important Business English market, which can provide some of the most exciting career options.
And if you are looking for a job anywhere in the world, **Section Four** has opportunities in over 100 countries.

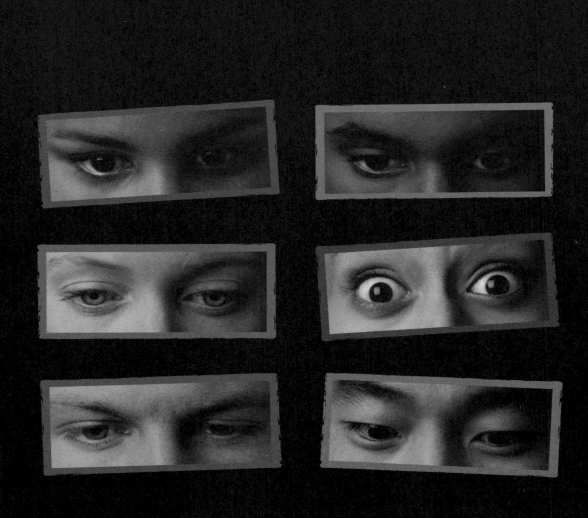

Don't let your students get caught off guard.

Contents

Section One: Becoming A Teacher

8   Routes Into EFL Teaching
9   Can I Teach EFL?
10 Starting Out
11 Basic Qualifications
13 RSA/Cambridge Certificate (CTEFLA) Courses
16 Trinity College Certificate In TESOL Courses
18 Initial Qualifications In Ireland
19 Getting Qualified In The USA And Canada
20 Getting Qualified In Australia And New Zealand
21 Overseas RSA/Cambridge Certificate (CTEFLA) Courses
25 ATT And RELSA Certificate Courses
26 Overseas Trinity College Certificate In TESOL And COTE
27 Introductory Courses
31 In-House Training
32 Distance Training In TESOL
34 Distance Learning Courses

Section Two: Further Qualifications

52 The Academic Ladder
53 How Will Qualifications Help Me?
54 RSA/Cambridge Diploma (DTEFLA) Courses
55 Trinity Licentiate Diploma In TESOL Courses
56 Overseas RSA/Cambridge Diploma (DTEFLA) Courses
57 UK University Courses
58 UK University/College Certificate Courses
59 UK University Diploma Courses
61 UK University Degree Courses
61 MA's In North America
62 US University Certificate Courses
63 Canadian University Certificate Courses
64 US Masters Degree Courses
68 MA's In The UK
69 UK Masters Degree Courses
74 MA's In Australia And New Zealand
75 Australian University Certificate And Diploma Courses
76 Australasian University Masters Degree Courses
77 Specialising
78 Teaching Young Learners
80 Teaching Business English
81 Short Courses
82 RSA/Cambridge CEELT Courses
83 RSA/Cambridge DOTE Courses
87 Teaching Business English Courses

Section 3: Finding A Job

99   A Career In The Life Of
100 Working In The UK and Ireland
101 Summer Schools
105 Homestay
106 Working In North America
107 Working In Australia And New Zealand
108 Volunteering
109 Starting Your Own Language Business
111 TEFL And Beyond
113 How To Find Work

Section 4: World English

116 A New Career In A New Town
117 Medical Advice
121 Financial Advice
123 The European Union
137 The Rest Of Europe
146 North Africa And The Middle East
152 Sub-Saharan Africa
154 The Far East
162 The Rest Of Asia
164 Latin America And The Caribbean

Section 5: Business English

174 What Is Business English?
175 What Kind Of Business English?
178 Assessing The Language Needs Of Your Company
179 The Training Option
181 Business English Courses
189 The Technology Option
190 Recruiting English Speakers

Reference Section

196 Recognition Schemes
197 An Insider's Guide: Methodology
199 An Insider's Guide: The Internet
203 ELT Book Suppliers
205 Conference Calendar
206 RSA/Cambridge And Trinity College Centres
207 Addresses
215 Index Of Advertisers
216 Index

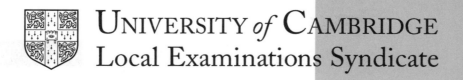

Becoming A Teacher

There are many routes to becoming a teacher of English. Each has its own advantages. The following pages explain how to select the best route for you with details of many of the initial training courses available throughout the world.

8 Routes Into EFL Teaching

9 Can I Teach EFL?

10 Starting Out

11 Basic Qualifications

13 RSA/Cambridge Certificate (CTEFLA) Courses

16 Trinity College Certificate In TESOL Courses

18 Initial Qualifications In Ireland

19 Getting Qualified In The USA And Canada

20 Getting Qualified In Australia And New Zealand

21 Overseas RSA/Cambridge Certificate (CTEFLA) Courses

25 ATT And RELSA Certificate Courses

26 Overseas Trinity College Certificate In TESOL And COTE Courses

27 Introductory Courses

31 In-House Training

32 Distance Training In TESOL

34 Distance Learning Courses

Routes Into EFL Teaching

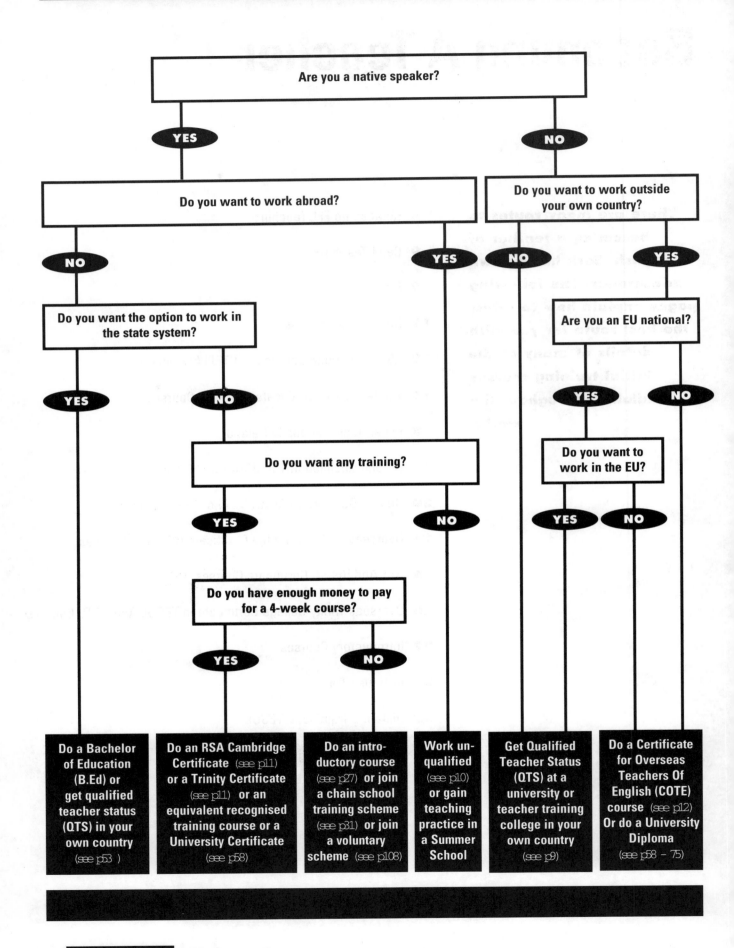

Are you a native speaker?

YES → Do you want to work abroad?

NO → Do you want to work outside your own country?

Do you want to work abroad?

NO → Do you want the option to work in the state system?

YES → (continues to "Do you want any training?" branch)

Do you want to work outside your own country?

NO → Get Qualified Teacher Status (QTS) at a university or teacher training college in your own country (see p9)

YES → Are you an EU national?

Do you want the option to work in the state system?

YES → Do a Bachelor of Education (B.Ed) or get qualified teacher status (QTS) in your own country (see p53)

NO → Do you want any training?

Are you an EU national?

YES → Do you want to work in the EU?

NO → Do a Certificate for Overseas Teachers Of English (COTE) course (see p12) Or do a University Diploma (see p58 – 75)

Do you want any training?

YES → Do you have enough money to pay for a 4-week course?

NO → Work un-qualified (see p10) or gain teaching practice in a Summer School

Do you want to work in the EU?

YES → Get Qualified Teacher Status (QTS) at a university or teacher training college in your own country (see p9)

NO → Do a Certificate for Overseas Teachers Of English (COTE) course (see p12) Or do a University Diploma (see p58 – 75)

Do you have enough money to pay for a 4-week course?

YES → Do an RSA Cambridge Certificate (see p11) or a Trinity Certificate (see p11) or an equivalent recognised training course or a University Certificate (see p58)

NO → Do an introductory course (see p27) or join a chain school training scheme (see p31) or join a voluntary scheme (see p108)

Final boxes:

- **Do a Bachelor of Education (B.Ed) or get qualified teacher status (QTS) in your own country** (see p53)
- **Do an RSA Cambridge Certificate** (see p11) **or a Trinity Certificate** (see p11) **or an equivalent recognised training course or a University Certificate** (see p58)
- **Do an introductory course** (see p27) **or join a chain school training scheme** (see p31) **or join a voluntary scheme** (see p108)
- **Work un-qualified** (see p10) **or gain teaching practice in a Summer School**
- **Get Qualified Teacher Status (QTS) at a university or teacher training college in your own country** (see p9)
- **Do a Certificate for Overseas Teachers Of English (COTE) course** (see p12) **Or do a University Diploma** (see p58 – 75)

Can I Teach EFL?

Before looking at the courses, qualifications and careers available in TEFL, here are the answers to some of the most common questions that new or potential teachers ask.

Do I have to get a qualification?

No. There are some countries where you can teach English unqualified (see p10). Remember that schools will pay more and generally treat you better if you are qualified.

Is it better to look for a job once I reach my destination?

It is often easier to get a job if you are already in the country where you want to work. Check in the local English language newspaper for job adverts or approach individual schools (see p123-171). Note that some countries will only offer work permits to teachers who have been offered work before they enter the country.

I am already a teacher. Can I teach EFL?

If you want to teach in the state educational system, you must achieve QTS (Qualified Teacher Status) such as a BEd or PGCE from the UK or State Certification in the US. If your qualification is not in the field of English Language teaching you will need a further qualification.

What is the basic TEFL qualification?

At present there are no standard international EFL qualifications. In recognised schools in the UK, only teachers with an externally validated certificate are seen as 'qualified' teachers. These are widely recognised and the courses last about a month. There are alternatives, some of which will be regarded highly by employers.

Are there shorter courses in TEFL?

There are various introductory courses in TEFL which give you a grounding even if not a formal qualification. They are worth considering if you do not want to commit yourself to a long time in TEFL. They also tend to be cheaper. Some schools run their own courses for unqualified teachers that train you in the methods of that particular school, which is worthwhile if you wish to work for that organisation (see p31). It may also be worth considering a course which combines distance learning with a short course.

Where can I train?

You can take TEFL courses throughout the world (see p21-26). The price reflects the economy and/or popularity of the country.

Do I have to have teaching experience to do a TEFL course?

No, although many people do teach first before doing a course.

Do I need to be a graduate to get on a course?

Most courses demand some sort of further education qualification, not necessarily a degree. Non-graduates may be required to do an introductory course. Some countries demand a degree before issuing a work permit.

How can I pay for my course?

In most countries QTS is paid for by the government. All full-time overseas students can work in Australia (see p107) and there are often teaching assistant jobs in the US and Canada. In the UK you cannot get a grant to do a teacher training course at a private institution, although some further education colleges offer subsidised courses and, if you have been unemployed for more than six months, you may be eligible for free training. (Contact your local DSS.) You may be eligible for a Career Development Loan - a government-backed scheme whereby banks make unsecured loans at preferential rates to students - call 0800-585505 for details.

Am I too old to teach EFL?

Many teachers start after retiring from their traditional careers. Indeed, if you have worked in a specialist field such as banking, you may have the expertise to teach ESP (English for Special Purposes), teaching French stockbrokers, for example (see p80).

Can I teach EFL if English isn't my mother tongue?

Yes, although most of these job opportunities will be within your own country unless you are completely fluent.

Can I train by post?

Some courses are offered partly by correspondence, partly with on-site training. Courses which are totally correspondence courses are not recognised by many employers (see p32).

Will the place I train at find me a job?

Most establishments will give you advice and some may offer you employment, especially if you have a good grade.

How much can I expect to earn?

This can vary greatly from country to country and school to school (see p123-171).

How do I know a school is reputable?

There are organisations that monitor schools. It is often useful to contact the local British Council or TESOL affiliate. Elsewhere, contact the local teaching union or relevant association.

What will my career prospects be?

There are further qualifications which can lead to specialist jobs (see p77). There are also spin-off careers like publishing (see p111).

Starting Out

Even if you have no formal TEFL qualifications, as a native English speaker you can still find teaching work almost anywhere.

The better jobs (in terms of pay and conditions) are almost always restricted to qualified teachers

here was a time when being able to speak English was the only qualification you needed to teach it. Many a world tour was funded by a bit of teaching on the side. With initiative you can still find work almost anywhere, however secure jobs at established schools now demand a qualification.

The EFL market is becoming much more professional and competitive leading to more rigorous teacher selection, especially in the well-established schools. The better jobs (in terms of pay and conditions) are almost always restricted to qualified teachers. In the more popular areas of the world even relatively poorly paid jobs can still demand a qualification. However, although the majority of EFL teachers are qualified and most language schools nowadays insist on formal qualifications and a minimum of experience, there are still job opportunities for unqualified native English speakers. How easy it is to find them depends on where you are and when you're there.

Western Europe

Many summer schools in the UK will consider graduates without an EFL certificate. A degree in modern languages or a Postgraduate Certificate of Education may be enough to persuade some. The emphasis is on you, however, to sell yourself.

The JET scheme recruits around 500 teachers each year

There are possibilities on the European Continent if you have business experience and can speak the native language. Your chances will obviously be better away from the more popular cities.

In Italy there are a number of language schools which train teachers themselves and do not require a formal qualification. Greece has always had a large number of jobs for unqualified teachers. It is also one of the few countries where non-native speakers with good English can find work.

In Southern Europe some language schools are more flexible with regard to qualifications. Some schools in Spain, for example, employ unqualified teachers to help state school students with their English exams. You will need to be relatively proficient in Spanish to get this kind of work.

Eastern Europe

Eastern Europe's new, dynamic market offers more opportunities for working unqualified than the West. There is a huge demand for English language teachers in both state and private schools in Poland, Hungary, the Czech Republic, the Baltic States and the Ukraine. but remember local teachers are often impressively trained and qualified.

The Far East

Many countries in the Far East employ unqualified teachers, yet few recruit from abroad. In Thailand, for instance, many schools recruit native English speakers on a temporary basis as they pass through the country. Wages are low, however, if you are unqualified. Until now Japan, Korea and Taiwan provided work for unqualified teachers, particularly those with experience in business. However, legislation on illegal workers has tightened up and unqualified teachers may fall into this category.

Teaching work is available, qualified or not, in Egypt, Morocco, Turkey and the larger Latin American countries as long as you are there and offering your services.

Government programmes

Many governments run programmes which accept unqualified teachers. Japan's Exchange and Teaching Programme (JET) is one such scheme. You can apply through any Japanese embassy and do not need experience or a teaching qualification, though candidates should be native English speakers under 35 with a university degree. The JET scheme recruits around 500 teachers each year to work in Japanese secondary schools. The salary is good (around UK£18,000) but the cost of living is very high. Air fares are also paid. Recruitment for the scheme begins in October for placement in the following July.

Basic Qualifications

A qualification greatly enhances your chances of finding a job. However, there is more than one type of qualification available and some are more useful than others.

Most employers consider certificates from courses lasting at least four weeks full-time to be the minimum requirement

nyone can teach English once their proficiency in the language reaches a high level, and it is often said that those who have learned English themselves are better placed to teach it. However, native speakers have a natural advantage and, indeed, a certain cachet when it comes to looking for employment outside their own country. Therefore, this section is aimed mainly at Americans, Britons, Australasians and the Irish.

Probably as a result of the recession, more and more people have been trying to find work in the area of EFL. Interestingly, the percentage of applications for training courses from more mature candidates with experience - such as engineers, bankers or mothers going back to work - has increased dramatically. The objective of most of these people is to find the quickest and cheapest route to a valid teaching qualification that will give them access to teaching jobs in the country of their choice.

Beginners courses can vary from a few days to a few years with corresponding variances in coverage and cost, but most employers consider externally validated certificates resulting from courses lasting at least four weeks full-time and including teaching practice to be the minimum qualification.

The most widely accepted qualifications in Europe are the RSA/Cambridge and Trinity certificates or state Qualified Teacher Status (QTS), preferably with a TEFL component

It is important to remember that most schools only recognise certain qualifications - which ones will vary depending on the school's status and location. Most American teachers will have completed an MA course (see p62), which will obviously cover considerably more than a four-week course. However it may not involve teaching practice, which is of fundamental importance to many employers and an important component of most certificate courses. The most widely accepted qualifications in Europe are the RSA/Cambridge and Trinity certificates or state Qualified Teacher Status (QTS), preferably with a TEFL component. These are generally seen as a minimum qualification.

This does not necessarily mean that alternative courses are not good. A qualification of some sort will certainly be considered preferable to no qualification at all. Make sure, though, that your course has a practical element.

At present there is no set policy in European countries towards other TEFL qualifications awarded by institutions in the United States, Canada, Ireland, New Zealand or Australia. This does not mean they are not recognised, but recruitment policy is to take each case as it comes. A teacher will be expected to have completed a course containing a balance of theory and practice. The British Association of TEFL Qualifying Institutions was set up in 1991 and is currently working on validating teaching qualifications within the UK.

Larger organisations such as the British Council, ELS, International House and the Bell Educational Trust would normally require a diploma or QTS in TEFL. The RSA/Cambridge or Trinity certificate may be accepted but only in certain centres, such as in the Middle East where there are relatively few locally qualified teachers. However, teachers already in a particular country should not be put off applying to such organisations if they only have the RSA or Trinity certificate, as recruitment often depends on local management.

Non-EU nationals who hold an RSA/Cambridge or Trinity certificate or QTS should not assume this is an automatic means of getting a job teaching in Europe - they will still need to obtain a work permit.

RSA/Cambridge Certificate

The RSA/Cambridge Certificate (also known as the RSA CTEFLA or the RSA Preparatory certificate) is a four-week intensive course with a strong practical element and an emphasis on teaching practice. It is the most widely recognised and respected basic TEFL qualification internationally. Although based in the UK, there are now 250 centres in 40 countries which run RSA/ Cambridge courses (see pp21-23). There is, for example, a growing number of centres in the USA and Australia. It can be cheaper to take the certificate course overseas than in the UK, though accommodation may be a problem.

The RSA/Cambridge courses are currently being revised. From this year new teachers who have received no previous training in language teaching and have little or no experience will be able to take a Pre-service Certificate in Teaching English to either adults or young learners. There will also be an In-Service Certificate in Teaching English to Young Learners for teachers with limited language teaching experience but no previous training.

These courses are open to native and non-native speakers. The certificate courses aim to develop a practical awareness of learners, the language and language learning materials. Candidates are expected to demonstrate this awareness in their ability to plan and carry out lessons. Teaching practice is an integral part of the course.

Courses are understandably demanding and if you don't have any teaching experience, some background reading is recommended before you embark on one. If you do not have a languages background and are unfamiliar with basic grammatical terms, find out about the tense system and common terminology first.

COTE/DOTE

The RSA/Cambridge COTE (Certificate for Overseas Teachers of English) and DOTE (Diploma for Overseas Teachers of English) are non-native English speaker courses. The courses take regional conditions into account and use local classrooms for teacher training. COTE requires that teachers are roughly at the standard of Cambridge First Certificate. The revised Diploma will merge DOTE and DTEFLA, and neither the new DTEFLA nor the revised COTE will differentiate between native and non-native speakers. See page 26 (COTE) and page 56 (DOTE) for further information on these courses.

Trinity Certificate in TESOL

Trinity College London run the Certificate in TESOL (Teaching English to Speakers of Other Languages). The number of validated centres

offering the course has grown rapidly in recent years. The qualification is now widely recognised worldwide and there is a number of centres outside the UK.

The Trinity syllabus has a basic set of requirements that all its validated centres must meet. However, the course designer in each centre is free to submit his or her own course design to supplement these requirements. This means that individual centres may give a different weighting to certain elements. For example, one course may focus more on phonetics, another on discourse analysis. This degree of flexibility has proven popular with trainees and teacher trainers alike, but check that the focus of the course meets your requirements.

Most Trinity centres also offer pre-sessionals before the one-month or six-week intensive course begins, giving the trainee some basic grounding. Several institutions offer a correspondence module in addition to the 130 tuition hours. The Trinity syllabus may include teaching practice at centres with young learners, and cover the use and design of materials for children.

Trinity College has also developed a course on teaching young learners, called CertTeyl (Certificate in Teaching English to Young Learners). As with the Certificate in TESOL it does not differentiate between native and non-native speakers.

There are a number of other certificate courses of roughly the same level as the RSA and Trinity, which are listed on pages 24-25. They may not be as well known on a global level, but they are often very well respected within their own geographical sphere.

University courses

In addition to degree and diploma courses (see Section Two), universities also run EFL certificate courses (see p59). These can either be independent free-standing courses or a module in a degree or teacher training course. Make sure they contain teaching practice with foreign students, not just with other teachers.

RSA/Cambridge Certificate (CTEFLA) Courses

College	Course length	FT/PT	Fees	Start dates	Entry requirements	Contact	Comments	Max no of students
Anglia Polytechnic University, Cambridge	4 weeks	Full-time	£875	1 July, 29 July	'A' level or equivalent	Anne Dovet	—	15
Anglo Continental School of Language, Bournemouth	4 weeks	Full-time	£905	5/2, 4/3, 19/8	University entrance level. Age 20+	Ms J. Haine	—	10
Angloschool, London	4 weeks	Full-time	£800 (approx)	26 February, 22 April	20+ Degree or good edu. + experience.	David Bartlett	Help with accomodation	8
Basil Paterson, Edinburgh	4 weeks	Full-time	£877 (inc. VAT and Assessment fee	12/2, 11/3, 8/4, 6/5, 3/6, 1/7, 29/7 26/8, 23/9, 21/10, 18/11	2 'A' levels or 4 Highers. Degree preferred	Mary Beresford-Pierse	Full until April	15
Brasshouse Centre, Birmingham	2 terms	Part-time	£900 approximately	October	Interview	Deborah Cobbett	—	16
Bedford College	Sept-March	Part-time	£695 (provisional) £62 for those on benefit (provisional)	23 September	Degree preferred. Min. 2 'A' levels.	Ken Wilford	—	12
The Bell Language School, Cambridge	30 weeks	Part-time	£895 + exam fee	October	University entrance level.	Sue Sheerin	—	15
	4 weeks	Full-time	£895 + exam fee.	Throughout the year	University entrance level.	Sue Sheerin	An intensive course.	15
The Bell Language School, Norwich	4 weeks	Full-time	£895 + exam fee	Throughout the year.	University entrance level.	Sarah Knights	An intensive course	15
Cheltenham International Language Centre	Full-time 5 wks Part-time 9 months	Both	£945 inc. VAT and Cambridge Registration	Throughout the year.	University entrance level. Degree preferred	CTEFLA Course Tutor	An intensive course. Entry by interview	12
Chichester College of Arts, Science and Technology	24 weeks	Part-time	On application	September	As per UCLES	Brenda Pike	—	12
City of Bath College	4 weeks	Full-time	On application	25/3, 19/4, 1/7	University entrance level.	EFL Reception	Campus self catering or accom with family P/T course also available	15
Concorde International, Folkestone	4 weeks	Full-time	£798 + UCLES fee	29/4, 24/5, 3/6, 28/6, 8/7, 2/8, 12/8, 6/9, 9/9, 4/10	20+ Teaching exp. and foreign language pref.	Anne Kennedy	Job offers for successful + overseas contacts	15

RSA/Cambridge Certificate (CTEFLA) Courses

College	Course length	FT/PT	Fees	Start dates	Entry requirements	Contact	Comments	Max no of students
Devon School, Paignton	4 weeks	Full-time	£798	26/2, 6/5, 26/8, contact school for later dates	As UCLES/RSA requirements	Principal	Assistance with accom. and job search	12
Eastbourne College of Arts and Technology	24 weeks or 9 weeks	Part-time	£320	24 wks Sept. 9 wks 15 April	As UCLES/RSA requirements	John Pomeroy	1 or 2 eve/day a week	18
	4 1/2 weeks	Full-time	£320	24 June	As UCLES/RSA requirements	John Pomeroy	First half week input session + peer teaching	18
Eastbourne School of English	4 weeks	Full-time	£350	15/4, 29/7, 26/8 23/9	Degree preferred. Age 20+	Dorothy S. Rippon	Cost inc. RSA /UCLES fee. Accomm. available from £70 per week	18
ELT Banbury	4 weeks	Full-time	£860 + £64.50 Cambridge Fee	8/1, 4/3, 6/5, 1/7, 19/8	As per Cambridge	Dr T. J. Gerighty	—	12
English Language Unit, SOAS, London	4 weeks	Full-time	£840	8 July	Minimum 'A' levels, degree preferred	Fiona English	—	16
Frances King School of English, London	4 weeks	Both	£799	8/1, 12/2, 18/3, 22/4, 27/5, 1/7, every 5 weeks thereafter.	As per UCLES	Natalie Ivemy	—	12
GEOS, Brighton & Hove	4 weeks	Full-time	£835 inc. VAT and RSA registration fee	5/2, 4/3, 29/4, 28/5, 8/7, 5/8, 2/9, 30/9, 28/10, 25/11	Age 20+. Educated to 'A' level standard. Interview	GEOS	—	—
Gloscat, Cheltenham	6 weeks	Full-time	£750	September, January, April.	Interview	Paul Burden	—	14
Hammersmith and West, London College	6 months	Part-time	£550	24 September	As per University entrance	Course Information Centre	—	15
	1 month	Full-time	£550 + Cambridge exam fee	20/1, 3/3, 25/4, 30/6, 28/7, ,26/9, 11/11	As per University entrance	Course Information Centre	—	15
Harrow House International College, Swanage	4 weeks	Full-time	£792	19/2, 22/4, 20/5, 2/8, 7/10, 11/11	Age 20+. 2 'A' Levels	Teacher Training Dept.	Host Family Accomm. (Full Board) £65 per week	10
Hendon College, London	33 weeks	Part-time	£720	September	As per UCLES	Course Enquiries	Tuesday evenings + approx 16 daytime attendances.	14
Hilderstone College, Broadstairs	4 weeks	Full-time	£815 + £65 exam fee	15/1, 22/4, 14/10, 18/11	Age 20+, native speaker, good general education	Valerie Horne	Accomm. available	12
International House Hastings	4 weeks	Full-time	£805 + £64.50 Cambridge entrance fee	4/3, 9/4, 7/5, 3/6, 1/7, 29/7, 2/9, 30/9, 28/10, 25/11	Interview	Adrian Underhill	Accomm. services available.	18
ILI Leeds	4 weeks	Full-time	£825	Monthly	Interview	Steven Procter	—	10

RSA/Cambridge Certificate (CTEFLA) Courses

College	Course length	FT/PT	Fees	Start dates	Entry requirements	Contact	Comments	Max no of students
International Teaching and Training Cent. Bournemouth	4 weeks	Full-time	£826 + RSA fee.	Monthly	2 'A' levels	Pilar Diaz-Caneja	—	18
Leeds Metropolitan University	4 weeks	Full-time	£700	17/2, 12/4, 16/5, 24/6, 29/7. Sept., Oct., Nov. dates tba.	Interview	Felicity Henderson	Accomm. arranged on request.	18
Loughborough College	4/5 months	Part-time	On application	Mid September	Succesful study at H.E. level	Jan Sanders	—	15
Newnham Language Centre	4 weeks	Full time	£865 + £65 assessment fee	4/3, 29/4, 1/7, 29/7, 27/8, 21/10	Degree from a British University.	Marie-Louise Banning	—	16
North Trafford College, Manchester	28 weeks	Part-time	£480	September	At least 2 'A' levels, nat ive or bi-lingual speaker	Admissions	—	12
Pilgrims, Canterbury	4 weeks	Full-time	£1,020	January, April, July, August, October	Native speaker, 'A' levels + interview	Ms Sam Preston	—	6
Regent School (Oxford and London)	4 weeks	Full-time	£775	Monthly	2 'A' levels or degree	Declan McNally	—	12
St. Giles College, Brighton	4 weeks	Full-time	£860	Monthly	University entry level. Min. age 20.	Dermot A. Tobin	Accomm. service	15
Skola Teacher Training, London	4 weeks	Full-time	£830	12/2, 18/3, 22/4, 28/5, 1/7, 5/8, 9/9, 14/10, 18/11.	University entrance level preferred	Sandra Stevens	—	15
Stanton Teacher Training, London	4 weeks	Full-time	£738 inc. the issue of the UCLES certificate	Every month	University matriculation, 20 years of age.	David Garrett	—	18
Stoke-on-Trent College	12-13 weeks	Part-time	£700	April	Min. 2 'A' levels	Enquiries, Stoke-on-Trent College	—	12
Studio School, Cambridge	4 weeks	Full-time	£795	4 March, 29 April, 29 July, 23 September, 18 November	3 'A' levels	Lucy Purvey	—	12
University of Hull EFL Unit	4 weeks (full-time) 20 weeks (part-time)	Both	£840.15	June/July	20+. Degree, English of native speaker. level	Debra Marsh	—	12
Westminster College, London	5 weeks	Full-time	£625	Monthly	21+. Degree or equivalent, native speaker of English	Frances Jagodzinska	—	—
Wigston College of FE, Leics.	1 year	Full-time	Refer to College	Refer to College	Refer to College	Student Guidance Services	—	—

College	Course length	FT/PT	Fees	Start dates	Entry requirements	Contact	Comments	Max no of students
Aberdeen College	7 months	Part-time	Tba	September, May	Degree or equivalent	Anne Bain	—	10
Abon Language School, Bristol	1 year (30 weeks)	Part-time	Tba (approximately £700)	1 October	2 'A' levels or equivalent	Heather Crispin	—	12
Bradford and Ilkley College, Bradford	Full-time 4 weeks. Part-time 30 weeks	Both	£600	Full-time Feb, May, July, Oct Part-time Oct-June	Min. 2 'A' levels. Degree or equivalent preferred.	Nancy Hall	—	16
Cicero Languages International, Tunbridge Wells.	4 weeks	Full-time	£745 + exam fee.	Throughout year	'A' level + interview	Mrs Maureen Binns	Accomm. available	10
Colchester Institute	8/10 weeks	Full-time	£600 (including exam fee)	April, September, January	Graduate or equivalent	Barbara Stewart	—	10
Edinburgh Tutorial College	4 weeks	Full-time	£785 inclusive of moderator's fee	19/2, 15/4, 20/5, 1/7, 5/8, 9/11, 14/10, 11/11	Degree preferable	Michelle Sweeney	—	14
Gateshead Training Consultancy	4 weeks	Full-time	Tba	5 August	Trinity specified	TEFL Organiser	Accomm. can be arranged	—
inlingua Teacher Training and Recruitment, Cheltenham	5 weeks	Full-time	£850 (inc. VAT and materials) + moderation fee.	Throughout year	University entrance level	Dagmar Lewis	Split 3 weeks Germany or France 2 weeks UK	10
ITS English School, Hastings	4, 5 or 2+2 weeks	Full-time	£740	5/2, 1/4, 22/4, 22/7, 16/8, 14/10, 11/11	—	John Palim	—	12
Kingsway College, London	Full-time 8 wks Part-time 13 wks	Both	£595	Jan, May, Oct	By interview	Felicity Henderson	—	18
Leeds Metropolitan University	32 weeks	Part-time	£424	October	Age 21+. Graduate or equivalent	Janet Poveda	Evening attendance plus some days	18
Oaklands College, Borehamwood	12 weeks Jan/Sept 6 weeks July	Full-time	£595	January, September, July	Good educational background	EFL Admin Office	Day-time course Monday - Thursday	14
	32 weeks	Part-time	£595	September	Good educational background	EFL Admin Office	1 evening per week + d/time teaching practice	14
Oxford House College, London	4 weeks full-time 13 weeks part-time	Both	£650 + moderation fee full-time, £750 + moderation fee part-time	Throughout year	As per Trinity requirements	Michael Hamsworth	Also available full and part-time in Barcelona £595 inclusive.	16
Park Lane College, Leeds	1 year	Part-time	£295 + moderation fee	September	Minimum 2 'A' levels and native speaker	Anita Taylor	—	15
Regency School, Kent	4 weeks	Full-time	£850	Monthly	On application	Teacher Training Dept.	—	12

College	Course length	FT/PT	Fees	Start dates	Entry requirements	Contact	Comments	Max no of students
The Richmond Adult & Community College	1 year	Part-time	£800 approx	September	Degree or equivalent	Barbara Beaumont	—	14
St Brelades, Jersey	4 weeks	Full-time	£700 plus exam fee	March and September	Degree or 2 'A' levels	Mr D. Brown	Accomm. available	—
St George's School of English, London	4 weeks	Full-time	£579	Throughout year	Interview	David Collard	Central London accomm. available	12
Saxoncourt Teacher Training, London	4 weeks	Full-time	£725	Throughout year	Interview	Ann Hardy	—	12
Sheffield Hallam University	Full-time 4 weeks + 12 weeks Dist. L.	Mixed	£910 + Trinity examfee	Throughout year	First degree	Gill King	First part of teacher education programme	18
South East Essex College, Southend	1 year	Part-time	£365 + moderation fee	2nd week in September	Interview	Marketing Section	1 evening a week + 3 - 4 Saturdays.	Variable
Southwark College, London	5 weeks	Full-time	£570 + moderation fee	22 April	Normally degree or equivalent	Philip Jakes	—	10
Students International Ltd, Melton Mowbray	4 weeks	Full-time	£765 inc. moderation fee	Throughout year	Interview, minimum age 20, good educational background	Alison Blythe	Course offers experience in junior and adult learners	12
Surrey Language Centre, Farnham	4 weeks	Full-time	£750 inclusive of VAT	14/2, 15/4, 24/6, 29/7	Minimum 20 years old, good standard of education	Jill Woodley.	—	N/A
Sutton College of Liberal Arts, Surrey	32 weeks	Part-time	£480	October	'A' level English or equivalent	Sonja Compton	Course held on Thursday mornings	14
Thurrock College, Aveley	4 weeks	Full-time	£575	November, February	Degree and/or teachers cert.	John Saunders	—	8
Universal Language Training, Ockham	4 weeks full-time, 16 weeks part-time	Both	£830	Throughout year	Minimum age 20, good educational background	Bodile Streeten	Course also run in Salamanca Spain	16
University of St. Andrews, Fife, ELT Centre	6 weeks	Full-time	£805	22 June	Over 20 years of age, native speaker	Alison Malcolm Smith	To be validated by Trinity College in January	12
Waltham Forest College, London	Full-time 6 weeks Part-time 2 terms	Both	Tba	Full-time Mid June Part-time Mid September	University entrance level	Programme Co-ordination Centre TESOL	—	12
Windsor Schools	Full-time 4 weeks Part-time 4 months	Both	£840 + Trinity fees	FT 7/5, 10/6, 1/7, 12/8 PT 4/3	2 'A' levels	Jacintha McSherry	—	15
Woking and Chertsey Adult Education College	4 weeks	Full-time	£550 approx	March, June, November	'A' levels or equivalent	Ursula Over	Course leaflet/ application form available	12

Initial Qualifications In Ireland

Although many UK qualifications are acceptable in Ireland, domestic qualifications are becoming increasingly standardised.

Language schools in Ireland are now trying to find common ground to ensure there is more consistency in their qualification system

In the past the EFL qualification system in Ireland was rather unstructured. Although the country has a long tradition of quality English language training and there have always been a large number of Irish teachers working overseas, there has frequently been confusion over their qualifications. In the last few years, however, there have been a number of moves towards creating a more formal system of accreditation, thus making courses more respected and more widely known.

To teach in Ireland, a degree is required but, until recently, the regulations of the Advisory Council on English Language Schools (ACELS) have allowed recognised language schools to employ anyone with a TEFL qualification, including one of the huge variety of short-course certificates. Many of these short courses are run within Irish colleges, but last less than 20 hours. The problem with them is that foreign students generally go to Ireland only in the summer months (although this too is changing towards all-year courses), and outside this time trainee teachers simply do not have enough students to practise on.

Language schools in Ireland are now trying to find common ground to ensure that there is more consistency in their qualification system.

RELSA

The Recognised English Language Schools Association is the main association of EFL schools in Ireland, and in 1992 it decided to introduce its own teacher training Certificate. The course, known as the RELSA Preparatory Certificate lasts 70 hours and involves teaching practice, observation and a project. The cost is in the region of £220 and schools generally offer students the choice of either an intensive full-time or a part-time course of study.

At present there are 12 schools licensed to run such courses. The RELSA Preparatory Certificate is considered an acceptable qualification in some schools

The Universities of Dublin and Cork offer a teacher training course, the College Certificate in EFL, which is considered as an equivalent to the RSA/Cambridge Certificate

overseas, who were previously baffled by the diverse range of certificates Irish teachers presented them with. According to RELSA, over 1,000 teachers have taken their Certificate since it was introduced. However, the RELSA course is still shorter and less well-known internationally than the RSA/Cambridge Certificate. See p25 for RELSA Certificate course details.

ATT

The Association for Teacher Training in TEFL is an association of nine schools concerned with standards of teacher training in Ireland. At the forefront of curriculum innovation, they run a Preliminary Certificate (40 hours), an International Certificate (106 hours). They also offer 40-hour Refresher courses for both Native and Non-Native Teachers, as well as a Distance Learning course.

The Preliminary Certificate is designed to persuade trainee teachers away from the less reputable short courses. The International Certificate is comparable to the RSA and Trinity College Certificates. Course fees range from 150 to 450 Irish punts. The courses enjoy recognition by a number of schools in Europe and overseas, and standards are assured and maintained by the ATT's own panel of moderators. See p25 for course details.

RSA/Cambridge and Trinity Certificates

The RSA/Cambridge and Trinity College Certificates are respected in Irish schools. RSA/Cambridge courses are available at two centres and the Trinity Certificate is available in Dublin.

State sector qualifications

The state EFL sector is fairly small in Ireland, although the Universities of Dublin and Cork offer a teacher training course, the College Certificate in EFL, which runs in conjunction with the Higher Diploma in Education over two years. This is considered as an equivalent to the RSA/Cambridge Certificate.

Getting Qualified In The USA And Canada

The rapidly rising demand for EFL (or ESL) has led to an increase in both the number and variety of courses currently available for teachers.

Hundreds of English teaching positions do not require an advanced degree in the United States, particularly in private language schools

At present there are no absolute equivalents to the RSA/ Cambridge Certificate in the United States, but the situation is changing. Many individual states with burgeoning immigrant populations are pressing for more flexible and effective certification programs at all levels. An increasing number of universities are offering comprehensive non-degree, certificate programmes that combine theoretical considerations with practical applications, including a required student teaching practice component.

Several RSA and RSA-style certificate programmes have sprung up across the country, particularly on the West Coast where at least six are currently on offer. Meanwhile, it is still possible in some states - California is one - to obtain an adult credential or secondary authorisation to teach ESL to adults. A large number of non-profit, community-based organisations offer effective, free training programmes for volunteers who wish to teach English and many teachers are ex peace corps volunteers.

McGill University in Montreal, Quebec, and Toronto University in Ontario both offer an array of teacher training programs

The minimum qualification to enter most programmes is a BA or BS degree. However, university BA programs in TESOL and many of the private, intensive teacher training schools or volunteer programs will accept trainees with a High School diploma. You do not need any previous teaching experience to enter one of these programs. However, it is a rare program today that does not encourage, if not require, teaching practice and classroom observation as part of the curriculum. The fact that Georgetown University, Washington, has begun running RSA/Cambridge Certificate courses is a sign that English language teaching in the United States is changing.

In the past, English language teaching in the United States meant TESL (Teaching English as a Second Language). For decades TESL operated mainly at the university level with academic students. Beginning in the 1970s and well into the 1980s, the United States experienced a mass migration of non-English speaking immigrants with special needs, many of whom lacked basic literacy skills in their own language. As these individuals began to enter both schools and the workplace, a strong need for eclectic methodology arose.

Today, with the encroaching 'global village', a new recognition of the importance of teaching English as a foreign language is gaining currency.

Most of the better jobs at state-run institutions in the United States are for TESL and generally require an MA degree. However, hundreds of English teaching positions do not require an advanced degree, particularly in private language schools where overseas experience and an RSA or similar certificate may be more useful than an MA.

Canada

In Canada the basic English as a Second Language teacher training qualification for instructing adult learners consists of an undergraduate degree, a recognised ESL teacher training course, and a standard of spoken and written English equivalent to that of an educated native speaker of English.

Canada has become well known as a destination for teachers who wish to improve both their knowledge of linguistic theory and their practical teaching skills. The proximity of the western coast to the Far East and its large immigrant community have increased the demand for ELT and subsequently made it popular as a teacher training destination. The International Teacher Training Institute at Vancouver Community College, British Columbia, specialises in short programmes. Outside British Columbia, McGill University in Montreal, Quebec, and Toronto University in Ontario offer an array of teacher training programmes, including short summer courses which have been designed for teachers whose mother tongue is not English.

Prospective students must have passed a university course or hold a certificate. RSA/Cambridge qualifications are also available in Canada.

Getting Qualified In Australia And New Zealand

The EFL sector is experiencing rapid growth in Australasia as is the number of training courses available to teachers.

It may be possible for teachers to get work with as little as a certificate in TESOL in some institutions, but most colleges require the equivalent to NEAS minimum qualifications

There are schools in both Australia and New Zealand offering Cambridge or Trinity qualifications. There is also a variety of homegrown training programs approved under official accreditation schemes.

Australia

EFL courses for adults are mainly taught in accredited ELICOS (English Language Intensive Courses for Overseas Students) institutions. The National ELICOS Accreditation Scheme (NEAS) has set minimum standards for teacher qualifications within such institutions. These guidelines state that teachers must have at least:

EITHER a recognised pre-service teaching qualification (minimum three years) plus or including an appropriate TESOL qualification,

OR a recognised degree or diploma (minimum three years), plus at least 800 hours classroom teaching experience, plus an appropriate TESOL qualification.

To be deemed 'an appropriate teaching qualification', the course must have a content focus on English language learning and teaching, a practical component including at least six hours supervised and assessed practice teaching, and no less than 100 contact hours. The course must also be accredited by the appropriate accrediting body. For more details of the NEAS policy, contact: NEAS, Locked Bag 2, Post Office, Pyrmont, NSW 2009.

A certificate along with a degree is the accepted qualification for NZQA (New Zealand Qualification Authorities) accredited schools

Recently the Australian government relaxed its rules to allow students from some countries to study on tourist visas and on such 'Study Tour' courses teacher qualifications are unregulated. It may be possible for teachers to get work with as little as a certificate in TESOL in some institutions. However, most colleges require the equivalent to NEAS minimum qualifications.

A wide range of teacher training courses, from introductory level upwards, are available. In Sydney, the Australian TESOL Training Centre offers RSA Certificate and Diploma courses, as well as an introductory one-week course. The Australian Centre for Languages has an intensive four-week and part-time RSA Cambridge certificate courses. The Insearch Language Centre, part of the University of Technology, Sydney, also offers a four-week full-time or five-month part-time RSA Cambridge certificate.

The University of Southern Queensland offers courses from graduate certificate level upwards, some pre-service and some for practising teachers. Also in Queensland, Bond University offers a Graduate Certificate in TESOL. The University of South Australia offers a graduate certificate for trained teachers with at least one year's experience. In Western Australia, RSA Certificate courses are provided by the Milner International College and in Victoria by the Holmesglen Institute of TAFE.

EFL in Australia is entering a growth period, and this provides more opportunities for teachers wishing to get higher level teaching positions in ELICOS centres. Generally, employers would expect a coordinator or head teacher to have a qualification at RSA Diploma level or above, and there are many courses available at the level of graduate certificate or diploma and MA which prepare teachers for a senior teaching position. See p73 for details.

New Zealand

The export of education is the fastest growing industry in New Zealand, and this growth in demand has led to the increased popularity of short, intensive teacher training courses. A certificate along with a degree is the accepted qualification for NZQA (New Zealand Qualification Authorities) accredited schools.

Languages International in Auckland was the first school to offer the RSA Cambridge CTEFLA, now also run by the Capital Language Academy in Wellington. and Dominion English Schools in Auckland. The Trinity Certificate in TESOL course is available at Seafield School of English in Christchurch, the International Academy of Languages in Auckland and the International Pacific College in Palmerston North.

Overseas RSA/Cambridge Certificate (CTEFLA) Courses

College	Course length	FT/PT	Fees	Start dates	Entry requirements	Contact	Comments	Max no of students
Auckland Language Centre, Auckland City, New Zealand	4 weeks	Full-time	NZ$2,750 (includes exam fee)	8/1, 10/6, 2/8, 11/11	Min age 20, university entrance qualification, English of educated native speaker standard	Nick Marsden	—	12
Australian Centre for Languages, Sydney, Australia	4 weeks full-time, 15 weeks part-time	Both	AUD$2,080 full-time AUD$2,230 part-time	Full-time 1 July Part-time 17 February	Min age 20 years, English of educated native speaker standard	Sonia Ortega	—	12
Australian TESOL Training Centre, Bondi Junction, Australia	4 weeks full-time, 12 weeks part-time	Both	AUD$2,090	Full-time every month, part-time April and September	Matriculation	Gloria Smith	—	12
Bell Language School, Geneva, Switzerland	4 and 5 weeks	Full-time	SFR 3,600	July 4 weeks, January 5 weeks	—	Director of Training	—	10
	12 weeks	Part-time	SFR 3,600	February, September	—	Director of Training	—	12
Bell Language School, Zurich, Switzerland	4 and 5 weeks	Full-time	SFR 3,650	August 4 weeks, February 5 weeks	University entrance level	Head of Studies	—	12
	12 weeks	Part-time	SFR 3,650	March and September	University entrance level	Head of Studies	—	12
British Council, Istanbul, Turkey	5 weeks full-time, 4 months part-time	Both	£800	May full-time, October part-time	University entrance level	Dorothy Gwillim	Some help with accomm.	12
British Council, Izmir, Turkey	4 weeks	Full-time	£800	17 June	Graduates preferred, selection by pre-course tasks and interview (may be by phone)	Steven Darn	—	18
British Council, Milan, Italy	4 weeks full-time, 15 weeks part-time	Both	2,400,000 lire	Full-time 24/6, end of September Part-time 10 February, mid September	Min age 20, university entrance standard, native speaker	Amanda Bourdillon	—	12
British Council, Muscat, Oman	15 January - 13 February inc. Feast holiday break	Full-time	R.O 595	15 January	Min. age 20 years, at least 2 'A' + 3 'O' levels, interview.	Michael Manser	Further courses to be offered subject to usual UCLES reapproval process	12
	10 weeks	Part-time	R.O. 595	2 March	20+, at least 2 'A' levels and 3 'O' levels plus succesful interview	Michael Manser	—	12

Overseas RSA/Cambridge Certificate (CTEFLA) Courses

College	Course length	FT/PT	Fees	Start dates	Entry requirements	Contact	Comments	Max no of students
British Council, Naples, Italy	Tba	Full-time	2,600,000 lire	17 June	Application form + grammar test + interview	Frank C. De la Motte	—	16
British Language Centre, Madrid, Spain	4 weeks full-time, 10 weeks part-time	Both	£650	Throughout year	—	Alistair Dickinson	Accomm. provided	12
British School of Milan, Italy	4 weeks full-time, 15 weeks part-time	Both	2,100,000 lire + 100,000 lire enrolement fee	17 June full-time, 13 February part-time	20+, native speaker standard, 2 'A' levels or equivalent	Janine Thomas	—	12
CALUSA, Adelaide, Australia	4 weeks full-time, part-time equivalent	Both	A$2,000	FT January, July PT March, September p	21+, higher ed entrance level,	Ms Caroline Rannersberger	Open to both native and non-native speakers	12
Cambridge School, Lisbon, Portugal	4 weeks	Full-time	£750	July, August	As per UCLES	Jeffrey Kapke	Help with accomm., interview poss. in UK	12
Cambridge School, Verona, Italy	Tba	Both	FT 2,300,000 lr PT 2,4000,000 lr	FT 17 June PT November	Good standard of general education	Anne Parry	—	12
Campbell College Valencia, Spain	4 weeks	Full-time	120,000 pts	1 July, 4 November	University entrance level, native speaker competence	Seamas Campbell	Some help with accomm.	12
Capital Language Academy, Wellington, New Zealand	4 weeks	Full-time	NZ$2,700	January, May, October	Min. age 20, Bursary/ University entrance	Fliss Hope	Contact college for exact course dates	12
Center For English Studies, International House New York, USA	4 weeks	Full-time	$1,925 (includes RSA fees)	25/3, 22/4, 17/6, 15/7, 12/8, 9/9, 7/10	Four-year u/graduate degree, for. lang. learning exp., written app. + int.	International House Teacher Training	—	15
Centre For English Lang. Learning, Melbourne, Australia	Full-time 4 weeks Part-time 16 weeks	Both	$1,800(includes RSA fees)	Full-time every second month Part-time every semester	20+, high level of written and spoken English	RSA Administrative Officer	—	12
Coast Language Academy, Portland, USA	4 week full-time, 8 week part-time	Both	$1,975 (including course books)	24/2, 6/7, 8/8, 9/9 full-time, 12/4, 16/10 part-time	As per UCLES requirements	John Myers	FT course also available in Santa Monica 3/2 and 6/7	—
Dominion English Schools, Auckland, New Zealand	4 weeks	Full-time	NZ$2,750	24 June, 12 August	Edu to 3rd lvl, good language awareness, pre-interview task, interview	Andrew Williams	—	12
English International, San Francisco, USA	4 weeks	Full-time (includes 30 hours of self study using tasks provided by the centre)	US$2,350	Monthly	Normally BA/BS degree + some knowledge of a foreign language	Deanne Manwaring	Professional job guidance during/after course. 11 courses per year.	12

Overseas RSA/Cambridge Certificate (CTEFLA) Courses

College	Course length	FT/PT	Fees	Start dates	Entry requirements	Contact	Comments	Max no of students
Georgetown University, Centre for Lang. Ed. Development Washington, USA	5 weeks	Full-time	$3,000	8 July	Degree plus fluency in a foreign language	Mary Marggraf	—	18
Holmesglen Institute of TAFE, Victoria, Australia	FT 4 wks PT 18 wks Semi intensive 10 wks	Both	A$1,800	All year	As per UCLES	Director of Studies	—	12
ILA South Pacific Ltd., Christchurch, New Zealand	4 weeks	Full-time	NZ$2,800	15/2, 2/5, 6/6, 3/10, 7/11	Minimum University entrance	Julie Van Dyk	—	12
Insearch Language Centre, University of Technology Sydney, Australia	4 weeks full-time, 5 months part-time	Both	NZ$2,100	Full-time 4/3, 22/4, 6/8, 11/11 Part-time 20/5	Min. age 20 School leaving certificate, native speaker English proficiency	Teacher Training Department	—	18
International House, Barcelona, Spain	4 weeks	Full-time	138,000 pesetas	Throughout year	University entrance level	Jenny Johnson	Help with accomm.	15
	4 months	Part-time	138,000 pesetas	March	University entrance level	Jenny Johnson	Help with accomm.	18
	Full-time 4 weeks Part-time 6 months	Both	120,000 pesetas	Part-time January, Full-time February	University entrance level	Jenny Johnson	RSA/Cambridge CTEFL Young Learners. Help with accomm.	15
International House, Budapest, Hungary	12 weeks	Part-time	£670	26 February	Degrees preferred but not essential	Eva Baricz	Help with accomm.	15
	4 weeks	Full-time	£670	15/1, 17/6, 15/7, 5/8	Degrees preferred but not essential	Eva Baricz	Help with accomm.	15
International House, Lisbon, Portugal	4 weeks	Full-time	180,000 pte	February-June (pilot)	Pre course interview and task	Paula de nagy	Contact school for further dates	15
International House, Madrid, Spain	Tba	Both	130,000 pesetas	Full-time 3/5, 31/5, 28/6, 2/9 Part-time 2/10	Cambridge requirements	Steven Haysham	Help with accomm.	12
International House, Paris, France	4 weeks	Full-time	8,960.00 FF	12/2, 9/4, 3/6, 1/7, 5/8, 2/9, 30/9, 4/11	Degree	—	—	18
International House, Prague, Czech Republic	4 weeks full-time, 18 weeks part-time	Both	26,775 CZK full-time 18,900 CZK part-time	Full-time 27/5, 8/7 Part-time 10/1	Education to University entrance lvl.	Jim Chapman	Accomm. can be provided for full time courses	12 -18
International House, Queensland, Australia	4 weeks	Full-time	A$2,300	12/2, 17/6, 2/8	Tertiary level education. over 20.	Simon Bradley	—	12
International House, Rome, Italy	8 months	Part-time/Semi Intensive	2,400,000 lire + RSA/UCLES fee	Part-time Mid October Semi Intensive 4/3	UCLES requirements	The Director	—	15

College	Course length	FT/PT	Fees	Start dates	Entry requirements	Contact	Comments	Max no of students
International House, Rome, Italy	4 weeks	Full-time	2,260,000 lire + RSA/UCLES fee	June, July, September	UCLES requirements	The Director	Help given with accomm.	15
International Language Institute, Nova Scotia, Canada	4 weeks	Full-time	C$2,000.00	May, July, August	Min. age 20, undergraduate degree	Raissa Musial	—	12
Language Centre of Ireland, Dublin	4 weeks 9 weeks	Both	IR£750	January, June, September	Degree + interview	David Doyle	—	12
Language Resources, Kobe, Japan	4 months	Part-time	285,000 Y	April	Bachelor's degree	G Rupp	—	10
LSC, Language Studies, Toronto, Canada	4 weeks	Full-time	$1,700 Canadian	11/3, 6/5, 2/7, 29/7, 26/8, 23/9	Native proficiency, 20+, university degree	Crystal Han	—	12
Languages International, Auckland, New Zealand	4 weeks	Full-time	NZ$2,750	April, June, August, November	As per CTEFLA guidelines	Julia Donovan	—	12
Milner Int. College of English, Perth, Aus	4 weeks	Full-time	A$1,995	4/2, 6/5, 5/8	Tertiary entrance	Linda Wrighton	—	12
NSTS English Language Institute, Valletta, Malta	4 weeks full-time, 12 weeks part-time	Both	799 BGBP	Full-time 15 April, 10 May Part-time 29 March	As per UCLES entry requirements	Norman Shaw	Maximum ratio 6 trainees per tutor	18
RMIT Centre for English Lang.Learning, Melbourne, Australia	Full-time 4 weeks Part-time 16 weeks	Both	$1,800	FT 4/3, 29/4, 29/7, 7/10, 18/11 PT 19/2, 15/7	20+ high level of written and spoken English	RSA Administration Officer	—	12
Polyglot Institute, Ruwi, Oman	Tba	Part-time	RO 545/-	2 March	As per UCLES requirements	Aleya James	—	8
St Giles' Language Training Cent., San Francisco, USA	4 weeks	Full-time	US$2,125	25/3, 6/5, 17/6, 9/9, 21/10	Written exercise and oral interview	Arlyn Bull	—	12
St Mark's International College, Perth, Australia	12 weeks	Part-time	A$2,090	9/4, 2/7, 24/9	Over 20, tertiary education, native speaker	Director of Studies		18
TBI, Jakarta, Indonesia	4 weeks	Full-time	US$1,750	20 May, 11 November	—	Ken Trolland	—	12
University of Waikato, Hamilton, NZ	4 weeks	Full-time	$NZ2,700	'96 June, Nov. '97 Jan, Feb.	20+, university entrance level	Jean Young	—	12
University of Wollongong, NSW, Australia	105 hours (3 weeks full-time) +18 hours teaching pract.	Full-time & part-time options	A$1,990+ £62 sterling	Tba	High school graduation	—	—	15

Overseas RSA/Cambridge Certificate (CTEFLA) Courses

College	Course length	FT/PT	Fees	Start dates	Entry requirements	Contact	Comments	Max no of students
Volkshoch-schule Zurich, Switzerland	On application	Part-time	On Application	may, October	Application form	Margaret Stark	—	12
Worldwide Teachers Development, Boston, USA	Full-time 4 weeks Part-time 3 months	Both	On Application	On Application	—	—	Global placement guidance	—

ATT And RELSA Certificate Courses

College	Course title	Course length	FT/PT	Fees	Start dates	Entry requirements	Contact	Comments
Alpha College of English, Dublin	RELSA Preparatory Certificate	2 weeks, 70 hours	Full-time	£235	4/3, 10/6, 9/9, 25/11	21+, 3rd level degree or equivalent	Ian Brangan	Help with job placement
Bluefeather School of Languages Dublin	ATT Preliminary Certificate	3 weeks to 3 months	Part-time	£160 and £495 (incl. exam fees)	Every month	Good standard of education	Greg Rosenstock	Also offers part-time Int. Certificate
Centre of English Studies, Dublin	RELSA Preparatory Certificate	70 hours	Both	£235	All year	Degree or equivalent; min age 20	—	Job advice given.
Dublin School of English	RELSA Preparatory Certificate	4 weeks evening or 12 days	Day and evening courses	£235	Regular	Degree/exper-ience or equivalent	Barry Crossen	—
Emerald Cultural Inst., Dublin	RELSA Preparatory Certificate	3 weeks	Full-time	£230	Contact school	—	Mr Mauro Biondi	
Excel International College of Lang., Cork	ATT Preliminary Certificate	40 hours (Monday to Friday 9-6)	Full-time	Ir£170 inclusive of £10 exam fee	Fortnightly	Native speaker, good standard of education	Martin Murray	—
Foyle Language Centre, Derry	ATT Preliminary Certificate	40 hours (2-6pm. Mon - Fri) or 10 wk night class	Both	£160	—	Native speakers with good standard of English	Paul Murray	
Galway Language Centre	RELSA Preparatory Certificate	4 weeks (70 hours)	Part-time	£225	4/3, 22/4, 10/6, 12/8, 23/9, 4/11	BA. Mature students also accepted	B. Bazler	—
Irish College of English, Dublin	ATT Preliminary Certificate	40 hours	Both	Ir£160	On application	University entrance level, min. age 18	Peter Gibson	Includes teaching practice
Language Centre of Ireland, Dublin	RELSA Certificate	70 hours	Part-time	Ir£210	—	Degree	David Doyle	—
TEFL Training Institute of Ireland, Dublin	ATT Prelim/ International Certificate	40 hours	Both	Ir£160	On application	University entrance level, min. age 18	Peter Gibson	Includes teaching practice
Westlingua Language School, Galway	RELSA Preparatory Certificate	2 weeks	—	£225	End of March, mid-June, mid September.	3rd level qualification.	Eoghan Garvey	—
Words Language Service, Dublin	ATT Preliminary Certificate	8 weeks	Full-time	£150 + £10 examination fee	April, June July, Aug, Oct	Leaving Cert/ 'A' levels	TEFL Dept.	—

Overseas Trinity College Certificate In TESOL Courses

College	Course length	FT/PT	Fees	Start dates	Entry requirements	Contact	Comments	Max no of students
Abu Baker Cultural & Scientific Institution, Al Ain, UAE	—	Part-time	Tba	—	—	—	Short intensive course	—
Centro Anglo Paraguayo, Asuncion, Paraguay	—	Part-time	On application	On application	On application	Carlos Caruallo	Contact school for further details	—
Dickens Institute, Montevideo, Uruguay	—	Part-time	Tba	—	—	—	—	—
Grafton Tuition Centre, Dublin	Full time 4 weeks, part-time 6 months	Both (includes part time with Dist. Learning block)	Tba	—	—	Denis O'Donaghue	Assistance with finding accomm.	
Novalingua/ Oxford House College, Barcelona, Spain	4 weeks	Full-time	Tba	—	—	—	—	
Saxoncourt, Chiba, Japan	4 weeks	Full-time	NT$40,000 (approx)	3 times a year	Degree, fluency in English	Saxoncourt Taiwan/Saxon court UK	—	—
Seafield School of English, Christchurch, New Zealand	4 weeks	—	Tba	—	—	—	Assistance given with finding accomm.	—

RSA/Cambridge COTE Courses

College	Course length	FT/PT	Fees	Start dates	Entry requirements	Contact	Comments	Max no of students
American University in Cairo, Egypt	14 weeks	Full-time	LE 1500	—	—	Dr Christine Zaher	—	—
Asociacion Cultural Peruano Britanica, Lima Peru	6 months	Part-time	$800 approx	July	300 hours teaching experience, CEELT 1	Pilar Ferreyros	—	15
Centro Anglo Paraguay, Asuncion, Paraguay	5 months	Part-time	US$700	February	UCLES requirements	Maureen Finn	—	10
English Prep School, Mersin, Turkey	1 year	Part-time	On application	September - June	First degree, English or Foreign Language	—	—	15
Instituto-cultural Anglo-Uruguayo, Montevideo, Uruguay	February to October	Part-time	Tba	February	300 hours of classroom experience and CPE levels of English	Ursual Krieger	—	16
PROFILE, Athens, Greece	6 months (160 hours)	Part-time	350,000 Drs	January	300 hours experience	Kate Wakeman	—	25

Introductory Courses

If you are unsure whether TEFL is the job for you or simply cannot afford the time and money for full-time training, an introductory course can be a good way to test the water.

he full-length RSA/Cambridge or Trinity Certificates are an excellent introduction to, and basic preparation for, the world of EFL teaching. However, they also represent a substantial investment of both time and money. If you are unwilling or unable to make such a commitment but are keen to undertake some kind of training in EFL, there is a wide range of introductory courses available. Most of these courses are about one week long and are therefore limited in what they can teach. Unless you already have teaching experience in another discipline, they are not generally considered sufficient to enable you to go straight into the classroom. The basic aim of these courses is to provide an introduction, not a qualification. They are, however, a useful first step into the world of TEFL and have provided plenty of teachers with their first jobs.

Vacation Work In Summer Schools

Such courses really come into their own if you are interested in vacation work. During the summer in the UK and Ireland there are hundreds of EFL jobs at schools. This is the busy period for schools as they tend to run numerous Summer Schools for overseas students who visit the UK or Ireland to spend some time (usually a month to six weeks) living and studying in an English language environment. See pp101-103 for information on schools which run Summer courses.

There are also plenty of vacancies in Australia and New Zealand over the Christmas period (their Summer). This surge in demand for teachers means that there are more vacancies to be filled than there are teachers with RSA or Trinity Certificates. The experience of a short course would give you an advantage over many applicants who may have no experience or qualifications at all. Your effectiveness and confidence as a teacher will also tend to be better than that of the completely unqualified teacher. This is of benefit to both you and your students.

For those whose interests in TEFL are likely to stretch beyond the summer, then an introductory course has a wide variety of uses. Centres who offer such courses may be able to help you find a permanent job and are likely to have some knowledge of which schools tend to offer employment to teachers without a full certificate.. This help generally takes the form of careers advice or specific classes in job seeking. In some cases, however, the school may even be able to place you in one of its own overseas schools. Students who undertake the inlingua Introduction To TEFL, for example, are offered the possibility of being placed abroad in an inlingua school after the successful completion of their course.

Introductory Courses Linked To Certificates

Introductory Courses not only help you test the water to see if this is the job for you, but they can also serve as a valuable introduction to a full training course. Some UK centres offer introductory training courses linked to certificates. These are particularly useful if you do not hold a degree (a usual requirement for starting the RSA certificate). Even if an introductory course is not specifically linked with a fully-fledged certificate course, you may find that a school will consider your application for a full course more favourably if you have already displayed interest and aptitude in TEFL.

Whether you decide to take an introductory course as part of a long-term career move or simply to help with a Summer job, you want to ensure that the course you are taking is worth the time and money. Courses inevitably vary in quality and teaching standards. Try to ensure that the course you select has a clear set of goals and offers an organised syllabus. Where possible, look for a balance between theory and practice and the opportunity to practice regularly with foreign students, not just peer groups, i.e. other trainee teachers.

If you find the right course, it will have a lot to offer as the introduction to the vast and varied world of EFL teaching.

Introductory Courses

College	Course length	FT/PT	Fees	Start dates	Entry requirements	Contact	Comments	Max no of students
Aberdeen College, Aberdeen, UK	30 Hours	Both	£65	Various	—	Anne Bain	—	15
Abon Language School, Bristol, UK	25 Hours	Full-time	£125	22/1, 25/3, 24/6, 16/9, 11/11	—	Heather Crispin	Certifiacte upon completion.	10
Australian TESOL Training Centre, NSW, Australia	One Week	Full-time	$375	4/3, 13/5, 22/7, 30/9, 9/12	—	Gloria Smith	—	18
Bedford College, Bedford, UK	22 Hours	Part-time	£90 approximately	13/1, 7/4, 23/9	Degree pref'd. Others considered	Ken Wilford	—	16
Brasshouse Centre, Birmingham, UK	One Week	Full-time	£110	March, May, October	—	Deborah Corbett	—	10
The British Language Centre, Madrid, Spain	One Week	Full-time	£290	Throught the year	—	Alistair Dickinson	Practical & fun!	12
Canterbury Christ Church College, Canterbury, UK	One Week	Full-time	On request	On request	On request	Stephen Bax	Further details available upon request	15
CELT, Athens, Greece	75 Hours	Both	£400	Full-time Jun, Jul, Sep. Part-time Jan, Mar, Apr, Oct	—	Harisa Constantinides	Teaching practice component included	10
Colchester Institute, Colchester, UK	20 Hours	Full-time	£80	June 1996/7	—	Barbara Stewart	—	15
Eastbourne College of Arts & Technology, Eastbourne, UK	11 weeks	Part-time	£98	Jan, Apr, Sep	'A' levels or equivalent	John Pomeroy	Classes held in evenings, 6-9pm.	16
	2 weeks either side of Easter. Total hours: 40	Full-time	£98	Varies according to date of Easter	2 'A'-levels or equivalent.	John Pomeroy	1 course per year.	16
Edinburgh Tutorial College, Edinburgh, UK	2 weeks	Full-time	£390	Every Monday from 15 Jan.	Advanced level of English.	Michelle Sweeney	—	12
Frances King School of English, London, UK	—	Both	£149	5/2, 11/3, 15/4, 27/5, 1/7.	—	Natalie King Sean Leahy	—	12
Globe English Centre, Exeter, UK	Full-time 1 week Part-time 3 months	Both	Upon application	On demand, usually May & Sept.	Higher Education, teaching experience preferred.	Gill Heaton	—	10
Harrow House International College, Swanage, UK	1 Week	Full-time	£185	Throughout the Year	—	The teacher Training Department.	Host Family accomm. from £65 p.w.	10 max.

Introductory Courses

College	Course length	FT/PT	Fees	Start dates	Entry requirements	Contact	Comments	Max no of students
Hendon College, London, UK	2 terms (1 term possible)	Part-time	£188 per term	September (But enrolment also possible in January for 1 term)	Good FCE, CAE or CPE lvl in English language, interest in TEFL	Course Enquiries	Introduction to TEFL and preparation for CEELT.	16
Hilderstone College, Broadstairs, UK	6 Days	Full-time	£190	8/1, 15/4, 7/10	Age 20+ Good general education	Valerie Horne	Accomm. available.	12
Holmesglen Institute of TAFE, Victoria, Australia	30 Hours	Both	A$ 450	Throughout the year	Completion of Year 12	Larry Foster	—	15 max.
inlingua Teacher Training, Cheltenham, UK	2 Weeks.	Full-time	£320	June, August, December	Degree or equivelent	Dagmar Lewis	Possibility of being placed abroad upon successful completion of course.	10
Insearch Language Centre, University of Technology Sydney, Australia	1 Week	Full-time	$395	12/2, 27/5, 9/8, 16/12	Intermediate level of proficiency in English.	Teacher Training Dept.	—	15
International House, Hastings, UK	2 Weeks	Full-time	£445	17/6, 15/7, 12/8	By application	Adrian Underhill	Introductory course for non-native students and teachers. Accomm. available.	15
International House, Lisbon, Portugal	40 Hours	Both	PTE 50.000	Full-time September Part-time January	Pre-course interview and task	Paula de Nagy	Other courses available. Apply direct.	15
JKM Language and Educartion Centre, Alton, UK	2 Days	Full-time	£80	Monthly throughout year	Age 18+	Kay Marchment	Centres thoughout UK. Free advice on TEFL courses upon request.	15
King Alfred's College of Higher Ed., Winchester, UK	10 Weeks	Part-time	£85	Termly	—	TEFL Department	Practical and intensive.	12
The Language Project, Bristol, UK	1 Week	Full-time	£130	Throughout the year.	Interest in language and people.	Dr. Jon Wright.	Accomm. can be arranged. Help with jobs sometimes available	10
University of Manchester, UK	Full-time 4 weeks Part-time 4 months	Both	£700	Full-time July Part-time February	First Degree	CELSE Secretary	Foundation certificate in TESOL Inc. teaching pract.	20
Milner International College of English, Perth, Australia	From 2 to 10 weeks	Both	A$400 per week	Groups by arrangement	Tertiary entrance	Linda Wrighton	—	18

Introductory Courses

College	Course length	FT/PT	Fees	Start dates	Entry requirements	Contact	Comments	Max no of students
Multi Lingua, Guildford, UK	Full-time 4 weeks Part-time 6 months	Full-time	£820 plus £65 moderation fee	FT - 5/2, 4/3, 8/4 6/5, 3/6, 1/7, 29/7, 26/8, 23/9, 21/10, 18/11 PT - 6/2, 17/9	Good educational background and knowledge of grammar	Dr G P Connolly	Prepares the student for classroom teaching	12
	5 Saturdays	Part-time	£215	24 February	—	Dr G P Connolly	Thorough introduction to the theory and practice of TEFL.	10
Northumbria House, Blaydon-on-Tyne, UK	1 week	Full-time	£225	Throughout year	Interest in teaching EFL	Course Director	Intensive practical course in TEFL, including a job workshop	10
Oaklands College, London, UK	—	Part-time	£35	May	Good educational background	EFL Admin Office	—	14
Primary House Group, Bristol, UK	80 hours	Practical week end 20 hours + self study (optional) 60 hours	£250	Throughout the year	Over 18, native speaker	Anne Lang	—	16
Profile (Professionals in Language and Education) Athens, Greece	50 hours	Both (Saturdays/ weekdays/ intensive)	110,000 DRS	January, October (Sats), February, October (P/T) June, Sept (Intensive)	Proficiency holder	Profile	—	20
Saxoncourt, Taipei, Taiwan	1 week	Full-time	Tba	Tba	Good knowledge of English	Saxoncourt Taiwan	—	Tba
Skola Teacher Training, London, UK	1 week	Full-time	£175	5/2, 11/3, 15/4, 20/5, 24/6, 29/7, 2/8, 7/10, 11/11, 16/12	None	Sandra Stevens	—	15
Study Space, Thessalonika, Greece	4 months regular, 3 weeks intensive	Part-time	£350	Regular Feb/October, Intensive June/Sept.	None	Christine Taylor	—	8
Surrey Language Centre, Farnham, UK	1 week	Full-time	£175 inc. VAT	Tba	—	Jill Woodley	—	—
University of Sussex, Brighton	1 week	Full-time	£100	18/3, 1/7, 16/12	'A' level or equivalent	Margaret Khidhayir	Intensive and practical	20
Wigston College of FE, UK	2 terms	Part-time	Refer to college	Refer to college	Refer to college	Student Guidance Services	—	—
Windsor Schools TEFL, Windsor, UK	1 week	Full-time	£195	12/2 11/3, 12/6	'O' level English	Dean Pateman	—	10
Youngstown State Univ., USA	1 year for all classes if taken full-time	Full-time	Vary	September, January, March	Application to university	Steven Brown	From Sept. will offer 8 ELT related classes	20 (approx)

In-House Training

Some organisations own chains of schools and run short courses for prospective teachers. These can lead to a job in the school you trained in or another in the chain.

Although there are universally accepted varieties of EFL teaching methods, a number of schools train their teachers in their own in-house methodology. Many of these schools will be keen to accept unqualified teachers (who are less likely to come to the course with a set of preconceptions about how language should be taught). The successful applicant will then be taught the EFL methodology favoured by that school - although they may also be given some tuition in other pedagocial theories - before being placed in one of the school's own centres (though this is not always guaranteed). Obviously, having been trained to work in one specific chain of schools may be a disadvantage later if you want to find work outside that particular chain. However, most of these courses are highly respected and a qualification from them should count in your favour. Moreover the opportunity to be trained and then employed by the same school may appeal to some teachers and certainly takes some of the stress out of both job hunting and the first few weeks working as a qualified teacher. Here are some of the major chains:

BERLITZ (320+ SCHOOLS WORLDWIDE)

This long-established chain has branches throughout the world and offers introductory courses in the Berlitz method. The courses are mainly for experienced or EFL-qualified teachers but they will also consider people who have worked abroad, are language graduates or have skills in specialist fields, such as law or accountancy.

Courses last for one to two weeks and are only open to native English speakers and incorporate CD-ROM facilities. If you work outside the UK, Berlitz may pay you a modest sum to see you through the course. The school provides extra training courses for its teachers during working hours in skills such as Business English and English for Children. These courses are also based on Berlitz's own teaching methods.

Contact: Berlitz International Inc., Research Park, 293 Wall Street, Princeton NJO8540 USA or Berlitz School, Wells House, 79 Wells Street, London WIA 3BZ, UK. Written applications only.

GEOS

Geos Corporation provides teacher-training courses for native English speakers recruited as teachers for its chain of schools in Japan.

Contact: Geos Corporation, PO Box 512, Ark Mori Building, 33rd Floor, 1-12-32 Akasaka, Minato-Ku, Tokyo 107, Japan.

Geos also runs courses for non-native English speaker teachers in January in the UK.

Contact: Geos English Academy, Teacher Training Department, 55-61 Portland Road, Hove, Sussex BN3 5DQ, UK. Tel: 01273 73975

INLINGUA (250 SCHOOLS WORLDWIDE)

inlingua adopts the direct method of teaching. The school's in-house teacher training courses qualify teachers to work for inlingua's chain of language schools. The organisation teaches and uses its own specially designed course books.

The school prefers applicants to have a degree (not necessarily in languages) and to be of British or Irish nationality.

Contact: inlingua Teacher Training and Recruitment, Rodney Lodge, Rodney Road, Cheltenham, GL50 1JF, UK. Tel: 01242 253 171

LINGUARAMA (35+ SCHOOL WORLDWIDE)

This international chain runs both intensive introductory teacher-training courses for non-experienced graduates and in-house training programmes for Linguarama teachers already employed. The one-week introductory courses take place on a monthly basis in Birmingham and Manchester and consist of 40 hours' theory and short teaching practice sessions. Linguarama frequently recruits teachers for its international school network from these courses. Only native English speakers are accepted.

Contact: Linguarama, Queen's House, 8 Queen Street, London EC4N ISP, UK.

MULTI LINGUA

Multilingua forms part of the General Education Group, a teacher training and recruitment organisation, and provides its own introductory courses throughout the year. All courses can be attended either on a full or part-time basis. Multilingua places teachers who have attended its courses in schools across the world. Applicants are not obliged to have a degree or any teaching experience, but they are required to pass an aptitude test. In addition Multilingua provides a course for non-native English speakers and courses in teaching Business English. All courses are run in the UK.

Contact: Multilingua Administration Centre, St. Michael's House, 53 Woodbridge Road, Guildford, Surrey GU1 4RF, UK.

Distance Training In TESOL

For those who are unable to spare either the time or the money for a full-time teacher training course, Distance Learning is becoming an increasingly popular option.

Distance training offers the opportunity to follow a substantial course of professional training at a much lower fee

hether you are an experienced EFL teacher looking for an advanced diploma course, or someone considering a career in teaching English to speakers of other languages, a distance-training programme can provide a viable alternative to full-time study, although a distance-learning qualification without teaching practice may not be enough to give you qualified status in the eyes of many employers unless you have classroom experience. In the past, distance learning has had to shake off a 'second best' reputation inherited from the old 'correspondence course'. However it is a study method with its own advantages and, as this sector of the profession moves towards better regulation, it deserves serious consideration.

Distance-learning courses can be divided into two types: free-standing programmes, where the whole course is carried out at a distance, and Hybrid courses, where there is an element of face-to-face study, for example teaching practice.

Free-standing Programmes

Full-time study generally offers three main advantages. It is normally undertaken without job distractions. There is immediate access to resources, human as well as library and departmental, and support from the other members of the course.

Many of today's distance programmes set out to mirror face-to-face teaching and training wherever possible

Free-standing distance training, however, also offers many advantages, including the opportunity to follow a substantial course of professional training at a much lower fee; the possibility to work from home at one's own pace and the opportunity to continue working and earning whilst following the course; the very considerable saving of time and money, through not having to travel to a place of study and not having to meet any residential costs involved.

There is a wide range of distance only courses available. Several institutions offer introductory courses which can be completed in some sixty to seventy hours, are not usually very expensive and can be a good first step into TESOL. However, there are

a number of cowboy operators working in the distance field so always check out a course thoroughly before enrolling. If you are not sure of the credentials of an organisation check them with a professional body such as your local British Council or TESOL.

Hybrid Programmes

The full-time training leading to an RSA or Trinity Certificates equips trainees with reasonably effective classroom management skills and teaching techniques; but there is a limit to the amount of theory and background knowledge that can be absorbed in four weeks. Preceding such a course with a sound distance-training element, it is possible to provide a depth of knowledge simply not viable in a four-week programme. A growing number of institutions now offer initial combined courses of distance training followed by a residential block. Trinity Certificates are available on this route as well as a selection of certificates offered by UK universities. Some also offer combined programmes leading to diplomas. These are usually very flexible, taking from nine months to three years to complete.

Duration of Distance Courses

A major advantage of both distance and hybrid courses is the time flexibility. In the case of hybrid programmes one can start as early as one wishes and in the case of free-standing distance programmes one should, within reason, be able to take as long as one needs. No two people work at the same pace, have similar commitments, identical workloads or study time available. Someone able to commit him or herself to fifteen hours home study time per week will complete a 150-hour course in ten weeks. Another person able to find only five to six hours will take some six months. Therefore, it is usual to describe course length in terms of hours.

What about Teaching Practice?

There is, of course, no substitute for teaching practice. In the case of experienced practising teachers it is not always necessary - which is why

Make sure your course leads to a certificate or diploma that will be acceptable to schools and institutions able to offer you employment.

Distance Learning can be most suitable for experienced teachers seeking to gain further qualifications. For the unqualified teacher a 120-hour distance-only programme leading to a Certificate of Educational Studies in TESOL with Associate Teacher status can be a valid route to teaching abroad as a 'semi-qualified' teacher. Many overseas schools have teaching practice schemes in apprenticeship form enabling an associate to work closely with an experienced teacher during the first few weeks.

Quality Assurance

The College of Preceptors, the Chartered Body of the Teaching Profession, has played an important role in providing academic quality assurance and assessment in TESOL distance-training in the UK. Under the terms of its Royal Charter, the College is empowered to offer professional qualifications for teachers in the UK and overseas. For many years the College has offered an optional paper in the Teaching of English as a Foreign or Second Language for Part II of their LCP (a licentiate diploma equivalent to a degree).

At present the College externally validates a 250-hour course leading to the Cert(TM)TESOL as well as a 450-hour Dip(TM)TESOL programme. It also awards its own ACP(TESOL) qualification following a 250-hour distance-training programme.

A good certificate course will take some 200 hours' study time to complete

The recent launch of the Accreditation Council for TESOL Distance Education Courses (ACTDEC) is another important development. ACTDEC, a non-profit-making quality control body, has introduced a code of practice for institutions offering distance programmes covering such areas as course publicity, pre-course information, course structure and content, administration, course evaluation and quality assurance. ACTDEC also aims to establish an accreditation scheme and regular audit for courses leading to five distance education and training qualifications at four separate levels.
Level 1: 70-hour Introductory Distance-Training Courses leading to the Preliminary Certificate of Educational Studies in TESOL: TESOL Assistant

Level 2: 120-hour Distance-Training Courses leading to the Certificate of Educational Studies in TESOL: Associate Teacher of ESOL
Level 3: 250-hour Distance-Training Courses leading to the Certificate in the Theory and Methodology of TESOL: Accredited Teacher Status
Level 4: 400-hour Distance-Training Courses leading to the Diploma in the Theory and Methodology of TESOL or TESP and the qualification Dip(TM)TESOL or Dip(TM)TESP: Senior Teacher Status

Which Course?

As discussed earlier, Distance-Learning still has its disreputable element. So how do you sort the wheat from the chaff?

If the course is not accredited by an external examining body or ACTDEC, then make sure it leads to a certificate or diploma that will be acceptable to schools and institutions able to offer you employment. Do not simply be seduced by a school or qualification with an impressive-sounding name - what matters is if the school and its courses are recognised by any of the main schools or ELT institutions.

Does the length of the programme seem suitable? A good certificate course will take some 200 hours' study time to complete; a diploma 400 hours or longer.

Ask to see a copy of the syllabus. Does it state the course objectives? Does it cover the areas you are interested in? Does it list all the topics you would expect to be covered in such a course?

Does the programme incorporate a range of interactive features? Will you, for example, receive weekly or fortnightly feedback from a tutor, as well as personal direction and guidance, throughout the course?

If you have any questions or queries, don't hesitate to telephone or visit the training institution. If they are genuine, they will be glad to be of help.

College	Course title	Course length	Accrediting Body	Fees	Start dates	Entry requirements	Contact	Comments
Chrysalis Language Courses, Exeter	Foundation Certificate in EFL	150 hours	Chrysalis Language Courses (ACTDEC Accreditation being pursued)	Notified on enquiry	Throughout year	Good educational standard - usually commensurate with 2 'A' levels	Miss Y. C. Doney	Course based on a tutorial system. Study notes, concise grammar reference and bibliography provided
Eurolink Courses, Sheffield	Cert (TM) TESOL	250 hours	College of Preceptors/ ACTDEC	UK £295 EU £325 Oseas £345	Throughout year	Degree (any discipline)	B Winn-Smith	—
	ACP (TESOL) (Associate of College of Preceptors)	250 hours	College of Preceptors	UK £295 EU £325 Overseas £345	Throughout year	University entrance (degree preferred)	B Winn-Smith	—
	Dip (TM) TESOL	450 hours	College of Preceptors/ ACTDEC	UK £431 EU £460 Overseas £475	Throughout year	Two years TESOL experience	B Winn-Smith	—
Grafton International, Dublin	Cert (TESOL)	150 hours	Trinity College London	£775	—	Good educational background	Denis O'Donoghue	4 week residential block
	LTCL (TESOL) Diploma	450 hours	Trinity College London	£1100	—	2 years full-time TESOL experience	Denis O'Donoghue	2 week residential block
International House, London	RSA/Cam. DTEFLA written exam preparation	January - May	RSA/Cam.	£400	January	Those required for RSA/Cam DTEFLA	Susan Bagley	For students retaking written section of DTEFLA
Language 2 Associates, london	Certificate in TESOL - ACP	250 hours	College of Preceptors	£295	Throughout year	Preferably teacher with at least one years experience	The Secretary	Modular course leads to the Diploma
	Diploma in TESOL	450 hours	College of Preceptors	£450	Throughout year	Degree level, teaching experience	The Secretary	5 or 6 modules, - development from ACP certificate
London Montessori Centre	Montessori ELT Diploma	3 units of work + 2 week workshop	ODLQ, BAC	£275 course, £200 w/s £50 exam	Throughout year	'O' level English or equiv. Cambridge First Cert.	Correspond-ence Dept.	Teaching English as a second language to children.
Lynda Hazelwood Language Services, Bristol	Certificate of Education Studies in TESOL	120 hours (+ optional introductory week-end)	ACTDEC (Going through accreditation)	Course £180 Intro week-ends £85 Stud. and Unemp. reductions	Course anytime. Intro monthly	None for intro. Otherwise academic background	Lynda Hazelwood	Practical base backed up by sound theory. Also offer Teaching Bus. English
ROBACO, London	Preliminary Certificate of Ed. Studies in TESOL	70 hours	ACTDEC	£245	Throughout year	Good general education, preferably 2 'A' levels	Robert M. Barrett	Also offer Certificate and Diploma in TEFL
TEFL Training, Witney	Certificate in TEFL	80 hours	—	Residential £215 Video/ Distance £150	Monthly	Fluent English	Tony Crofts	Intensive introduction in direct contact seminar or on video

Key to UK Certificates

NORTH & SCOTLAND

	PAGE
Aberdeen College	42
Basil Paterson	42
Bradford & Ilkley College	42
Edinburgh Tutorial College	41
Leeds I.L.I	39
Sheffield Hallam	42

CENTRAL & WALES

		PAGE
Bell Language School:	Cambridge	36
	Norwich	36
	Saffron Waldon	36
ELT Banbury		
Regent School Oxford		40
Students International:	Leicestershire	41
Studio School:	Cambridge	42

LONDON

		PAGE
British Council		44
Frances King		42
Hammersmith & West London		39
International House		37
Kingsway College		36
London Guildhall University		38
Regent School :	London	40
Southwark College		42
Stanton Teacher Training		38
Trinity College		37
Westminster College		40

SOUTH

		PAGE
City of Bath College		40
Colchester Institute:	Essex	36
Concorde International:	Kent	41
Devon School of English		41
Eastbourne School of English		38
GEOS:	Brighton	39
	Hove	39
Harrow House		39
Hilderstone College:	Kent	38
International House:	Hastings	37
ITS Hastings		39
ITTC Bournemouth		39
Multilingua		41
Regency School:	Kent	40
Regent School	Oxford	40
St Giles:	Eastbourne	36
	Brighton	36
University of Portsmouth		41
Windsor Schools		40

CHANNEL ISLANDS

		PAGE
St Brelades:	Jersey	42

1936 - 1996

60 years of quality
English Language Teaching

EASTBOURNE SCHOOL OF ENGLISH

Non-profit-making Educational Trust
Registered Charity No. 306381

RSA/CAMBRIDGE DIPLOMA in TEFLA

- **Full-time and part-time courses**

RSA/CAMBRIDGE CERTIFICATE in TEFLA

- **4-week full-time courses**

COURSES FOR OVERSEAS TEACHERS OF ENGLISH

- **Cambridge Examination in English for Language Teachers (CEELT I and II)**

- **Advanced Language Development and Aspects of British Culture**

- **Communicative Methodology and Advanced Language Development**

Eastbourne School of English (EFLG),
8 Trinity Trees,
Eastbourne, E. Sussex BN21 3LD.
Telephone: +44 (0)1323 721759 Fax: +44 (0)1323 639271

Key to Overseas Certs & Diplomas

	PAGE
NORTHERN EUROPE	
ATT	49
Excel International	47
Foyle Language Centre	47
Galway Cultural Institute	47
International House Paris	45
International House Hastings	45
University College Cork	49
CENTRAL & EASTERN EUROPE	
International House Budapest	46
International House Prague	45
SOUTHERN EUROPE	
British Council Naples	46
British Language Centre Madrid	46
Cambridge School Lisbon	44
Campbell College Spain	46
CELT Athens	47
International House Barcelona	44
International House Madrid	43
International House Portugal	46
International House Rome	46
NSTS Malta	44
THE AMERICAS	
English International	48
Hawaii Pacific University	45
International House New York	49
University of California Riverside	48
University of Waikato	47
Worldwide Teachers Dev. Institute	48
AUSTRALIA/ASIA	
Australian Centre for Languages	49
British Council Hong Kong	44
ECC Thailand	46
Insearch language Centre	49
University of Southern Queensland	43

University of California, Riverside

Programs in

Teaching
English to
Speakers of
Other
Languages

The TESOL Certificate Program is designed to provide participants with the major competencies and knowledge necessary to be specialists in the ESL field.

• **TESOL Methodologies Workshop: 4-Week Program**
    For those who already teach English in their own countries and wish to improve their skills and learn about new developments in the field.

• **TESOL Certificate: 1-Year Program**
    For those would like to teach English but are not prepared to enter the field.

Classes combine theory and practice to help develop and improve teaching skills. Most classes are composed of both American and international participants. Enrollments can be made in any quarter.

"The TESOL Program is really great! The teachers are excellent and very friendly. But what I like best about TESOL is that the program is very practical. As a student-teacher, I need this in order to be prepared for the real world."

Carmen Paladino, TESOL
Student
From Brazil

For more information, please contact:

International Education Programs
University of California Extension
1200 University Avenue, Dept. ELT,
Riverside, CA 92507-4596 U.S.A.
PHONE: (909) 787-4346
FAX: (909) 787-5796
E-mail: ucriep@ucx.ucr.edu
Web site: http://www.unex.ucr.edu/
    iephomepage.html

American English in Boston
"USA's Academic Capital"

The Boston Course®/Certificate in Teaching English as a Foreign Language (C.T.E.F.L.)

• Four-week Intensive Course Monthly

• Three-month Part-time Certificate Course

• Teacher Training Provided

• No Second Language Necessary

• Global Placement Guidance

• Harvard University Club or other accommodations

Also available complete American Business English Programs

Thomas A. Kane, Ph.D., Admissions Director
WORLDWIDE TEACHERS
Development Institute
266 Beacon Street
Boston, Massachusetts 02116 USA
Tel: 617-262-5766   Fax: 617-262-5722
Email: BostonTEFL@aol.com

To ensure that we have up-to-date details of all your courses, send or fax details to:

ELT GUIDE RESEARCH DEPARTMENT
10 Wrights Lane
Kensington
London W8 6TA
Fax: +44 171 937 7534

RSA/Cambridge CTEFLA for Americans

• 4-Week Courses Start Monthly
• Maximum of 12 Participants Per Course
• Unique Pre-Course Assignment
• Job Guidance Service for Our Graduates
• BA/BS & Some Foreign Language Knowledge Required

We are the only center which specializes exclusively in offering quality CTEFLA courses for teachers of American and Canadian English.

English International

655 Sutter (Suite 200), San Francisco, CA 94102, USA
Tel: (415) 749-5633   Fax: (415) 749-5629

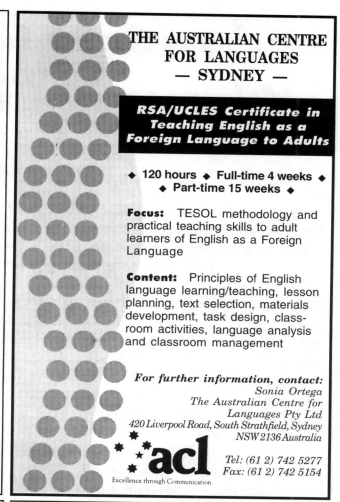

English Language Institute
University of Surrey
MA in Linguistics (TESOL)
by distance learning

Promoting Excellence in Education and Research

The English Language Institute of the University of Surrey offers its MA in Linguistics (TESOL) on a Distance Learning basis, making it possible for teachers to gain a higher degree without the necessity of leaving their post or having to fulfil residence requirements in the United Kingdom.

The course is one of the largest of its kind, with 300 students currently taking the course in 48 countries. The course materials are specially designed for students working away from the University, and include printed modules, tapes and bibliographies. The University provides a unique degree of personal tutorial support, and dissertation supervision. A distinctive feature of the University of Surrey degree is the range of module subjects, now totalling 17. All students study 8 core modules, and select two from the option module list.

Core Modules
**Syllabus Design   Discourse Analysis   Pedagogic Grammar   Sociolinguistics
Phonetics   Methodology   Testing   Second Language Acquisition**

Option Modules
**Bilingualism   Computers and Applied Linguistics   ELT Management
Learner Independence   Literature   Statistics and Empirical Research Methods
Scientific English   Typology   Written Genres**

Assessment is by assignment on 10 modules, and a dissertation of 12,000 words. Submission of work, feedback and dissertation supervision may be by traditional methods (post, fax, audio tape), or using the Internet where available. The English Language Institute also maintains a useful World Wide Web site.

Internet: http://www.surrey.ac.uk/ELI/eli.html

The English Language Institute also offers **Pre-sessional courses** throughout the academic year, and a **Summer programme**, for students of English.

For further information on any of these courses, including fees and application forms, please contact:

**Dr Glenn Fulcher
English Language Institute, University of Surrey, Guildford,
Surrey GU2 5XH, United Kingdom**

Fax: + (01483) 259507   e-mail: g.fulcher@surrey.ac.uk

Further Qualifications

For experienced teachers keen to improve their skills or move into a specialist sphere of English Language Teaching, there is a vast range of courses offered by Universities, Colleges of Further Education and Private Language Schools. The following section gives details on many of these courses as well as advice on which qualifications might best suit your chosen career path.

52 The Academic Ladder

53 How Will Qualifications Help Me?

54 RSA/Cambridge Diploma (DTEFLA) Courses

55 Trinity Licentiate Diploma In TESOL Courses

56 Overseas RSA/Cambridge Diploma Courses

57 UK University Courses

58 UK University/College Courses

61 MA's In North America

62 US And Canadian University Courses

68 MA's In The UK

69 UK Master's Degree Courses

74 MA's In Autralia And New Zealand

75 Australian And New Zealand University Courses

77 Specialising

78 Teaching Young Learners

80 Teaching Business English

81 Short Courses

87 CEELT And DOTE Courses

89 Business English Courses

The Academic Ladder

After undertaking an initial training programme and gaining some practical experience a teacher wishing to progress in TEFL should start considering further qualifications.

If you have two or more years' experience, you can opt for a practical diploma such as the RSA/Cambridge or Trinity

espite its emphasis on successful classroom methods, Teaching English as a Foreign Language is still an academic discipline and it is important that you take time out to continue studying and researching as your career develops. Academic qualifications will definitely be a factor in obtaining high profile jobs, especially in the public sector.

If you start with a university degree and an RSA/Cambridge or Trinity Preparatory Certificate, obtained by doing a short training course, as discussed in Section One, (For short courses see pp81-86), what is the logical next step?

An EFL Diploma

If you have two or more years' experience, you can opt for a practical diploma such as the RSA/Cambridge or Trinity. These contain both written papers and a practical, two lessons, each with a different class, taught by you, observed by an examiner and marked accordingly. Courses take around 10 weeks full-time or one year part-time.

Distance Learning is a good option at this level although the RSA/Cambridge and Trinity programmes insist on some elements of on-site teaching practice. A distance-learning RSA Diploma has also been offered for many years by International House. However, to take the examination you will need to be registered with a recognised school. Other institutions offer distance-only programmes which may be an option if you are interested in a theoretical approach.

A diploma or other further qualification is likely to be an essential part of your job-seeking armoury.

In Britain, Ireland, Australia and New Zealand a diploma is often a prerequisite for a good job, particularly one in Academic Management (such as Director of Studies) or Teacher Training.

Experienced teachers may opt for a UK Diploma in Education, specialising in EFL. This is also a one-year university degree course that is equivalent to the general Postgraduate Diploma in Education (DipEd). It qualifies teachers in other subjects to

teach in secondary schools.

The Master of Arts (MA)

Academically, EFL is an application of linguistics and many teachers choose to do a one-year MA in Applied Linguistics. As part of your MA course you have to do research for a short dissertation. This may allow you to pursue areas of special interest, for example the use of media or the use of video in ELT. If this is the case, you should look for colleges that have a special interest in this area, such as the University of Westminster or the Language Centre at Brighton Polytechnic. Although an MA is often regarded as a theoretical rather than a practical course of study, it is also possible to study for an MA which is more directly related to teaching EFL, such as the University of Warwick's MA in English Language Teaching or the University of Sterling's MSc in CALL and TESOL. See page 68 for more details.

Doctorate in Philosophy (PhD)

Qualified teachers who intend to undertake a university teaching career may wish to study for a doctorate. Doctorates involve researching and writing a dissertation on your chosen area of research and they can last from between two years (full-time research) to what can sometimes seems like a lifetime (part-time). The subject for your doctoral research must be agreed by a university at the outset and a research supervisor will be assigned to you.

Some universities - London is one - offer a one-year MPhil (Master in Philosophy) which counts towards the full doctorate. This might be appropriate for a practising teacher who has done the Diploma and wants to approach doctorate work without doing the MA.

Whichever academic course you decide to follow, it is important to remember that in the UK and USA competition for jobs in ELT is fierce at the moment. A diploma or other further qualification is likely to be an essential part of your job-seeking armoury.

How Will Further Qualifications Help Me?

There is a wide variety of further qualifications for experienced EFL teachers looking to improve their knowledge and employability.

I am an experienced native English-speaking teacher of EFL but I have no qualification. What should I do?

It is a good idea to get a qualification. You do not necessarily need to do a certificate course, which is the course most teachers of EFL will initially take. If you want to work in the private sector and you have more than two years' experience, you could do an RSA or Trinity Diploma (see p 54). Note, however, that some centres may prefer you to do the RSA Certificate before they will let you do the Diploma. If you want to work in the state system, you must achieve Qualified Teacher Status. With two years' teaching experience you can do a Masters degree or a diploma.

Does a qualification guarantee a job?

There is a popular myth that if you do a Masters degree, you will automatically get a better job. This is not necessarily true. Jobs which require MAs do generally pay well, but they are thin on the ground with far too many teachers with MAs chasing them. There is, however, a shortage of experienced teachers with diplomas.

Is a university diploma equivalent to an RSA or Trinity Diploma?

It can be equivalent if it contains teaching practice, but generally it is a completely different qualification (see p57).

Are MA's much the same price?

The cost of an MA varies from country to country. In general, MAs in Australia and Canada are relatively cheap. Most EU countries, have comparable costs. MAs for non-residents are more expensive. If you are a British teacher who has been outside the EU for a long time, you may be classed as an overseas teacher in the UK.

Are all MA courses similar?

Not really. Because some universities are inevitably better equipped with staff and materials in some fields, MA courses at such universities will also be stronger in those fields (see pp62, 69, 75).

I am interested in computers/literature/drama. What should I do?

There are courses that focus on a specialised area of teaching. You can choose from a range of subjects as diverse as video, audio and computers in teaching to English through theatre or designing and creating materials (see pp81-89).

How can I pay for further training ?

If you are an EU citizen, you may be eligible for a Career Development Loan - ask your college. If you do a course in Australia, you have automatic, limited work rights, whatever your nationality. In the US and Canada you can only work legally on the college campus, but jobs as a teaching assistant are fairly common. In the UK you can do a part-time RSA Cambridge or Trinity Diploma while you are working. There is also an increasing number of UK MA courses which are part time, modular or offer distance-learning options.

I want to train to get into management. What should I do?

You could do an MBA (Masters in Business Administration). Many EFL teachers are now turning to this qualification as a way of either getting into management within EFL, or of broadening out of EFL into general management. Bristol University run a management stream as part of their MA in TEFL. West Sussex University also run a management course. Some other British MAs also incorporate management training elements. IATEFL (the International Association of Teachers Of English as a Foreign Language) has a Special Interest Group (SIG) dedicated to management.

I want to teach English as a Second Language in the UK. What should I do?

Many EFL teachers change to ESL as an opportunity to have a clearer career structure. It also offers the means to remain teaching in your native country in the primary or state sector.

I want to teach English for Specific Purposes What is the best thing to do?

Teaching English in specific subjects such as English for Banking is a growing area. If you have a specialist background, you could be in demand (see p77 and p81). Training courses in ESP, although not obligatory, are a common requirement for teaching ESP.

I am a primary specialist. Which is the best course for me?

There are various short courses that incorporate such experience (see pp81-86) and some Masters programmes also specialise in this.

Will I automatically get more money if I am better qualified?

Unfortunately not. There is no incremental system as such within the private EFL sector, and salaries can vary quite widely for teachers with the same qualifications. Your location can have as much effect on your salary as your qualifications. Only state schools and major employers, such as the British Council, have a rigid incremental system.

RSA/Cambridge Diploma (DTEFLA) Courses

College	Course length	FT/PT	Fees	Start dates	Entry requirements	Contact	Comments	Max no of students
Bell Language School, Cambridge	27 weeks	Part-time	£950	October	2 years' teaching experience	Sue Sheerin		15
Bell Language School, Norwich	10 weeks	Full-time	£1,300	April	2 years' teaching experience	Sarah Knight	—	15
Bell Language School, Saffron Walden	10 weeks	Full-time	£1,300	March	2 years' teaching experience	Robin Davis	Intensive	15
Chichester College of Art, Science + Technology	32 weeks	Part-time	On application	September	Degree + 2 years' teaching experience	Brenda Pike	—	15
Eastbourne College of Art And Technology	8 months	Part-time	£400	September	As UCLES/RSA requirements	Barbara Garside	—	16
Eastbourne School of English	9 weeks	Full-time	£1,200	January	Min. 2 years' TEFL experience	Dorothy S. Rippon	Cost exc. exam fee but inc. post course dist. learning	12
	9 months	Part-time	£750 (to be confirmed)	October	2 years' TEFL experience and currently in TEFL post	Dorothy S. Rippon	1 eve per week for 30 wks + 3 Saturday workshops	12
GLOSCAT, Cheltenham	36 weeks	Part-time	£700	September	Interview, CTEFLA and/or teaching experience	Paul Burden	—	14
Hammersmith & West London College	1 year	Part-time	£550	12 September	Degree, 2 years EFL experience. CTEFLA preferred	Course Information Centre	—	15
Hilderstone College, Broadstairs	9 months	Part-time	£975 + exam fee of £162	October	Native speaker 2 years exp., high lvl of ed.	Valerie Horne	—	12
ILI Leeds	2 terms Dist + 1 term part-time	Part-time	£1100	September	On application	Steven Procter	—	—
International House Hastings	8 weeks and 9 weeks	Full-time	8 weeks £1,340 9 weeks £1,450 Both + £157 Cambridge Entrance Fee	9 weeks 4 March, 8 weeks 30 September	RSA/Cam. Cert plus 2 years' experience	Adrian Underhill	Accomm. service available	12
International House London	300 hours min.	Part-time	Tba	October	Initial TEFL qualification preferred + equivalent of 2 yrs teaching experience with adults	Susan Bagley	Dist. learning course + 2 wk face to face orientation Closing date for apps, mid-April	—
International Teaching and Training Centre, Bournemouth	8 weeks/28 weeks	Both	£1,268 plus RSA fee	Full-time Feb, Apr, Oct. Part-time Oct.	University Degree	Pilar Diaz	—	18

RSA/Cambridge Diploma (DTEFLA) Courses

College	Course length	FT/PT	Fees	Start dates	Entry requirements	Contact	Comments	Max no of students
Mid-Cheshire College, Northwich	9 months	Part-time	On application	September	Degree + 2 years experience	Barbara Murphy		16
Skola Teacher Training, London	8 weeks + written assignments over following 9 months	Full-time	Tba	July	Min. 2 years' experience	Sandra Stevens	—	12
University of Edinburgh, Institute of Applied Lang. Studies	10 weeks	Full-time	£1,400	March	Degree/ teaching qualification + 3 years exp.	Registration Secretary		8
Waltham Forest College, London	1 year	Part-time (2 evenings a week)	Tba	Sept-June	Currently in EFL + 2 years' experience	Programme Co-ordinator	—	12

Trinity Licentiate Diploma In TESOL Courses

College	Course length	FT/PT	Fees	Start dates	Entry requirements	Contact	Comments	Max no of students
Aberdeen College	2*10 weeks	Part-time	£330	Various	2 years' experience	Anne Bain	—	10
Bradford and Ilkley College	34 weeks	Part-time	£1000	October	TEFL cert. + 2 years' full-time experience	Nancy Hall	—	16
ITS English School, Hastings	11 months (220 - 270 hours)	Part-time	£850 - £1,250	1 August	2 years recent TESOL experience	John Palim	Dist. Learning course + res. block. Optional supervised teaching pract.	10
The Language Project, Bristol	20 weeks	Part-time	£550 + exam fee	Jan/August	2 years' experience	Dr Jon Wright	—	10
Oaklands College, Borehamwood	9 months	Part-time	£695	Varied	2 years' experience	EFL Admin Officer	—	10
Oxford House College, London	Full-time 6 weeks, Part time (Dist.) up to 3 years	Both	£990	Throughout year	As per Trinity requirements	Michael Harmsworth	Dist. Learning includes 2 wk London block	Full-time 4 Part-time n/a
St. George's School of English, London	1-2 years	Part-time	£800	Anytime	2 years' TEFL experience + Trinity Cert. or equivalent	Max Loach	Dist. Learning course with 2 wk residential block.	—
Sheffield Hallam University	Part-time Dist 42 weeks Full-time 4 weeks	Mixed	£1,400 + Trinity College Fee	7 October	Cert. TESOL + 1-2 years experience	Gill King	Second part of teacher training programme	25
Students Intenational, Melton Mowbray	9 months	Part-time	On application	October	Interview + 2 years' experience	Alison Blythe	—	12
Woking and Chertsey Adult Education Institute	30 weeks	Part-time	£400 approx	October	2 years' ESOL teaching experience	Ursula Over	Course leaflet/ application form available	16

College	Course length	FT/PT	Fees	Start dates	Entry requirements	Contact	Comments	Max no of students
Australian TESOL Training Centre, Bondi Junction, Australia	Full-time 8 weeks Part time 20 weeks	Both	Aus$3,150	Full-time 5 Feb. Part-time 2 Sept.	Substantial exp. EFL to adults, degree and/or teaching qual.	Gloria Smith		12
British Council Milan, Italy	8 months	Part-time	2,400,000 lire (excl exam fee)	end of September	—	David Gibbon	—	15
British Council Izmir, Turkey	8 months	Part-time	£900 plus exam fee	October	RSA CTEFLA or equivalent, 2 years relevant teaching exp.	Steven Darn	—	—
The British Language Centre, Madrid, Spain	Full-time 8 weeks, Part-time 6 months	Both	240.000 pts	Throughout year	Degree + CTEFLA pref.	Alistair Dickinson	Accomm. provided	12
British School Milan, Italy	30 weeks approx	Part-time	L2.200.000 (95/96 fee)	Last Friday in September	UCLES Cert. TEFLA + 2-3 yrs' experience	Susan Swift	Course sessions held every Friday	10
Cambridge School Verona, Italy	—	Full-time	L2.400.000	October	Degree, RSA Cert. pref., 2 yrs' experience	Anne Parry	—	12
CELT Athens, Greece	1 year (210 hours + 40 hrs of elective subjects)	Part-time Oct-June + full-time Summer blocks	£1,600	June	BA or Teachers Cert., exp. + basic training	Marisa Constantinides	Internal Practical Assessment scheme	—
Centre of Lang. Ed., Univ. of Wollongong, NSW, Australia	210 hours (6 weeks full time) + 36 hrs practice teaching	Full-time + Part-time options	Tba	Tba	High School (Year 12) graduation	—	Students with RSA Cert only need complete 105 hrs + 18hrs teaching	15
Centro Anglo Paraguayo, Asuncion, Paraguay	—	Part-time	On application	Tba	On application	Maureen Finn	—	—
International House Budapest, Hungary	6 weeks	Full-time (in three blocks)	£790 plus £162 examination fee	3/1, 31/3, 13/5	Min. 2 years' post CTEFLA experience	Eva Baricz	Assistance with accomm. in Budapest	12
International House Lisbon, Portugal	Full-time 8 weeks Part-time 8 months	Both	275,000 pte	Full-time July Part-time October	CTEFLA + 2 years' experience	Paula de Nagy	Interview	12
International House Madrid, Spain	—	Part-time	210,000 pesetas	14 October	2 years' post CTEFLA exp., working in travelling dist. of Centre	Steven Haysham	—	12
International House Rome, Italy	8 weeks	Full-time	On application	July, September	UCLES requirements	The Director	Help given with accomm.	12
The Language Centre of Ireland, Dublin	9 months	Part-time	IR£850	September	Degree, 3 years' experience	Tom Doyle	—	12
St Mark's International College, Perth, Australia	8 months	Part-time	$2,600 + $350 exam fee	18 September	Min. 2 years' EFL experience + degree	Director of Studies	—	12

UK University Courses

There is a vast array of University courses for both the new and highly experienced EFL Teacher.

It is possible to take a university certificate in most Anglophone countries instead of the more widely known RSA/Cambridge or Trinity Certificate

here are too many EFL teacher training courses offered by universities to list here, but the following information describes courses leading to certificates, advanced certificates and diplomas. Remember that there are many new UK universities, as changes in legislation have enabled British polytechnics to run degree courses and become universities.

Pre-experience certificates

The term 'certificate' generally refers to a short course between three and six months in length. Most certificates in the UK are initial teacher training courses open to native and non-native speakers. It is possible to take a university certificate in most Anglophone countries instead of the more widely known RSA/Cambridge or Trinity Certificates. However, if you take a university course, make sure it includes teaching practice with foreign students and not just peer teaching with other teachers on your course. Many employers will not recognise such a qualification unless it includes teaching practice.

Post-experience certificates

Recently there has been a growth in advanced certificates for experienced teachers wishing to specialise in defined areas of EFL teaching

These are usually called 'advanced certificates' and last three to six months. They are designed for people who either have experience but no previous qualifications, or who have training and need further qualifications without having the time to do a full Masters degree. Recently there has been a growth in advanced certificates for experienced teachers wishing to specialise in defined areas of EFL teaching such as English For Academic Purposes, Teaching Young Learners or teacher training.

Postgraduate diplomas

These are usually a year in length, and are for native or non-native English speakers with teaching experience (usually a year minimum). They are not automatically seen as equivalent to the RSA/Cambridge or Trinity College Diplomas (see p54) unless they include a substantial amount of teaching practice with EFL students.

The advantage of such courses is that they have easier entry requirements than Masters programmes, and they should be more practical and less academic - although this is not always the case. The disadvantage of such courses is that too many universities offer exactly the same courses for Diplomas or Masters. Either check the contents of the course carefully, or make sure that you opt for a course that allows you to move over from a diploma to a Masters if you do well enough.

There is also an infinite variety in academic level between one Diploma and another. This is partly because there is no validation scheme for diplomas in the UK. Universities validate their own degrees, and while control of degree awards such as Masters are strictly regulated by mastership committees, diploma status seems to be more easily conferred. In effect, a diploma is any course that is not a Masters, although the British Association of Applied Linguistics (BAAL) is trying to rectify this.

Masters degrees

Teachers of EFL/ESL in the United States generally hold an MA in TESL or Applied Linguistics as a minimum qualification, largely because there is no widely recognised equivalent to the RSA/Cambridge or Trinity Certificates (see page 19). The only problem with this system is that many MA courses offer theoretical tuition with too little practical guidance. For this reason, teachers are not adequately prepared to teach in the classroom. It is therefore vital to check that the Masters degree has a solid teaching component.

Elsewhere, teachers of EFL tend to take a Masters degree as a way up the career ladder (see pp61 - 76). Remember that there are now many EFL teachers who hold a Masters degree, far more than there are jobs that require them. Therefore it may be more useful to do the RSA/Cambridge or Trinity College Diplomas (see p54) with its stronger practical teaching component.

College	Course title	Course length	FT/PT	Fees	Start dates	Entry requirements	Contact	Comments
Canterbury Christchurch, College	Certificate in TEFL	1 term	Both	£1,715	October 1996 January 1997	Two years' teaching experience	Stephen Bax	Information sheet comparing course to RSA/Cam available on request
College of St Mark and St John, Plymouth	Certificate in Principles and Practice of Materials Production	3 months	Full-time	£2,750	At an agreed time	Teachers with substantial classroom experience	Director, INTEC	—
	Certificate in Teaching Reading in EFL	10 weeks	Full-time	£2,750	January	Teachers, curriculum developers, materials & textbook writers	Director, INTEC	—
	Cert. in Primary Teacher Training for ELT	1 term	Full-time	£2,750	At an agreed time	Teacher trainers, inspectors, supervisors	Director, INTEC	—
	Certificate in Teaching English for Specific Purposes	3 months	Full-time	£2,750 (currently)	January and April	Practising teachers of English and ESP, materials writers, ESP programme designers and managers	Director, INTEC	—
	Certificate in Classroom Research	3 months	Full-time	£2,750	At an agreed time	Teachers, trainers, project managers, curriculum developers	Director, INTEC	—
	Certificate in Resource Centre Management	1 term	Full-time	£2,750	At an agreed time	Teachers, teacher trainers, personnel who would run resource centre	Director, INTEC	—
	Cert. in the Principles. and Practice of In-Service Training for ELT(PRINSELT)	3 months	Full-time	£2,750	January and April	Teachers, teacher trainers and supervisors, in-service training programme co-ordinators	Director, INTEC	—
	Research Certificate in Readability Of School Textbooks And Other Educational Materials	1 term	Full-time	£2,750	At an agreed time	Curiculum developers, materials writers, editors etc.	Director, INTEC	—

UK University/College Certificate Courses

College	Course title	Course length	FT/PT	Fees	Start dates	Entry requirements	Contact	Comments
Aston University, Birmingham	Certificate in Principles of ESP	10 weeks	Full-time	£2,045	October, January	Degree + 2 years' experience	Secretary, Language Studies Unit	EFL experience unnecessary
	Advanced Certificate in Principles of TEFL	6 months	Distance Learning	£1,100	January	Teaching qualification + 2 years' experience	Secretary Language Studies Unit	EFL experience unnecessary
The Queen's University of Belfast TEFL Centre	Certificate in TEFL	4 weeks	Full-time	£385	1 July, 29 July	Native or near native speakers only. Degree desirable	Janice Witherspoon	—
	Graduate Certificate in TEFL	9 months	Part-time	£435 (under review for 96/97)	23 September	Degree essential, knowledge of foreign languages and teaching or presentation experience desirable	Janice Witherspoon	Undergoing validation procedure this year for Trinity Certficate in TESOL
University of Edinburgh	Advanced Certificate in Teaching English for Specific Purposes	10 weeks	Full-time	£1,400	January	Teaching qualifcation + 3 yrs' experience	Registration Secretary	—
	Advanced Certificate in ELT	10 weeks	Full-time	Full-time £1,400 Distance Learning £1,250	Full-time October Dist/ Learning January or May	Full-time Degree/ teaching qualification + 2 years' experience (3 years for Dist. Learning)	Registration Secretary	Distance Learning includes 2 week Residential Mode
University of Liverpool	Certificate in TEFL/ESP	Full-time 6 weeks, Part-time 6 months	Both	£950	January, July	Degree	TEFL Admissions Tutor	Initial training in TEFL, most applicants are native speakers
University of Portsmouth	Introduction to TEFL	Full-time 1 week, Part-time 9 weeks	Both	Full-time £165 Part-time £99	Full-time 25 March, 17 June Part-time 18 April	N/A	David Palmer	An introduction - does not lead to a certificate
	TEFL Refresher	2*1 week	Full-time	£395	24 March, 14 July	Teacher of Seniors + 1-2 years' exp. + degree/ teacher training certificate	David Palmer	—
University of Wales Aberystwth	Option course within PGCE Secondary course	30 hrs within full-time PGCE course	—	N/a	September	Degree and admission to PGCE Secondary Course	PGCE Secondary Course Secretary	Provides an introduction to TESL/TEFL but no practical teaching experience. It does not lead to a separate qualification

UK University Diploma Courses

College	Course title	Course length	FT/PT	Fees	Start dates	Entry requirements	Contact	Comments
Aston University	Diploma in TE/TESP	6 months 1-2 years	Both + Distance Learning	EU £1,550 Non EU £3,250	January, October	Degree + 3 years' experience	Secretary, Language Studies Unit	CTEFLA useful, DL available in specific countries
University of Brighton (The Language Centre)	Diploma In TEFL	Full-time 1 year Part-time 2 years	Both	Full-time £900 Part-time £350 Non-EU £5,700	23 September	Degree or teaching qualification with some EFL experience	Departmental Secretary	—
University of Leeds (School of Education)	Post Graduate Dip. in TESOL	Two semesters	—	—	October or February	3 years' experience	Hywel Coleman	—
	EdD (TESOL)	3 years	Both	—	October, February	MA, MEd or equivalent	Dr Martin Bygate	—
University of Manchester (School of Education)	Diploma in TESOL	9-12 months	Both	EU £2,430 O/seas £5,890	September January	Degree, teacher training, 1-2 years' exp.	Secretary CELSE	5 obligatory modules and long essay
University of Sheffield (Department of English Language and Linguistics)	Diploma in Applied Linguistics	Full time 9 months Part-time 21 months	Both	Full-time £2,430 Part-time £823 (95/96 fees)	September	Degree	Secretary	IELTS score of 5.5 overall or equivalent
University of Warwick (Centre For English Language Teacher Education)	Diploma in English Language Teaching and Administration	9 months	Full-time	EU £2,430 Overseas £5,955	October	Degree, training, 2 years' experience	Anne Beale	—

UK University Degree Courses

College	Course title	Course length	FT/PT	Fees	Start dates	Entry requirements	Contact	Comments
Anglia Polytechnic, Cambridge	BA in English Language Studies (Subject to validation)	3 years	Full-time	£5,400	September	'A' level equivalent + minimum of IELTS 5.5	Anne Dover	Students can combine Eng Lang. with Arts/Humanities, Business or TEFL
Chichester Institute of Higher Education	Minor Route in Language Studies within BA Humanities Programme (Modular)	—	Full-time	Tba	October	To be accepted on BA Humanities programme	Angela Karlsson	—
University of Leeds (School of Education)	BA TESOL	2 years	Full-time	—	October	Initial training, 5 years' experience	Lynne Cameron	—
University of Stirling (Centre for English Language Teaching)	BA in English Language Training	3 years	Full-time	On application	16 September	University entrance qualifications and IELT 5	Mrs S. Tyler	For non-native speakers of English only

MA's In North America

North America has an impressive range of Master's programs covering all areas of EFL and ESL.

There are around 200 TEFL-related MA courses in the USA

In the last twenty-five years, TESOL or the Teaching of English to Speakers of Other Languages, has grown into an international profession with its own association. The overwhelming concern for training qualified practitioners has led to the establishment of the MA degree as a standard professional qualification often taken as an initial training course.

There are around 200 TEFL-related MA courses in the USA. With such a dazzling array of options available, it is very difficult to know which one best suits your needs. Start with your interests and whether or not you intend to teach abroad.

The core of MA programmes in the US contains a series of skills aimed at developing effective teaching. They include: English linguistics, psycholinguistic and sociolinguistic processes, pedagogy and testing, cultural study and teaching practice.

English linguistics refers to the nature of language, linguistic descriptions, contrastive analysis among other languages and aspects such as grammar, and semantics. The University of Pittsburgh, UCLA, Colorado at Boulder, Ball State, Illinois at Chicago all have good programs; Harvard and MIT have well-known programs in pure linguistics.

When choosing a particular program, keep in mind the school location and whether it has access to a wide range of non-native speakers

Psycholinguistic and sociolinguistic processes refer to how we learn languages, factors that affect language learning and differences in learning styles. The University at Southern California, UC Santa Cruz, San Francisco State University, UCLA and The University of Hawaii at Manoa all have a reputation for second language acquisition specialities. The University of Alabama and Hunters College in New York are known for learning style research.

Pedagogy and testing refer to the methods of teaching, lesson planning and assessment. Teachers College New York, the School for International Training, University of San Francisco, and Minnesota are quite strong in pedagogy. The University of Hawaii, UCLA, Georgetown University and Michigan are strong on testing.

Cultural studies include knowledge of the cultural influences on learning, study of intercultural communication theory and sociocultural issues affecting language learning. The universities of Colorado at Denver, Brigham Young in Utah, The Monterey Institute of International Studies in California and The School for International Training, Vermont all excel in this area.

Teaching practice includes guided observation, group feedback and supervised teaching practice; sometimes programs even offer teaching practice overseas. All of the better known programs now contain this component. The University of Hawaii, Teachers College New York and San Francisco State University are particularly strong.

Many MA programs require students to undertake the study of a foreign or second language concurrently with other studies, usually second language acquisition. Multimedia applications in language teaching are increasingly being introduced as new course elements.

MA degrees are generally offered under many different university departments and in very diverse subject areas. Georgetown University in Washington, for example, offers an MA in TESL under the Department of Linguistics while an MA in TESOL at Azusa Pacific University near Los Angeles comes under the Department of International/Inter-cultural Studies. When choosing a particular program keep in mind the school location and whether it has access to a wide range of non-native speakers. Although all universities that offer MA degrees have ESL programs for foreign students, those programs situated in multi-ethnic regions in the United States offer many more opportunities to gain broader teaching experience.

Bilingualism is the speciality of many Canadian programmes, with Concordia and McGill, both in bilingual Quebec, taking the lead. The University of British Colombia is doing pioneering work in the area of content-based instruction.

US University Certificate Courses

College	Course title	Course length	FT/PT	Fees	Start dates	Entry requirements	Contact	Comments
University of California (International Education Programs)	TESOL Certificate	1 year	Part-time	$1,850	Year round	550 TOEFL score (Uncond.) 500 TOEFL score (cond.)	Co-ordinator of TESOL programs	Classes are composed of Americans and internationals
University of California Irvine Extension	TESL Certificate plus TEFL Seminar	Cert. 5 1/2 months Seminar 4 weeks	Both	Cert. $3,900 Seminar $950	Cert. 8 July Seminar 5 August	Cert. TOEFL 530 Seminar TOEFL 530 + 2 yrs' teaching	Dr Jia Frydenberg	—
Eastern Washington University (Department of Mod. Lang. and Literatures)	Certificate Program in TESOL (also a Minor Endorsement for the State of WA)	One academic year, 27 quarter credits or two summers	Full-time	$75 per credit hour, $752 resident tuition	23/9 for academic year 24/6, 22/7, 19/8 for 1996 Summer sessions	BA or part of u/graduate work. Can be taken as a Cert. Prog. without completed BA	Mary Brooks	—
Goshen College, Indiana	Minor in TESOL	20 credits (6 courses) 1 year	Full-time	Full-time $4,950/semstr, Part-time $475 (for 13 cr class)	4 September, 7 January	2 years of college + 2 semesters of some foreign language	Carl Barnett	—
	1 Year Certificate in TESOL	1 year (30 credits)	Full-time	Full-time $4,950/semstr, Part-time $475 (for 13 cr class)	4 September, 7 January	2 years of college + 2 semesters of some foreign language	Carl Barnett	Designed for students who are not seeking a full BA
	ESL Teaching Endorsement	1 year (24 credits)	Full-time	Full-time $4,950/semstr, Part-time $475 (for 13 cr class)	4 September, 7 January	2 years of college + 2 semesters of some foreign language	Carl Barnett	With a state teaching license course entitles one to teach ESL in public schools (In Indiana at least)
Georgetown University, Washington DC	BA Language and Linguistics	4 years	Full-time	On application	September	120 credit hours	Faculty of Language and Linguistics	—
Hawaii Pacific University, Honolulu	TESL Certificate	24 Semester credit hours (Full-time 9 months, Part-time usually 1-2 years)	Both	Full-time $3,350/semester Part-time $375/course	September, January, May, June every year	Complete Bachelor's degree	Dr Edward F. Klein	Even balance among theory, pedagogy & practicum
	BA in TESOL	Full time 4 years Part-time varied	Both	$3,350/ semester	September, January, May, June every year	On application	Dr Edward F. Klein	Strong practical program
University of Northern Iowa	Bachelor's Degree in TESOL or TESOL/Modern Languages	4 years	Full-time	$1,193 resident $3,231 non resident per semester	26 August	High School Diploma, English Language proficiency	Dr Cheryl Roberts	—
The American University of Paris	TESOL Certificate Program	3 months	Full-time	20,000 Francs (includes 6 US college credits)	October each year	BA or equivalent; 600 on TOEFL or interview for non-native speakers - full application dossier	Danielle Savage	Graduate viewbook sent to local schools/ institutions at end of course

US University Certificate Courses

College	Course title	Course length	FT/PT	Fees	Start dates	Entry requirements	Contact	Comments
Sam Houston State University, Texas	Endorsement in ESL	—	—	On application	On application	ExCET English as a Second Language, one year succesful teaching, valid Texas teaching credentials.	College of Education and Applied Science	—
Wright State University, Ohio	Graduate TESOL Certificate	22 quarter hours (4 hr prerequisite) Full-time 3 qtrs Part-time 6 qtrs	Both	Ohio Resident $137/qtr hr Non resident $244/qtr hr	September, January, March, June	Baccalaureate, GPA 2.7 or better (600 TOEFL 50 TSE)	Director, Program in TESOL	—
	Undergraduate TESOL certificate	22 qtr hrs (4 hr prerequisite) Full time 3 qtrs Part-time 6 qtrs	Both	Ohio Resident $107/qtr hr Non Resident $214/qtr hr	September January March June	High School Diploma (600 TOEFL, 50 TSE)	Director Program in TESOL	—

Canadian University Certificate Courses

College	Course title	Course length	FT/PT	Fees	Start dates	Entry requirements	Contact	Comments
University College of the Cariboo, BC	Overview of Teaching ESL (UCC with VCC)	30 hrs	Part-time	$225 approx	Vary - 1 Fall, 1 Summer	None	Elizabeth Templeman	Occasionally run a second short course
Universite Laval, Quebec	Baccalaureat en enseignement de l'anglais, langue seconde	3 years	Full-time	$3,005 (Can)	Autumn	Recognised High School Diploma	Alan Manning	—
Saint Mary's University, Nova Scotia	An Overview to Teaching ESL/EFL	45 hours plus 20 hour practicum	—	$650 Canadian	17 April, 8 July, 5 August	—	Maureen Sargent	—
University of Saskatchewan (CERTESL Program, Extension Credit Studies)	Certificate in TESL	Full-time less than 1 year Part-time 2-5 years	Both	Canadians $297 (Can) per course, plus texts & materials International Students $668.25 (Can) plus t&m	September, January	Complete secondary level standing and access to ESL learners	Grace Milashenko	Students must complete four core courses, one elective course, plus a supervised practicum or professional project
University of Western Ontario	Certificate in Second Language Teaching	Five full courses or equivalent, including a practicum	Part-time	Currently Certificate credit courses $295 Full-time $627.47 (95 fees, will change in 96) Admin Fee $50 Fee for overseas students higher	Application deadline 11 April	Applicants must be admitted to the University. Admission is competitive and enrolment limited	Megan Fletcher	Program designed to be pursued concurrently with an undergraduate degree. Non degree candidates and graduates may also apply
University of Winnipeg, Manitoba	Linguistics/ Multi Cultural Education	36 hours (half course credit)	—	$300 (Can) per course	September, January	High School Diploma	Elizabeth Madrid	—

College	Course title	Course length	FT/PT	Fees	Start dates	Entry requirements	Contact	Comments
Adelphi University, New York	MA TESOL	3-4 Semesters	Both	$400 per credit hour. Fees $150	Any semester	BA with GPA of 2.75 (full matric.) 2.25 (provisional)	Prof Eva M. Roca	—
Arizona State University	Master of TESL	2 semesters (30 hours)	Both	In State $889 per 12+ credit hours Out of State $3,642	September	BA with GPA of 3.0 or equiv., Non native speakers require min. TOEFL 550 plus TSE of 220	Karen L. Adams	—
Azusa Pacific University, California	MA TESOL	6 quarters	Both	$245 per unit plus $50 access fee and $80 graduation	Fall or Spring	BA with GPA of 3.0 or equiv., Non native speakers require min. TOEFL 550	Director Graduate TESOL Program	—
Ball State University, Indiana	MA in TESOL	Full-time 2 years Part-time 4 years	Both	$3,300 tuition per semester, out of State, plus student fees (1995)	Fall or Spring semester	Undergraduate degree, GPA of 3.0 (4.0 scale), 2 years foreign language, 3 letters of recommen-dation, writing sample, statement of purpose	Robert D. Habich	Assistantships available on a competitive basis, dpt offers instruction in computer-aided teaching, high placement rate for graduates.
Biola University, California	MA in TESOL	4 semesters plus interterm	Both	$272 per semester unit	Fall preferred	Degree, GPA 3.0, letters of rec., TOEFL 550	—	For students from the evangelical Christian community
Brigham Young University, UT	MA TESL	2 semesters in addition to TESL Cert. course	Both	$1,435 (Latter Day Saints) $2,152 (Others)	Beginning of semester	Degree, GPA 3.6, letters of rec., TOEFL 580	Melvin J Luthy	—
University of California, Los Angeles	MA TESL	2 years	Full-time	Out of State $8,000pa Fees $4,800 pa	Fall	Degree, GPA, letters of rec., TOEFL, work sample	Lyn Repath-Martos	—
California State University, Northridge	MA Linguistics	4 semesters	Both	In State $958 per semester Out of State $246 per unit plus $166	Beginning of semester	Degree, GPA 3.0, TOEFL 550	TESOL Co-ordinator	—
Columbia International University	MA TEFL/ Intercultural Studies	1 or 2 years	Both	$3,460 per semester	Fall	Degree, GPA 2.7, TOEFL 600	Dr Nancy Cheek	—
University of Delaware, Educational Studies	MA in ESL/Bi-lingualism	Full-time 3 semesters (33 credits)	Both	$9,800 approx. for out of state students	August or February	Undergraduate cumulative index of 3.0 (B), Graduate Record Examination	ESL Co-ordinator	Student teaching at local schools and in the University available
Eastern Michigan University (TESOL Program)	MA TESOL	Full-time 1 1/2 years	Both	Michigan res. $136/cr hr + fees of $13.33/ cr hr. non res. £317/cr hr + $13.33/cr hr fees	End of August beginning of January	2.5 GPA undergraduate, 2 years' foreign language	TESOL Advisor	—

US Masters Degree Courses

College	Course title	Course length	FT/PT	Fees	Start dates	Entry requirements	Contact	Comments
Eastern Washington University	MA TESOL	2-4 years	Both	Resident $1,250 10-18 credits, Non resident $3,800 Health $40	15/9, 3/1 1/4, 20/6, July and August	GRE native, TOEFL non natives	LaVona Reeves PhD	Transfer 12-15 credits from an accredited graduate school
Fairfield University	MA TESOL Methods and Materials for 2nd Language Teaching	Fall, Spring semester 1 class per week, Summer 4 week sessions	—	$915 per course	September, January, June	2.67 GPA, Special Status up to 9 credits	Sr. M. Julianna Poole SSND EdD	—
	MA TESOL Practicum in Teaching	Ditto above	—	$915 per course	September, January, June	2.67 GPA, Special Status up to 9 credits	Sr. M. Julianna Poole SSND EdD	Numerous other courses
The Florida State University	MA Education (TESOL specialisation)	3 semesters	Both	Resident $1,400 per semester Non Resident $4,400 per semester	Fall	Degree, GPA 3.0, GRE 1000, TOEFL 570+, letters of rec.	Dr Frederick Jenks	—
Georgetown University, Washington DC	MAT (TESOL)	36 credit hours	Full-time	On application	September	Degree	Graduate School	—
	Phd Applied Linguistics with TEFL Base	—	Both	On application	September	Masters Degree + 24 credit hours + dissertation	Graduate School	
Grand Canyon University, Phoenix	MA ESL	36 credit hours	Both	$249/credit hour	Continuous enrolment Spring Jan 2, Fall Aug 22	Degree, GPA 2.8, MAT or GRE at satisfactory level, 3 refs	College of Education	Overseas practicum experience available
University of Hawaii at Manoa	MA ESL	4 semesters	Both	Resident $1,045 Non Resident $3,228 (per semester) Fees $55	Spring or Fall	Degree, GPA 3.0, TOEFL 600, knowledge of at least one foreign language	Dr Charlene Sato	—
Hunter College of the City University of New York	MA TESOL	1-2 years	Both	$145 per credit	Summer or Fall	Degree, GPA 2.7, 12 credits from foreign language study	TESOL Co-ordinator	—
University of Illinois at Chicago	MA Applied Linguistics	2 semesters plus Summer	Both	Resident $2,149 per semester Non resident $5,042 per semester	Spring or Fall	Degree, GPA 4.0, TOEFL 580	TESOL Co-ordinator	—
Illinois State University	MA courses	2 years	Full-time	Out of state $2,787.55 In state $1,154 per semester	Fall semester mid-August Spring semester mid-January	Bachelor's degree	William Woodson	Teaching assistantship with tuition waiver available
Iowa State University	MA in English, Specialisation in TESL/ Linguistics	Can be completed in 2 years	Full-time	$1,417/ semester in state $4,172/ semester out of state	20 August each year	Undergraduate degree	Dan Douglas	Some teaching assistantships available that pay stipends and reduce fees to in-state level or below

College	Course title	Course length	FT/PT	Fees	Start dates	Entry requirements	Contact	Comments
Michigan State University	MA TESOL	3-4 semesters	Both	Out of state $3,411.25 per 9 credits In state $1,159 per 9 credits	Fall	Bachelor's degree, TOEFL 600	Course Director	—
University of New Hampshire	MA English Language and Linguistics (speciality in TEFL)	Full-time 1 year Part-time optional	Both	$12,840 per year, full-time tuition and fees	1 September	TOEFL 550, GRE aptitude test, degree	Director of Graduate Programs	—
University of Nevada, Reno	MA TESL	3 semesters plus a Summer	Both	Out of state $2,375 per semester In state $81 per credit	Beginning of semester	Bachelor's degree, GPA 3.0, TOEFL 550	Course Director	—
North Eastern Illinois University, Linguistics Dept.	MA courses	2-3 years	Part-time	$86.50 per credit hour plus $74.25 incidental fees	January, July, September	BA with 2.75 GPA and 9 hours study of a foreign language	Audrey L. Reynolds	—
University of Northern Iowa	MA in TESOL MA in TESOL/Modern Languages	3-4 semesters	Full-time	Tuition per semester: $1,417 (resident) $3,493 (non resident)	26 August	Bachelor's degree, English Language proficiency	Dr Cheryl Roberts	BA in TESOL or TESOL/Modern Languages also available
Old Dominion University, Virginia	MA Applied Linguistics	33 semester hours 1 1/2 years (11 courses)	Full-time	$170 per semester hour	29 August, 8 January	BA or equivalent, B average in major (570 on TOEFL for international students)	Dr Janet Bing	Co-operative program with English Language Centre
University of Pittsburgh	MA Linguistics with TESOL certificate	Full-time 2 years	Both	$3,717 per term in state $7,386 per term out of state	September (1st February enrolment deadline for financial aid)	BA or equivalent plus GRE scores	Alan Juffs, PhD	—
Saint Michael's College	MA TESL	3 semesters	Both	$235 per credit	Beginning of semester	Degree or equivalent, 3 letters of rec., TOEFL 550	M. Kathleen Mahnke	—
San Francisco State University	MA English (Emphasis on ESL/EFL)	4 semesters	Both	Resident $417 per semester (up to 6 units) $729 per semester (6 or more units) Non resident $246 Fees $199	Beginning of semester	Degree GPA 3.0, TOEFL 570	TESOL Co-ordinator	—
School for International Training, Vermont	MAT Program	9 months plus thesis	Full-time	Tuition $15,800 fees $650 Room and Board $4,350	1 Sept	BA; 550 TOEFL	Fiona Cook	Includes winter semester internship
	SMAT Program	Two 8 week Summers plus interim year practicum	Full-time	Tuition $16,500 fees $650 Room and Board $4,450	22 June	BA; 550 TOEFL	Fiona Cook	Requires a full-time job for interim year, US public school certification available

US Masters Degree Courses

College	Course title	Course length	FT/PT	Fees	Start dates	Entry requirements	Contact	Comments
Seton Hall University	MA's include Computer Applications in the Bilingual Curriculum, Applied Linguistics, TESL, General Linguistics, Socio-linguistics and Bicultural Ed.	30 hours	Both	Registration fee $85, Tuition $1,248	16 August, 18 January	MAT or GRE, TOEFL for international students	Dr William E. McCartan	College preparation ESL program available for limited English proficient students
Southern Illinois University (Department of Linguistics)	MA TESOL	1-2 years	Full-time	Average $2,500 per semester	Mid August every year	Bachelor's degree with 3.0 GPA 570 TOEFL for non native speakers	Diane Korando	—
Teacher's College of Columbia University	MA TESOL	3-4 semesters	Both	$520 per credit. Fees $100 approx	Fall	BA (minimum average B), 600 TOEFL	TESOL Co-ordinator	—
University of Texas at Austin	MA	3 semesters	Both	Resident $798.87 per 9 semester hours Non Resident $1,968.87 per 9 semester hours	Beginning of semester	Degree, TOEFL	Graduate Advisor	—
Texas Women's University	MEd TESOL	Semester 4 courses	Both	$207.09 per 3 hours	2 September, 15 January, 8 June, 9 July	BA, 3.0 GPA	Dr Rudy Rodriguez	—
Wright State University, Ohio	MATESOL	52 qtr full-time 4-6 quarter hrs Part-time 8 quarters	Both	Ohio resident $137/quarter hour, non resident $244/quarter hour	September, January, March, June	Baccalaureate GPA 2.7 or better (TOEFL 600, TSE 50)	Director Program in TESOL	—

Further Colleges Offering US Masters Degree Courses

The following Colleges should be contacted direct for information on their courses:

The University of Alabama, University of Alabama in Huntsville, The American University, The American University in Cairo, University of Arizona, Boston University, Bowling Green State University, University of California, Davis, California State University, Dominguez Hills, California State University, Fresno, California State University, Hayward, California State University, Long Beach, California State University, Sacramento, Cardinal Stritch College, Central Connecticut State University, Central Michigan University, Central Missouri State University, Central Washington University, University of Colorado at Boulder, University of Colorado at Denver, Colorado State University, East Carolina University, Eastern College, Eastern Kentucky University, Fairleigh Dickinson University, The University of Findlay, Florida International University, Fordham University, Fresno Pacific College, University of Georgia, Georgia State University, Hofstra University, University of Houston, University of Houston-Clear Lake, University of Idaho, University of Illinois at Urbana-Champaign, Illinois State University, Indiana State University, Indiana University, Indiana University of Pennsylvania, Indiana University of South Bend, Inter American University of Puerto Rico, Jackson State University, Jersey City State College, University of Massachussets at Boston, University of Mississipi, University of New Mexico, New York University, Notre Dame College, Oregon State University, University of Pennsylvania, Rhode Island College, San Jose State University, University of South Carolina, University of Washington.

MA's In The UK

An MA can improve your practical and theoretical TEFL skills as well as your employment opportunities.

The MA represents a very different qualification to the Certificate or Diploma

 anguage teachers sometimes regard the MA as a natural step in their career, or at least qualification, path. First comes the Certificate, then the Diploma and then the MA. This is far from the case. Indeed many students undertaking an MA in linguistics have never studied or taught EFL.

The MA represents a very different qualification to the Certificate or Diploma. Usually run by the EFL Unit or Language Centre of a University an MA is not necessarily going to improve your teaching skills. The courses are often of an academic/theoretical nature - you'll get far more teaching experience from an SRSA/Cambridge or Trinity Diploma. Some MA's may be of help in your career - where they teach specific management or teaching skills - but in general an MA should be viewed as a means to study more deeply in a field that interests you.

For clarity's sake we have referred throughout to MA's, however there are also MEd's, MScs and MPhils which cover various aspects of ELT. Although broadly similar, as a (very) rough rule of thumb, an MEd is likely to be the most practical and an MPhil the most theoretical. There is, however, substantial variety between courses.

The Cost Of Study

If you wish to move into the academic side of English Language study, then an MA is essential

One problem with undertaking the MA is the investment of time and money. In some respects, however, this is improving. Although grants are increasingly hard to come by, there are now many part-time courses which enable you to carry on earning while you are studying (though bear in mind that there is a lot of work involved in an MA so you must be sure that you'll be able to meet your work and study commitments without completely wiping out your social life). For an EFL teacher this obviously holds out the possibility of mixing teaching with studying. The University of Manchester, for example, offers two MEd's which can be undertaken through distance study combined with a full-time Summer course. This is the sort of timetable that might suit many teachers, although

for an EFL teacher working in the UK private sector the summer is the busiest time of year.

Whether or not you manage to carry on earning while you are studying, an MA still represents a substantial commitment of time and money, so it is important you select the right course. Since an MA is far more specialist than either the Certificate or Diploma, it should be possible to find a course that exactly fits your interests - although the variety of choice can be intimidating at first. Some MA's are highly theoretical with a strong research element, others are more practical: it is up to you to decide what best suits your needs and interests.

With the growth of the ELT market and of the number of people wishing to make a more long-term career out of it, there is an increasing number of MA's of direct relevance to ELT teachers. A number of Universities run MA s in English Language Teaching. The University of Durham runs MA's in Applied Linguistics with reference to a number of TEFL areas including ELT and ESP. Teachers interested in moving into a more specialist area of ELT might undertake an MA in ESL or Teaching Young Learners. For those wishing to enhance their practical skills in general ELT teaching, there are MA's in areas such as Materials Development and Classroom Management as well as courses which deal with Technology in the classroom. These courses are of obvious practical benefit to a teacher as well as enhancing their employment prospects.

Although an MA should not be seen specifically as a career move, it can obviously be of some assistance. If you wish to move into the academic side of English Language study, then an MA is essential. For those wishing to stay in teaching, then an MA can still be of use, particularly one of the more practical courses. In an ever more competitive market a teacher seeking work in the UK may find a Diploma is often a minimum requirement, so an MA can be an important additional string to your bow. Teachers seeking to move up the TEFL career ladder may consider undertaking an MA in Teacher Training and ELT Management.

College	Course title	Course length	FT/PT	Fees	Start dates	Entry requirements	Contact	Comments
Canterbury Christ Church College	MA English Language Education	1 year	Full-time	£5,300	October	Degree and three years' TEFL experience	A. Holliday	
Chichester Institute of Higher Education	MA ELT Management	1 year	Full-time	£2,400 (UK/EC) £5,900 (non UK/EC) approx	October	Degree or equiv., mini. 3 years' TEFL exp., IELTS 6.5	Fred Chambers	—
CELT Athens	In assoc. with College of St Mark and St John and Univ of Exeter MEd (Exon) in ELT/BPhil (Exon) in ELT	2.5 years	Part-time	£6,000 approx	Easter	BA plus 3 years' experience	M Constantinides	Course taught on a 'home & away' basis. Two Easter blocks at CELT, two Summer blocks in Plymouth
College of St Mark and St John, Plymouth	MEd Teacher Training	1 year	Full-time	£5,550	October	First degree plus 3 years' experience	Director, INTEC	—
	MEd Teaching English for Specific Purposes	1 year	Full-time	£5,550	October	Teachers of ESP/teacher trainers. First degree plus 3 years' experience	Director, INTEC	—
	MEd English Language Teaching	1 year	Full-time	£5,550	October	Teachers, Teacher Trainers, first degree plus 3 years' experience	Director, INTEC	—
Moray House Institute of Education, Edinburgh	MA TESOL	1 year	Full-time	£5,955 Full-time £4,710 Distance Learning	Full-time October Distance Learning Open	Relevant 1st degree or equivalent plus 3 years' experience	The Registrar	—
Aston University	MSc TE/TESP	Full-time 1 year Dist. Learning 2-3 years	Full-time or Distance Learning	Full-time EU £2,550 Non EU £5,875 Dist L. £4,300	January, October	Degree plus 3 years' EFL experience	Secretary Language Studies Unit	CTEFLA useful. DL in specific countries
University of Brighton	MA in TEFL	Full-time 1 year Part-time 2 years	Both	Full-time £2,350 Part-time £900 per year	23 September	Degree plus 2 years' EFL experience	Departmental Secretary	—
	MA in Media Assisted Language Learning	Full-time 1 year Part-time 2 years	Both	Full-time £2,350 Part-time £900 per year	23 September	Degree plus 2 years' EFL experience	Departmental Secretary	—
University of Bristol, School of Education	BEd	2 years	Full-time	£6,282	October	Teaching Qualification plus 2 years' teaching experience	School of Education	—
	MEd	Full-time 1 year Part-time 2-5 years	Both	Full-time £2,430 UK/EC £6,282 Overseas Part-time £203 per unit (UK/EC)	Beginning of any term.	Degree or equivalent plus 1 years' experience	School of Education	

College	Course title	Course length	FT/PT	Fees	Start dates	Entry requirements	Contact	Comments
University of Durham, Department of Linguistics and English Language	MA Applied Linguistics with Reference to ELT/ESOL/ESP/ ELT,CALL and Educational Technology/ELT and Materials Development/ FLT - German/ French/Spanish/ Arabic/Japanese	9 months	Full-time	On application	October	Good first degree or equivalent, 3 years experience in second language teaching	Martha Young-Scholten	Assessed by coursework and dissertation. Discontinuous enrolment option.
	MA Applied Linguistics with Reference to Translation	12 months	Full-time	On application	October	Good degree or equivalent, fluency in both source and target language	Martha Young-Scholten	Assessed by coursework and dissertation. Discontinuous enrolment option
	MA Applied Linguistics	9 months	Full-time	On application	September	Good first degree or equivalent.	Martha Young-Scholten	Assessed by coursework and dissertation. Enquire about discontinuous enrolment
	MA Language Acquisition	9 months	Full-time	On application	September	Good first degree or equivalent.	Martha Young-Scholten	Assessed by coursework and dissertation. Enquire about discontinuous enrolment
	MA Linguistics	9 months	Full-time	On application	September	Good first degree or equivalent.	Martha Young-Scholten	Assessed by c/work and dissertation.
University of Edinburgh, Department of Applied Linguistics	MSc Applied Linguistics	1 year full-time 2 year part-time	Both	£2,450 (UK/EC) £6,220 (Overseas)	October	Degree and relevant experience	Admissions Secretary	Also offer higher degrees, Mlitt and PhD
University of Essex	MA Applied Linguistics	9/12/24/36 month programmes	Both	Approximately £2,430 per term	October	Good first degree (2:1 or above)	Graduate Admissions Secretary	—
University of Exeter, Department of Applied Linguistics	MA Applied Linguistics	1 year	Both	£2,445 (UK/EC) £6,180 (Overseas)	October	Degree	Dr Reinhard Hartmann	Coursework plus dissertation
University of Hertfordshire	MA Module (Part of Linguistics)	14 weeks	Part-time	£200	October	Degree in language related subject. Teaching experience	Pat Morton	—

UK Masters Degree Courses

College	Course title	Course length	FT/PT	Fees	Start dates	Entry requirements	Contact	Comments
University of Hull, Language Institute	MA Applied Language & New Technologies	Full-time 1 year Part-time 2 years	Both	Full-time £2,430 Part-time £700 (Overseas £5,800/£2,900)	23 September	Good degree (2:1) in a language and IELTS 8 if not native speaker	—	—
University of Leeds, School of Education	MEd TESOL	11 months	Both	Write for rates	October or February	First Degree, initial training qualification, 3 years experience	Jayne Moon	—
University of Leicester	MA in Applied Linguistics and TESOL	Full-time 12 months Part-time 24 months	Both	Full-time EU £2,430 Overseas £5,850 Part-time £1140 (95/96 fees - new fees still to be finalised)	September	UK 2nd class hons degree or equivalent + appropriate TESOL exp. Non native speakers must show evidence of English proficiency	Julie Thomson	The ELT unit offers a range of courses for international students both before and during their MA studies
University of Liverpool Applied English Language Studies Unit	MA Language Teaching & Learning	1 year	Full-time	£2,800	October	First Degree	MA Admissions Tutor	Stong on discourse analysis and its application to language teaching
University of London (Royal Holloway), English Dept.	MA Modern English Language and Stylistics	Full-time 1 year Part-time 2 years	Both	Full-time £2,430 Part-time £1,215	September	Normally a good second class degree in English or its equivalent.	English Department Office	Subject to validation TESOL will be added to the list of options
University of Manchester, Centre for English Language Studies and Education	MEd Educational Technology and TESOL	Tba	Both	UK/EU£2,430 Overseas £5,890	October, January	First degree or equivalent, teacher training qualification, 3 years' teaching experience	Secretary, CELSE	Flexible modular structure - 6 months and dissertation.
	MEd Educational Technology for ELT	Summer attendance and Distance-Learning	N/A	£3,300	Variable for Distance-Learning, summer attendance June - August	First degree, teacher training qualification, 3 years' teaching experience.	Secretary, CELSE	Can be delivered entirely by distance using Internet 6 modules and ~~dissertation.~~
	MEd ELT	Summer Attendance	N/A	£3,300	Variable for Distance-Learning, summer attendance June - August	First degree, teacher training qualification, 3 years' teaching experience.	Secretary, CELSE	Flexible modular structure, 6 modules plus dissertation
	MEd TESOL	1 year	Both	£2,430 UK/EC £5,890 Overseas	October January	First degree, teacher training qualification, 3 years' teaching experience.	Secretary, CELSE	Flexible modular structure, 6 modules plus dissertation
University of Nottingham	MA English Language Teaching	Full-time 1 year Part-time 2-4 years	Both	Full-time £2,430pa UK/EU Overseas £6,144 pa Part-time £850pa or £352/module	October (full-time)	Contact Faculty of Education for details	Mrs Joyce West	—

College	Course title	Course length	FT/PT	Fees	Start dates	Entry requirements	Contact	Comments
University of Portsmouth	MA Applied Linguistics and TEFL	Full-time 12 months Part-time 24 months	Both	Full-time EU £2,430 O'seas £6,000 Part-time £575 + £85 dissertation fee	October	2 years' experience	Dr Paul Rastall	Accumulation of credits system enables flexible completion
University of Reading	MA TEFL	3* module	Full-time	UK £1,560 O'seas £2,460 for modules 1+2 Dissertation materials UK £610, Overseas £920	July, October, March	4 years' teaching practice	Amanda Horn	Accomm. available catered/ s/catering. Full university faculties+ support
St. Mary's University, Twickenham	MA Applied Linguistics	Full-time 1 year	Both	£180 a module. £5400 O'seas students	January, April	Degree + 3 years' experience in education	—	—
University of Sheffield, Dept. of English Language and Linguistics	MA Applied Linguistics	Full-time 1 year Part-time 2 years	Both	Full-time £2,430 Part-time £823 (95/96 fees)	September	Degree + min. 2 years' teaching experience	—	IELTS score of 6 overall (or equivalent)
Sheffield Hallam University TESOL Centre	MA TESOL	Part-time DL 10 months Full-time phase 6 weeks	Mixed	£2,400	13 May, 28 October	PG Diploma in TESOL	Gill King	Final part of the teacher education programme
University of Southampton, Faculty of Educational Studies	MA (ED) Language in Education	Full-time 1 year Part-time 2 years	Both	Full-time £2,430 UK/EC £5,985 Overseas Part-time £745 pa	October	Degree or equivalent, 2 years' experience	Assistant Registrar	—
	MA Applied Linguistics for Language Teaching	1 year	Full-time	£2,430 UK/EC £5,985 Overseas	October	Degree or equivalent, 2 years' experience	Assistant Registrar	—
University of Stirling, Centre for ELT	MSc CALL and TESOL	1 year	Full-time	UK/EU £2,500 approx. Overseas £6,000 approx.	16 September	A first degree in a relevant subject	Mrs S. Tyler	—
University of Surrey	MA in Linguistics (TESOL)	27 months	Part-time (Distance Learning)	£5,000	1 March, 1 October each year	Degree plus two years' teaching experience	Dr G Fulmer	8 core modules, 2 option modules + 12,0000 wd dissertation.
University of Sussex, School of Cognitive Sciences	MA Applied Linguistics	1 year	Full-time	On request	October	Degree	Dr Max Wheeler	—
University of Wales, Cardiff,	MA Applied Linguistics	1 year	Full-time	On request	September	First degree or equivalent	Secretary, Centre for Language + Commun.	—
University of Warwick,	MA English Language Teaching	1 year	Full-time	Full-time £2,430 Part-time £5,955	October	First degree, 3 years' experience	Anne Beale	For teachers, trainers and curriculum developers

MA's In Australia And New Zealand

There are good language-based MA courses in Australia and New Zealand for both teachers and academics alike.

In both Australia and New Zealand the rapid growth of the EFL sector has encouraged Universities to offer MA's of direct and practical relevance to English Language Teaching as well as more theoretical linguistic courses.

Australia

Australia offers overseas students a relatively low-cost option for university study. Relatively low fees, a moderate cost of living, and work rights which permit part-time employment all add up to an attractive package.

Most of the Australian courses can be taken either full-time or part-time, but student visa regulations stipulate that overseas students must study full-time.

As well as Masters programmes many universities offer Graduate Diploma courses in Applied Linguistics, TESOL or Adult/Multi-cultural Education. These programs have always been popular with teachers of English as a Second Language in schools and migrant education centres as well as with teachers of literacy. They are now increasingly popular with ELICOS (English Language Intensive Courses for Overseas Students) teachers, partly due to the growing emphasis in the language school sector on formal teacher qualifications, and postgraduate qualifications in particular, to enhance promotion prospects.

Several Australian Masters programs in Applied Linguistics include not only predictable linguistic and TESOL-related subjects, but also practical subjects such as curriculum design, research methods, language testing, translation, and ELT programme management. However, there is still a fairly common perception in the ELICOS sector that Masters courses, even in Applied Linguistics, are theoretically rather than practically oriented. Many private sector EFL teachers in particular opt for an RSA/UCLES or comparable course, and many ELICOS employers prefer to recruit teachers with such credentials. (RSA/UCLES courses are available at Certificate and/or Diploma level in Sydney, Melbourne and Perth.)

Australia is also the leading centre for the study of Hallidayan Systemic Linguistics, although since Halliday's retirement from the University of Sydney a few years ago, the University of Sydney's dominant position in this area has been somewhat eclipsed by the very active School of Linguistics at Macquarie University, also in Sydney.

Another option at a number of Australian universities is correspondence study, available both to overseas students (most takers are in Asia) and to expatriate Australian teachers. The University of New England in New South Wales and Deakin University in Victoria are well known for their long history of specialisation in distance education programs, but are not alone in offering TESOL or Applied Linguistics courses in this form.

Many Australian universities offer two- or three-tiered qualifications, with students having the possibility of obtaining credit as they move from one tier to the next. For example, Macquarie University's new Graduate Certificate in TESOL feeds into the Graduate Diploma course, which in turn feeds into the Masters. Both the Postgraduate Certificate and the Graduate Diploma include practice teaching, whereas the Masters does not.

New Zealand

New Zealand has a small, but growing number of Master's courses. Most students are language graduates, although teachers with extensive practical experience will be considered if they have a degree in another field or have the Diploma in TESL.

The Victoria University of Wellington runs an MA in Applied Linguistics, covering language learning theory, literary linguistics, curriculum development, and English as an international language.

Contact the University of Otago, Massey University, Waikato University and Lincoln University for details of their courses.

Australian University Certificate And Diploma Courses

College	Course title	Course length	FT/PT	Fees	Start dates	Entry requirements	Contact	Comments
Bond University, English Language Institute	Graduate Certificate in TESOL	3 weeks	Full-time	$1,810	8 January, 25 June	University degree or equivalent	Dr Ron Holt	
University of Canberra, School of TESOL and International Education	Graduate Certificate in TESOL	1 semester	Both	$A4,750 (Tuition only)	12 February, 15 July	Degree or equivalent and English language requirements (IELTS 6.5 or TOEFL 550 with 4.5 in the Test of Written English)	Ms Sue Wharton	—
	Graduate Diploma in TESOL	2 semesters	Both	$A9,500 (Tuition only)	12 February, 15 July	Ditto above	Ms Sue Wharton	—
La Trobe University, Melbourne	Graduate Diploma in LOTE Teaching	1 year	Full-time	$A11,000	February	Bachelor's degree (Teaching/Education) + extensive LOTE teaching experience	School of Education	—
	Graduate Diploma in TESOL	1 year	Full-time	$A11,000	February	Bachelor's degree plus 2 years' relevant teaching experience	School of Education	—
Macquarrie University, Sydney	Postgraduate Diploma in Language and Literacy Education	Full-time 1 year Part-time 2 years	Both	Local $A4,000 O'seas $A12,000	February, July	Degree and/or significant teaching experience	Irene Chung	Full application pack available
	Postgraduate certificate in TESOL	1 semester (1/2 academic year)	Both	Local $A2,000 O'seas $A6,000	February, July	Degree and 1 years' ESL teaching experience	Irene Chung	Full application pack available
University of South Australia, Centre for Applied Linguistics (CALUSA) Adelaide	Graduate Certificate in TESOL	Full-time 6 months or Part-time equivalent	Both	$A5,500	January, July	3 yr teaching qualification, relevant employment and 1yrs' experience, working knowledge of language other than English	Ms Anny Be	In-service program for practising teachers. Succesful students may apply for up to 50% advanced status in Grad Diploma
	Graduate Diploma of Education	Full-time 1 year Part-time equivalent	Both	$A11,000	January, July	Ditto above + writtent evidence of access to appropriate TESOL context while studying	Ms Anny Be	Ditto above Course allows teachers to undertake TESOL studies in the context of their own work situation

Australian University Certificate And Diploma Courses

College	Course title	Course length	FT/PT	Fees	Start dates	Entry requirements	Contact	Comments
University of Southern Queensland	Graduate Certificate in Teaching Second Languages	1 year	Part-time	$A3,200	February, July	A teaching qualification or equivalent	Dr Francis Mangubham	Includes teaching practice
University of Wollongong, Keiraville, Australia	Graduate Diploma in TESOL	1 year	Full-time (Part-time options)	Tba	Variable	3 year Bachelor's degree or equivalent	Lesley Neggo	—

Australasian University Masters Degree Courses

College	Course title	Course length	FT/PT	Fees	Start dates	Entry requirements	Contact	Comments
University of Canberra	MA in TESOL	4 semesters (2 academic years)	Both	$A9,500 (Tuition only)	12 February, 15 July	Degree, TEFL exp, IELTS 6.5, TOEFL 550, 4.5 in the Test of Written English	Ms Sue Wharton	—
Macquarrie University, Sydney	MA Applied Linguistics	Full-time 1 year Part-time 2 years	Both	Local $A4,500 O'seas $A12,000	February, July	Degree and/or significant teaching experience	Irene Chung	Full application pack available
University of Melbourne	MA in Applied Linguistics	Full-time 1 year Part-time 2 years	Both	$A2,814	March or July	Honours degree plus professional experience	Dr Brian Partridge	Preliminary programme for applicants w/out Honours degrees
	MEd Language and Literacy Education	Full-time 1 year Part-time 2 years	Both	On application	—	Teacher Training & Hons Postgrad Diploma	Professor Frances Christie	—
University of South Australia CALUSA	MEd TESOL	Full-time 1 year or Part-time equivalent	Both	$A12,000	January, July	4 yrs Higher Ed with teaching qualification. Pref. profess-ional exp.	Charles Clennell	For exp'd TESOL practitioners aiming for management positions
	MEd - Research TESOL	Full-time 2 years Part-time equivalent	Both	$A12,000	January, July	Completion of MEd at USA, submission of dissertation proposal	Dr James Pandian	—
University of Southern Queensland	MA in Applied Linguistics (Hons or Coursework)	Hons Ft 1 1/2 yrs Pt 3 yrs Cwrk FT 1 yr Pt 2 yrs	Both	Hons $A8,720 Coursework on application	Feb on campus, Feb and July Dist. Learning	4 years tertiary training	Dr Francis Mangubham	Hons-research bsd thesis. C/work- t'ching practice
University of Waikato, Hamilton, NZ	MA (Applied) in Applied Linguistics	Full-time 1 year Part-time 2 years	Both	$NZ2,796	May	First degree, Dip TESOL	Academic Administrator	—
Victoria University of Wellington, NZ	MA in Applied Linguistics	12 months	Both	NZ$2,250 for NZ residents NZ$15,000 overseas	March each year. July start also possible	Degree and 2 years teaching experience	Chairperson Eng. Lang. Institute	MA can be completed by c/wk or thesis Phd also offd.
University of Wollongong, Keiraville, Aus.	MEd TESOL	1 year	Both	Tba	Variable	4 yr degree with major study in Ed.	Lesley Neggo	—

Specialising

For teachers seeking to make themselves more attractive to employers and to make their work more interesting, a specialist skill offers a number of opportunities.

To make the most of a specialisation from both a personal and professional point of view, you would be well advised to choose an area in which you have a genuine interest

The world of English Teaching is becoming increasingly more fragmented or specialised. Although a majority of your teaching is likely to be General English, if you are able to offer any specialities, then you are likely to find yourself more employable and your work more interesting. Some of the key, and most rapidly growing, areas of specialisation are Teaching Young Learners, ESL and Teaching Business English, and these are covered in some depth over the next few pages. However, there is a multitude of other possibilities, some of which are considered below.

So how do you become specialised? In some cases your previous experience outside TEFL may be of relevance to some of your students. It is also possible to take a short course that is relevant to the area in which you wish to specialise. However to make the most of a specialisation from both a personal and professional point of view you would be well advised to choose an area in which you have a genuine interest. Teaching Business English is a substantial market but you are unlikely to find it particularly fulfilling if the Business Pages of your newspaper are just something you use to wrap your chips in.

English for Academic Purposes (EAP)

If you have some EFL experience, you can do a course in ESP which is teaching English towards a specific objective

EAP courses are generally run for non-native English speakers who wish to attend Anglophone higher educational establishments. Courses give students the language skills to understand lectures or write essays, for example. Alternatively, an EAP teacher may provide support work on a course, working with the tutor to ensure that students have the relevant vocabulary and background knowledge before each lecture/tutorial.

Probably the best way to become involved in EAP is to do a related short course and apply for a support service position within a university in a non-Anglophone country. This will give you the academic background. If you succeed in this competitive field, senior university positions and their respective salaries will follow. With the increasing number of overseas students attending UK higher education establishments in English-speaking countries, there are also vacancies for support staff. EAP programmes are common in the States, Australia, New Zealand and, increasingly, the UK. Most jobs require a Master's degree.

English For Specific Purposes (ESP)

If you have some EFL experience, you can do a course in ESP, which is teaching English towards a specific objective. A specialist background, in business for example, will make you particularly suitable for this sphere. If your students want to be doctors or pilots, they will need specialised English, so ESP is job - rather than exam - orientated. Indeed the teaching demands can be fairly unusual. You may, like one teacher, find yourself training a group of Algerian engineers the vocabulary they needed to work on the construction of a power station. It's a challenging and unusual environment but can be very rewarding. Another entry into this market is a Homestay course which may offer a specialised section where students can stay with a teacher with relevant experience (e.g. a lawyer, doctor, engineer). See the Homestay article on page 105 for details.

Cultural Studies

Some students are only interested in language learning, but for others an understanding of the history and culture of your country is also of interest - and may also be of use to them in their career. Therefore a number of centres are starting to offer cultural studies. Finding teachers for this can present a problem since it's either done by someone with a background in history or sociology but little knowledge of the students' linguistic needs or by a qualified EFL teacher who lacks specialist knowledge of their country's history or culture. The teacher who combines cultural and linguistic knowledge is therefore at an advantage. There are opportunities for this sort of course overseas and also in the home market where some schools offer their students cultural tours/events as part of their course.

Teaching Young Learners

Being confronted by a classroom of children can be a bit daunting for the new native speaker EFL teacher. Fortunately there is an increasing amount of training available.

> **The skills required to teach children are very specific and very different to those required in teaching adults**

Many teachers' first experience of EFL is in a summer school where the students tend to be teenagers or young adults. Increasingly, however, when recently trained teachers arrive at a new job in a new country, they are likely to find themselves spending a considerable amount of their time teaching Young Learners.

The ever increasing importance of English as a language of business combined with very varied standards of language teaching in the state sector means that parents, keen to give their children a headstart, are willing to make substantial sacrifices in order to pay for additional lessons for their children. There are other influences as well, some specific to individual countries, so the demand is not constant across the globe. It is particularly high, however, in Spain, Italy and Greece. In the Far East, it is also becoming the trend to start English language learning at an earlier age.

Although the skills required to teach children are very specific and very different to those required in teaching adults, it is an area of teaching that, until recently, has not received a particularly high profile on the various teacher training programmes. Having trained with classes of highly motivated adults, a new teacher confronted by a classroom of eight-year-olds is likely to feel that they've been rather dropped in at the deep end.

> **It is increasingly likely, though by no means certain, that a general teacher training course will contain a TYL element**

There are already courses available for teachers in the UK, but few specific (or recognised) exam-based qualifications. There are short courses offered by, among others, Trinity College, Shane School, The Bell Language Schools, International House; and a number of Universities also offer courses, some leading to a certificate in teaching young learners. It is also increasingly likely, though by no means a certainty, that a general teacher training course will contain a TYL element, although there is no guarantee that these courses will include classroom practice. Companies that run teacher training courses specifically for teachers intending to work in their schools are also likely to include a TYL element

where children are likely to make up a substantial proportion of students.

Before undertaking a course, it could be worth your while to find out exactly what age levels you'll be working with. Young Learners has become something of a 'catch all' phrase - to some it refers specifically to children of primary school age, others use it to refer to teaching teenagers as well.

Not all these courses will include exams, and some of the general teacher training courses, while including a TYL element, will not actually include that in the exam. Therefore it is difficult for a teacher to provide incontrovertible proof of their training or skills as a teacher of young learners. This situation, too, is changing.

Recognised Courses

There is already a Trinity College CertTEYL (Certificate of Teaching Young Learners) which is aimed at both native and non-native teachers who already have some experience of teaching primary level children but wish to have specialist TESOL knowledge. The course time is at least 140 hours, of which approximately 20 are made up of teaching practice.

The new, integrated, Cambridge syllabus will include both a Certificate and Diploma in Teaching Young Learners. Both courses will cover aspects of teaching children and teenagers. As with the Trinity Certificate both courses will be open to native and non-native teachers. The Certificate, like its Teaching Adults equivalent, will be open to students with no previous teaching experience. Teachers wishing to study for the Diploma, however, will have to have had some previous experience of teaching young learners.

As well as changes from the teacher training aspect, UCLES are developing a new exam for young learners. The STYLE exam syllabus aims to assess young learners' linguistic skills without providing the sort of demotivation that exams can represent. The course will have three levels: Starters, Movers, and Flyers. The STYLE exam will also be integrated with a range of CD-ROM products being developed by Homerton College in Cambridge.

Other Courses

If you are unable to enrol in the Trinity or Cambridge Certificate courses but are interested in teaching young learners, there are a number of short courses that will give you some knowledge (and in some cases experience) of teaching young learners.

These courses do not represent teaching qualifications in their own right. Rather, you should consider them as a top-up or supplement to a qualification you already have. They will make you more attractive to an employer and make teaching young learners somewhat less intimidating to you.

In The Classroom

So how does teaching young learners differ from teaching adults? One of the skills which is particularly important for a teacher to possess is classroom management. It is a lot easier to lose control of a class of children than adults and a lot harder to get it back. Yet while controlled, the classroom must not be allowed to become restrictive or sterile.

The teacher must also be very patient. Children do not have the same linguistic or cognitive foundations to build on as older students, so do not expect pupils to grasp concepts or carry out tasks in English that they are not able to handle in their own language. Although children often seem to learn quickly, they also forget easily, so it is important to keep on activating and recycling the language you have taught in different ways.

Although children can be less inhibited than adults when it comes to speaking in a new language, they can also be very easily discouraged. Therefore it is important that you find English language tasks for your pupils that are challenging without being over-taxing. If the task is beyond them, they'll lose their confidence and, in the absence of constant and

sympathetic encouragement, they may begin to think of themselves as poor language learners. If this happens, then they can easily give up trying and become bored.

Boredom is the bane of any teacher's life but with children it is a particular problem as it can easily lead to disruptive behaviour. Vary activities as much as possible during the lesson. It may help to use videos and cassettes so that they can see and hear English outside the classroom and also have a break from more formal work while still being exposed to language. However, you should have a clear objective in mind with whatever you play or show the children. They may think they're watching a cartoon; you know that they're learning colours

It is also possible, and often highly useful, to use games and physical activities to get children doing things in English which are purposeful, relevant and enjoyable in their own right, rather than simply practising language for its own sake. Try to use songs and music with repetitive choruses and actions to involve your pupils as much as possible.

It is important to bear in mind, however, the culture you are in and the attitude of your pupils. In some countries children (and their parents) may be suspicious of non-traditional teaching methods and become dissatisfied and demotivated if lessons are too informal. Don't be patronising or approach a class with too fixed an idea of how young learners should be taught. Some children may not share your enthusiasm for games and songs and may work better (and more happily) in a more formal environment.

Both you and your class can benefit from lessons which are not purely language-based. Find ways to expand your pupils' knowledge of the real world, improve their social skills and enhance their general understanding.

Above all, be enthusiastic. If you can convince the children in your class that learning English can be fun and rewarding, then it will be - both for them and you.

There are a number of short courses that will give you some knowledge (and in some cases experience) of teaching young learners

Children do not have the same linguistic or cognitive foundations to build on as older students

Teaching Business English

With English perceived in many countries as the language of international business, there are great opportunities for teachers.

Working with business people is an area of teaching that can favour the more mature teacher

business English is becoming an increasingly popular market within TEFL and also an increasingly demanding one. As with all areas of teaching, students' expectations are higher and the days when a cursory glance through a copy of the FT was all it took to prepare for a Business English lesson are long gone. Fortunately with the increase in demand has come an increase in the specialist teacher training courses which will prepare you for the lessons.

Working with business people demands special skills, knowledge and interests. It is also an area of teaching that can favour the more mature teacher since many business students may be wary of being taught by someone significantly younger than themselves.

The wariness of students may extend to more than the age of their teacher. Although students will generally be highly motivated, since the course has clear advantages for them within their company or career in general, they might also feel uncomfortable with any suggestion that they're going back to school. Senior executives may have difficulty adapting to the role of learners (it is important that the teacher does not relate language competence to professional competence or seniority) and they may not relax in a classroom environment and, as a result, be reluctant to contribute. A group from the same company may also contain its own hierarchical structures with some students unwilling to risk embarrassing themselves in front of senior or junior colleagues. Age can also be an issue with older employees sometimes being ill at ease in a class of much younger students. All this requires sensitivity and diplomacy on the part of the teacher

A group from the same company may also contain its own hierarchical structures with some students unwilling to risk embarrassing themselves in front of senior or junior colleagues

Lesson Preparation

The presentation of classes and use of materials is very different in a business environment than when teaching a more general course. Business people may need to be sold an exercise by having its purposes and benefits clearly spelled out. They often want to learn everything in a minimum amount of time so classes have to be very practical and pragmatic.

The teacher also needs to be highly flexible. Business English is a 'catch all' phrase but not only will each company have different and often quite specific language needs, so will each student. A receptionist will not need the same range of vocabulary as a senior executive, but you might find yourself teaching them both on the same day. You may also be called upon to teach English for very specific purposes. One teacher remembers being given three days to prepare two Italian businessmen for a trip to New York "There was a slight clash of interest. I was supposed to be teaching them English for use in business, they were more interested in learning English for use in nightclubs."

Self presentation as much as lesson presentation is one of the keys to the role of teaching English for Business. This refers to the time in the company not just in the classroom. The teacher will often be going into a company and may be expected to discuss students' progress and course plans with either the Training or General Manager.

The Business English teacher has to maintain a consistent professional image, be logical, well-organised, an excellent communicator, and most importantly, be interested in and have a good understanding of business - especially the business of the company in which you are working. A high degree of patience and understanding is also beneficial since the needs of the company are always going to come first. You may find you have spent an hour travelling out to a company only to find the lesson cancelled because of something that has cropped up in the workplace.

If you earn your students' respect and have respect for them, then teaching Business English can be a very stimulating and exciting area of EFL teaching. It is an opportunity to gain experience of a world outside the classroom and make a useful contribution to its development. If this appeals to you then turn to page 89 for details of training courses for teachers of Business English.

Short Courses

College	Course title	Course length	FT/PT	Fees	Start dates	Entry requirements	Contact	Comments
Abon Language School, Bristol, UK	Teacher's Refresher Course	1-2 weeks	Full-time	£295 first week, £215 second week (includes homestay)	15/1, 9/4, 8/7, 5/8	—	Heather Crispin	For non native teachers of English. Opportunuty to examine methodology and brush up language at the same time
Anglia Polytechnic University, Cambridge, UK	Refresher Course for Teachers of English	1 weeks	Full-time	£250	8/7, 29/7, 19/8	Qualified TEFL teachers at secondary school level and above	Anne Dover	This course is for non-native speakers of English. The fee includes self-catering accomm.
Anglo-Continental School of English, Bournemouth, UK	Overseas Teachers Course	2-4 weeks	Full-time	£420-£740	17/6, 1/7, 15/7, 29/7, 12/8, 4/11, 18/11	Teachers of English	Steve Millar	—
Bradford and Ilkley College, Bradford, UK	Introduction to Computer Assisted Learning	1 week	Full-time	£250	July for individuals, by arrangement with groups	Must be practising language teacher	Nancy Hall	Excellent intro to CALL with use of Computerised Language Laboratory
	Refresher Courses for Overseas Teachers of English	4 weeks	Full-time	£600	July for individuals, by arrangement with groups	Must be practising overseas teachers of English	Nancy Hall	Excellent up-dating of methodology and language skills
British Council Izmir, Turkey	ELT Workshop	—	—	Free to Teachers' Centre Members	—	—	Steven Darn	Regular fortnightly ELT workshops throughout academic year.
	Teaching ESP	2 week intensive - 3 month part-time (flexible)	Both	Negotiable	On demand, as from October 1996	—	Steven Darn	Designed for native and non native speakers contracted to teach ESP, EAP and Business Eng.
British Council Milan, Italy	Courses in teaching i) Business English ii) Young Learners	3 1/2 days or 5 mornings over 5 week period	Both	350,000 lire	To be decided	For practising teachers	Amanda Bourdillon	—
	Refresher Workshops	—	—	50,000 lire	Held from November to May on Wednesday mornings	—	Amanda Bourdillon	Practical workshops designed to give fresh ideas or help.
British Language Centre Madrid, Spain	Pre-Diploma course	8 weeks	Part-time	£225	January	—	Alistair Dickinson	Preparation for DTEFLA

College	Course title	Course length	FT/PT	Fees	Start dates	Entry requirements	Contact	Comments
Camosun College, Victoria, Canada	Teaching Grammar One: Theory and Practice	6 sessions	Part-time	$388	27 April	On application	Carol Fengstad	—
	An Introduction to Curriculum Development	1 session	Part-time	$63	2 March	On application	Carol Fengstad	—
	Intercultural Skills for the TESL Instructor	4 sessions	Part-time	$74	15 February	On application	Carol Fengstad	—
CELT Athens, Greece	Available on a variety of topics	Usually 1 or 2 days	—	£30-£60	Throughout year	—	Marisa Constantinides	—
	Language skills for Teachers of English	To be announced	—	To be announced	On application	—	Marisa Constantinides	—
Chichester Institute of Higher Education, Chichester, UK	Course for Overseas Teachers of Young Children	3 weeks	Full-time	£685 for 3 weeks tuition + £285 food and Accomm.	8th + 29th July	Currently teaching	Gilly Lloyd	—
	Certificate/ Diploma Advanced Educational Studies (ELT Administration)	5 weeks per certificate, 6 months diploma	Full-time	UK/EU £470 approx. Non EU £1,300 approx. per certificate	October	3 years' English language teaching	Angela Karlsson	—
	Certificate in Advanced Educational Studies Management and Curriculum Development	10 weeks	Full-time	Tba	Throughout year	Qualified teacher, graduate, IELTS 4.5	Angela Karlsson	—
College of St Mark and St John, Plymouth, UK	Trainer Development	3 weeks	Full-time	£585	14 July	—	Ross Lynn	—
	Teaching English for Specific Purposes	3 weeks	Full-time	£585	4 August	For teachers	Ross Lynn	—
	Teaching English to Young Learners (Nursery or Primary)	3 weeks	Full-time	£585	14 July	For teachers	Ross Lynn	—
	Teacher Development Course	3 weeks	Full-time	£585	14 July, 4 August	For teachers	Ross Lynn	—

Short Courses

College	Course title	Course length	FT/PT	Fees	Start dates	Entry requirements	Contact	Comments
Eastbourne School of English, Eastbourne, UK	Adv. Language Development and Aspects of British Culture	2 weeks	Full-time	£360	January	For practicing non-native speakers of English	Dorothy S. Rippon	Accom. available from £70 per week
Edinburgh Tutorial College, Edinburgh, UK	Communicative Song + Game in the Primary Classroom	2 weeks	Full-time	£390 exclusive of accomm.	1/7, 15/7, 29/7, 12/8, 26/8	Advanced level of English	Michelle Sweeney	—
Harrow House International College Ltd., Swanage, UK	Overseas Teacher Refresher courses	2 weeks	Full-time	£210 per week (including full board, host family)	30/3, 13/7, 27/7 10/8	—	Anne McLintock	£40 enrolment fee.
Hilderstone College, Broadstairs, UK	Language and Creative Teaching	2 weeks	Full-time	£570 including accomm.	30/6, 14/7, 28/7, 11/8	Overseas teachers of English	International Students Office	CEELT available on courses starting in July
	Language and Learner Centred Teaching	2 weeks	Full-time	£570	14 July	Overseas teachers of English	International Students Office	CEELT available
	Langauge + Teaching Young Learners	2 weeks	Full-time	£570 including accomm.	28 July	Overseas teachers of English at Primary level	International Students Office	CEELT available
	New Perspectives on Teaching Grammar	1 week	Full-time	£295 including accomm	30 June	Native and non-native teachers of English	International Students Office	—
	From Teacher to Teacher Trainer	1 week	Full-time	£295 including accomm.	7 July	Native and non-native teachers of English	International Students Office	—
Holmesglen Institute of TAFE, Victoria, Australia	Specialist courses in aspects of EFL Methodology and Language Awareness	Variable	Both	Dependent on duration	All year	Usually practising teacher	Director of Studies	—
	A refresher course for teachers of ESL/EFL	30 hours	Both	Full-time $450 or $90 per module	All year	EFL/ESL qualified teacher	Director of Studies	Highly practical workshops
inlingua Teacher Training and Recruitment, Cheltenham, UK	inlingua Specialised Orientation Seminar	1 week	Full time	£170 inc. VAT and materials	April, June and September	Teaching cert + experience	Dagmar Lewis	Courses prepare for placement abroad with inlingua schools.
International House Barcelona, Spain	TEFL to Young Learners	2 weeks	Full-time	60,000 pesetas	July, September	CTEFLA or equivalent, 1 year's experience	Jenny Johnson	Help with accomm.
	Director of Studies Training Course	1 week/30 hours	Full-time	40,000 pesetas	July	Extensive EFL experience	Jenny Johnson	Help with accomm.

Short Courses

College	Course title	Course length	FT/PT	Fees	Start dates	Entry requirements	Contact	Comments
International House Budapest, Hungary	Teaching Young Learners	6 weeks	Part-time (one evening per week)	£56	29 Jan	CTEFLA or equivalent, plus 6 months' TEFL experience	Eva Barics	—
International House Hastings, UK	Teaching EFL to Young Learners	5 days 2 weeks	Full-time	5 Days - £235 2 weeks - £445	5 days - 15 Jan 2 weeks - 1 July	By application	Adrian Underhill	For exp'd native and non native speakers. Accomm. service available.
	Modern English Literature & Culture	2, 3 and 4 weeks	Full-time	£210/ £240 per week Guest House £280 per week University Halll of Residence	2 weeks Jan, Feb, July. 3 weeks July, August, 4 weeks July	By application	Adrian Underhill	Located at Peterhouse College, Cambridge. Suitable for native and non native speakers.
	Communicative Language Teaching	2 weeks	Full-time	£445	5 February	By application	Adrian Underhill	For native and non native speakers. Accomm. service available.
	Methodology Refresher	2 weeks	Full-time	£445	19/2, 15/7, 12/8	By application	Adrian Underhill	A refresher course for non native speakers. Accomm. service available.
	Sound Foundations - Living Phonology	4 days 5 days	Full-time	4 days - £200 5 days - £235	4 days - 2 Jan 5 days - 1 July	By application	Adrian Underhill	For native and non native speakers. Accomm. service available.
	The Skills of Teacher Training	2 weeks	Full-time	£470	5 February, 15 July	By application	Adrian Underhill	For exp'd native and non native speakers. Accomm. service available.
	New Trends in English Language Teaching	4 days and 5 days	Full-time	4 days - £200 5 days - £235	4 days - 2 Jan 5 days - 29 Jan, 29 July	By application	Adrian Underhill	For native and non native speakers. Accomm. service available.
	The Skills of Academic Management	2 weeks	Full-time	£470	15 January, 12 August	By application	Adrian Underhill	For native and non native speakers. Accomm. service available.

Short Courses

College	Course title	Course length	FT/PT	Fees	Start dates	Entry requirements	Contact	Comments
International House Madrid, Spain	Teacher Development Course	—	Part-time	Stated locally	Various dates throughout the year	Practising teacher of English	Steven Haysham	A variety of short courses are offered during the year
International House Rome, Italy	TEFL course for teaching young learners	2 weeks	Full-time	1,000,000 lire	September each year	Min. TEFL certificate	The Director	Help given with accomm. in Italian families or pensione
International Language Academy, Christchurch, New Zealand	Language improvement + methodology	—	Full-time	£350	2/1, 5/2, 4/3, 1/4, 29/4, 22/5, 17/6, 1/7, 15/7, 29/7, 12/8, 27/8, 23/9, 18/11	For practising English teachers (non native speakers)	Mr N. P. Kenny	—
ITS English School, Hastings, UK	Advanced Conversations + Methodology	2 weeks	Full-time	£250	1 July, 8 July	Practising teacher of English. Non native speaker	John Palim	—
	Certificate in Teaching Practice	25 hours	Both	£185	By arrangement	Introductory course or experience	John Palim	—
The Language Project, Bristol, UK	Teaching Translation	1 week	Full-time	£200	January, June, July, August, September, December	French/German teachers of English	Dr Jon Wright	Accomm. can be arranged
	Modern Literature and Culture	1 or 2 weeks	Full-time	£200 or £350	Jan, Feb, June, July, August, September, December	Overseas teachers.	Dr Jon Wright	Accomm. can be arranged
	Language Intensive + Media Studies	1 or 2 weeks	Full-time	£200 - £350	Jan, Feb, June, July, August, September, December	Overseas Teachers	Dr Jon Wright	Accomm. can be arranged
	Language Intensive + Practical Teaching Ideas	1 or 2 weeks	Full-time	£200 - £350	Jan, Feb, June, July, August, September, December	Overseas Teachers	Dr Jon Wright	Accomm. can be arranged
LTS, Training & Consulting, Bath, UK	Designing ESP Courses	1 week	Full-time	£360	June, December	TEFL qualification + 2-3 yrs' exp.	Adrian Pilbeam	First Part LCCI Cert TEB
	Developing ESP Materials	1 weeks	Full-time	£360	July, December	TEFL qualification + 2-3 yrs' exp.	Adrian Pilbeam	Second Part LCCI Cert TEB
Multi Lingua, Guildford, UK	Multi Lingua TEFL Diploma Course (ML Dip. TEFL)	Full-time 8 weeks Part-time 12 months	Both	£1,295 plus £145 Moderation fee	Full-time 15 January, 15 July. Part-time 16 January, 17 September	Either two years' full-time English language teaching experience or a teaching certificate and one year's experience	Dr G P Connolly	A Professional Qualification designed for experienced teachers wishing to continue their ELT careers in a DoS or Management position

College	Course title	Course length	FT/PT	Fees	Start dates	Entry requirements	Contact	Comments
Netherhall International College, London, UK	In-service teacher improvement courses for non-native speakers	Full-time Intensive 6 hrs per day, semi intensive 3 hrs.	Both	Intensive £330-£400 2 wks, £585-£675 4 wks: Semi intensive £200-£250 2 wks, £330-£400 4 wk	Tba	Teaching experience	The Manager	—
Norwich Institute for Language Education (NILE), Norwich, UK	MLA69 (SAT1) + MLA (JUL)	4 weeks	Full-time	US$ 1960/£1300	MLA 69 (SAT1) 7th January. MLA69(JUL) 14 July	Degree + teaching experience. Exceptions can be considered	NILE	Award bearing professional development courses
	ELT Management	2 weeks	Full-time	£690	MAN1 96 31 March MAN2 96 1 September	—	NILE	—
	Innovation And Reflection In The Classroom	2 weeks	Full-time	£690	30 June	Experience as an EFL teacher	NILE	Numerous other courses - apply NILE for details
NSTS English Language Institute, Valletta, Malta	Methodology Courses	2 weeks (30 lessons per week)	Full-time	GBP 280	17 August, 30 August, other dates to be announced	Experienced teachers	Norman Shaw	—
Oxford House College, London, UK	English for English Teachers	Up to 8 weeks	Part-time (part of full-time course in May)	From £176 for 2 weeks- £500 for 8 weeks	From 1 July	Good standard of English	Michael Harmsworth	—
Phoenix English Language Academy, Perth, Australia	Professional Development Courses for Non native speakers of English EFL teachers	Varied	Both	On application	On application	Experienced English teachers	Ms Kate Tarrant	Can cater for specific areas such as teaching Business, Academic,, Medical English etc.
Pilgrims, Canterbury, UK	Specialist Courses For Teacher Trainers	2 weeks	Full-time	£955 all inclusive	July, August	—	Sasha Beavis	—
Saxoncourt, Taipei, Taiwan	Certificate in Teaching Young Learners	Tba	Tba	Tba	Tba	Tba	Saxoncourt Taiwan	—
Swan School of English, Stratford upon Avon, UK	Teachers' Refresher Course	2 weeks	Full-time	£480per course (includes a theatre ticket)	15/7, 29/7, 19/8	Practising teacher or graduate pre-experience	Anne Holmes	—
University of Edinburgh, UK	Teaching English For Specific Purposes	3 weeks	Full-time	£657	22 July	2 years' relevant experience	Registration Secretary	Also Teaching English For Medical Purposes - 2 weeks £450
	Drama For TEFL	3 weeks	Full-time	£657	12 August	Open to practising teachers	Registration Secretary	—
University of York, EFL Unit, York, UK	Teaching English To Young Learners	9 months	Full-time	£2,599 excl. accomm., meals, travel costs	14 October	Practising teachers, non-native speakers of English	Secretary EFL Unit	Also 2 or 3 week courses on same subject

College	Course length	FT/PT	Fees	Start dates	Entry requirements	Contact	Comments	Max no of students
Aberdeen College	2 weeks	Full-time	On application	Various	FCE 'A' pass or CAE/CPE	Anne Bain	Certificated or practising teachers preferred	15
The Bell Language School, Norwich	3 weeks	Full-time	£1,040 (including tuition, accom. and special programme)	July	Practising overseas teachers	Head of Studies	Intensive preparation for CEELT exams	14
Brasshouse Centre, Birmingham	4 weeks	Full-time	On application	July or August	FCE level or above	Deborah Cobbett	Course may run during year depending on demand	15
British Council, Izmir	6 months	Part-time	£75 + exam fee	October - thereafter on demand	Qualified teacher status, appropriate langauge competence	Steven Darn	Available at both CEELT I and CEELT II levels	12
CELT Athens	60 hours per course	Both	£320 approx	Full-time summer Part-time October	Language Examination	Marisa Constantinides	CEELT I level not available in Greece	10
Centro Anglo Paraguayo,	3 months	Part-time	£5 registration fee, £18 monthly tuition fees, exam fee £55	March	Good pass at FCE	Lorraine Jackson	—	15
Eastbourne School of English	4 weeks	Full-time	£540	1 July	Minimum level FCS	Dorothy S. Rippon	Accomm. avaliable from £70 per week	12
ELT Banbury	2/3/4 weeks	Full-time	£175 per week	July, August	Teacher of English	Dr T. J. Gerighty	—	10
The English Preparatory School, Turkey	One semester (approx 17 weeks)	Part-time	On application	September	First degree	Edward Casassa	—	15
Globe English Centre, Exeter	Min 1 week (15-33 hours/week)	Both	From £178/week (15 hours tuition)	On demand	Teacher of English	Catherine J Borgen	—	6
Gloscat, Cheltenham	2-4 weeks	Full-time	£150 per week	July	Advanced English	Paul Burden	—	14
Hammersmith and West London College	3 months	Part-time	£190	September, January, April	Cambridge Proficiency level English	Course Information Centre	—	20
Instituto Cultural Anglo-Uruguayo	9 months	Part-time	To be published Feb 96	April	FCE for CEELT I CPE for CEELT II	Ursula Krieger	—	12
International Language Academy, Cambridge	3 weeks	Full-time	£525	29 July	For practising non-native speaking teachers	Mr N.P.Kenny	—	15
Kingsway College, London	10 weeks	—	EU £175 Overseas £195	January, September	—	David Rosewarne	—	18
Norwich Institute for Language Education	3 weeks	Full-time	£990	14 July	Experience as an EFL teacher	NILE	—	16

RSA/Cambridge CEELT Courses

College	Course length	FT/PT	Fees	Start dates	Entry requirements	Contact	Comments	Max no of students
Phoenix English Language Academy, Western Australia	4 weeks	Full-time	A$950	4/3, 6/5, 24/6, 29/7, 4/11	Level 1 520 TOEFL 5, IELTS Intermediate Level 2 580 TOEFL 6 IELTS Upper Intermediate.	Ms Kate Tarrant	Exam fee A$200. Includes half day per week practicum. 30 hours per week teaching	10
Richmond Adult & Community College	20 weeks (Jan-June) 13 weeks (Sept - Dec)	Part-time	Jan-June £308 Sep-Dec £210	8 January, 16 September (testing on 9 Sept.)	At least a Grade B at First Certificate	The Secretary, Dep't of Languages & Business Studies	Students can enrol after the beginning of the course.	24 (Av. 18)
Skola Teacher Training, London	1, 2 or 3 weeks	Part-time	£80	Any Monday from 15 July	FCE level of English. Teaching experience preferred	Sandra Stevens	—	10
Study Space, Thessalonika	4 months 2 months	Part-time	£175	February/ October	Either practising EFL teacher or following methodology course	Christine Taylor	—	8

Diploma For Overseas Teachers Of English (DOTE) Courses

College	Course length	FT/PT	Fees	Start dates	Entry requirements	Contact	Comments	Max no of students
Asociacion Cultural Peruano Britanica, Lima, Peru	15 months	Part-time	$2,000	April 1997	600 hours teaching experience, CEELT 2	Pilar Ferreyros	—	15
CELT, Athens, Greece	1 year, 16 months	Full-time (Summer blocks), Part-time Oct-June	£1,600	June	BA or equivalent, experience + basic training	Marisa Constantinides	—	10
English Preparatory School, Mersin, Turkey	2 years	Part-time	On application	September	Degree, 2 years teaching (CEELT II preferred)	Edward Casassa	—	15
Middle East Technical Univ., Ankara, Turkey	2 years	Part-time	£250	First week of October	3 years teaching experience, proficiency in English	Suna Yazar	Practical, with some theoretical. Seminar/ workshops/ discussions	15
PROFILE, Athens, Greece	2 years (300 hours)	Part-time	850,000 DRS	October	2 years exp., initial training, degree (not oblig.)	PROFILE	—	25
Study Space, Thessalonika, Greece	18 months	Part-time	£1,750	January 1997	3 years TEFL experience	Christine Taylor	—	8
University of Edinburgh, UK	3 weeks	Full-time	£657	12 August	Good pass at FCE	Registration Secretary	Lang. Skills for Lang. Teachers (CEELT Prep)	12
Volkshoch- schule, Zurich, Switzerland	—	Part-time	approx SFr. 800	October	—	Mrs Margaret Stark	—	16

Teaching Business English Courses

College	Course title	Course length	FT/PT	Fees	Start dates	Entry requirements	Contact	Comments
Frances King School of English, London	LCCI Certificate in Teaching English for Business (LCCI Cert. TEB)	2 weeks	Both	£299	Available on application	Teaching qualification + 1 year TEFL or 6 month TEFL and a business backgound	Natalie Ivemy	—
International House, Barcelona	Business English	Full-time 2 weeks Part-time 6 weeks	Full-time	39,000 pesetas	July, September	CTEFLA or equivalent, 1 year's experience	Jenny Johnson	Help with accomm.
International House, Budapest	Teaching Business English	10 weeks	Part-time (1 evening per week)	£98	11 March	CTEFLA or equivalent, 6 months TEFL experience	Eva Baricz	—
International House, Hastings	Teaching Business English	5 days & 2 weeks	Full-time	5 days £235 2 weeks £445	5 days 29 January 2 weeks 12 August	By application	Adrian Underhill	For native and non-native teachers. Accomm.
International House, Lisbon	Teaching Business English	1 week	Full-time	41.000 pte	September	Pre-course interview and task	Paula de Nagy	—
London Guildhall University	LCCIEB Certificate/ Diploma in Teaching English for Business	Cert. 2 weeks Dip. 2*3 weeks	Full-time	Cert. £435 Dip. £1,490	Cert. 8 January 15 July, Dip. 15 July	Initial TEFL Qualification Dip. Degree + ELT Qualification + experience	The Secretary, English Language Centre	2*3 week courses in successive years + project in intervening year. Course available by arrangement overseas
LTS Training & Consulting, Bath	LCCI Cert in Teaching English for Business	2 weeks	Full-time	£700	June, July, December	TEFL Qualification + 2-3 yrs exp.	Adrian Pilbeam	Also seminars in UK and overseas incl. LCCI Cert TEB
Multi Lingua, Guildford	Teaching English for Business Certificate Course (ML Bus. TEFL)	5 Saturdays	Part-time	£390	24 February 28 September	Relevant teaching qual. + at least 1 yr's general ELT experience	Dr G P Connolly	Highly intensive course.
Pilgrims, Canterbury	Teaching Business & Professional People	2 weeks	Full-time	£955	July, August	—	Mrs Sasha Beavis	—
Regent Capital London	Business English Course	—	Full-time	£699	4/3, 24/6, 30/9, 9/12	Degree, teaching qualification, TEFL experience	Vicky Timperley	The first centre to run an LCCIEB Cert. TEB course
University of Edinburgh	Teaching English for Business Purposes	2 weeks	Full-time	£450	12 August	2 years' relevant experience	Registration Secretary	—

Key to UK Diplomas

NORTH & SCOTLAND

	Page
Moray House	90
Sheffield Hallam	94
University of Edinburgh	91
University of Leeds	94
University of Liverpool	93
University of Manchester	92
University of Sheffield	95
University of Stirling	94

CENTRAL & WALES

Aston University	95
University of Hertfordshire	95
University of Wales	93
University of Warwick	91

LONDON

International House London	91
St. Georges	91

SOUTH

University of Essex	90
University of Reading	92
Chichester Institute of HE	93
Canterbury Christchurch College	94
University of Southampton	95
The Language Project, Bristol	95
St. Mary's University	95

The University of Reading

MA in TEFL

The Centre for Applied Language Studies offers experienced EFL teachers a modular course leading to an MA in the Teaching of English as a Foreign Language. The course offers a flexible programme of study. The MA can be completed in a 12-month study route or in an extended time frame if you return each year to complete a module. Entry dates are in January, July and October.

For further details, or advice about a programme of study to suit you, please contact:

The MA Course Administrator (ELTG), Centre for Applied Language Studies, The University of Reading, Whiteknights, PO Box 241, Reading RG6 6WB. Tel: (01734) 318512. Fax: (01734) 756506.

A centre of excellence for university teaching and research.

Centre for
Applied Language Studies

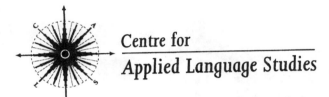

UNIVERSITY of STIRLING

CENTRE for ENGLISH LANGUAGE TEACHING

Situated on a beautiful campus in central Scotland with excellent sports facilities, shopping and arts centre, the University offers the following:

- ☐ MSc in TESOL (1 year)
- ☐ MSc in CALL and TESOL (1 year)
- ☐ BA in ENGLISH as a FOREIGN LANGUAGE
- ☐ BA in ENGLISH LANGUAGE TEACHING
- ☐ ENGLISH LANGUAGE COURSES (all year)
- ☐ PRE-SESSIONAL COURSES (April-September)

For a brochure and further information please contact:

The Associate Director, CELT
University of Stirling
Stirling FK9 4LA, Scotland, UK
(01786) 467934
Fax (01786) 463398

- PROVIDING HIGHER EDUCATION AND RESEARCH -

Canterbury Christ Church College

MA in English Language Education (TEFL/TESL) (University of Kent)

* 12-month advanced course for teachers, trainers, administrators, curriculum developers, project personnel
* Professional development in teaching, materials and curriculum design, management and evaluation
* Focus on social context and appropriate methodology

Diploma/MA in TEFL (University of Kent)

* 9-month course leading to Diploma
* Possibility of continuing to MA by dissertation
* Professional qualification for EFL teachers
* Practical work including teaching practice, lesson observation and work with teaching mentors

Certificates in TEFL

* Eleven-week practical courses
* Certificates can be used as credit for Diploma

These courses begin in October 1996 and are open to teachers from all countries.

For a copy of our prospectus and application form contact:
International Programmes Office,
Canterbury Christ Church College, Canterbury CT1 1QU
Tel: 01227 458459   Fax: 01227 781558

The University of Leeds

School of Education

COURSES FOR TEACHERS OF ENGLISH

BA TESOL (2 years - starts Oct)
MEd TESOL (11 months - starts Oct or Feb)
EdD TESOL (3 years, partly taught)
MPhil/PhD degrees (2/3 years, by thesis)
Graduate Diploma in TESOL (Sept-June)
Grad Certificates in TESOL (Oct-Dec, or Feb-June)
  • For information: Tel. +44 (0) 113 233 4528

Specially Arranged Short Courses and Attachments
  • For information: Tel. +44 (0) 113 233 4579

For information, contact:

Dr Martin Bygate
School of Education, University of Leeds
Leeds LS2 9JT
Fax +44 (0) 113 233 4541
E-mail *M.Bygate@education.leeds.ac.uk*

TESOL CENTRE

Trinity College Licentiate Diploma in TESOL
MA TESOL

These courses are part of the TESOL Centre's teacher education programme Certificate/Diploma/MA TESOL. Each part contains distance learning, full-time direct contact and research phases. The certificate and diploma courses are accredited by BATQI.

The diploma course also leads to the University's Postgraduate Diploma in TESOL, and earns credit towards the MA in TESOL. It starts in October and consists of

- **30 week distance learning phase**
- **12 week research phase**
- **four week full-time direct contact phase**

The MA in TESOL focuses on a workplace-based research project. It starts in May and October and consists of

- **eight week distance learning phase**
- **six week full-time direct contact phase**
- **32 week research phase**

For further information please contact
TESOL Centre
Sheffield Hallam University
Totley Campus Totley Hall Lane
Sheffield S17 4AB
Telephone 0114 253 2816
Fax 0114 253 2832

Sheffield Hallam University
Education for business and the professions

 **University of Hertfordshire**

Linguistics and TEFL (Undergraduate level: February entry)

A theoretical introduction to fundamental issues in second language learning. *1 module: 2 hours per week contact.*

Linguistics and Language Teaching
(Master's level: October/February entry)

Forms part of the modular Master's degree in Linguistics and its Applications.

Examines the processes of learning a second language drawing on teachers' experience across various languages, levels and contexts.

Contact: Pat Morton, School of Humanities and Education, Watford Campus, Wall Hall, Aldenham, Watford, Herts WD2 8AT.

The University of Hertfordshire is a Registered Charity committed to the furtherance of education.

Centre for Language in Education
(Faculties of Arts and Educational Studies)
- MA in Applied Linguistics for Language Teaching (full-time)
- MA(Ed) in Language in Education (part-time)
- Research degrees (MPhil/PhD) in Language/Literature/Applied Linguistics

These courses are recognised for the award of ESRC studentships.

For further details, apply to: Ms Rachel Ryan, Faculty of Educational Studies, University of Southampton, Southampton SO17 1BJ. Tel (01703) 592763. Fax (01703) 592687.

 University of Southampton

A centre of excellence for university research and teaching

ST MARY'S
UNIVERSITY COLLEGE
Strawberry Hill
A college of the University of Surrey

MA APPLIED LINGUISTICS & ELT, MA LINGUISTICS IN EDUCATION CERTIFICATE/DIPLOMA IN ELT

Why not advance your career by taking out modular MA programme?
whether you are:
- teaching ELT as a second or foreign language
- teaching language
- training teachers
- involved in ELT administration
- a native or non-native speaker

Courses look at theory and practice in applied linguistics. Programme offered on a full-time or part-time.
ACCOMMODATION ARRANGED FOR OVERSEAS STUDENTS
For further information pleas contact:
Mona Farrugla, The Registry, St Mary's University College Strawberry Hill, Twickenham, TW1 4SX. Tel: 0181 892 0051 ext. 249

---

the LANGUAGE *project*

Fun and affordable courses with something for everyone!

✱ Introduction to TEFL...............................for anyone

✱ Trinity Licentiate Diploma....for experienced teachers

✱ Short courses.......................for non-native teachers

✱ Intensive courses.......................for foreign students

The Language Project
78-80 Colston Street
Bristol BS1 5BB
Tel/Fax: (0117) 927 3993

ELGAZETTE
ENGLISH LANGUAGE JOURNAL OPENING DOORS ACROSS THE WORLD

EL*GAZETTE* **is the worldwide journal for the English Language industry. The** *GAZETTE* **regularly runs features on MA Courses in the UK and around the world and presents an ideal opportunity for universities to promote their courses.**

For further details on feature schedules, contact Shaun Collins on +44 171 938 4639

  ## UNIVERSITY OF SHEFFIELD

DIPLOMA and MA in APPLIED LINGUISTICS
modular programme: one year full-time; two years part-time.

(4 modules for Diploma; 6 modules or 4 modules + dissertation for MA.)

For further details contact:
Dr Mike Reynolds
Department of English Language and Linguistics,
University of Sheffield, 5 Shearwood Road,
Sheffield S10 2TD
Tel: +44 (0)114 282 6042   Fax: +44 (0)114 276 8251

Aston University

Courses for your career development

MSc in TESP
1 year full-time (Oct start)

MSc in TESP or TE
2 or 3 years by **distance learning** (Jan start)
Centres in Spain, Turkey, Greece, France, Italy, and Japan as well as UK
Also: **Diploma** in TESP or TE, 1 or 2 years

Certificate in Principles of TESP
3 months full-time (Oct/Jan/Apr start)

Advanced Certificate in Principles of TEFL
Individually-based distance learning (Jan-Jun) plus short practical classroom component in August

Introductory Certificate in TEFL
1 month full-time (July and Aug)

Further details:

Language Studies Unit,
Aston University,
Birmingham B4 7ET, UK.
Tel: 0121 359 3611 (ext. 4242/4236)
Fax: 0121 359 2725
Email: lsu@aston.ac.uk

Finding A Job

Whether you are a newly qualified teacher seeking your first job or an experienced teacher looking to return to his or her own country, this section offers advice on finding work in the English-speaking nations. There is also advice for teachers seeking to use their **TEFL** experience to develop their career in other spheres.

99 A Career In The Life Of

100 Working In The UK And Ireland

101 Summer Schools

105 Homestay

106 Working In North America

107 Working In Australia And New Zealand

108 Volunteering

109 Starting Your Own Language Business

111 TEFL And Beyond

113 How To Find Work

A Career In The Life Of

For some, TEFL might be a short-term career to fund time spent living abroad. However, it can be the beginning of a long and varied career, as this example demonstrates.

Skills which EFL teachers gain can stand them in good stead in their further careers

 he careers followed by people in EFL are as different as the people involved in it and as varied as their initial reasons for getting involved in English teaching.

Having studied languages at Sheffield University, Helen Mattacott Cousins was intending to take up a job at The National Westminster Bank. However, Sheffield University was twinned with the University of Upper Brittany in Rennes and Helen was offered a temporary (1-year) lecturer's post. Half thinking she might do an MA, Helen turned her back on banking and took the first steps into EFL.

Moving Abroad

Her first contact with EFL was at the University of Upper Brittany, but the course she taught there was neither particularly intensive or practical. It was very academic with an emphasis on linguisitics and phonetics. However, a tutor on the course was very aware of EFL and inspired Helen in that direction.

Having been in contact with the British Council in Morrocco, Helen went to work for them as a very temporary temp. At this stage, despite her academic background, she felt neither qualified nor prepared for teaching English. However, after gaining valuable firsthand experience, her tempory job developed into a full-time contract. The British Council also sponsored her to do an RSA Diploma through International House's Distance Learning scheme. This was very beneficial to her teaching and under-standing of EFL and led to her becoming a teacher trainer advising teachers in Secondary Schools.

There are not enough Director of Studies jobs to go round

After four years in Morocco Helen was offered a one-year contract working in China. Once again her role was that of teacher trainer - working with heads of department from schools in and around Nanjing. After this it was back to England in order to take an MA in Applied Linguistics at Reading University.

Back In The UK

Having qualified, she then returned to work as one of three Assistant Directors with the British Council in Indonesia. On returning to the UK her first job was as marketing manager for the EL Gazette. However the world of teaching won her back and she went on to become Director of Regent Capital Executive Centre which ran Business English Courses for executives.

From May 1994 Helen has been working at ARELS as the Education and Welfare Officer. Her job is concerned with raising standards of education and welfare in the EFL industry, particularly among ARELS members. This involves providing advice, training and information via publications, speaking at conferences and consultancy.

So what was it that kept Helen in EFL? The attraction of EFL teaching, she believes, is the challenge and opportunity of meeting people from overseas and, of course, living overseas. There is also the freedom and independence that is more a part of TEFL than banking. Skills which an EFL teacher gains that can stand them in good stead in their further careers include communication, counselling and personal confidence. A succesful EFL teacher will be strong on initiative and flexibility and (hopefully!) have the added bonus of having acquired one or more languages in their travels.

On the downside is the moderate salary. Few people get rich working in EFL. Part of the problem is the continued lack of a career structure. In theory one can progress, as Helen did, from teacher to teacher trainer to Assistant Director of Studies - although she acknowledges that her career is actually fairly unusual: she has been lucky to move up the ranks with such seeming smoothness. From there things get harder since one can come across something of a bottleneck. There are not enough DOS jobs to go round and, since there are even fewer Principal jobs DOS's can remain in place a long time. It is for this reason that people like Helen look for jobs outside of teaching. However, she does feel that the experience of being your own boss and emphasis on originality and dynamism that comes from a background in EFL has held her in good stead in her non-teaching work.

Working In The UK And Ireland

Job prospects and living conditions.

United Kingdom

English language teaching has been an important industry in the UK since the fifties. During the summer, towns like Oxford, Cambridge and Hastings are flooded with foreigners who are studying English and living with host families.

It can be quite difficult for a new teacher to find permanent work. The British Council recognition scheme has strict rules on staff qualifications, so recognised schools prefer diploma-qualified teachers. New teachers often work in schools outside the council's accreditation scheme or as freelancers.

There is a lot of work in the summer when schools employ vast numbers of teachers who have just finished certificate courses or returned from teaching abroad. (See page 101 for details)

Visas and work permits: Unless you are an EU citizen, it is extremely difficult to obtain a work permit. Employers must apply on behalf of teachers before they enter the country and prove that EU citizens can't do the job. Your only real chance is if you have some very specialist skill. It can take several months for entry to the UK to be cleared.

Members of the EU are entitled to work in Britain, but they must still arrange a National Insurance number before starting work. Europeans cannot receive unemployment benefit while looking for work unless they have lived in Britain before. Many private schools require 'native speakers' as teachers.

Citizens of Commonwealth countries aged between 17 and 27 can come to Britain on a working holiday allowing part-time or casual work, which could include teaching in summer schools.

Spouses of foreigners who have work permits or are studying full-time at a British university may work in the UK. Full-time students can work part-time if they gain permission from the Department of Employment. Study must continue to be independently funded.

Cost of living: Expensive in London, cheaper elsewhere.

Salaries and taxes: Rates vary considerably. Schools in Oxford and Cambridge pay well, while rates in London are relatively low. You should get around £10 per hour in the private sector and double that in the state sector or if you have a specialised skill.

The basic rate of tax is 24%.

Accommodation: Expect to pay around £50 per week for a room in a shared house in London and the south of England. Rents are less elsewhere in the UK. A standard deposit is one month's rent.

It is relatively easy to find accommodation, especially if you pair up with somebody else. Most leases are for six or twelve months but it is often possible to get one for nine months in student areas.

Health insurance: Health care is free for everybody on the National Health Service. There are long waiting lists for non-urgent operations, so private health care is becoming increasingly popular.

Newspapers: Look for teaching jobs in the EL Gazette, Tuesday's Guardian and the Times Education Supplement.

Ireland

Work in Ireland is very seasonal, with the vast majority of students coming to Dublin in July and August. Schools tend to have a skeleton staff of experienced teachers working all year-round then hire large numbers of other teachers for two to four months.

Summer work in Ireland is extremely popular with Irish teachers on short contracts abroad. Large numbers of British and American teachers apply for summer school work but, without a mailing address in Ireland, you should expect to go to the bottom of the pile. Schools are unlikely to hire somebody they haven't interviewed and students expect to be taught by Irish teachers.

With such a large number of highly qualified teachers trying to work in Dublin during the summer, unqualified teachers will find work hard to come by. Decentralisation has seen a growth in the number of schools in tourist towns such as Cork, Kerr, Limerick and Galway.

Visas and work permits: UK citizens do not need a work permit. For other nationalities, employers must arrange permits, convincing the authorities that no Irish citizen could do the job.

Cost of living: Many visitors are surprised at how expensive Ireland is: expect usual West European rates.

Salaries and taxes: A good hourly wage during the summer would be Ir£9-15, but many schools pay less. Basic tax is around 35%.

Accommodation: Short-term accommodation is primarily targeted at business visitors and it can therefore be expensive.

Summer Schools

There are plenty of seasonal opportunities for teachers during the school holidays.

As students have the time to travel and study English during their long summer holidays, schools put on special courses. There is a boom in July and August especially in the UK, US, Ireland and Canada, when the European schools are on holiday. In Australia and New Zealand the busy time is between December and March, when schools in Japan and the Far East are on holiday.

Established language schools run summer courses, as do colleges and universities, but EFL agents and teachers may hire out public buildings to run their own seasonal summer schools. With so many courses being run, staff are in huge demand but salaries are not that good. Often courses are split into half a day of language learning and half a day of recreation - perhaps sightseeing trips or sports activities - so courses need people to be lively administrators as well as competent language teachers.

In Britain there are courses combining English with just about everything from horse riding to sailing. In Australia and New Zealand it is also possible to combine teaching English with activity holidays, including sports such as scuba diving and even bungee jumping. So if you have any experience in such activities, you may be in demand.

Summer school contracts usually run for one to two months. As with any job in EFL, some sort of TEFL qualification will ensure you get a better-paid job. Experienced teachers may also be able to become course directors or Directors of Studies. In Britain, state sector colleges and, increasingly, universities also run summer courses where pay tends to be higher than in private schools.

Summer courses are traditionally where newly qualified teachers have their first classroom experience. Demand for teachers is so high that unqualified people have a good chance of being taken on. The courses are usually quite intensive and cater for multinational students. If you are interested in finding out more about teaching summer courses, read Teaching English on Holiday Courses by Nick Dawson, part of Longman's Handbook for Teachers series. Schools with a high level of young learners prefer teachers with primary rather than TEFL experience.

Unfortunately summer schools in Britain have often had a bad press, with stories of exploitative agents employing inexperienced teachers on inadequate premises. There has been a move to crack down on such operations. One result of this has been to push students away from the established centres, such as the south coast of England, to the north of England, Ireland and Scotland. Students have found such areas less crowded, cheaper and friendlier. Prospective teachers can thus find potential employment throughout the British Isles. Pay can still vary considerably, with Cambridge reportedly commanding the top rates. London has the highest cost of living and too many teachers available to pay well.

Some schools offer full board and accommodation on residential summer courses, which is valuable for teachers returning from abroad for the summer, but they may pay badly and you may be expected to look after the students outside class hours.

Tips for summer school teachers:

Apply early. Christmas is a good time to get an interview and secure a place at a favoured school.
Check salary rates. Telephone a number of centres in your chosen area to get an average. Around £7 an hour should be the minimum in the UK with extra for social activities.
Look for professionalism during the interview.
Be prepared for a lot of hard work - often you will be living, eating and socialising with your students for the duration of the course.
Make sure the school includes a proper training day.
Teachers should check pay, tax and insurance conditions, especially if the school is less well known.
Some UK schools offer full board and accommodation in residential summer schools but they may offer very low salaries and you may be expected to look after the students outside class hours.

UK SUMMER SCHOOLS DIRECTORY

The following list is of some of the language schools which run summer courses. The list is by no means definitive - it's worth checking with any language school in your area. Most universities also run summer schools.

Abbey College, Wells Road, Malvern Wells, Worcestershire, W14 4JF. Tel: 01684 892 300

Aberdeen Centre For English, 68 Polmuir Road, Aberdeen, AB1 2TH Tel: 01224 580 968

Abon Language School, 25 St. John's Road, Clifton, Bristol, BS8 2HD Tel: 0117 973 035

Alexanders International School, Bawdsey Manor, Bawdsey, Woodbridge, Suffolk, IP12 3AZ Tel: 01394 411 633

Anglo Continental School of English, 29-35 Wimborne Road, Bournemouth, BH2 6NA Tel: 01202 557 414

Anglo European School of English, 55 Lansdowne Road, Bournemouth, BH1 1RN Tel: 01202 558 658

Anglo European Study Tours, 8 Celbridge Mews, Porchester Road, London, W2 6EU Tel: 0171 229 443

Anglo World London, Park Lodge, 8 Queens Road, Hendon, London, NW4 2TH Tel: 0181 202 435

Anglo World Oxford, 108 Banbury Road, Oxford, OX2 6JU Tel: 01865 515 808

Basil Patterson College, 22-23 Aberchomby Place, Edinburgh, EH3 6QE Tel: 0131 556 769

BBC English Summer School, PO Box 76, Bush House, London, WC2B 4PH Tel: 0171 257 825

Buckswood Grange, Church Street, Uckfield, East Sussex, TN22 3PU Tel: 01825 761 666

Bell Language School Cambridge, 1 Red Cross Lane, Cambridge, CB2 2QX Tel: 01223 247 242

Bell Language School Norwich, The Old House, Church Lane, Eaton, Norwich, NR46NW Tel: 01603 456 321

Bell Language School London, 34 Fitzroy Square, London, W1P 6BP Tel: 0171 637 833

Bournemouth International School, 711-713A Christchurch, Bournemouth, Dorset, BH7 6AF Tel: 01202 393 112

Bridge International School of English, 3 Bennet Street, Bath, Avon, BA1 2QQ Tel: 01225 465 453

Cambridge Academy of English, 65 High Street, Girton, Cambridge, CB3 0QD Tel: 01223 277 230

Cambridge School of Languages, 119 Mill Road, Cambridge, CB1 2AZ Tel: 01223 312 333

CELT Centre for English Teaching Ltd., 3 Foster Drive, Penylan, Cardiff, CF3 7BD Tel: 01222 452 800

Central School of English, 1 Tottenham Court Road, London, W1P 9DA Tel: 0171 580 286

Cheltenham School of English, 87 St George's Road, Cheltenham, Gloucestershire, GL50 3DU Tel: 01242 570 000

Chichester School of English, 45 East Street, Chichester, West Sussex, PO19 1HX Tel: 01243 789 893

Cicero Languages International, 42 Upper Grosvenor, Tunbridge Wells, Kent, TN1 2ET Tel: 01892 547 077

Colchester English Study Centre, 19 Lexden Road, Colchester, Essex, CO3 3PW Tel: 01206 44422

Concorde International, Arnett House, Hawks Lane, Canterbury, Kent, CT20 2AT Tel: 01303 256 752

Coventry International English Studies, 9 Priory Row, Coventry, CV1 5EX Tel: 01203 223 379

Devon English Centre, 1 Victoria Road, Exmouth, Devon, EX8 1DL Tel: 01395 265 068

Devon School of English, The Old Vicarage, 1 Lower Polsham Road, Paignton, Devon, TQ32AF Tel: 01803 559 718

Edinburgh School of English, Cranston House, 271 Canongate,

The Royal Mile, Edinburgh, EH8 8BQ Tel: 0131 557 920

Edinburgh Tutorial College, 29 Chester Street, Edinburgh, E3 7EN Tel: 0131 225 988

EFA International School, Seadown House, Worthing, West Sussex, BN11 2BE Tel: 01903 209 244. Longest established English School in West Sussex. Open all year - Adults, students, juniors. Variety of courses, reasonable prices, social prog.

EFA International School of English London, 74 Roupel Street, London, SE1 8SS Tel: 0171 401 839

EL International School Cambridge, 221 Hills Road, Cambridge CB2 2RW Tel: 01223 240 020

Elizabeth Johnson Organisation, West House, 19/21 West Street, Haslemere, Surrey, GU27 2AE Tel: 01428 652 751

Embassy Language & Training Centre, 7 Wilbury Villas, Hove, East Sussex, BN3 6GB Tel: 01273 721 135

Embassy Language & Training Centre, 7 Warrior Square, St. Leonards on Sea, East Sussex, TN37 6BA Tel: 01424 720 282

Embassy Study Tours, 44 Cromwell Road, Hove, East Sussex, BN3 3ER Tel: 01273 207 481

English & Cultural Studies Centre, 40 Village Road, Enfield, Middlesex, EN1 2EN Tel: 0181 360 411

Eurocentre Bournemouth, 26 Dean Park Road, Bournemouth, BH1 1HZ Tel: 01202 554 426

Eurocentre Brighton, Huntingdon House, 20 North Street, Brighton, BN1 1EB Tel: 01273 324 545

Frances King School of English, 195 Knightsbridge, London, SW7 1RE Tel: 0171 838 020

Greylands School of English Ltd, 315 - 317 Portswood Road, Southampton, SO17 2LD Tel: 01703 315 180

Harrogate Language Academy, 8A Royal Parade, Harrogate, North Yorkshire, HG1 2SZ Tel: 01423 531 969

Harrow House International College, Harrow House, Harrow Drive, Swanage, Dorset, BH191PE Tel: 01929 424 421

Hastings English Language Centre, St Helen's Park Road, Hastings, East Sussex, TN34 2JW Tel: 01424 437 048

Inlingua Cheltenham, Rodney Lodge, Rodney Road, Cheltenham, Gloucestershire, GL50 1JF Tel: 01242 250 493

Interlink School of English, 126 Richmond Park, Bournemouth, Dorset, BH18 8TH Tel: 01202 290 983

International House, 106 Picadilly, London, W1V 9FL Tel: 0171 491 259

International House Northumbria, 14-18 Stowell Street, Newcastle Upon Tyne, Tyne & Wear, NE1 4XQ Tel: 0191 232 955

International House Torquay, Castle Road, Torquay, Devon, TQ1 3BB Tel: 01803 299 691

International Language Academy Oxford, 7 Norham Gardens, Oxford, OX2 6PS Tel: 01865 516 402

International Language Centres, International House, White Rock, Hastings, East Sussex, TN34 1JY Tel: 01424 720 100

International Language Institute, County House, Vicar Lane, Leeds, LS1 7JH Tel: 0113 242 8893

International Teaching & Training Centre, 674 Winbourne Road, Bournemouth, Dorset, BH9 2EG Tel: 01202 531 1355

Irwin College, 164 London Road, Leics, LE2 Tel: 0116 255 2648

ITS English School Hastings, 43-45 Cambridge Road, Hastings, East Sussex, TN34 1EN Tel: 01224 438 025

Kingsway English Centre, Northwall House, 11 The Butts, Worcester, WR1 3PA Tel: 01905 27511

King's School of English, 58 Braidley Road, Bournemouth, Dorset, BH2 6LD Tel: 01202 293 535

King's School of English, 25 beckenham Road, Beckenham, Kent, BR3 4RP Tel: 0181 650 589

Lewis School of English, 33 Palmerston Road, Southampton, SO13 1LL, Tel: 01703 228 203

Linguarama, 28 Princes Street, Manchester, M1 Tel: 0161 228 398

Linguarama, 1 Elm Court, Arden Street, Stratford Upon Avon, Warwickshire, CV37 6PA Tel: 01789 296 535

Linguarama Birmingham, New Oxford House, 16 Waterloo Road, Birmingham, B2 5UG Tel: 0121 632 592

Living Language Centre, Highcliffe House, Clifton Gardens, Folkestone, Kent, CT20 Tel: 01303 258 53

London House School of English, 51 Sea Road, Westgate on Sea, Kent, CT8 8Ql Tel: 01843 831 216

Lydbury English Centre, The Old Vicarage, Lydbury North, Shropshire, SY7 8AU Tel: 01588 680 233

Marble Arch Intensive English, 21 Star Street, London, W2 1QB Tel: 0171 402 927

Mayfield College, 24 Holland Road, Hove, East Sussex, BN3 1JJ Tel: 01273 202 389

Mayflower College of English, 34-36 Pier Street, The Hoe, Plymouth, Devon, PL1 3BT Tel: 01323 734 335

Merrion House Centre For English Studies, 60 Penn Road, Beaconsfield, Buckinghamshire HP9 2LS Tel: 01494 673 769

Milner School of English, 32 Worple Road, Wimbledon, London, SW19 4DB Tel: 0181 944 880

Multilingua, St Michael's House, 53 Woodbridge Road, Guildford, Surrey, GU1 4RF Tel: 01483 35118

Newnham Language Centre, 8 Grange Road, Cambridge, CB3 9DU Tel: 01223 311 344

Nord Anglia International, 10 Eden Place, Cheadlem Cheshire, SK8 1AT Tel: 0161 491 419

Oxford House College, 3 Oxford Street, London, W1R 1RF. Tel: 0171 580 978

Oxford House School of English, 67 High Street, Oxford, OX33 1XT Tel: 01865 874 786

Parkland International, Leighton Park Street, Shinfield Road, Reading, Berks, RG2 7DH Tel: 01734 313 214

Pilgrims Ltd, Pilgrims House, Prchard Street, Canterbury, Kent, CT2 81P 01227 762 111

Regency School of English, Royal Crescent, Ramsgate, Kent, CT11 9PE Tel: 01843 591212

Regent Oxford, Godmer House, 90 Banbury Road, Oxford, OX2 6JT Tel: 01865 515 566

Regent Park House, Park House, Hyssington, Montgomery, Powys, SY15 6DZ Tel: 01588 620 611

Regent Summer Schools, 3rd Floor, 19-23 Oxford Street, London, W1R 1RF Tel: 0171 636

Schiller English language Institute, Wickham Court, Layhams Road, West Wickham, Kent, CT20 2PX Tel: 01303 850 007

SELS College London, 64/65 Long Acre, Covent Garden, London, WC2E 9JH Tel: 0171 240 258

Shane English School, 59 South Molton, London, W1Y 1HH Tel: 0171 499 853

Sidmouth International, May Cottage, Sidmouth, Devon, EX10 8EN Tel: 01395 516 754

Solent Language Centre, 54 The Avenue, Southampton, SO1 2SY Tel: 01703 672 444

St Brelades College, Mont Les Vaux, St Aubin, Jersey, Channel Islands, JE3 8AF Tel: 01534 41305

St Giles College, Regency House, 3 Marlborough Place, Brighton, East Sussex, BN1 1UB Tel: 01273 682 747

St Hilary School of English, 2/4 Midvale Road, Paignton, Devon, TQ4 5BD Tel: 01803 559 223

St Peter's School of English, St Alphege Lane, Canterbury, Kent, CT1 2EB Tel: 01227 462 016

Swan School of English, 11 Banbury Road, Oxford, OX2 6JX Tel: 01865 53201

Swandean School of English, 12 Stoke Abbott, Worthing, West Sussex, BN11 1HE Tel: 01903 231 330

Thames Valley Cultural Centre, 15 Park Street, Windsor, Berks, SL4 1LU Tel: 01753 852 001

The Trebinshun Group, Trebinshun House, Near Brecon, Powys, LD3 7PX Tel: 01874 730 635

UTS Oxford Centre, Wolsey Hall, 66 Banbury Road, Oxford, OX2 6BR Tel: 01865 516 162

Vacational Studies, Pepys Oak, Tydehams, Newbury, Berks, RG14 6JT Tel: 01635 523 333

Winchester School of English, Beaufort House, 49 Hyde Street, Winchester, Hants, SO23 7DX Tel: 01962 851 844

Young English Studies, 11 Yourk Terrace, Regents Park, London, NW1 4PT Tel: 0171 935 263

Homestay

Norman Renshaw of Intuition Languages explains why Homestay is popular with students and teachers alike.

Homestay offers the motivated adult student shorter, more intensive courses

ne-to-one teaching can and should offer a rewarding and pleasurable experience to both teacher and student where the teacher too can learn from the experience of a cultural exchange.

Home English is a system of one-to-one tuition where the student lives in the home of a qualified EFL teacher and his or her family giving them total immersion in English language and culture. The average length of stay is one to two weeks and the standard format is for 15, 20 or 25 lessons per week plus full board for the student. The students benefit from receiving quality one-to-one tuition and also being assured of a host family that is educated and open to foreign visitors, offering a comfortable and hospitable environment. It is more flexible in terms of course dates and offers the motivated adult student shorter, more intensive courses. There is no peer pressure from other classmates and the student is not surrounded by other speakers of his or her mother tongue.

It is also a popular form of tuition from the teacher's perspective, meeting the needs of an increasing number of teachers who demand a more flexible working pattern without forfeiting their earning potential. It allows them to work from home and yet not be contracted or committed to any particular school. The added convenience of no travelling time to work and the opportunity of tutoring in a more convenient environment is also a big plus. It also suits teachers who live outside the main EFL centres. The flexibility comes from being able to choose when you want to accept a student. The work is on a freelance basis but if teachers work through an agency, they should receive full and professional support, in terms of course materials and guidance.

The advantage of an agency is not only the stronger marketing effort but also the perceived credibility it gives individual teachers

There are also a number of less definable advantages. The students themselves tend to be motivated and rewarding to teach, they arrive with a positive attitude and this makes for a rewarding exchange. Many have chosen one-to-one because they want to study hard but are also keen to become immersed in family life and culture. Some Homestay courses include an ESP element - students electing to stay in a family with a shared professional interest. For example a student may stay with a lawyer or doctor to improve their specialist as well as general English.

Teachers find home tuition fits their lifestyle, whether they are teacher trainers themselves working in other parts of the EFL industry as freelancers, or whether they are a qualified EFL teachers but also writers, or musicians, or have a family to look after and find normal classroom hours too much of a commitment away from home.

Home English is open to any qualified EFL teacher living in a comfortable and hospitable home but it does demand commitment from the teacher to be prepared to show an active interest in the development of students' language skills.

There are several ways of becoming a host teacher. Some teachers may have their own leads built up from teaching overseas, which will be sufficient to provide them with students when they require them.

An alternative method is to work through an agency that promotes your home as part of a network of teachers. This gives the teacher the benefit of working with an organisation that markets the network to a wider market of students. There are several agencies that cover this form of tuition. Some have a national network of teachers and others operate in a local area. It is up to the agency to brief the student accurately on what to expect on their course and also to brief the teacher on the student's profile, level and needs, plus all arrival details.

Agencies deal with the finances of the course by invoicing the student and paying the teacher. Rates vary but a qualified teacher should expect a minimum of £210 a week in the UK for 15 hours tuition plus accommodation.

The British Council has just set up a recognition scheme for Home English and the Irish are expected to follow suit. With the advent of recognition, Home English is becoming a valued part of the EFL industry.

Working In North America

Job prospects, terms and conditions in the USA and Canada.

United States Of America

Government cuts have drastically affected state-funded English language programs for immigrants but there are still two huge markets in the States. Adults learn English in the private sector - which includes the universities - and children learn English in the state-owned public schools.

This means that before you can teach children, you must have state certification from an American university. To teach adults, a Master's degree is the minimum qualification. The RSA Diploma is often accepted as the equivilant of an MA, but it is much harder for non-Americans to find work.

Adult education is broken up into various sectors, including intensive English programs in universities and private language schools and longer courses at universities.

To find work, contact the schools in the area you are interested in or approach TESOL - fax: +1-703-836 7864 - and ask about their placement and resume-holding services.

Many trade schools or semi-professional training schools and programs also hire English teachers to meet the increasing demand for foreign students who wish to enter programs designed for native English speakers. Neither credentials nor MAs are required.

Visas and work permits: You should have a green card of permanent residence or a work permit, although it is often possible to work while on a student or cultural visa. It helps to be qualified before getting your papers in order. It is unwise to work illegally, as there are stiff penalties.

To get a J1 visa for teachers, ask the head of a school to give you a form to return to the Foreign Student Department. The school doesn't need to employ you. The FSD will tell you which consulate to approach to pick up your visa.

The HIB working visa can be obtained if you are sponsored by a US company and it is processed by the Immigration and Naturalisation service, as well as the Department of Labor.

Cost of living: Consumer goods are amongst the cheapest in the world.

Salaries and taxes: Teachers can earn anything from $15 to $34 per hour. The tax depends on the state and the salary level.

Accommodation: Apartments are easy to find, but tend to be expensive. A small apartment can cost between $500 and $700 per month. Rooms in shared houses are cheaper: expect to pay around $400 per month.

Three months' rent is usually expected upfront. One month is a non-returnable deposit and the other two months are for the first and last months of the lease.

Health insurance: Essential.

Canada

Canada is an increasingly popular destination with Latin American students who feel it is safer and cheaper than the US. There are opportunities for qualified teachers in private schools in large cities.

Other opportunities exist in both the state and private sectors teaching the large immigrant population. Canada's open immigration policies are accompanied by massive public-funding English courses which can last up to six months. Qualifications are necessary unless you are working as a community-based volunteer.

There is demand for English language teachers in the French-speaking province of Quebec. Business English is booming, despite the vocal independence movement , as the French speakers realise that English is the key to successful international relations.

As well as private language schools in Quebec, there are employment opportunities in the state sector for teachers of English as a foreign language.

Visas and work permits: You have to prove that you are more suitable for a job than prospective Canadian candidates. This rarely happens since there are so many highly qualified Canadian teachers.

Cost of living: The standard of living is high.

Salaries and taxes: Wages range from $12 per hour in the private sector to $25 per hour in the public sector. Tax tends to be between 18 and 30 per cent.

Accommodation: Although accommodation is easy to find, it can be expensive in Toronto and Quebec.

Health insurance: Health care is free for all residents. Otherwise, it is worth taking out private cover.

Working In Australia And New Zealand

Job prospects, terms and conditions.

Australia

Australia's TESOL Industry is divided into two sectors (ESL and EFL), both of which are booming. The ESL sector is government funded and aimed at permanent residents from non-English-speaking backgrounds. Courses are organised through the Adult Migrant Education program and the Department of Technical and Further Education. Teachers involved in ELICOS (English Language Intensive Courses for Overseas Students) can be employed on a casual hourly basis for relief work and short periods of time; teachers employed for more than four and less than 40 weeks must have a seasonal contract which provides some continuity of employment and includes some provision for sick leave and recreation leave.

If you have an overseas qualification and intend to apply for teaching or Director of Studies positions, it is advisable to have your qualifcations formally assessed for equivalence. This can be done through the National Office of Overseas Skills Recognition, Commonwealth Department of Employment, Education and Training (Tel: 06-276 8111, Fax: 06-276 7636).

Visas and work permits: To work in Australia, you need either resident status, a working holiday visa or a full-time overseas student visa, which allows you to work up to 20 hours a week. Permanent residents are assessed for immigration on a points system, but English language teaching does not earn any points on the assessment.

It is relatively easy for British teachers aged between 18 and 26 to get a working holiday visa which is valid for a year. It allows you to work for each employer for up to three months. This means it is only really feasible to work as a casual relief teacher in the state sector or in the private sector.

Salaries and taxes: Rates for teachers working in ELICOS centres are covered by a union-negotiated pay award.

Tax is around 30 per cent provided you have a tax file number (if not then the rate is 48%). If you have an overseas student visa, you will have to take out Overseas Student Health Cover which costs around A$65 per six months. Permanent residents and those on working holiday visas will have a levy deducted from their pay.

Accommodation: Costs are higher in Sydney than elsewhere but it's easy to find. A room in a shared flat will cost around A$90-110 per week in Sydney, A$60-70 elsewhere.

Health insurance: Residents and those on working visas will have a levy deducted from their pay as a contribution to the government's Medicare health plan.

Inoculations: Yellow fever, if coming from an infected area.

New Zealand

Demand for English in New Zealand varies seasonally, with the peak demand during the Japanese and Thai holiday periods, between February and May and between July and October. It is only possible to find work if you are a qualified native speaker or completely bilingual.

There are opportunities in both EFL and teaching English as a Second Language to immigrants. Other than general English, there is demand for teachers in some specialist areas of English teaching, specifically teachers of English for academic purposes and those who teach High School preparation. There are some private classes to be had, but opportunities are limited. Auckland tends to be the best place to look for work.

Visas and work permits: Australians do not need any documentation to work in New Zealand. People under 27 of other nationalities can get a working holiday visa. You should apply to your local New Zealand embassy.

Work permits for older non-Australians are difficult to obtain since the employer has to prove that no New Zealander can do the job. There are temporary work permits which can be obtained by teachers with exceptional qualifications or experience. It is illegal to work on a tourist visa.

Cost of living: Relatively cheap, but consumer durables are more expensive.

Salaries and taxes: Teachers earn between NZ$27,000 and $36,000 per annum. The tax rate is around 25 per cent.

Accommodation: Schools tend not to help teachers find accommodation. However, it should not be too difficult to find accommodation for yourself. A room in a shared flat costs between $60 and $110 per week, while a one-bedroom flat costs between $150 and $170. Two weeks' rent is payable in advance as a bond.

Health insurance: All visitors need private health insurance. An accident compensation levy is paid by employees and employers.

Volunteering

Teaching English can be a means of becoming involved in the voluntary sector. Even here, however, qualifications are becoming increasingly important.

There are various organisations that recruit people to work as English teachers overseas, often in the developing world. Most developing countries are realising the importance of using experienced and qualified volunteers for their needs, and the days when people could simply take off for a year's adventure with most voluntary organisations have gone.

Today a volunteer's average age is 30. Most organisations prefer to recruit teachers with at least two years' experience. Graduates sometimes find that two years' experience volunteering revitalises their career, with head teachers keen to take them on in the state sector when they return. The British Council are sometimes interested in former volunteers, and OXFAM and the ODA (who fund VSO) often recruit people who have worked in the developing world. Listed below are some of the key organisation you should contact if you are interested in volunteering.

Voluntary Service Overseas (VSO)

VSO offers placements in a wide range of skill areas including education, technical trades, small business development, health, agriculture, social work/community development and sport. Contracts are usually for 2 years although shorter placements may be offered in selected skill areas. VSO place around 900 volunteers each year in 58 countries in Africa, Asia, the Pacific, the Caribbean and Eastern Europe. VSO pays for flights, health insurance, national insurance contributions plus grants towards equipment and re-settlement. Accommodation and a modest living allowance are provided by the local employer. A majority of the posts offered are suitable for volunteers aged between 23 and 55. Volunteers must have a qualification and a skill, be aged 20 - 70, be without dependents and have un-restricted right of re-entry to the UK.

United Nations Volunteers (UNV)

VSO recruit and sponsor volunteers to work through the United Nations multinational programme, the UNV. Work tends to be specialised, but allowances are larger and UNVs may be posted with their spouse and up to two children.

East European Partnership (EEP)

EEP is a branch of VSO, set up to contribute to the development of Eastern European countries. They are particularly interested in recruiting child carers and ELT/secondary level teachers for their projects in Albania, Bulgaria, the Czech and Slovakian Republics, Hungary, Poland and Romania. A TEFL qualification is preferred for their teacher training projects and teachers with specialist knowledge are in demand. Volunteers are paid a local salary and provided with accommodation and free medical services. Posts are for one to two years.

Peace corps

Peace corps volunteers are particularly active in Eastern Europe. Returning volunteers are now offered state teaching jobs in the USA while they study for MEds.

WorldTeach

WorldTeach is a programme of Harvard University's social service organisation in America, and they have operations in Africa, Asia, Central America and Eastern Europe. Most volunteers teach EFL on a one-year contract. Volunteers do not need any qualifications except a degree. Volunteers pay a fee of around $3000 to cover insurance, airfares and support services. They are then paid a local salary, and get free accommodation.

Overseas Service Bureau (OSB)

OSB is a non-government organisation which provides opportunities for Australians to live and work in developing countries in a range of programmes including the Australian Volunteers Abroad Program.

Returned Volunteer Action

Returned Volunteer Action (RVA) provides a range of different information publications looking at the opportunities in volunteering and the issues involved. RVA also run 'Information Days' when you can meet former volunteers.

Other voluntary organisations

Catholic Institute of International Relations, 22 Coleman Fields, London N1 1UL, UK.
Designers for Development Ltd., Campden Hill, Ilmington, Shipston-on-Stour, Warwickshire CV36 4JF UK. Fax: 01608 82643. (Min. 3-month contracts in Vietnam).
Skillshare Africa, 3 Belvoir Street, Leicester LE1 6SL UK.
Volunteer Service Abroad, VSA House, 31 Pipitea St., Thorndon, Wellington, New Zealand.

Starting Your Own Language Business

Many experienced EFL teachers - as well as a few business entrepreneurs - have seen how lucrative it can be to open their own language teaching business.

You can expect at least a two-year slog before your school is likely to break even

There comes a stage in the career of many EFL teachers when they decide that they have had enough working for other schools or waiting for senior positions to become available. It's then that teachers often consider setting up their own school. This can happen if you're working overseas or have returned to your own country. The temptations are obvious - there are some very successful, privately-owned schools around, but there are many pitfalls as well.

You must be prepared to spend time and effort learning the ins and out of running an efficient business. You can be the best teacher in the world, but if you don't understand cash flows then you're unlikely to make a great success of running your own school.

If you are considering opening a language school, remember that you can expect at least a two-year slog before your school is likely to break even. Many schools in the UK have not survived this period, partly because the British Council only recognises private language schools which have been operating for two years. Without this, it can be difficult to attract students. Once you reach the two-year limit, make sure you meet the recognition standards.

Find out what competition you have from other schools in the area, and try and offer something none of them have

It is vital to ensure that you have the financial backing to survive the first few years. Consult an accountant to see how much money you will need to get going. You will need money for market research and advertising and you must pay rent, the teachers' salaries, your own salary, tax, and bills. Check your cash-flow - some clients may take up to 120 days to pay invoices. It can take six months from making your first payment to receiving your first income.

Within the EU, changes in VAT laws relating to EFL operations could help you to cut your tax bill by a hefty sum. A specialist accountant will advise you on the latest EU regulations. Education is normally VAT-exempt, so if your school only supplies EFL tuition, you will not have to pay VAT. However, if you are running residential courses and have to buy in travel services, it is mandatory to use the Tour Operators Margin Scheme (TOMS) to work out your VAT bill. The EFL element is VAT-exempt while excursions, accommodation and catering carry a 17.5% VAT rate. Transport was zero-rated, but from the beginning of this year it has become liable for VAT.

If you are considering opening a school abroad, check out the legalities first. In Greece, for example, it is hard for a foreigner to open a school unless they at least have a Greek partner, although if you are an EU citizen, this is technically illegal.

Do your market research before you make a final commitment. Marketing people often refer to the USP (Unique Selling Point) of a product. Although you may hesitate to regard your school as a product you need to ask yourself what would make a student apply to your school rather than another. One school, targeting Business English, felt it worth their while to accept the greater overheads of being based near Harrods for the benefit such a location would bring to their students. It is important to consider other areas of investment and how they might benefit your company. If you don't invest, you'll limit your school's potential for growth but, at the same time, you must be clear why you're spending the money and what return it will bring to the school - even if that return is some years away. For example, will the money you spend on taking your students to the Opera be wasted or will it justify itself in the increased prestige and reputation you develop? Find out what competition you have from other schools in the area, and try and offer something none of them have - Business English or classes for younger learners, for example.

Think carefully about how to make your business efficient. Investing in a good PC will ease administration, and a laser printer, though representing a substantial outlay, will help you to do your own professional advertising. Choose suppliers you can trust. Try to arrange discounts on bulk orders of office and teaching materials. If you offer excursions or study trips, make sure your tour operator is reliable.

You must also consider how you will recruit teachers. If you want to recruit from an English-speaking country, will it be worth offering to pay their airfare? Will you recruit highly-qualified teachers, knowing they will expect higher salaries? Will you be strictly 'legal' and pay their tax and insurance contributions, or will you find loopholes to avoid this? All these factors will affect your prices, and the quality of your school.

Decide on a marketing campaign to attract clients. Mailshot your list of contacts and try the personal approach by following it up with a telephone call or a visit. It helps if you can offer to tailor your courses to fit clients' requirement. Ensure that your most important clients are taught by your best teachers.

Setting up your own business can be daunting and requires immense amounts of work and energy. However it can be very rewarding. Helene Panzarino, who set up the Bella school in London after the school she was working in closed down, acknowledged that it had been very hard work but that she was the only person who got off the train every morning with a smile on her face.

Ten Tips For Starting A Business

Ian Peters, Head of NatWest's Small Business Services offers the following ten points for consideration by the budding entrepreneur.

1. Think it through carefully. Why do you want to be self-employed? Do you really have the drive, training and skills to make a go of it?

2. Don't underestimate the financial and personal commitments that successful self-employment needs. Make sure your family are on your side.

3. Use all sources of free advice available to you such as, in the UK, Local Enterprise Agencies, Training and Enterprise Councils and NatWest Small Business Advisers.

4. Always keep your bank manager and professional advisers fully informed.

5. Research your market and product. Ensure your business idea is viable. Make sure there is sufficient demand for your product.

6. Plan realistically for success. Fill in cashflow forecasts and operating budgets making sure that break-even point is set at a comfortable level. Monitor performance against forecasts.

7. Work out how much finance you will need: it may be more than you think. Make the best use of grants, bursaries or cheap loans which you may be eligible for. Take advice on the best way to borrow - consider fixed rate loans for start-up costs, leasing and hire purchase for machinery. An overdraft facility for working capital needs is appropriate.

8. Don't forget the legal side. Protect your product. Understand tax and employers' obligations. Take professional advice from solicitors and accountants.

9. If you give credit, make sure your invoices are clear and legally binding. Chase debtors on time and be firm. Treat creditors as you would wish to be treated yourself.

10. You are your business' greatest asset - make sure you and your business are insured. Be prepared to work long hours but take time to enjoy achieving your self-employment goal.

Educational consultancies

If your budget does not run to equipping school premises, but you have the contacts to teach a large number of clients, it may be worth starting an educational consultancy. In this way you will only need an office, from which you can deal with your clients and your teachers.

Consultancies supply businesses or individuals with teachers at the client's premises. Investment will be less than for a school, but the same sound business principles of research, marketing and recruitment will apply. Once you have a reputation for supplying quality teachers, an agency can become a sound business.

TEFL And Beyond

Even if you've decided to move out of TEFL, the skills you have gained can stand you in good stead. Chris Graham of English Worldwide considers the options.

s there life after TEFL? Both James Joyce and Anthony Burgess proved that there was by quitting the classroom for literary careers, but for mere mortals like us, what is there beyond the classroom?

The first choice for most teachers wishing to leave the classroom is to stay in the TEFL business but in a different capacity. So what are the options? 'Limited' is the immediate answer to that. Within the school setting, becoming an Assistant Director of Studies and eventually director of Studies (DoS) is one possible avenue. Another is moving into teacher training. However, both in the UK and overseas these jobs are few and far between and are very rarely advertised. If a promoted post in a school is on your agenda, then the larger TEFL organisations such as International House, the Bell Language Schools, the British Council and the American ELS chain do offer a career structure of sorts which, given persistence and a willingness to work in several different locations, can allow you to move up the school ladder.

As a sideline to teaching, you may consider becoming an examiner. Money earned from marking exam papers can be a useful income supplement and may lead to work as a setting examiner for one of the EFL examining boards such as UCLES, Trinity College London, Pitman Examinations Institute and the University of Oxford Delegacy.

Publishing perhaps offers the most professional opportunities within TEFL but outside the school structure. Jobs in publishing divide crudely into selling and editorial and while there is certainly an interface between them, people usually start and stay in one sector or the other. Many sales people are ex-teachers and will use their knowledge of TEFL to sell to other teachers through seminars and teacher training sessions. Jobs can involve travel and working overseas. However, selling is selling and you have to be happy with that. My friends in publishing often mention that teachers and selling can sit uncomfortably together.

The editorial side of publishing is (at least initially) desk-based and can involve lots of very tedious work, getting more interesting once you've gained more experience and can move towards commissioning and managing projects. The drawbacks of publishing are its low pay and strident commercialism which may be a culture shock to an EFL teacher returning to their home country after a period of living abroad. This, however, is a problem that will need to be addressed with any move out of teaching, and on the bonus side there is a career structure if you stick with it.

A publishing-related career for EFL teachers is lexicography, or dictionary writing. The entry requirement for this career will vary from publisher to publisher. However an MA in linguistics and some TEFL experience would stand you in good stead. As with many TEFL-related jobs it may be a good idea to seek work initially as a freelancer while still doing some teaching. This will allow you to see if it is a career you are really after as well as enabling you to build up contacts and work while still having another source of income.

Life After TEFL

What about outside the TEFL business? What do your EFL qualifications and experience prepare you for? The main things that you are likely to have acquired would seem to include a knowledge of languages, excellent communication skills, a better than average command of English and a high degree of cultural sensitivity. Sounds unbeatable, doesn't it! Let's begin with the language skills. Translating and interpretation are obvious directions to go in, though, however fluent you are, you will probably need to undertake further studies since they are both very distinct skills. They are also usually badly paid and do not offer long-term employment, the whole business depending upon small armies of freelancers. If your skills are really good, then the EU and the UN do employ linguists but these jobs are highly sought after. UK Government service through the Foreign Office does offer careers for linguists: again they are very popular jobs so look for the annual open competition advertised in the national press and apply early. Some companies employ linguists in their export departments but companies in English-speaking countries are way behind their international competitors in this respect. The seriously well-paid jobs are for bi-lingual accountants or lawyers but the general assumption is that it's easier to teach a lawyer or accountant a language than it is to convert a linguist into a lawyer or accountant.

The communication skills that EFL teachers are assumed to possess lend themselves to a range of different career options ranging from counselling (which teachers often do well at) to sales. The problem is that everyone thinks they can communicate and it is sometimes difficult to convince an employer that your three years' teaching in Bilbao means that you can get their message across effectively and efficiently. One other point to consider is that, while sales might appeal in theory, in practice I see many CVs from teachers who have left teaching for sales and then, frustrated and unsuited, gone back into teaching. Overall, teaching shields you from the naked capitalism that much of the rest of the world makes its living in and leaving it can require a cultural leap.

A good command of English should apply to anyone who has passed through a university degree but it does seem fair to assume that EFL teachers know the language better than most. But apart from writing fiction like Messrs Joyce and Burgess this is a little required skill these days. Journalism may be one choice but sadly if you're far over 23 very few newspaper-sponsored training schemes will want to look at you. The BBC/ITN journalism trainee posts are also just a little oversubscribed. However, many people get into journalism without undergoing a training course through talent and persistence. Your TEFL experience should help you with both.

Copywriting jobs with advertising and PR agencies are an alternative to look at although initially low salaries and intense competition for what are seen as glamorous jobs are a drawback. If you have a science or technology degree, then technical writing may also be a viable option. Publishers are often on the look-out for people with that elusive mix of

scientific and linguistic ability.

The high degree of cultural sensitivity and understanding mentioned above can be an asset in many jobs. Administration work with, say, the British Council or a multi-national often requires this skill as can a post either in the UK or overseas with one of the international charities or aid organisations. As usual these are sought-after jobs but an ex-EFL teacher who has lived and worked in, for instance, an Arabic or Chinese culture should be well placed. Teachers who have spent part of their careers as volunteers will be even more attractive. The travel business in all its aspects can be an interesting destination for ex-EFL teachers. The opportunities range from flight and holiday sales (which will often require an excellent geographical knowledge) to guiding (requiring an in-depth knowledge of just one or two areas). The money isn't all that good but cheap travel opportunities will often compensate ex-teachers with itchy feet.

So there are opportunities if you do decide to leave TEFL. The important thing, whatever job you are applying for, is to sell your TEFL experience properly. Don't dismiss it as an extended holiday in which you did some teaching.

1991 - 1994 Teaching English in Portugal

makes it and you look a waste of time. Make it clear what your job involved and the emphasis is on clear

1991 - 94 Portugal - EFL (FCE, CAE, CPE) ESP (LCCI) and input on RSA CTEFLA

won't mean much to an outsider. Just explain what you did and more particularly what skills you think you got from your teaching. The other problem with TEFL is that anyone can do it (we all speak English, don't we?), so that many people have taught English at some time in their lives without qualifications. You therefore will need to give a brief summary of your TEFL teacher training so that whoever reads your CV will see that it is a profession and not just a holiday job. In essence you will need to sell TEFL as well as yourself.

How To Find Work

Some of the best places to start your search for a job.

Newspapers

The following newspapers and newsletters regularly carry EFL, and ESP recruitment advertisements.

WORLDWIDE

EL Gazette (monthly) - available for £1.50 (1 issue), £23.50-UK, £27.50 - Europe, £31.50 - Rest of the world (yearly subscription) from 10 Wrights Lane, London W8 6TA, UK, or specialist bookshops in Britain.

Globetrotters, PO Box 741, Pwllheli, Gwynedd, LL53 6WA, UK.

The Guardian (Tuesdays and Saturdays) - Education supplement (UK edition only) carries job advertisements.

Overseas Jobs Express (twice monthly) - available from PO Box 22, Brighton BNI 6HX.

Times Educational Supplement (Fridays).

TESOL Newsletter - available from TESOL.

International Herald Tribune (daily).

IRELAND

Irish Independent (daily); **Irish Times** (daily).

JAPAN

The Language Teacher (monthly) - available from JALT

UNITED KINGDOM

ARELS bulletin will place free 'jobs wanted' ads and circulate them to member schools in the UK - write to Arels, 2 Pontypool Place, Valentine Place, London SE1 8QS. The Department of Employment's Overseas Placing Unit (OPU) has a list of vacancies in the EC, and can be contacted via any Jobcentre in the UK.

Jobshops

Japanese Association of Language Teachers (JALT) have a job Information Centre with about 100 employers who give interviews to qualifying applicants.

TESOL job shop. Contact TESOL.

Recruitment agencies

Sending a CV to an EFL specialist recruitment agency may be better than approaching individual employers. Agencies generally charge employers a percentage of salary, so it is in their interest that you earn a good salary. See p207 for addresses unless listed below:

European Council of International Schools (ECIS). Recruit for Europe, Africa and the Far East. Prefer teachers with specialist subjects to teach English in independent international schools.

English Worldwide. Recruit for Europe, the Middle East, the Far East and South America.

English and Spanish Studies (for Spain only).

Foreign Language Services. Recruit for Greece. Contact Alexis Pournatzis, Gounari 21-23, 262 21 Patras.

Central Bureau for Exchange arrange teaching exchanges in Europe. They also recruit for the **Japan Exchange and Teaching (JET)** scheme (see p10).

Hilderstone College. Recruit for secondary schools in Japan.

Language Matters, 4 Blenheim Road, Moseley, Birmingham B13 9TY, UK.

Nord Anglia International Ltd. Recruit for UK and abroad.

Saxoncourt (UK) Ltd, Recruit for Japan, the Far East and Europe, Eastern Europe, and Africa.

Salisbury School. recruits teachers for Sweden on behalf of British Centre run by Folk University in Stockholm.

Teach Asia. Recruit for Asia and the Far East. Contact Jon Felperin, Workforce 2000 Associate, especially for vacancies in Korea and Japan, Tel/Fax: 415-585-3220.

Teachers in Greece (for Greece only), Taxilou 79, Zographou, 15771 Athens, Greece.

Major employers

The following are major employers who have branches worldwide, and may be worth approaching for potential employment.

American Language Academy (USA).

ARA (UK- recruit for Middle East).

Berlitz International (USA). Berlitz School (UK).

Bell Educational Trust (UK - offer good conditions but prefer well-qualified teachers).

Benedict Schools (Switzerland).

British Aerospace (UK - recruit males for Saudi Arabia).

British Council (UK - for Commonwealth nationals only.) Sometimes recruit locally, but well-qualified teachers are offered lucrative London contracts. Expect to be moved every three years.

Centre for British Teachers (UK - run projects in Europe, the Middle and Far East - primary and secondary EFL).

ELS International Inc (USA). ILC Recruitment (UK).

inlingua (Switzerland and USA). Also inlingua Pedagogical Department, UK Branch, Essex House, 27 Temple Street, Birmingham B2 5DB, UK.

International House, London (UK - have branches and affiliated schools around the world).

International Language Services (UK - for Sweden only).

Linguarama Ltd (UK).

British Council Teaching Centres

QUALITY LANGUAGE LEARNING WORLDWIDE

Europe   North Africa   The Middle East
Latin America   The Far East

The British Council is the largest international ELT employer with an expanding network of over 80 teaching centres worldwide, employing a staff of over 1,500 teachers and managers.

Each year we recruit about 150 teachers through London. These posts offer attractive salaries, airfares, baggage allowance, medical cover and paid leave. For mobile staff a central pension scheme is available. Contracts are usually for a period of 2 years, and are often renewable. Staff are encouraged to transfer to other centres within the network at the end of their contracts, giving the opportunity for career progression for suitably qualified and experienced teachers. Almost all middle and senior managers are recruited from within the network.

Our teaching centres are well equipped and offer excellent resources and support. Staff are encouraged to develop in all areas of interest, such as computer assisted language learning (CALL), teacher training, materials development, young learners and skills through English. Training awards are available to help with further study.

Details of vacancies appear in the Guardian and Guardian International.

Come and work with us!

For further details and a brochure contact:

CMDT Recruitment
The British Council
10 Spring Gardens
London SW1A 2BN

Telephone: 0171 389 4931
Fax: 0171 389 4140

The British Council

Registered in England as a charity no. 209131, is Britain's international network for education culture and development.

World English

Armed with a qualification and, sometimes, some teaching experience, many teachers of EFL set their sights on working abroad. The following pages give details on working conditions in over 100 countries plus addresses of schools and other useful contacts.

116 A New Career In A New Town

117 Medical Advice

121 Financial Advice

123 The European Union

137 The Rest Of Europe

146 North Africa And The Middle East

152 Sub-Saharan Africa

154 The Far East

162 The Rest Of Asia

164 Latin America And The Caribbean

A New Career In A New Town

The chance to live abroad is the key motivation behind many people's study of TEFL. However, life abroad is not without its downside, as Patrick MacDonald remembers.

although a TEFL training course prepares you for many things, it does not, however, prepare you for that windswept evening when you step off the train at Gare Du Nord and suddenly think "What is it I'm doing here?". Whether it's Paris, Berlin or Moscow, I imagine it must be the same. After a summer of dreams - fuelled by the fun of teaching in a summer school - you suddenly come up against reality with a bump. New town - no job.

I suppose I was lucky in that I had somewhere to stay in my first couple of weeks. Accommodation is important because, if like me, you haven't lined a job up, then finding somewhere to rent (even if you've brought plenty of savings with you) can be a real bind. Can you imagine many landlords in London or Boston renting out a flat to an unemployed foreigner who was 'hoping to get a job teaching'? Even when you find work there's likely to be a problem with accommodation. EFL is not the best paid work in the world, especially when you're just starting out, and so your first view of a foreign city - particularly if you don't know anyone in it - is likely to be through a very small window.

Four Steps To Settling In

Having done some reading around the subject since moving back to the UK, there seems to be a recognised pattern to the emotional ups and downs of starting work abroad. Although everyone's experience of living and working abroad will be unique, studies of these experiences do highlight certain consistent themes. Essentially the experience tends to break down into four stages.

Stage 1: The shock of the new; although it can be daunting, most people will initially be carried along by the euphoria of living in a new and challenging environment. Setbacks will tend to be ridden out as part of the experience.

Stage 2: The sense of doubt; After about two months the novelty has worn off and a degree of insecurity is likely to have set in - particularly if the job hunt hasn't been as rewarding as first hoped.

Stage 3: How low can you go? The period around the fourth month in a country tends to be the most challenging. There is a tendency to cling to fellow nationals and get into escapism (i.e. eating and drinking) rather than absorbing the new environment. What makes matters worse is that most teachers tend to arrive in their new country in September/October so their mood worsens with the weather.

Stage 4: The Road Back: Provided you don't allow yourself to retreat completely into a shell, by the fifth month in a country things tend to be on a much firmer footing. Your knowledge of the language and culture are better, you have more contacts, if not friends, among the population and basically feel more at home.

Merging In

Even the most enthusiastic traveller will have moments of homesickness but there are ways to reduce the low moments while making the most of your new environment. In fact, making the most of your new environment is the secret to overcoming the worst of the culture shock. Knowing the history, economy, political and social attitudes of your new home will make it more interesting and allow you to become more involved in conversations - rather than limiting yourself to discussions of your own country.

It is important to mix as much as possible with locals and (while not cutting yourself off completely) avoid spending too much time in the company of homesick ex-pats. Obviously meeting new people can be a challenge but your students may often be keen to meet outside the classroom. It's also of great importance to get to know your local area. Being recognised in shops or bars can be a real boost to flagging morale.

Above all, however, it's down to your attitude. Remember why you came to a new country and make the most of what it has to offer. It is likely to be one of the best experiences of your life.

Medical Advice

Part of the enjoyment of teaching abroad is the sense of adventure. Like every adventure, however, it is best to be prepared for the unexpected.

Teaching abroad is stimulating and exciting, but coping with different climates and social environments can put people under great psychological stress, as well as exposing them to physical risks. Yet while people generally take out health insurance on holiday, they don't always think of it when planning a longer stay. "What has to be considered are the different facilities, or lack of such facilities, when abroad. In addition there are language complications, and although one of the family may be fluent in several languages, it does not always follow that the spouse and children will have that same expertise," says Neil Horseman of BUPA.

Pre-departure check-ups

You must take some general health precautions before going to work abroad. Some countries will insist on this before allowing you a visa anyway. The required check-up may be just an overall medical or may include specific tests such as HIV.

Even if a health check is not a prerequisite of gaining admission to a country, it males sense to have one as any problems that can be sorted out in your home country could save you a lot of time and trouble later. You should have a full medical and dental check-up. A visit to the optician for an eye test or change of glasses is also advisable. You must of course be up to date with all injections and vaccinations. If not, do not leave them to the last minute. Vaccination programmes should be started at least six weeks prior to departure. If the family are travelling with you, don't forget to make sure the children have been vaccinated against the usual infections and illnesses, eg, rubella, measles and tetanus.

European Union

If you are an EU citizen, you and your family are entitled to the same level of medical cover as the nationals of any other EU country in which you are staying. In order to take advantage of this reciprocal arrangement, you must obtain the relevant form prior to your departure. In the UK, it is known as Form E111 and is available from the Department of Health and Social Security.

Social Security services

If you are staying for more than a few months in a country, then it is likely that you will start paying taxes and/or making social security contributions. It is important that you find out if you are making such contributions (and if your employer is also

contributing to the scheme) and what your contributions entitle you to.

Once you are clear what you are entitled to within the state system you must then assess the standards of care and efficiency that the system offers before deciding whether they are sufficient to give you complete peace of mind or whether you would be happier investing in a private health care scheme.

Travel insurance packages

If you are not intending to be a long-term resident in a country, then there are a number of 'extended stay' travel insurance packages available. Although these are often adequate for essential needs, you may be better covered at a lower premium under a tailor-made policy.

Private medical insurance

Having private medical insurance can take the worry and uncertainty out of health care abroad. It gives you control over where you are treated and ready access to treatment when you need it. Some employers will offer medical insurance as part of your job package. If your employer offers this benefit, check the scheme to ensure that it provides adequate cover. If your employer does not provide cover, you should consider taking out your own policy.

If you are taking out private medical insurance make sure you understand what you are paying for and be certain that you are sufficiently covered for your circumstances. Most schemes provide a generous annual maximum for the costs of hospital accommodation, specialists' fees, in-patient charges such as x-rays, drugs and dressings, and out-patient consultations and treatment.

It is important to be aware of what your scheme does not offer as well as what it does. Some schemes limit the number of nights spent in hospital for eligible treatment in any one year. Also there are others that have restrictions on sporting activity cover, so it is important to check the details.

New options

Low-cost options have been introduced which do not include out-patient benefit and are approximately 20 per cent cheaper than standard schemes. They provide the same comprehensive cover for in-patient and day-case treatment as well as all the other benefits of the standard schemes.

Medical Advice

Most insurers will now tailor schemes to provide cover for additional health care costs, such as General Practitioner consultations, emergency dental treatment, and professional nursing care in your own home.

Evacuation cover

An important service that can also be provided is optional evacuation cover with 24-hour emergency service. Many people think of this service as one of helicopters and air ambulances flying the sick and injured to hospitals from remote areas. But it has other features, such as the fact that the subscriber is never more than a telephone call away from multilingual medical help. This can be of great importance if you, a child or partner are seriously ill in a

country whose language and culture you are still unfamiliar with. A telephone call will put you in touch with doctors and specialists who could advise you on exactly what to do depending on the medical emergency.

They may suggest the nearest Medical Centre if that will meet the needs. It may be necessary to move the patient to another hospital or even to evacuate them to another country. The policy also allows the patient's spouse to accompany them, or a parent to travel with their child if necessary on medical grounds.

Being ill can be a worrying thing in a foreign country. Be sure that you go adequately prepared, not just for the job and new lifestyle but for your health as well.

You take care of the children's future – but who takes care of yours? Now that you're embarking

on a new and exciting phase of your career with a posting abroad, you're going to

need someone to help **EDUCATION** you take care of your

financial future. No one is better qualified to do

that than Eagle Star International Life. Our track record and excellent historical

pedigree has helped us grow into a leading provider in the highly competitive field of

international financial planning. After all, when you're earning good money abroad it's a

golden opportunity to make your finances work harder for you. So talk to Eagle Star as

soon as you can and we promise to help you tailor an investment plan that suits

your needs–not ours! Then when you return to the UK you'll have

more to show for your time away than a load of happy memories.

EAGLE STAR
International Life

Head office: *Eagle Star International Life, Eagle Star House, Athol Street, Douglas, Isle of Man IM99 IEF. British Isles. Telephone: + 44 1624 662266 Telefax : +44 1624 662038*
Sales Management Centre : *Eagle Star International Life Services, Abbey Gardens, 4 - 6 Abbey Street, Reading, Berkshire RG1 3BA. Telephone: +44 1734 567666 Telefax : +44 1734 585186.*
Eagle Star International Life is the business name of Eagle Star (International Life) limited which is regulated by the Personal Investment Authority.

Financial Advice

Although financial reward is unlikely to be a key motivation when working abroad, it is important to make sure that your finances are in order and you are not losing money.

he idea of being able to find work wherever takes your fancy is very attractive. However, such a lifestyle has inherent financial disadvantages unless simple arrangements are made prior to departure. Below are the areas which could have a fundamental effect on your financial well-being. Most of this information applies to teachers of all nationalities, but, where specific details are mentioned, non-British teachers should consult their relevant authorities.

Financial reward is not the first objective which comes to mind when considering a career in EFL. If you are approaching your first job abroad, the chances are you will not be earning a fortune. However, many teachers find that if they are working in a country with low income tax, they can save considerable sums of money. This may be because their living expenses are very low, or because on completion of their contract they are entitled to a surprisingly generous bonus payment. These payments may be taxed in the country where they are earned, or they could be taxed on the teacher's return to their native country even if the bonus is tax-exempt in the country in which it was earned.

Taxation

Although your salary may be relatively low, you still need to be aware of the taxation system both in your home country and in the country you are intending to work in. Without a reasonable amount of care it is possible to find yourself liable for tax in both countries. For teachers to avoid unnecessary tax payments on income earned abroad, they must establish their personal status. First see if the country where you are going to work has a reciprocal agreement with your country - contact your local tax office. If this is not the case, taking the UK as an example shows just how intricate tax laws can be and how great the need for expert advice is in this field.

Under UK law, if you are away for at least 365 days, and visits to the UK are less than 62 consecutive days (or one-sixth of a total period abroad), you are eligible for exemption, but you are not considered to be non-resident. To obtain non-resident status, you must work full time abroad for more than a whole tax year (i.e. from April to April) without visiting the UK for more than three months per annum.

The difference between non-resident status and exemption is that non-residents are not liable for tax on unearned income arising overseas (such as interest on offshore bank accounts) and capital gains. However, non-resident status does not exempt you from all UK tax by any means. Most non-residents are still considered to be domiciled in the UK as determined by the courts. This means that income obtained in the UK is still taxable, and that your estate - in other words your worldwide assets - is liable to UK inheritance tax.

Remember also to keep a record of any payments you have made whilst abroad - this will ensure you are not taxed again on your return to your native country. See also the Inland Revenue leaflet IR6-Double Taxation Relief.

National Insurance / Health Insurance

While you are working abroad, you may lose your entitlement to

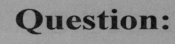

social security if you fail to keep up your contributions. To qualify for a full UK state retirement pension, you must have paid the minimum contribution each year for at least 90% of your working life. If you miss some payments, then you will generally receive a reminder from the Department of Social Security. This will not be a demand for money but will simply point out that you have not made your full year's quota of payments. You are then offered the opportunity of making up the payments so that you are still on course to receive a state pension. It is then up to you to decide whether to make up the missing amount - depending on your future career plans and other pension arrangements.

If you are from the UK, obtain leaflet NI38 (SA29 if you will be working within the EU) from the Overseas branch of the

Department of Social Security (Tel. 0191 213 5000). This explains the effect on benefits of working abroad.

If you are working in a country with a reciprocal agreement with the UK for a certain period, you will be subject to the UK social security scheme for that period, and will have to pay Class 1 contributions. After this period you can pay Class 2 (self-employed) or 3 (voluntary) contributions to the UK scheme and remain eligible for benefits.

If you are working in a country with a permanent reciprocal agreement with the UK, you must pay contributions to that country's scheme - which could be substantially higher than the scheme in the UK. Check these figures before you go.

The European Union

One of the most popular teaching destinations, and for UK and Irish citizens, it offers many opportunities

T he dawn of the single market has made it extremely easy for citizens of European Union member states to move from country to country. British and Irish nationals should have far fewer headaches with paperwork than in other countries, although they will often still need to apply for residency permits and tax numbers. Unfortunately, this makes employing teachers from outside the community a far less attractive proposition. Schools often have to go through a maze of red tape in order to give contracts to Americans, Australians and New Zealanders. Applying for visas and work permits from home also makes it far more difficult to come out and look for work on spec. Traditional markets like Spain and Italy are becoming saturated but there are far more job opportunities for new teachers in Central and Eastern Europe.

However, Western Europe remains an extremely rewarding place to teach. English is in great demand wherever you go and people are very keen to practise with you. It can be hard to find work in the great cities like Paris, Rome, Madrid, Lisbon and Vienna, but there are always opportunities in smaller, provincial towns.

If you do decide to work in one of the great capital cities, don't expect to get a full-time contract for the first year or two. Most teachers survive through a series of part-time contracts at various language schools and private classes. It can take a while to build up enough work to live on so it does help to save money beforehand, maybe by working for a year in the Far East.

Some places have very little demand for English teachers, especially in Northern Europe. You need fluent Danish to work in Denmark; there are no universities in Luxembourg, so people from the tiny, landlocked country often take degrees in the UK or the USA.

If you want to work in any of these countries, the local British Council should be able to give you more information.

Austria

Knowledge of German is a basic requirement for working in Austria and there is stiff competition for teaching jobs from the ex-pat community. Now Austria is in the EU, British and Irish teachers can apply for teaching jobs in state schools although the most commonly available work is part-time and company-based. In the summer, there is always the chance of working for a summer camp. Apply to Young Austria or Village Camps. Unqualified teachers should be able to find private classes.

Visas and work permits: EU nationals can now compete with Austrians to apply for jobs, including teaching jobs in the state sector. Although there are no longer work permits, EU citizens must apply for an ID card after three months in the country. Other nationals require visas and work permits which must be applied for outside Austria. It is difficult to obtain a work permit.

Cost of living: Food is expensive, but restaurants and drinks are cheap. Otherwise, costs are high, especially in Vienna.

Salaries and taxes: The hourly rate can be lower than AS200, which is often cash-in-hand. On contract, expect AS15,000 per month, with an income tax of around 40 per cent.

Accommodation: A one-bedroom flat in Vienna or Salzburg will cost around AS6,000 per month.

Health insurance: Advisable.

English language newspapers: The Vienna Reporter, Austria Today, ELT News.

List of Schools in Austria

American International School, Salmannsdorferstasse 47, A-1190, Wien. Tel: 603 02 46

Amerika-Institut, Operngrasse 4, 1010 Wien. Tel: 512 77 20

Austro-British Society, Wickenburgasse 19, 1080 Wien. Tel: 431 141

Berlitz Sprachschule, Rotenturmstrasse 1-38, 1060 Wien.

Berufsforderungsintitut, Kinderspitalgasse 5, 1090 Wien. Tel: 408 3501

Business Language Centre, Trattnerhof 2, 1010 Wien. Tel: 533 70 010

Danube International, Guderunstrasse 184, A-1100, Wien. Tel: 01 603 0246

Didactica Akademie Fur Wirtschaft Und Sprachen, Schottenfledgasse 13-15, 1070 Wien. Tel: 526 2287

English For Kids, 1230 Vienna A-Baumgartner -Str 44 A/7042. Tel: 43 1 667 4579 Full immersion summer camps in Austria (age 10-16) summer courses in England (age 14-18)

English Language Centre, In der Hagenau 7, 1130 Wien.

Graz International Bilingual School, Klusemannstrasse 25, A-8053, Graz. Tel: 0316 1050

inlingua Sprachschule, Neuer Markt 1, 1010 Wien. Tel: 5122225

Innsbruck International, Highschool, Schonbeg 26, A-6141, Innsbruck. Tel: 05225 4201 3992

Institut CEF, Garnisongasse 10, 1090 Wien. Tel: 42 04 03
International House Vienna, Schedenplatz 2/55, 1010 Wien. Tel: 535 5746
The International Montessori Preschool Vienna, Mahlerstrasse 9/13, A-1010 Wien Tel 01 512 8733.
Jelinek & Jelinek, Privatlehrinstitut, Rudolfsplatz 3, 1010 Wien.
Kindergarten Alt Wien, Am Heumarkt 23, A-1030, Wien. Tel:
Lizner International School, Aubrunnerweg 4, A-4040, Linz. Tel: 0732 245 8670
Mini Schools & English Language Day Camp, Postfach 160, 1220 Wien. Tel: 227717
Salzburg International Preparatory School, Moosstrasse 106, A-5020, Salzburg. Tel: 0662 844 485
Sight & Sound Studio Gesmbh, Schubertring 12, 1031 Wien. Tel: 512 67 520
Spidi-Spracheninstitut Der Industrie, Lotringerstrasse 12, 1031 Wien. Tel: 715 2506
Sprachstudio J-J Rousseau, Untere Viaduktgasse 43, 1030 Wien. Tel: 712 2443
Sprachinstitut Vienna, Universitatstr. 6, 1090, Wien. Tel: 422227
Super Language Learning Sprachinstitut, Florianigasse 55, 1080 Wien. Tel: 408 4184
Verband Wiener Volksbildung, Wiener Volkschochschulen, Hallergrasse 22, 1150 Wien.

Belgium

English is becoming much more prevalent in Brussels because it is the centre of the European Union. But this means there is a lot of competition from the spouses of diplomats and Belgian teachers who speak excellent English. Unqualified teachers will find it hard to get work in Belgium. Teaching young learners is one area where it is relatively easy to find work. Teachers generally need to combine various contracts with private lessons.

Visas and work permits: Non-EU nationals should apply to their local embassy, with proof of employment.

Cost of living: High. Food is cheap.

Salaries and taxes: BFr550 is the standard hourly rate. On a contract, expect to earn between BFr45,000 and BFr50,000. Employers pay tax and health insurance if you are on a contract. Rates vary for freelancers.

Accommodation: Outside Brussels, rent costs a minimum of BFr10,000 per month, while in the capital it costs BFr15,000.

Health insurance: Advisable for self-employed teachers.

English language newspapers: The Bulletin (weekly) and Newcomer (bi-monthly).

List of schools in Belgium

Access Bvba Taalbureau, Atealaan 5, 2200 Herentals. Tel: 014 22 61 92
Access Taal & Commumicatie, Abdy Van Tongerlo, Abdystraat 40, B-2260 Westerlo.
Applied Language Centre, 21 rue D'Eosse, 1060 Brussels. Tel: 02 649 7462
Belgo - British Courses, 21 Rue D'ecosse, 1060 Brussels. Tel: 537 8775
Berlitz Language Centre, 28 Rue Saint Michel, 1000 Brussels. Tel: 219 0274
Berlitz Language Centre, 10 Place Stephanie, 1050 Brussels. 02 512 44 04
Berlitz Language Centre, Westinform 17-19, Monnikenwerve, 8000 Brugge.
Berlitz Language Centre, 172 Leuvenselaan, 3300 Tienen.
Bilingua, 6 rue Renier Chalon, 1060 Brussels. Tel: 347 4534
The British Council, rue Joseph 11, Jozef 11 Straat 30, 1040 Brussels. Tel: 0032 2 219 3600
The British School Of Brussels, Leuvensesteenweg 19, 3080 Tervuren. Tel: 02 767 4700
Brussels Language Centre, 55 Rue Des Drapiers, 1050 Brussels.
Crown Language Centre, 9 Rue Du Beguinage, 1000 Brussels.
The English Institute, 77 Rue Lesbroussart, 1050 Brussels.
inlingua School Of Languages, 62 Limburgstraat, 9000 Gent.
Institute of Modern Languages and Communications S.A., 20 Av De La Toison D'or, Bte 21, 1060 Brussels.Tel 512 6607
Institut Pro Linguis SC, Place De L'eglise, 6717 Thiamont.
Linguarama, Avenue Des Arts, Kunstlaan 19, 1040 Brussels. Tel: 217 9055
May International, 40 Rue Lesbroussart, 1050 Brussels. Tel: 2 640 8703
Mitchell School Of English, 156 Rue Louis Hap, 1040 Brussels. Tel: 734 8073
Peters School, 87 Rue Des 2 Eglises, 1040 Brussels. Tel: 02 280 0021
Phone Languages, 65 rue Des Echevins, 1050 Brussels. Tel: 2 647 4020
Practicum, 24 Reep, 9000 Gent. 09 223 5442
School Voor Europese Talen, 28 Charlottalei, 2018 Antwerpen. Tel: 03 218 7370

Denmark

With local unemployment running at an average of 11%, the prospects of finding a teaching post in Denmark are very poor, particularly as the number of children of school age is decreasing, and schools and universities are cutting back on staffing.

Accustomed to free education, the private schooling sector continues to be small, and the problem of finding posts in the Danish public sector is only exacerbated by the need for non-native teachers to possess a sound knowledge of Danish. Some opportunities may be found in institutes running part-time courses and evening classes, particularly in Business English, and it is in this area that job-hunting efforts should be concentrated.

Minimum salary: Salaries vary according to teachers' qualifications and the type of institution they work for.

Tax: 53%.

Visa Requirements: Virtually impossible for non-EU nationals.

Accommodation: In and around Copenhagen, the cost of accommodation averages out at 8,000-10,000 kroner per month. Elsewhere it can be considerably less, and standards are high.

Other information: Danish state teachers enjoy some of the highest salaries in the EU, primarily because they are expected to be able to teach any subject to students of any age. As a result, the majority of Danish teachers have a very high standard of proficiency in English, with little need for native English speakers.

List of schools in Denmark

Access, Hamerensgade 8, 1267 Copenhagen K - branches in Odense & 4 other cities. Tel: 014 22 6192
Activsprog, Rosenvægets Alle 32, 2100 Copenhagen - also Odense, Ärhus & Aalborg.
Ais Language Training Centre, Kongevejen 115, 2840 Holte - also Odense, Silkeborg, Esbjerg.
Babel Sprogtræning, Vordingborggrade 18, 2100 Copenhagen.
Berlitz International, Vimmelskaftet 42a, 1161 Copenhagen.
Bis Sprogskole, Rolfsvej 14-16, 2000 Frederiksberg.
Cambridge Institute, Vimmelskaftet 48, 1161 Copenhagen. Tel: 33 13 33 02
Elite Sprogcentret, Hoffmeyersvej 19, 2000 Frederiksberg.
Erhvervs Orienterede Sprogkurser, Betulavej 25, 3200 Helsinge.

European Education Centre Aps (Inlingua), Lyngbyvej 72, 2100 Copenhagen.
FOF, Lyngby-Taarbaek, Hovedgade 15D, 2800 Lyngby, Denmark. Tel: 42 88 25 00
FOF, Sonderalle 9, 8000 Arhus C. Tel: 86 1229 55
Frit Oplysningsforbund, Vestergrade 5,1, 5000 Odense C. Tel: 66 13 9813
Ibi Sproginstitut, Rosenvaengets, Alle 32, 2100, Copenhagen.
Linguarama, Hvilevej 7, 2900 Hellerup.
Master-Ling, Sortedam Dossering 83, 2100 Copenhagen.
Praktisk Sprog Traening, Faksegade 13, 2100 Copenhagen.
Sprogklubben, Vendersgade 6, 1363 Copenhagen.

Finland

More than 90 per cent of Finnish children learn English at school so it's relatively easy for qualified teachers to find work. As well as young learners, the adult market is also booming.

Private and state-sponsored schools tend to recruit locally. The best time to look for work is in the spring when schools start recruiting for the following September. Contracts are usually for nine months. If you find work before you leave your home country, the package will probably include a flight and accommodation.

Visas and work permits: If you job-hunt in the spring on a tourist visa, you need to apply for a work permit and then leave the country. Papers can take two to three months to come through.

Cost of living: Eating and drinking out are very expensive.

Salaries and taxes: Teachers can earn anything from 80 to 250 markka per hour. Tax is around 25 per cent.

Accommodation: It's fairly easy to find somewhere to live, but schools often arrange it. Expect to pay 1,000 markka per month for a room in a shared flat, with one or two months' rent as a deposit. Rent includes heating, a real bargain during the long, cold winters.

Health insurance: Good healthcare system.

List of Schools in Finland

AAC-Opisto, Kauppaneuvoksentie 8, 00200 Helsinki Tel:.358 0 682 1411. The leading language school for companies and organisations in Finland, own materials testing, course planning, teacher training, convenient facilities.

The Federation of Finnish-British Societies, Puistokatu 1bA, 00140 Helsinki, Tel: 639625
International House, Mariankatu 15 B 7, 00170, Helsinki. Tel: 0 90 177 266
IWG Kieli-Instituutti, Nasilnnankatu 27d, 33200 Tampere. Tel: 31 147573
Lansi-Suomen opisto, (Private School) 32700 Huittinen. Tel: 8 3267866.
Richard Lewis Communications plc, 107 High Street, Winchester, Hants SO23 9AH, UK - recruits Business English teachers.

France

The majority of French companies are required by law to spend a fixed percentage of turnover on vocational training. Many allocate a large proportion of this to the development of their employees' English language skills. Therefore Business English and English for Special Purposes (ESP) are two areas of opportunity, while the best paid jobs are often found at the Chambre de Commerces who do much of the training (including English teaching) for smaller firms.

It is also possible for teachers to pick up bits of work as a part-time "vacateur", especially in the big EFL centres such as Paris, Toulouse and Strasbourg. For all English teaching, although a degree is often enough, a TEFL qualification is preferred and most schools will expect a good knowledge of French.

Legislation at EU level is forcing developments within the French public teaching sector, opening access to a number of posts for non-nationals. For those wishing to keep in touch with these rapidly changing developments, it is advisable to obtain the Bulletin Officiel du Ministère de l'Education Nationale. An additional source of useful information on working and teaching in France is the "Centre d'Information et Documentation Jeunesse" (CIDJ). In Paris, the English Teaching Resource Centre aims to provide support to English teachers on a membership basis, and provides a sound base of materials and ideas.

Salaries and taxes: Salaries for teachers vary immensely in France and will usually be considerably lower in the provinces than in Paris due to the lower cost of living. In universities the hourly rate may be as high as FF230, but paid three months later and with no long-term guarantee of work. Private language schools vary, but the lowest rate currently stands between FF50-100 per hour.

English language teachers in France fall into two categories - a

"salarié" (employee) or a "travailleur indèpendent" (self-employed). Status implies different rights and obligations. As a "salarié", social security contributions are deducted by your employer before you receive your pay slip and you are entitled to sick leave, holiday pay and certain other advantages. "Travailleurs indèpendents" are paid in "honoraires" (fees) which should be set significantly higher than salaries, due to the fact that social security contributions are paid separately. If you only teach a few hours a week you may not be covered by the French social security system.

Visas and Work Permits: EU nationals need a "carte de Séjour de ressortissant de la CEE", which should be applied for within three months of arrival in France, or as soon as you find work. Non-EU residents will need different documentation and should check with the relevant sources before setting off.

Accommodation: From around FF3,500 per month for a one-bedroom flat in Paris, about FF1,800 in rural areas. It is fairly cheap to live outside Paris.

English language newspapers: International Herald Tribune (D); Paris Passion (US magazine).

List of schools in France

AABC, 20 Rue Gonot de Mauroy, 75009 Paris. Tel: 1 42661311.
Academie des Langues Appliquees, 60 Rue de Laxou, BP 3736-54098 Nancy.
Alexandra School, 32 Rue Amiral de Grasse, 66130 Grasse.Tel: 93368801.
Alpha Formation, 51 Rue Saint-Ferreol, 130001 Marseille. Tel: 91330072.
The American Centre, Belomeau, Avenue Jean-Paul Coste, Paris. Tel: 1 42384238.
Anglesey Language Services (ALS), 1 Bis Avenue Foch, 78400 Chatou. Tel: 80 65 15
Arc Langue, Chemin de la Haie, 64100 Bayonne. Tel: 5955 0566.
Audio-English, 44 Allees de Tourny, 33000 Bordeaux. Tel: 56445405.
BEST, 24 Bd Beranger, 37000 Tours. Tel: 47 05 55 33.
British Connection International, 279 Rue Crequi, 69007 Lyon. Tel: 72730255.
British Council, English Language Teaching Resource Centre, 3rd Floor, 24 Rue Childerbert, 69002 Lyon. Tel: 7842 8670
British Council, 9/11 Rue De Constantine, 75000 Paris.Tel: 49 55 73 00
British Institute (University of London), 11 Rue De

Constantine, 74340 Paris, Cedex 07

Business English Service & Translation, 24 Bd Beranger, 37000 Tours. Tel: 47 05 55 33

BTS Language Centre, 226 Route de Philipeville, 6001 Marcinelle. Tel: 71313076.

Centre D'Etudes Des Langues, Z.I. Du Brockus, BP 278, 62504 St Omer. Tel: 21 93 78 45

Cybee Langues, 7 Rue D'Artois, 75008, Paris. Tel: 89 18 26

Collegium Palatinium, Dept EFL/CP, Chateau de Pourtales, 61 Rue Melanie, 67000 Strasbourg. Tel: 88 31 01 07.

Formalangues, 106 Blvd Haussmann, 75008 Paris. Tel: 45229912

Forum, 66 Rue De La Bretonnerie, 45000 Orleans. Tel: 38625245

Fointainbleu Langues et Communication, 15 Rue Saint-Honore, BP 27, 77300 Fountainbleu. Tel: 64 22 48 96

International House, 152 Alles De Barcelona, 31000 Toulouse. Tel: 61 23 00 42

International House, Centre D'Anglais D'Angers, 16 Rue De Deux Haies, 49000 Angers. Tel: 41 87 01 06

International House, 20 Passage Dauphine, 27 Rue Mazarine, 75006 Paris. Tel: 44 41 80 20

Rapid English, 2 Rue Du Marechal Gallieni, 76600 Le Havre. Riviera Plus, 22 Boulevard Dubouchage, 06000 Nice.

Rothman Institute, 21 Avenue du Major General Vanier, 1000 Troyes. Tel: 258 03041

Sarl Executive Language Services, 25 Blvd Sebastapool, 75001 Paris

Wood Language Studies, 33 Cours De La Liberte, 69003 Lyon.

Germany

Native speakers are in demand in Germany. As companies pick up from the recession, they reintroduce company classes. It is possible for unqualified teachers to find work through word-of-mouth. Speaking German helps a great deal.

The main market is for business and technical English, often in-company outside office hours. Most full-time jobs are with language schools which have a high staff turnover as teachers get lucrative freelance contracts.

The excellent state education system means that there is a high level of English. Many secondary schools employ native speakers as assistant teachers through the UK's Central Bureau.

There are many private language schools, with Linguarama, inlingua and Berlitz being particularly well-represented. It's possible to find work speculatively if you have plenty of time. Try getting in

touch with the English Language Teachers Association in the region where you most want to work for advice and lists of schools. There is a list of ELTAs below.

Visas and work permits: Although EU citizens can work in Germany, they still have to register with the local authority. Other nationalities should arrange employment and apply for a work permit before they leave. It may take a couple of months or more.

Cost of living: High.

Salaries and taxes: Schools pay DM20-25 per hour, while freelance teachers can earn DM50-120. EU nationals can work tax-free for the first two years, but they pay 13 per cent of their income towards social security. If they stay longer than two years, they are liable for 33 per cent back tax.

Accommodation: A one-room studio will cost around DM5/600 per month in Cologne, more elsewhere. Three months' rent is payable as a deposit, but landlords will normally accept double rent for three months if you can't afford to pay that much up-front.

Health insurance: Essential for freelance teachers.

English language newspapers: Spotlight and World Press.

Other useful information: These are the phone numbers for the main ELTAs in Germany:
Dresden: 351- 2210 172
Frankfurt: 6131-479 915
Hamburg: 40-796 7996
Munich: 89-692 4670
Ravensburg: 752-222 109
Rhine: 220-313 266
Stuttgart: 70-238 084

List of employers in Germany:

Administration Office for Examinations Ltd, Platanestr 5, 07549 Gera Tel: 365-388 519 Fax: 365-388 536

Anglo-German Institute, Christopherstr 4, 70178 Stuttgart Tel: 711-603 858 Fax: 711-640 9941

ASK Sprachenschule, 1 Kortumstr 71, 44787 Bochum Tel: 234-12910

Bansley College, Str Des Friedens 35, 03222 Lubbenau, Brandenburg Tel: 354-244 407 Fax: 354: 244 408

Benedict School, Gurzenichstr 17, 50667 Koln Tel: 221-212 203

Berlitz, Friedrich-Willhelm-Strasse 30, 47051 Duisburg

British Council: Hardenbergstrasse 20, 10623 Berlin Tel: 3110990

Christopher Hills School of English, Sandeldamm 12, 63450 Hanau Tel: 49-6181 15015 Fax: 49-6181 12121

Collegium Palatum, Adenauerplatz 8, 69115 Heidelburg Tel: 62-2146 289 Fax: 62-2118 2023

Didacta, Hohenzollernring 27, 95440 Bayreuth Tel: 921-27 555

English Language Centre, Altonaer Chausee 89, 22869 Schenefeld Tel: 830 2421

English Language Institute, Sprachenchule 4, Ubersetzer Am Zwinger 14, 33602 Bielefeld Tel: 521-69353

Europa-Universitat Viadrina, Sprachenzentrum, Grosse Scharrnstr 59, 15230 Frankfurt (Oder)

FBD Schulen, Katharinenstr 18, 70182 Stuttgart Tel: 711-21580

GLS, Sprachenzentrum, B Jaeshke, Pestalozzistr 886, 10625 Berlin Tel: 30-313 5025

Hallworth English Centre, Frauenstrasse 118, 89703, Ulmponau Tel: 731-22668

inlingua Spachschule, Konigstrasse 61, 47051 Duisburg Tel: 203 241334

Intercom Lang. Services, Muggenkampstr 38, 20257 Hamburg

International House, Poststrasse 51, 20354 Hamburg. Tel 352041

Knowledge Point, Hohenzollernstrasse 26, 80801 Munchen Tel: 089 33 3405

Lingotek Institut, Schlueterstrasse 18, 20146, Hamburg Tel: 40 459 520

Neue Sprachscule, Rosastrass 1, 79098 Freiburg Tel: 761-24810

NSK Language and Training Services, Comeniusstr 2, 90459 Nurnburg Tel: 911-441 552

Sprachstudio Lingua Nova, Thierschstrasse 36, 80538 Munich Tel: 89-221 171

Stevens English Training, Ruttenscheider Strasse 68, 45130 Essen Vorbeck-Schule, 77723 Gengenbach Tel: 7803 3361

Wirtschaftwissen-schaftliche Fakultat Ingolstadt, Auf der Schanz 49, 85049 Ingolstadt

Greece

There is a huge demand for English in Greece. Recruitment is normally made locally in May/June or September, although posts are often advertised overseas. There is such a large expatriate community in Athens that jobs in the capital are often found through word-of-mouth.

Teachers need a degree, preferably in English, to get a work permit, but teaching qualifications are often not necessary. Look for work in Athens or in the tourist areas. There are a number of unreliable 'cowboy' operations in Greece who do not always pay their teachers so try to insist on a contract.

Greece is one of the few countries where non-native speakers can find work. It helps if you can also teach your mother tongue.

Visas and work permits: In common with other EU countries, British and Irish citizens only need a residency permit. Non-EU citizens need a work permit, which is arranged by your school. You will need to give them a translated copy of your degree certificate and a doctor's certificate. Permits should take two months, but in practice they take far longer. It is feasible to work while your papers are pending. You can claim full residency if you are of Greek descent.

Cost of living: Relatively cheap.

Salaries and taxes: An English language teacher might earn £4 per hour, an extremely low rate. This sum doubles for private classes. Taxes are around 20 per cent.

Accommodation: Prices can be high, especially around Athens. Expect to pay around £200 per month, with two months' rent as a deposit. There is a ten-year waiting list for phone installation so look for somewhere with a phone if you want private classes.

Health insurance: Advisable.

English language newspapers: The Athens News.

List of schools in Greece

A Trechas Language Centre, 20 Koundouriotou St, Keratsini. Tel: 1 432 0546

Alpha Abatzolglou Economou, 10 Kosma Etolou St, 54643 Thessaloniki. Tel: 31 830535.

A Andriopoulou, 3, 28 Octobrio, Tripolis.

Athens College, PO Box 65005, 15410 Psychico, Athens. Tel: 1 6714621.

British Council, Ethnikis Amynis 9, PO Box 50007, 54013 Thessalonika. Tel: 00 30 31 235 236

English Tuition Centre, 3 Pythias Street, Kypseli 1136, Athens.

Enossi Foreign Languages (The Language Centre), Stadiou 7, Syntagma, 10562 Athens. Tel: 3230 356/3250081.

Eurocentre, 7 Solomou Street, 41222 Larissa.

Hambakis Schools of English, 1 Filellinon Street, Athens. Tel: 1 3017531/5.

Hellenic American Union, 22 Massalias Street, GR-106 80 Athns.

Homer Association, 52 Academias St, 10677 Athens. Tel: 3622887.

International Language Centre, 35 Votsi Street, 26221 Patras.

Institute of English, French, German and Greek for Foreigners, Zavitsanou Sophia, 13 Joannou Gazi St, 31100 Lefkada.

Institute of Foreign Languages, 41 Epidavrou St, 10441 Athens.

ISIAA 93, Lamia 35100. Tel: 23 121028.

Makritis School of English, 2 Pardos G Olympion St 60100 Katerini. Tel: 35122859.

G Michalopolous School of English, 24E Antistasis, Alexandria, 59300 Imathias, Thessaloniki. Tel: 333 322890.

New Centre, Arkarnanias 16, Athens 11526.

Peter Sfyrakis School of Foreign Languages, 21 Nikiforou Foka St, 72200 Ierapetra, Crete. Tel: 84228700.

Protypo English Language School, 22 Deliyioryi Street, Volos 38221.

School of English, 8 Kosti Palama, Kavala 65302.

School of Foreign Languages, 12 P Isaldari St, Xylokastro, 20400 Korinth. Tel: 74324678.

SILITZIS School of Languages, 42 Koumoundourou, 412 22 Larissa.

Universal School of Language, 66 M Alexandrou St, Panorama, Theaaslonika 55200 Tel: 031 341 014

Zoula Language Schools, Sanroco Square, Corfu. Tel: 66139330.

Italy

Strangely enough, although Italy is going through a recession and people seem to be cutting back on English classes, Italian students still top all the league tables for overseas study. It still remains a very popular destination for teachers, so it tends to be quite hard to find work. Teachers need to be qualified to at least certificate standard. There are very few opportunities for non-native speakers.

Visas and work permits: It is easy for British and Irish citizens to get a work permit. Other nationalities also need permits, but it is more difficult. Officially, teachers shouldn't work on a tourist visa.

Cost of living: Italy is no longer a cheap country.

Salaries and taxes: Between 1.5million lira and 2million lira. The tax rate is around 30 per cent.

Accommodation: It is easy to find accommodation, but it tends to be expensive. Schools sometimes help teachers find somewhere to live. A one-roomed flat will cost around 1 million lira and two or three months' rent is required as a deposit.

Health insurance: Advisable for people who aren't from the European Community.

Other useful information: Italy's economy is in a boom-bust cycle. When it's booming, everybody wants to learn English, but when it's in decline, people save their money to go abroad instead.

List of schools in Italy

Academia Britannica, Via Bruxelles 61, 04100 Latina. Tel: 773 491917.

Anglo American School, Piazza S. Giovanni in Monte 9, 40124 Bologna.

Anglocentre, Via A de Gasperi 23, 70052 Bisceglie (BA).

Arlington Language Services, cp99, 29100, Piacenza.

Bari Poggiofranco English Centre, Viale Pio XII 18, 70124 Bari.

Benedict School, Via Sauro 1/2, Bologna.

Berlitz, Via delle Asole 2, Milano.

The British Council, Via Manzoni 38, 20121 Milan. Tel: 00 39 2 782 016

British Institute, Fontane 109, Rome. Tel: 6491979. Fax: 64815549; via Marghera 45, 20149 Milan. Tel: 2 48011149.

The British Institute of Florence, Palazzo Feroni, Via Tornalbuoni 2, Florence. Tel: 55 298866.

The British Language Centre, Via Piazzi Angolo Largo Pedrini, 23100 Sondrio. Tel: 342 216130.

The British Language Centre, Via Piazza Roma 3, 20038 Serengo.

The British School of Bari, Via Celentano 27, 70121 Bari. Tel: 080 5247335. Fax: 080 5247396.

Cambridge Centre of English, Via Campanella 16, 41100 Modena. Tel: 59 24 1004.

Cambridge School, Via S Rochetto 3, Verona. Tel: 458003154. Fax: 458003154.

Cambridge School, Pal. Casa, Bianca Via Origlia 38, 84014 Nocera Inferiore, Salerno.

Canning School, Via San Remo 9, 20133 Milano.

Centro di Lingue, Via Pozzo 30, Trento. Tel: 461981733. Fax: 461981687.

Centro Internazionale di Linguistica Streamline, Via Piave 34/b, 71100 Foggia. Tel: 039 88124204.

Cento Lingue di Vinci Antonella, Via San Martino 77, Pisa.

Centro Lingue Tradint, Via Jannozzi 8, S Donato Milanese (N1).

Chandler, Viale Aventino 102, 00153 Roma.

Conner Language Services, Via Macchi 42, Milano.

Devon School, Contra Porti 4, Vicenza.

Dialogue International, Corso Re Umberto 61, 10128 Torino.

Elite, Corso De Gasperi 46, Torino.

English Centre, Via Promis 8, 11100 Aosta. Tel: 0165 235416.

The English Centre, Via Dei Mille 18, 07100 Sassari, Sardinia. Tel: 79 232154.

The English Connection, Via Ferro 1, 30027 San Dona di Piave.

English For Business, St. Coggiola n.8, 28100 Novara. Tel: 39 321 622 488. Outside company courses with Focused Learning Approach. Private lessons for adults, both one-to-one and groups. Examination preparation.

The English Institute, Corso Gelone 82, Siracuse, Sicily.

English House, Via Roma 177, 85028 Rionero, Potenza.

The English Language Studio, Via Antonio Bondi 27, 40138 Bologna. Tel: 51347394. Fax: 51505952.

Eurolingue, Via Chiana 116, 00198 Roma.

European Language Institute, Via IV Novembre 65, 55049 Viareggio (LU).

Filadelfia School, Via L. Colla 22, 10098 Rivoli.

Home School, Via F. Malvotti 8, Conegliano (TV).

inlingua, Piazza XX Settembre 36, Civitanova Marche (MC).

inlingua, Corso Vittorio Emanuel II 68, Torino.

inlingua, Via Leoncino 35, 37121 Verona.

inlingua, Via Monte Piana 42, Venezia.

International House, Via Manzoni 22, 00185 Rome. Tel: 6704768

International House, Via Risorgimento 9, 56126 Pisa. Tel: 50440 40

International House, Via Saluzzi 60, 10125 Turin. Tel: 00 39 11 669 95

International Language School, Via Tibullo 10, Rome. Tel: 66547796. Fax: 66547796.

Language Centre, Via Milano. 20, 21100 Varese. Tel: 0332 282732.

Language Centre, Via G Daita 29, 90139 Palermo.

Lb Linguistico, Centro Insegnamento, Lingue Staniere, Via Caserta 16, 95128 Catania, Sicily.

Lingua Due Villa, Pendola 15, 57100 Livrono.

Living Languages School, Via Magna Grecia, 89100 Regio Calabria. Tel/Fax: 39 965330926.

London School, Fabiola Cordaro, International House,Viale Emilia 34, 90144 Palermo. Tel: 00 39 91 52 524

Lord Byron College, Via Sparano 102, 70121 Bari. Tel: 80 232696.

Managerial English Consultants, Via Sforza Pallavicini 11, 009193 Rome. Tel: 6 654 2391. Fax: 6 6871159.

Modern English School, Via Giordano Bruno 6, 45100 Rovigo.

Tel: 425 200266.

Modern English Study Centre, via Borgonuova 14, 40125 Bologna. Tel: 51 227523.

Multimethod, I Go Richini 8, 20122 Milan. Tel: 2583042.

Oxford School of English, Via Dell Arcivescovad, 10121 Turin. Tel: 11 562 7456

Oxford School, San Marco 1513, Venice. Fax: 415210785.

The Professionals, Via F Carcona 4, 20149 Milan Tel: 2 48000035. Fax: 2 4814001.

Regency School, Via Arcivescovado 7, 16121 Turin. Tel: 11517456. Fax: 11,541845.

Regent International, V.U. Da Pisa 6, Milano.

Regent International, Corsa Italia 54, 21047 Saronno.

The RTS Language Training, Via Tuscolana 4, 00182 Roma.

Scuola The Westminster, Via Tevere 84, Sesto Fiorentino (FI).

Spep School, Via della Secca 1, 40121 Bologna.

Studio Linguistico Fonema, via Marconi 19, 50053 Sovigliana-Vinci (Fl). Tel: 571 500551.

Studio professionale Apprendimento Linguistico Programmato, Via Ferrarese 3, Bologna. Tel: 051 360617. Fax: 051 368413.

Unimoney, Corso Sempione 72, 20154 Milano.

Victoria Language Centre, Viale Fassi 28, 41012 Capri.

Wall Street Institute, Piazza Combattento 6, 4100 Ferrara. Tel: 532200231

Netherlands

Amsterdam is a hugely popular destination for teachers and backpackers so it is necessary to stand out from the crowd. A certificate is essential, business experience a great help.

With very high levels of English in the school system, most work tends to be teaching business executives. Schools rarely offer contracts, depending instead on long-term freelance teachers. Self-employed teachers typically work for a number of schools or agencies and their incomes can fluctuate considerably. To find work, go through the list of language schools below and those in the Yellow Pages (look under 'talen institut') and expect to give an observation lesson before you are hired.

Visas and work permits: British and Irish nationals need to obtain a tax number from the police when they arrive. There are complicated rules for other nationalities: it can take three months to arrange a work permit. Teachers do work on tourist visas, but it is hard to find work in reputable schools without a tax code.

Cost of living: Expensive, but it is possible to live well.

Salaries and taxes: Freelance teachers tend to get paid between 30 and 50 guilders per hour. Most schools pay around 35 guilders. Tax is 30 per cent.

Accommodation: Accommodation is expensive, especially in and around Amsterdam. A one-bedroom flat would typically cost around 500 guilders a month, with a month's rent as a deposit.

Health insurance: Not necessary if you pay tax.

List of Schools in The Netherlands

Amerongen Talenpraktikum, De Kievit 1, 3958 Dd Amerongen.
Asa Studiecentrum, Kotterstraat 11, 1826 Cd Alkmaar.
Asco, Nassauplein 8, 1815 Gm Alkmaar.
AVC, Oringerbrink 43, 7812 Jr Emmen.
Avoc Teleninstituut, Heugemerweg 2d, 6229 As Maastricht.
Bell College, Afd English LanguageTraining, Stationsstraat 17, 6221 Bm Maastricht.
Berlitz Language Centre, Rokin 87-89, 1012 Kl Amsterdam.
Bltc, Keizersgracht 389, 1016 Ej Amsterdam.
Boerhave Opleidingen, Hoogstraat 118, 801 Bb Zwolle.
Bressler's Business Language, Buiksloterdijk 284, 1034 Zd Amsterdam.
Class International, Bijlwerffstr 28b, 3039 Vh Rotterdam.
Dinkgreve Handelsopleiding, Wilemsparkweg 31, 1071 Gp Amsterdam.
Dutch College, P Calandlaan 42, 1065 Kp Amsterdam.
Educational Holidays, Beukstraat 149, 2565 Xz Den Haag.
Eerste Ned Talenpraktikum, Singel 355, 3311 He Dordrecht.
Eerste Nederlandse Talenpraktikum, Kalverstr 112, 1012 Pk Amsterdam.
Elseviers Talen, Jan Van Galenstraat 335, 1061 Az Amsterdam.
Elseviers Talen, Westelijke Parallelweg 54, 3331 Ew Zwijndrecht.
Erasmus College, Planetenlaan 5, 2024 Eh Haarlem,Hendrik Ido Ambacht.
Europa Talenpraktikum, Vosselmanstraat 400,7311 Cl Apeldoorn.
Fikkers Handelsinstituut, Anna Paulownastr 37a, 2518 Bb Den Haag.
Gouwe College, Turfsingel 67, 2802 Bd Gouda.
Instituut Meppel, Tav Dhr J G Rijpkema, Postbus 263, 7940 Ag Meppel.
Instituut Schoevers, Markt 17, 5611 Eb Eindhoven.
Instituut Schoevers, Postbus 10486, 5000 Jl Tilburg.
Interlingua Taalsupport Bv, Wijnhaven 99, 3011 Wn Rotterdam
Interlingua Talenpraktikum, Burg van Royensingel 20 - 21, 8011

ct Zwolle.
International Studiecentrum, voor de Vrouw Concertgebouwplein 17, 107 LM Amsterdam. Tel: (020) 6761437
Interphone Opleidingen, St Jorisstraat 17, 5361 Hc Grave.
Language Partners, Wtc Beursplein 37, 3011 A Rotterdam.
Leidse Onderwijsinstelling,Tav Mr Wirtz, Leidsedreef 2, 2352 Ba Leiderdorp.
Linguarama Nederland, Wtc Strawinskylaan 507, 1077 Amsterdam.
Linguarama Nederland, Venestraat 27, 2525 Ca Den Haag.
Linguaphone Instituut, Peperstraat 7, 6127 As Grevenbicht, Huis Van Bewaring, de Koepel Afd Onderwijs,Harmenjansweg 4, 2031 Wk Haarlem.
Mieke Boot Instuitut, Waterbergseweg 13, 6815 Al Arnhem.
Notenboom, Kerkakkerstraat 34, 5616 Hc Eindhoven.
Onderwijsinstituut Netty Post, Haverstraat 2, 1447 Ce Purmerend.
Scholengem. G K Van Hogendorp, Postbus 290725, 3001 Gb Rotterdam.
School Of English, Eerste Wormenseweg 238, 7331 Nt Apeldoorn.
Stichting Volwasseneducatie Deventer, Afd English Language Training, Postbus 639, 7400 Ap Deventer.
Talenpraktikum Twente, Tav Dhr P De Wit, Ariensplein 2, 7511 Jx Enschede.
Trait D'union, Argonautenlaan 24a, 5631 Ll Eindhoven.
Zeeuwse Volksuniversiteit, Afd English Language Training, Postbus 724, 4330 As Middleburg.

Portugal

The level of English tends to be high in Portugal since it is well taught in the state schools and foreign language films are subtitled rather than dubbed. It is still, however, quite easy to find a job, especially teaching children. Work which is advertised abroad usually involves some kind of contract while local recruitment is for hourly-paid evening and weekend work.

There is work for teachers, whether they have a diploma or have just left university. Most work is in small language schools and it is far easier to find work away from Lisbon. Private lessons are easy to find. Working in-company can be very lucrative.

Visas and work permits: British and Irish citizens only need a residency permit. For non-EU citizens a lot of paperwork and waiting around is involved. This makes schools less likely to hire non-EU teachers.

Cost of living: It's not as cheap as many people assume. Similar to other EU countries.

Salaries and taxes: The going rate is between UK£7 and £12 per hour. If you are on a contract, you will get extra payments at Christmas and during the summer.

Your salary is free until you reach a certain threshold when you become liable for between 5 and 30 per cent tax. After two years, most teachers are entitled to big rebates.

Accommodation: Long-term residents still pay very low fixed rents but new teachers would have to pay around half their salaries on a two-bedroom flat. Two months' rent is expected as a deposit.

Health insurance: Advisable.

English language newspapers: The Anglo-Portuguese News, The Post.

List of schools in Portugal

American Language Institute, Rua Jose Falcao 15-5, 4000 Porto. Tel: 2 318 127
Berlitz, Av Conde Valbom 6-4, 1000 Lisboa.
Big Ben School, Rua Moinho Fanares 4-1, 2725 Mem Martins.
Bristol School, TV Dr Carlos Felgueiras, 12-3, 4470 Maia.
Bristol School Group: Oporto area (3), Inland (2), Azores (2). British qualified, experienced teachers (BA/equivalent + RSA TEFL course) Quality,Experience, Value, Integrity.. Tel: 2 948 8803
British Council, Rua De Sao Marcal 174, 1294 Lisbon Codex. 00 351 1 346 141
British Council, Rua Do Breyner 155, 4050 Porto. 00 351 2 200557
Cambridge School, Avenida de la Liberdade 173-4, 1200 Lisboa. Tel: 352 74 74, Fax: 353 47 29.
Casa de Inglaterra, Rua Alexandre Herculano 134, 3000 Coimbra.
Celfibocage, Av Luisa Todi, 288-2, 2900 Setubal.
CENA-Cent. Est. Norte Americanos, Rua Remedios 62 c/v, 1200 Lisboa.
Centro de Estudos IPFEL, Rua Edith Cavell 8, 1900 Lisboa.
Centro de Instrucao Tecnica, Rua Da Estefania 32- 10Dto, 1000 Lisboa.
Centro Internacional Linguas, Av Fontes P de Melo 25-1Dto, 1000 Lisboa.
Centro de Linguas de Alvide, Rua Fonte Nino, Viv Pe Americo 1, Alvide, 2750 Cascais.
Centro de Linguas Estrangeiras de Cascais, Av Marginal BI A-30, 2750 Cascais.
Centro de Linguas Intergarb, Tv da Liberdade 13-1, 8200 Albufeira.
Centro de Linguas de Quarteira, Rua Proj 25 de Abril 12, 8125 Quartiera.
Centro de Linguas de Queluz, Av Dr Miguel Bombarda 62-1E, 2745 Queluz.
Centro de Linguas de Santarem, Lg Pe Francisco N Silva, 2000 Santarem.
CETI, Av Duque de Loule, 71-2, 1000 Lisboa.
CIAL-Centro De Linguas, Av Republica 14-20, 1000 Lisboa, Tel: 351-1-3533733, Fax: 351-1-3523096.
Class, Rua Gen Humberto Delgado 40-1, 7540 Santiago Do Cacem.
Clube Conversacao Inglesa 3M, Rua. Rodrigues Sampaio 18-3, 1100 Lisboa.
Communicate Language Institute, Praceta Joao Villaret 12B, 2675 Povoa de Sto Adriao.
Curso de Linguas Estrangeiras, Rua Dr Miguel Bombarda, 271-1, 2600 Vila Franca De Xira.
Ecubal, Lombos, Barros Brancos, Porches, 8400 Lagoa
ELTA, Av Jose E Garcia 55-3, 2745 Queluz.
Encounter English, Av Fernao De Magalha, 4300 Porto. Tel: 567916.
English at PLC, Praca Luis de Camoes 26, Apartado 73, 5001 Vila Real.
English Institute Setubal, Av 22 Dezembro 88, 2900 Setubal.
The English Language Centre, Rua Calouste Gulbenkian 22-r/c C, 3080 Figueira Da Foz.
The English School of Coruche, Rua Guerreiros 11, 2100 Coruche.
English School of Loule, Rua Jose F Guerreiro 66M,Galerias Do Mercado, 8100 Loule.
Escola de Linguas de Agueda, Rua Jose G Pimenta, 3750 Agueda
Escola de Linguas de Ovar, Rua Ferreira de Castro 124-1 A/B, 3880 Ovar.
Eurocenter Instituto de Linguas, Av de Bons Amigos 4-1, 2735 Cacem.
Gab Tecnico de Linguas, Rua Hermenegildo Capelo 2-2, 2400 Leiria.
GEDI, Pq Miraflores Lt 18-lA/B, 1495 Alges.
IF - Ingles Funcional, Rua Afonso Albuquerque 73-A, 2460 Alcobaca.
IF Ingles Funcional, Rua Com Almeida Henriques 32, 2400 Leiria.

IF Ingles Funcional, Av Vidreiro, 95-2, 2430 Marinha Grande.
INESP, Rua Dr Alberto Souto 20-2, 3800 Aveiro.
INLINGUA, Campo Grande 30-1A, 1700 Lisboa.
INPR, Bernardo Lima 5, 1100 Lisboa.
Instituto Britanico, Rua Cons Januario 119/21, 4700 Braga.
Instituto Britanico, Rua Municipio Lt B - 1 C, 2400 Leiria.
Instituto Britanico, Rua Dr Ferreira Carmo, 4990 Ponte De Lima
Instituto Franco-Britanico, Rua 5 de Outubro 10-1Dto, 2700 Amadora.
Instituto Inlas do Porto, Rua S da Bandeira 522-1, 4000 Porto.
Instituto de Linguas, Rua Valverde 1, 2350 Torres Novas.
Instituto de Linguas do Castelo Branco, Av 1 Maio, 39 S - 1 E, 6000 Castelo Branco.
Instituto de Linguas de Faro, Av 5 de Outubro, 8000 Faro.
Instituto de Linguas do Fundao, Urb Rebordao Lt 17-r/c, 6230 Fundao.
Instituto de Linguas de Oeiras, Rua Infante D Pedro 1 e 3-r/c, 2780 Oeiras.
Instituto de Linguas de Paredes, Av Republica, Casteloes Cepeda, 4580 Paredes.
Instituto Nacional de Administracao, Centro de Linguas, Palacio Marquus de Oeiras, 2780 Oeiras.
Instituto Sintrense de Linguas, Rua Dr Almeida Guerra 26, 2710 Sintra.
Interlingua, Lg 1 de Dezembro 28, 8500 Portimao.
Interlingua, Rua Dr Joaquim Telo 32-1E, 8600 Lagos.
International House, Lisbon, Rua Marques Sa Da Bandeira 16, 1000 Lisboa - Branches throughout Portugal.
International Language School, Av Rep Guine Bissau, 26-A, 2900 Setubal.
ISLA, Bo S Jo de Brito, 5300 Bragan A, Manitoba,C Com Premar, l-72, 4490 Povoa De Varzim.
Know-How, Av Alvares Cabral 5-300, 1200 Lisboa.
Lancaster College, Rua C Civico, Ed A Seguradora 2, 6200 Covilha.
Lancaster College, Pta 25 Abril 35-1E, 4400 Vila Nova De Gaia. Tel: 2 306 495
Language School, Rua Alm Candido Reis 98, 2870 Montijo.
Linguacoop, Av. Manuel da Maia 46-10 D, 1000 Lisboa.
Linguacultura, Rua Dr Joaquim Jacinto 110, 2300 Tomar.
Linguacultura, Lg Sto Antonio 6-1 Esq, 2200 Abrantes.
Lisbon Language Learners, Rua Conde Redondo 33-r/cE, 1100 Lisboa.
Mundilingua, Rua Dr Tefilo Braga, Ed Rubi-1, 8500 Portimao.
Mundilinguas, Rua Miguel Bombarda 34-1, 2000 Santarem.
The New Institute of Languages, Urb Portela Lt 197-5B-C, 2685 Sacavem. Tel: 1 943 5238

Novo Instituto de Linguas, Rua Cordeiro Ferreira 19 C-1D, 1700 Lisboa.
PEC, Rua SA Bandeira 5385, 4000 Operto. Tel: 200 5077
PROLINGUAS, Rua Saraiva Carvalho, 84 - Pt2, 1200 Lisboa
Royal School of Languages, Av Dr Lourenco Peixinho 92-2, 3800 Aveiro. Tel: (034) 2956. Fax: (034) 382870. Also schools in Agueda, Ovar, Guarda, Porto.
Tell School, Rua Soc Farmaceutica 30-1, 1100 Lisboa.
Tjaereborg Studio, Av Liberdade 166-4F, 1200 Lisboa.
Weltsprachen-Institut, Qta Carreira 37 r/c, 2765 Sao Joao do Estoril. Tel: 4684032. Branch: Rua Dr Brito Camacho 22-A-1, 7800 Beja.
Whyte Institute, Lg das Almas 10-2E/F, 4900 Viana Do Castelo.
World Trade Centre - Lisbon, Av Brasil 1-5e8, 1700 Lisboa.

Spain

Saturation and the recession mean that the demand for English is decreasing and there are more than enough established teachers in Spain. The British Council now recommends that new teachers don't go to Spain. In fact, you should find something if you have the certificate, but don't expect a full-time contract.

If you do decide to work in Spain, it is essential to go out and look on spec. Most recruitment is done on the spot, especially when contracted teachers fail to turn up in September/October or January after the unexpectedly cold winter. Schools usually only have part-time work. It is practically impossible to find 12-month contracts, unless you are a director of studies. Unqualified teachers can only expect some private classes.

The main markets are for in-company classes, which are often at 8am, young learners and special courses. There are opportunities for private classes but they tend to be hard to come by. The main sources of job information are newspapers, magazines, agencies and noticeboards in universities, bookshops and schools. Most vacancies are unadvertised because so many teachers turn up on spec. Use our list of schools or look up 'acadamias de idiomas' in the Yellow Pages. One good way of finding work in Spain if you can afford it is to study for a certificate locally.

Visas and work permits: British and Irish nationals need a residency permit. All other nationalities must have visas and work permits which you apply for from home. As well as teachers working legally, there are people working semi-legally while they wait for their papers to come through. Non-Europeans are often employed.

Cost of living: Expensive in the major cities.

Salaries and taxes: It varies a lot. 100,000 Ptas has been the standard rate for a full-time contract since 1990, but schools at the top end of the market will pay between 130,000 and 160,000 Ptas. The going rate for private classes is 2,000 Ptas per hour which is usually tax-free.

Residents pay 15 per cent tax while those waiting for their residency to come through pay 25 per cent.

Accommodation: Rents often take up more than a quarter of a teacher's salary.

Expect to pay between 65,000 and 100,000 Ptas a month if you want to live on your own. For shared accommodation, the standard is around 30,000 per month.

Up to two months' deposit is essential. If you find accommodation through an agency, you will pay an extra months' rent on top.

Health insurance: Essential.

Important cultural differences: The Spanish start work early and leave late, with a long break for lunch.

Other useful information: After three years on contract, employees should become full members of staff, which makes it nearly impossible to fire them. After three years some companies sack employees and hire somebody cheaper.

List of schools in Spain

Academia Andaluza de Idiomas, Crta El Punto 9, Conil, Cadiz, Tel: 956 44 0552.
Academia Britanica, Rodriguez Sanchez 15, 14003 Cordoba.
Academia Saint Patricks, Calle Caracuel 1, 17402 Girona.
Academia Wellington House, Guiposcoa 79, 08020 Barcelona.
Acento - The Language Company, Ruiz De Alarcon 7, 21, 41007 Sevilla.
Afoban, Alfonso Xii 30, 41002 Sevilla.Tel: 95 421 8974
AHIZKE/CIM, Loramendi 7, Apartado 191, Mondragon Guipuzcoa.
Alce Idiomas, Nogales 2, 33006 Oviedo. Tel: 85 254543.
Aljarafe Language Academy, Crta Castilleja-Tomares 83, Tomares, Sevilla.
American Institute, El Bachiller 13, 46010 Valencia.

Apple Idiomas, Aben al Abbar 6, 46021 Valencia. Tel: 362 25 45.
Audio Jeam, Pza Ayuntamiento 2, 46002 Valencia.
Augusta Idiomas, Via. Augusta 128, 08006 Barcelona.
Aupi, Jesus 43, 46007 Valencia.
Berlitz, Gran Via 80-4, 28103 Madrid. Tel: 1 542 3586. Also schools around Spain.
Berlitz, Edif Forum 1 Mod, 3 Av Luis Morales, S/N 41018 Sevilla.
Big Ben College, Plaza Quintiliano 13, Calahorra 26500 La Rioja.
Brighton, Rambla Catalunya 66, 08007 Barcelona.
Bristol English School, Fundacion Jado 10 Bis 6, 48950 Erlandio, Vizacaya. Tel: 467 6332
Britannia School Of English, Juan Diaz De Sol_s 9, Bl 2 41010 Sevilla.
Britannia School, Leopoldo Lugones 3-1B, 33420 Lugones, Asturias. Tel: 85 26 2800. Also Raset 22, Barcelona 08021. Tel: 3 200 0100. Fax: 414 4699.
British Council, Bravo Murillo 25, 35003 Las Palmas, De Gran Canaria. Tel: 00 34 38 368 300
British Council, General San Martin 7, 46004 Valencia. Tel: 0034 6 351 8818
British Language Centre, C/Bravo Murillo 377, 28020 Madrid. Tel: 1 733 07 39.
Business & United Schools, G,nova 4, 1D 41010 Sevilla. Tel: 427 3183
Callan Method School of English, Calle Alfredo Vicenti 6 bajo, 15004 La Coruna.
Cambridge School, Placa Manel Montanya, 4, 08400 Granollers. Tel: 3 870 2001. Languages taught: English, German, Spanish for foreigners. Present staff of 28 native teachers with RSA qualifications. School neat Barcelona.
Centro Atlantico, Villanueva 2apdo, 28001 Madrid. Tel: 1 435 3661. Fax: 1 578 1435.
Centro Britanico, Republica De El Salvador 26-10m, (Edificio Simago), 15701 Santiago De Compostela, La Coruna. Tel: 8159 7490.
Centro Cooperativo De Idiomas, Clavel 2, 11300 La Linea, Cadiz.
Centro Estudios Norteamericanos, Aparisi y Guijarro 5, 46005 Valencia.
Centro de Estudios de Ingles, Garrigues 2, 46001 Valencia. Tel: 352 21 02.
Centro De Idiomas Liverpool, Libreros 11-10, 28801 Alcala de Henares, Madrid. Tel: 1 881 3184.
Centro De Ingles, Tejon Y Marin, S/N 14003 Cordoba.
Centro de Ingles Luz, Passage Luz 8bajo, 46010 Valencia. Tel: 361 40 74.

Centro Linguistico del Maresme, Virgen De Montserrat. Tel: 35 55 5403 (Jenifer Grau).
Centro Superior de Idiomas, Tuset 26, 08006 Barcelona.
Chatterbox Language Centre, Verge de l'Assumpcio 21, Barbera del Valles.
CLIC (Centro de Lenguas e Intercambio Cultural), Santa Ana, 1141002, Sevilla. Tel: 34-5-437 4500/438 6007. Fax: 437 18 06.
Collegium Palatinum, Calle de Rodriguez San Pedro 10, 28015 Madrid. Tel: 1 446 2349. Fax: 1 593 4446.
The English Academy, Cruz 15, 11370 Los Barrios, Cadiz.
English Activity Centre, Pedro Frances 22a, 07800 Ibiza. Tel: 7131 5828.
The English Centre, Apdo de Correos 85, 11500 El Puerto De Santa Maria, Cadiz. Tel: 34 56 850560, Fax: 873804.
English Language Centre, Jes·s Maria 9-1d, 14003 Cordoba.
English Studies, SA Avenida de Arteijo 8-1, 15004 La Coruna.
English Way, Platero 30, San Juan De Aznalfarache, Sevilla.
Epicenter, Niebla 13, 41011 Sevilla.
Eurocentre, Puerta De Jerez 3-1, 41001 Sevilla.
Eurolingua, San Felipe 3, 14003 Cordoba.
European Language Studies, Edificio Edimburgo, Plaza Nina, 21003 Huelva. Tel: 34 59 263821. Fax: 34 59 280778.
Fiac School, Mayor 19, 08221 Terrassa, Barcelona.
FLAC, Escola DÆIdiomes Moderns Les Valls, 10 2/0, 08201 Sabadell, Barcelona.
Glossa English Language Centre, Rambla De Cataluna 9, 78 20 2A 08008 Barcelona.
Idiomas Oxford, Calvo Sotelo 8-1, 26003 Logrono.Tel: 4124 41332.
Idiomas Progreso, Plaza Progreso 12, 07013 Palma De Mallorca. Tel: 7123 8036.
Idiomaster, Los Maristas, 2 Lucena,Cordoba.
inlingua Idiomas, C/o Greforio Fernandez 6, 47006 Valladolid.
inlingua Idiomas, Maestro Falla 5, 2,12, Puerto del Rosario, 35600 Fuerteventura, Canary Islands.
inlingua idiomas, Tomas Morales 28, 35003 Las Palmas de Gran Canaria. Tel: 2836 0671.
The Institute of English, Santiago Garcia 8, 46100 Burjasot.
Interlang, Pl Padre Jean de Mariana 3-2, 45002 Toledo.
International House, Trafalgar 14 Entlo, 08010 Barcelona. Tel: 00 34 3 268 4511. I.H. Barcelona is a long-established and succeful teacher training centre with a world-wide reputation for excellence.
International House, Cale Zurbano 8, 28010 Madrid. Tel: 00 34 1 310 131
International House, C/Hernan Cortes 1, 21001 Huelva. Tel: (959) 246529.

International House, Pascual y Genis 16, 46002 Valencia. Tel: 352 06 42.
John Atkinson School of English, Isaac Peral 11 y 13, 11100 San Fernando.
Language Study Centre, Corredera Baja 15 Bajo, Chiclana De La Frontera, Cadiz.
Lawton School, Cura Sama 7, 33202 Gijon, Asturias. Tel: 8534 9609.
Lexis, Avenida de la Constitucion 34, 18012 Granada.
Linguasec, Malaga 1, 14003 Cordoba.
London House, Baron de S Petrillo 23bajo, 46020 Benimaclet.
Manchester School, San Bernado 81, 33201 Gijon, Alicante. Tel: 8535 8619. Fax: 8535 6932.
Modern School, Gerona 11, 41003 Sevilla.
Nelson English School, Jorge Manrique 1, Santa Cruz, Tenerife.
Ten Centro de Ingles, Caracuel 24, Jerez de la Frontera.
The New School, Calle Sant Joan 2, 2a Reus Tarragona.Tel: 77 330775.
Number Nine English Language Centre, Sant Onofre 1, 07760 Ciutadella De Menorca, Baleares. Tel: 7138 4058.
Onoba Idiomas, Rasco 19-2, 21001 Huelva.
Oxford Centre, Alvaro de Bazan 16, 46010 Valencia.
Oxford House, San Jeronimo 9-11, Granada.
The Oxford School, Maron Feria 4, 41800 Sanlúcar La Mayor, Sevilla.
Passport to English, Segura 14 - 16, 41001 Sevilla.
Piccadilly English Institute, Los Chopos 8, 14006 Cordoba.
Preston English Centre, Edif El Carmen Chapineria 3, Jerez De La Frontera, Cadiz.
Principal English Centre, Aptdo 85, Puerto De Santa Maria, Cadiz.
SALT Idiomes, Prat De La Riba, 86 08222 Terrassa (Barcelona). Tel: (3) 735 80 35. Adults, young learners, Business English, EAP, private semi-intensive, intensive courses; - the quality choice in foreign language learning.
San Roque School, Plaza San Roque 1, Guadalajara.
Skills, Trinidad 94, 12002 Castellon. Tel: 6424 2668.
Stanton School of English, Colon 26, 03001 Alicante. Tel: 65207581.
St Patrick's Caracuel, 1 Jerez De La Frontera, Cadiz.
The Tolkien Academy, Juan Bautista Erro 9, 20140 Andoain.
Top Class, Plaza del Chofre 20, 20001 San Sebastian.
Tower Centre, Asuncion 43, 41011 Sevilla.
Trafalgar idiomas, Avda Castilla 12, 33203 Gijon, Asturias. Tel: 85 332361.
Trinity School SL, C/ Golondrina (Plaza Jardines) 17 Bajo, 11500 Puerto De Santa Maria, Cadiz. Tel: 34-(9) 56-871926.

Wall Street Institute, Av República Argentina 24 P12 D, 41011 Sevilla.

Warwick House Centro Linguistico Cultural, Lopez Gomez 18-2, Valladolid 47002.

Westfalia, Chapineria 3, Edificio El Carmen, Modulo 310, 11403 Jerez de la Frontera.

William Halstead School of English, Camilo Jose Cela 12, 11160 Barbate de Franco.

Windsor School of English, Virgen De Loreto 19-1, 41011 Sevilla.

Yago School, Maria De Molina 40-l, 28006 Madrid.

York House, English Language Centre, Muntaner 479, 08021 Barcelona. Tel: 32 113200.

Sweden

Most English teachers are employed by the Folk University, a kind of public university, similar to the Open University in Britain. It places teachers in its network of adult institutions,called British Centres, throughout the country. Roughly 50 per cent of the teachers are native speakers who already live in Sweden and the other 50 per cent are recruited through the Salisbury School. Contact them at 36 Fowler's Road, Salisbury, Wilts, SP1 2QU, UK (tel: +44-1722-331 011).

Expect a full-time contract for nine months, teaching everything from ESP to scientific writing. Other jobs and classes tend to be through contacts in the large English-speaking community.

Visas and work permits: Sweden joined the European Union in 1995, making it easier for British and Irish citizens to work there. Teachers from non-EU countries will need to be studying in Sweden or be married to somebody who works there since the Salisbury School only recruits British and Irish nationals.

Cost of living: Expensive. The standard of living is extremely high.

Salaries and taxes: A new teacher can expect to earn 11,000 Swedish crowns per month. Tax is from 31 per cent, local rates can be high.

Accommodation: Teachers normally spend between 25 and 35 per cent of their salaries on accommodation, but there is no deposit. One person will pay between SKr2,500 and 3,000, which includes hot water and heating.

Health insurance: Advisable.

Switzerland

Switzerland is in the European Economic Space, but it is exempt from the free movement of labour until 1998. There is a great deal of red tape before you can start work at a Swiss school.

Business and General English are in great demand but there is a very strong bias in favour of qualified teachers. A majority of the available work is on a part-time basis.

Visas and work permits: It is extremely difficult to get a job without a work permit which involves getting through a lot of red tape. Schools have to prove that no Swiss person could do the job.

It is possible to get temporary permits, called Permis A. There are quotas for nine-month contracts and four-month permits cost the employer a great deal of money.

Cost of living: High.

Salaries and taxes: It depends enormously on the school, the hours and the teacher's qualifications but salaries are generally high. The tax rate is around 15 per cent.

Accommodation: Relatively easy to find but expensive. Schools do not normally help teachers find accommodation. Rent depends on the size and the location. One month's deposit is usually required.

Health insurance: Essential.

English language newspapers: There are no Swiss-based English language papers, but all the British papers are readily available.

Important cultural differences: Lots of kissing, shaking hands and regulations.

List of Schools in Switzerland

Basilingua Sprachschule, Birsigstrasse 2, 4054 Basel. Tel: 61 281 3954

Bell Language School, 12 Chemin des Colombettes, 1202 Geneva. Tel: 00 41 22 740 20

Berlitz, 14 rue De L'Ancien-Port, 1202 Geneva. Tel: 22 738 3200

Berlitz, Munzgasse 3, 4001 Basel. Tel: 61 261 6360

Markus Frie Sprachenschulen, Neugasse 6, 6300 Zug. Tel: 42 224 525

Village Camps, 1296 Coppet. Tel: 22 776 2059

The Rest of Europe

Primarily countries of the former Soviet Bloc, some of which now offer good job prospects, while others are only really accessible through voluntary organisations.

 The European countries which are not yet part of the EU are excellent places to look for work. English is big business in the former Communist countries of Central and Eastern Europe and there are at least as many opportunities in the region as there were in Spain, Italy and Greece in the seventies. Qualifications are not always necessary and teachers don't need large savings to get set up.

Not everywhere in Central and Eastern Europe has a huge demand for English teachers. If you want to work in Albania or Macedonia, contact the local British Council and voluntary organisations such as East European Partnership and the Peace Corps.

Despite years of isolation in Albania, the general level of English is actually quite good, especially in Tirana. English offers Albanians a means of leaving the country but it is still too poor to support many private language schools.

Likewise in Macedonia, the economy is volatile and rates of pay are low, although English is becoming more popular.

There will be a massive demand for English in Ukraine when the economy picks up. At the moment, if you want to work there, apply to the two International House schools or the Peace Corps.

There is less work in Latvia than in the other Baltic States, but the situation could improve if the economy begins to pick up. For more information contact the teachers' association: LATE, PO Box 194, Riga 047, Latvia.

In addition there are the 'Mediterranean Fringe' countries. Turkey, for example, shouldn't be neglected. There always seem to be opportunities in the country which straddles the divide between Europe and Asia.

Malta, where English is an official language, attracts a lot of students but most English language teaching is undertaken by Maltese nationals and it is extremely hard to get a work permit. There are more opportunities in Cyprus (see page 138).

In Norway, it is very hard to obtain a work permit unless you live with a Norwegian or have a very specialised skill, such as EAP. Unemployment is high, leading to fierce competition for jobs. Most foreigners in Iceland work in the fish processing industry, although there are at least four schools in Reykjavik. Your employer must arrange a work permit before you enter.

Bulgaria

Bulgaria has a surprisingly developed English language teaching structure and teachers have a high profile in the community. There is considerable enthusiasm for learning English.

Expect food shortages and fuel rationing, especially in winter. Basic necessities are not always easily obtainable.

Visas and work permits: All non-Bulgarian citizens need to get an entry visa which can be obtained from the Bulgarian Consular Service in any country. The system of registering with the police on arrival has been abolished for teachers in the state sector.

Cost of living: Very cheap in the provinces, reaching western levels in Sofia. Conditions are still extremely tough.

Salaries and taxes: Most teachers are paid at local rates - around 7,000 leva per month - but receive their air fares and furnished accommodation. The going rate for private classes is between 150 and 300 leva for 45 minutes or an hour.

Accommodation: Usually provided free by employers.

Health insurance: Essential.

Important cultural differences: Nodding your head means no, shaking your head means yes.

List of schools in Bulgaria

Alliance, Centre for Teaching of Foreign Languages, 3 Slaveikov Square, 1000 Sofia.
Centre for Language Qualification, National Palace of Culture, Administrative Bldg., 2nd Floor, Room 131, Sofia.
Institute of Tourism, Park Ezero, 8000 Bourgas.
Meridian 22, 6 Dimiter Blagoev Street, Sofia.
Pharos Ltd., 2 S.Vrachansky Street, Vasrajdane Square, Sofia

Croatia

Although the political situation is still fragile, English is booming in this former Yugoslavian republic and there is an understandable shortage of teachers. This means there are plenty of opportunities for teachers, usually in private language schools. However, many schools require teachers to have the diploma and it is not easy for unqualified teachers to find work.

Sometimes the British Council arranges to send teachers into state schools.

Jobs are often advertised abroad, but it's also possible to job-hunt on spec. Full-time contracts are the norm and there are opportunities for private lessons.

Visas and work permits: No visa is necessary for British or Irish citizens to enter the country as a tourist, but the employer must sort out a work permit. Other nationalities must have an entry visa as well as a work permit.

Cost of living: Cheap.

Salaries and taxes: Salaries are usually paid in hard currency, with tax deducted by the employer. The going rate is between 800 and 1,200 DM, while more experienced teachers might be able to earn more.

Accommodation: Rooms tend to be expensive and hard to find: a bedsit can cost 400 DM per month, paid for in hard currency. If you club together with other people, it works out much cheaper. A flat with two or three rooms will cost around 500 DM per month. There is usually a deposit of a month's rent, although landlords can ask for up to six months.

Health insurance: The employer normally provides it.

Inoculations: Hepatitis A, Polio, Typhoid

List of schools in Croatia

Centar za strane jezike, Vodnikova 12, 4100 Zagreb and Trg republike 2, 58000 Split.
Class, Jankomirska 1, 41000 Zagreb.
The English Workshop, Medulinska 61, 52000 Pula.
Interlang, Krisaniceva 7, 51000 Rijeka
Lancon, Jurisiceva 1, 4000 Zagreb.
Linguae, Radiceva 4, 51000 Rijeka.
LS Lukavec, Skolska 27, 41409 Donja Lomnica
Narodno sveuciliste, Skola za strane jezike, Trg Matice Hrvatske 3, 41430 Samobor
Octopus, Savska 13, 41000 Zagreb.
Radnicko sveuciliste, Bozidar Maslaric, 5400 Osijek.
Skola za strane jezike, Varsavska 14, 41000 Zagreb
Svjetski jezici, Varsavska 13, 41000 Zagreb
Verba, M. Gorkog 5, 51000 Rijeka

Cyprus

English is Cyprus' second language. It is taught from an early age in school and there are close links between Britain and the former colony through families, business, tourism and entertainment.

Unfortunately, it is not as easy to find work as the huge demand would suggest. In order to get your papers in order - and it is difficult to work on a tourist visa - it is necessary to have a first degree in the English Language or Linguistics. Sometimes, English Literature might be acceptable, but other graduates will find it difficult.

There is no local recruitment and you are unlikely to find work in the state sector unless you speak Greek. Write to the employers in the list below to see if they have any vacancies. Jobs tend to be full-time and there is scope to take private classes.

Visas and work permits: It's up to the employer to get the work permit. Don't go to Cyprus until you have it.

Cost of living: Cheap.

Salaries and taxes: Salaries and taxes vary considerably.

Accommodation: Flats cost UK£2/300 per month and up, but it's difficult just to rent a room. Deposits are not always necessary although one month's rent is sometimes expected.

Health insurance: Good healthcare available.

English language newspapers: Cyprus Mail, Cyprus Weekly.

List of schools in Cyprus

Ashley Janice, Arch Makarios III Avenue, Kanika Street, CDA
Coaching Centre, 5 Akritas Street, Larnaca.
Europa Language Centre, 3 Kypranoros Street, Nicosia.
Forum Language Centre, 47a Prodromou Street, Strovolos, Nicosia.
G.C. School of Careers, PO Box 5275, Nicosia
Language Centre, 49 Kennedy Avenue, Nicosia
Linguaphone Institute, 21 P Katelari Street, Nicosia.
Masouras Private Institute, D Lipertus Street, Zenia Zoe Court, Flat 103, Paphos.
PASCAL Institute, 3c Pantelides Street, Strovolos, Nicosia
Proodos Institute, 2 Asopios Street, Nicosia.

Richmond Institute, 9 Chr Kannaouros Street, Dasoupolis, Nicosia.
Themis Tutorial, 6a Einar Gzerstad Street, Larnaca.
Thomas Michaelides, 52 Golgon Street, Limassol. Limassol.

Czech Republic

The Czech Republic is an excellent place for qualified teachers to apply for a first teaching position, General English, Business English and teaching young learners are all common.

Although English is booming, most teachers have part-time contracts. It is easy to find private lessons. There are opportunities for non-qualified teachers, but non-native speakers will find it hard to find work.

In Prague, jobs can be found through word of mouth and the Prague Post. Otherwise, British Council noticeboards are essential. Other noticeboards can be found in cultural centres.

Visas and work permits: British citizens do not need a visa, although all nationalities do need a work permit and most others need an entry visa. You can apply for a work/residency permit while you are in the republic, but it is very bureaucratic and it can be difficult to obtain a permit.

Cost of living: Low.

Salaries and taxes: Private language schools have widely different terms and conditions. The tax rate is between 25 and 30 per cent.

Accommodation: It is very difficult to find accommodation and schools don't normally help teachers. Prices start from 2,000 KC per month and one month's rent is expected as a deposit.

Health insurance: Essential.

English language newspapers: The Prague Post.

Other useful information: Some people react very badly to the high levels of pollution in certain areas.

List of schools in the Czech Republic:

Agency Unitour, Libor Kivana, Senovazne 21, 110 00 Prague 1 Tel: 235 9917 Fax: 786 2153

Agentura Educo, Kurkova 2, 182 00, Prague 8 Tel: 848 035 Fax: 845 923
Anglictina Expres, Vodickova 39, Pasaz* Svetozor-galerie, 110 00 Prague 1 Tel: 290619
Bell School, Nedvezska* 29, 100 00 Prague 10 Tel: 781 5342
Cheb Free School, Kubelikova C.4, Cheb 350 02
Et Cetera Language School, PO Box 37, 130 00 Prague 3 Tel/Fax: 8944 84
Euro contact, Jankovskeho 52, 7 Hulesovice Tel: 801 527
GEJA, Seifertova 37, Prague 3 Tel: 225 375
International Language Centre Tel: 255 789
Jazykova Skola, Bitovska 3, 140 00 Prague 4 Tel: 420 595
London School of Modern Languages, Belgicka Ulice 25, 12 000 Prague 2 Tel: 256 859 Fax: 250 073
Prague 8 Language School, Buresova 1130, 18 000 Prague 8 Tel: 858 8028
Pro English 90, Mala Strana, 5 Helichova (4th floor), Prague 1 Tel: 534 551
Spusa Education Center, Navratilova 2, 110 00 Prague 1 Tel: 204 563/4
Statni Jazykova Skola, Narodni 20, 116 72 Prague 1 Tel: 203 814 Fax: 203 820

Estonia

It's very easy to find a job in Estonia, whether you have any qualifications or not. But Estonia, like many countries in the region, is becoming more discerning, and a teaching certificate will give you an edge.

There is a good noticeboard at the British Council and plenty of private schools where you can job-hunt speculatively. Arrive before the onset of winter in November.

Visas and work permits: It is relatively easy to obtain a work permit once you have found a job.

Cost of living: Fairly cheap.

Salaries and taxes: Local rates. Teachers need to take private classes to make ends meet.

Accommodation: The average rent for a two-bedroom flat in the dormitory suburbs is around US$200. Most flats are arranged through agencies which charge a month's rent.

Health insurance: Advisable.

Other information: The people of the Baltic States are the most business-minded of the former Communist countries of central and eastern Europe.

The seasons are very clearly defined: expect snow from November to March and hot summers.

Georgia

English is becoming the second language of Georgia and nearly everybody seems to be learning it. At the moment, there are very few native speakers, but there are thousands of Georgian teachers. The British Council Resource Centre in Tbilisi has 600 members and they estimate that this accounts for just a quarter of the English teachers in the capital!

Native speakers - whether or not they are qualified - should be able to pick up work by going out to Georgia on spec.

Visas and work permits: At the moment, it is extremely easy to work in Georgia and, amazingly, the authorities are quite flexible. Nobody seems to bother with work permits, institutions just ask for regular visa extensions on behalf of their teachers.

Cost of living: Extremely cheap. The standard of living is improving.

Salaries and taxes: Private language schools pay between US$3 and $4 per hour. The fee for private classes is generally negotiable: you could charge up to US$10 per hour or more. There isn't enough money in the state sector for a westerner to maintain a reasonable standard of living. Salaries are taxed at source but the rate is quite low.

Accommodation: Flats with two or three bedrooms cost between US$150 and US$200 per month. Deposits are not usually expected.

Health insurance: Essential.

Inoculations: Hepatitis A, Polio, Typhoid.

Important cultural differences: The Georgians are very hospitable and can be compared to the Italians.

Other information: The war has quietened down but some areas are still dangerous.

Hungary

English is in great demand in Hungary. It is an excellent place for a qualified teacher to find a first job and there are also opportunities for unqualified teachers in Hungarian-owned schools.

The main market is in General English. Prospective job-hunters can find work through the grapevine or going round all the schools in an area.

Only large schools offer full-time contracts but it is relatively easy to find private classes. Nine-month contracts are the norm.

Visas and work permits: British and Irish citizens do not need a visa, but other nationalities do. Everybody needs to apply for a work permit once they have found a job.

Cost of living: Fairly cheap.

Salaries and taxes: Students and schools pay between 500 and 1,000 forints for a 45-minute lesson.

Accommodation: It is very hard to find accommodation, even with help from schools. Rent tends to be cheap: between 30,000 and 60,000 forints for a one-bedroomed flat and between 100,000 and 125,000 forints for a larger flat which can be shared. One month's rent is payable as a deposit.

Health insurance: Advisable. Local health insurance is available but it doesn't cover repatriation.

Inoculations: BCG and Tetanus. You should also beware of ticks which carry Encephalitis.

English language newspapers: Budapest Sun, Budapest Week, Budapest Business Week Journal.

Other information: Hungary is very much a Central European country, rather than Eastern.

List of Schools in Hungary

The Budapest Pedagogical Institute, Horveth Mihaly Ter 8, Budapest 8 - recruits for schools in Budapest.
The English Teachers' Assoc. of the National Pedagogical Institute, Bolyai u.14, 1023 Budapest.
IH Budapest, POB 95, Budapest 1364.

recruits for schools outside Budapest.
RLC International, 27-28 George Street, Richmond, Surrey T9 1HY, UK - recruits for Hungary.

Lithuania

Although there are few opportunities for the unqualified, there are some opportunities for qualifed teachers. who should contact the Ministry of Education. The country's currency problems mean that materials and foreign expertise are hard to come by. The Soros Foundation has a centre in Vilnius, where the British Council has a resource centre.

Visas and work permits: UK passport holders do not require a visa though the situation varies for other EU citizens. For most nationalities the procedure to obtain work permits is relatively easy.

Salaries and taxes: Expect the equivalent of $50 a month.

Contact:

American English School, P.O. Box 731, Vilnius 2038. Tel: (0-03702) 731 514. A non-profit organisation offering English language lessons for children and adults throughout Lithuania; Summer Camps in Lithuania.

Poland

It's fairly easy to find work in Poland. English is in great demand, especially for the younger generation. Around 60 per cent of the work involves teaching young learners. There is also a substantial demand for Business English.

Although it does help to be qualified, particularly in the major towns and cities, being a native speaker is considered a great bonus, though local teachers are excellent.

Visas and work permits: There is no need for a visa but you will need to apply for a work permit if you wish to teach for more than a month. It is best to apply for a work permit from your home country. However, teachers do go to Poland on a tourist visa, find a job and then hop across the border to apply for a work permit in another country.

Cost of living: Cheap.

Salaries and taxes: Average salary is around US$80-100 per month

in the state sector for 18 contact hours a week. Some schools may offer extra hours. Private language schools pay more. The basic rate of tax is 21%.

Accommodation: It can be difficult to find accommodation. The cost varies enourmously depending on location. Schools in the smaller towns and private schools in the bigger towns may help teachers to find accommodation.

Health insurance: It's advisable to get it before you go.

English language newspapers: The Warsaw Voice.

Important cultural differences: Poles can be very direct.

Other useful information: The currency has recently changed from old zloties to new zloties. 1 million old zloties are the same as 100 new zloties. As always in these situations, expect some confusion for the foreseeable future as old habits die hard.

List of Schools in Poland
ABC, Uslugi Jezykowe, ul ZWM 6 m 29, Warszawa.
AJM, ul Klaudyny 30 m 100, 01-684 Warszawa.
American English School, Oddzial Warszawa-Cztery, Kondratowicza 25a m 33, 03-285 Warszawa.
Angloschool, ul Elblaska 65/84, Warszawa.
AS, Studio Jezykow Obcych, ul M L Kinga 13, 75-016 Koszalin
Bakalarz, Prywatne Studium Jezykowe, ul Rakowiecka 45/25, 02-528 Warszawa. Tel: 489 889.
Best, Prywatna Szkole, Jezyka Angielskiego, ul Wiktorsga 99, Warszawa.
Beyond 2000, Szkola Jezykow Obcych, ul Szuberta 39/5, 02-408 Warszawa.
British Council English Language Centre, Warsaw Technical University, ul. Filtowa 2, 00-611 Warszawa. Tel: 25 82 87.
The British School of Warsaw, Spzoo, ul Zielona 14, 05-500, Piaseczno.
Business and Educational English, ul Conrada 10 m 57, 01-922 Warszawa.
Compact School of English, Spolka Cywilna, Nowogrodzka 78/24, 02-018 Warszawa.
Discovery, Osrodek Nauczania Jezykow Obcych, Klub WAT-u, ul Kaliskiego 25a, 01-489 Warszawa.
Dominet, ul Pulawska 33, 05-500 Piassaczno
The Eagle English Centre, Al Stanow Zjednoczonych 26 m 25, 03-965 Warszawa.
Elan, Mokotowska 9 m 6, Warszawa. Tel: 25 19 91.

Elite Language School, ul Dunikowskiego 10 m 56, 02-784 Warszawa.

English is Fun, Warchalowskiego 2/13, Warszawa.

The English Language Academy, ul Narbutta 9 m 3, 02-564 Warszawa.

English Language School, ul Gleboka 49, 43-400 Cieszyn

English Language Studio, ul Jadzwingow 1 m 34, 02-692 Warszawa.

English Unlimited, Podmlynska 10, 80-885 Gdansk. Tel: 0048 68 31 35 73. Professional, dynamic school. General and Exam courses. Teachers must have RSA certificate and experience.

Falaland, Osrodek Nauczania Jez Obcych, Margerytki 52, 04-908 Warszawa.

Fast, Firma Prywatna, Jezyk Angielski-Lektoraty, Ewa Maszonska-Pazdro, ul Mickiewicza 74/58, 01-650 Warszawa.

Greenwich School of English Poland, ul Zakroczymska 6, 00-225 Warszawa.

Human, Agencja Jezykow Obcych, ul Swietokrzyshka 20 pok 317, 00-002 Warszawa.

Junior Art-Language Studio, ul Gwardzistow 8 m 5, 00-422 Warszawa.

Kajman, ul Felinskiego 15, 1 LO pokoj 57 (parter), 01-513 Warszawa.

Konwersatorium, Jezykow Obcych, Grojecka 40a m 13, 02-320 Warszawa.

Kozlowski I Rejman, Kusocinskiego 2, 31-300 Mielec

International House - Bydgoszcz, Pl Piastowski 5, 85-012 Bydgoszcz. Tel: 22 35 15.

Langhelp, Al Jerozolimskie 23/34, Warszawa. Tel: 21 44 34.

Lektor, Prywatna Szkola, Nauczania Jezykow Obcych, ul Sadowa 1, Warszawa.

Lexis College of Foreign Languages, ul Danilowiczowska 11m 18, Warszawa.

Lingua, Studium Jezykow Obcych, ul Moniuszki 4a, Lodz

Lingwista, ul Saska 59, 03-958 Warszawa, and Janowskiego 50, 02-784 Warszawa.

Mosak, ul Bonifacego 83/85 m 87, Warszawa.

Omnibus, Pl Wolnosci 5, 61-738 Poznan. Tel: 52 79 08.

The Orlik Language Centre, ul Rogalskiego 2 m 49, 03-982 Warszawa.

Perfect, Naucanie Jezykow Obcych, ul Wolnosci 2 bl 13 m 14, Maciej Musiala, Zielonka

Perfekt, Firma Oswiatowa, ul J Kaden-Bandrowskiego 2/16, 01-494 Warszawa.

Poliglota, Biuro Jezykowych, Dzialdowska 6, 01-184, Warszawa.

Prima, Osrodek Nauczania Jezykow Obcych, ul Rozana 7 m 3, 15-669 Bialystock

Promotor, Szkola Jezykow Obcych, Agencja Oswiatowa, Kraszewskiego 32a, 05-800 Pruszkow

Prymus, ul Jasna 2/4 pok 209, 00-950 Warszawa.

Pygmalion, Szkola Jezyka Angielskiego, ul Saska 78, Warszawa.

Success, ul Batalionow Chlopskich 14/50, 94-058 Lodz

Surrey Business and Language Centres, ul Gwardzistow 20, 00-422 Warszawa.

Studio Troll, Wrzeciono 1/22, Warszawa.

Urszula, Biuro Organizacji Kursow, Dworcowa 1 pok 13, 10-431 Olsztyn

Warsaw School of Commerce, Kursy Handlowe, al Chlodna 9, Warszawa.

Warsaw Study Centre, Osrodek Jezykowo-Szkoleniowy, ul Raszynska 22, 02-026 Warszawa.

World, ul Basztowa 17, 31-143 Krakow. Tel: 22 91 61.

Worldwide English School, ul Stoleczna 21 paw 24, 01-530 Warszawa.

Yes, ul Chelmonskiego 6 m 18, Lodz. Tel: 43 95 26.

Romania

English is the most popular foreign language in Romania and is widely studied. Most opportunities are to be found in the state sector, which is plagued by lack of resources, at either school or university level.

EEP, GAP, Central Bureau and SOL all have volunteer-teacher programmes in Romania and International House has an affiliate school in Timisoara which currently employs a small number of expatriate teachers on one-year contracts. Graduates with a teaching qualification should apply from their home country.

Most people will need to supplement their salary with private lessons or hourly-paid work in one of the growing number of private language schools.

Visas and work permits: Get a tourist visa at the point of entry and apply for a working visa from the Education Ministry.

Cost of living: Cheap.

Salaries and taxes: Teachers earn around US$100 per month, but need double that in order to live. However, with private classes bringing in between US$5 and $10 per hour, it isn't too difficult to earn enough money to maintain a fairly reasonable standard of living.

Accommodation: Flats tend to be expensive, but not too good. They cost from US$100 per month in Bucharest, less in the provinces. Sometimes there is no deposit although landlords can ask for up to six months' rent. State schools usually find teachers somewhere to live.

Health insurance: Essential.

Inoculations: Hepatitis A, Polio, Typhoid.

English language newspapers: Bucuresti, Nine O'Clock News. For private classes, advertise in the Romanian papers.

Other information: Romania is a welcoming country with attractive countryside, but conditions are not easy.

Addresses:
International House, Str Republicii 9, 1900 Timisoara
PROSPER-ASE Language Centre, Suite 4210, et 2, Calea Grivitei 2-2A, Bucharest. Tel: (01) 211 7800

Russia

English is becoming increasingly popular in Russia. Presently, a lot of the native speakers teaching English are unqualified students learning Russian who are trying to make ends meet.

Longer-term teachers normally start off working for a school and go freelance as soon as they can afford it to get the best rates. It is easier to get set up if you know people.

The main market is for General English. Business English seems to be getting more important, but there isn't much need for teachers of young learners yet.

Visas and work permits: To go to Russia, you need a student visa or an invitation from a company. The company doesn't need to employ you: it just needs to invite you for a two-month consultation trip.

Once you have a job, you need to apply for a working visa. It is complicated, but your company will usually put it through for you. It takes five weeks to process and you can pick it up in Finland. Don't forget to take a health certificate, your qualifications and references from previous employers.

Cost of living: Rents have now become expensive in Moscow.

Salaries and taxes: Employers normally pay people in dollars but declare a low salary in roubles to avoid the 40 per cent hard currency tax. In schools, teachers earn between US$500 and $600 per month, US$10-15 per hour. For private classes, you can charge US$15 or more per hour.

Accommodation: You can find a one-bedroom flat for US$150 per month. The deposit is one month's rent and if you don't speak Russian or have local friends, you can go through an agency which will charge a $200 fee.

Health insurance: Essential. Get it before you go.

English language newspapers: Petersburgh Press, Neva News.

Important cultural differences: Everything takes a long time: be patient.

Other information: Take decent winter clothers for cold weather

List of Schools in Russia

Anglo-American School, Penkovaya Ul. 5, St. Petersburg
Benedict School, Pskovskaya Ul. 23, St. Petersburg
Centre for Intensive Foreign Language Instruction, Sparrow Hills, Building 2, Moscow 119899.
Intense Language Business Centre, PO box 38, Ulitsa Gilyarovskogo 31/2, Moscow 125183
International Education Centre, School No. 56, Kutuzovski Prospekt 22, Moscow
Language Link School, BKC London-Moscow, Kashirskoe Shosse 54, Moscow 115409
Marina Anglo-American School, Leninsky Prospekt 39a, Moscow 117313
Moscow International School, 2nd Ulitsa Maryinoy Roshchi 2a, Moscow
Moscow MV Lomonosov University, Sparrow Hills, Moscow 117234.
Polyglot International School, 22 Volkov Pereulok, Flat 56, Moscow.
St Petersburg University, Universitetskaya, Naberezhnaya 7/9 B-164, St Petersburg 199164.
St Petersburg University Dept. of Foreign Languages, 15 Fuchika Str, 192238 St Petersburg Tel: 812 269 1925.
RISC Language School, Ulitsa Dekabristov 23a, Moscow
Russian Academy of Sciences, Universitetskaya Naberezhnaya 5, St Petersburg 199034.

Serbia and Montenegro

Although the political and economic climate is still far from ideal, many private language schools in Yugoslavia will welcome EFL teachers, as there continues to be a high demand for English.

Minimum salary: Average rates of pay for EFL teachers range from DEM 150-200 monthly in private language schools.

Visa requirements: Contact your local Embassy for details.

Accommodation: For a flat of approximately 40 sq. metres, it will cost roughly DEM 150 per month.

Slovakia

Although German is the second language of Slovakia - mainly due to its border with Austria - English is catching up fast. The Slovaks are keen to join the European Union and they see English as a means of getting important trade links. Commercial English isn't the only market, though, as interest is growing from primary schools.

At the moment, few organisations are involved in ELT in Slovakia, making it virtually impossible to go out on spec. Most jobs require a teaching qualification. Contracts are for full-time work and it is illegal to take private classes.

Visas and work permits: Once you have a job, you need to have a thorough medical and the police will check to see whether you have a criminal record. It's a long process, taking a couple of months with a lot of documentation. It's impossible without the backing of a sponsoring organisation.

Cost of living: Extremely low.

Salaries and taxes: Teachers are paid at local rates. At UK£4 per hour, teachers are considered extremely well-paid. Flights are usually provided. Employees of charities do not pay tax, otherwise it is around a third of income.

Accommodation: It's getting easier to find somewhere to live. Schools often put people up in residences until they find accommodation.

Health insurance: Essential. Get it before you go out.

English language newspapers: Slovak Spectator.

Important cultural differences: There is a limited range of food. The language is based on a case system, like Latin.

Other information: Slovakia is a very attractive destination for teachers. Bratislava has more of a small town feel than Prague in the other half of what used to be Czechoslovakia. There isn't much crime and it's easy to escape into the countryside for skiing and hiking.

Slovenia

There is a substantial demand for English, and unqualified teachers can find work easily. Only a small number of schools offer full-time contracts, but it is quite easy to find private classes.

After General English, the main markets are Business English, young learners and exam courses.

The best way of finding work is to apply from home or to go round all the schools.

Visas and work permits: Everyone needs a work permit and a visa, which you apply for at home. Unofficially, some teachers work on tourist visas.

Cost of living: Cheap.

Salaries and taxes: UK£10 per hour. Approximately half the gross salary goes towards taxes and national insurance.

Accommodation: It's not too difficult, but teachers usually have to go through an agency. Try to find one with a good reputation. Central heating, phones and TVs are fairly standard. Expect to pay £350 for a small, furnished flat, £450 for a bigger place. One month's rent is usually expected as a deposit, but six months is not uncommon.

Health insurance: Advisable. UK citizens are covered under a reciprocal agreement.

Other useful information: Slovenia is a proud new country, looking towards Western Europe. Sees itself as completely outside the conflict in the former Yugoslavia.

Although it is changing fast, it is still more stable than other former

Communist countries in the region, with more leisure activities. There is less of a gap between rich and poor.

Turkey

General English remains the main market, but Business English, English for academic purposes and young learners are all becoming increasingly popular. Jobs tend to be advertised abroad - try ELGazette, Tuesday's Guardian and the Times Education Supplement - and offer a package including a full-time contract, flight and accommodation.

There are plenty of opportunities for private classes and do not be surprised if people approach you in the street, asking if they can practise their English.

Visas and work permits: All nationalities need a work permit. It is better to apply from home as it can take up to six months to process applications in Turkey. However, many people do work on tourist visas, leaving the country every three months. There are heavy fines for overstaying your visit.

Only British nationals need a visa to enter Turkey. It must be purchased at the border using pounds sterling.

Cost of living: Relatively cheap, but there is an enormous inflation rate driving it ever-upwards.

Salaries and taxes: There is an enormous variation, but it tends to be between UK£200 and UK£500 per month, paid in the local currency. The tax rate ranges between nothing and 40 per cent but teachers tend to be quoted net salaries.

At the time of going to press, inflation was 70 per cent, so it is best to ask for mid-year salary increases or for your wage to be linked to a hard currency.

Accommodation: Schools tend to provide shared accommodation for full-time contracted teachers, but there is also plenty of private rented accommodation at a variety of rents. The average rent in the suburbs is around UK£120, but flats tend to be unfurnished. One month's rent is usually required as a deposit.

Health insurance: Advisable. Private health care is infinitely preferable to the state service.

Inoculations: Hepatitis A, Polio, Typhoid; Malaria in some areas.

English language newspapers: Turkish Daily News, Guardian Weekly and European Edition. Most English language papers are available one day late, but they tend to be expensive.

Important cultural differences: Bureaucracy and disorganisation can be frustrating for westerners. Tasks such as paying bills, getting money from the bank and even getting paid can be very time-consuming. Life tends to be harder for women than for men.

Other useful information: Check contracts very carefully and talk to teachers who already work at the school. Many schools are small, owner-directed operations and try to spend as little as possible on resources, training and administration.

List of schools in Turkey

Akademi School of English, PK 234, 21001 Bahar Sokar No 2, Diyarbakir. Tel: (90) 83242297. Fax: 83217908.
Ankara University, Rektorlugu, Beslevler, Ankara. Tel: 41234361.
Best English, Mesrutiyet Caddesi no 2/8, Ankara. Tel: 4172536.
Dilko English Centres, PO Box 152, Kadilkoy, 81300 Istanbul. Tel: 1 3380170.
Elissa English, Ihsaniye Mah 41, Sokak 48, Bandirma, Balikesir.
The English Centre, Rumeli Cad. 92/4, Zeki Bey Apt., Osmanbey, Istanbul. Tel: 1 470983.
English Fast, via Mr. K. Humphries, 9 Denmark Street, London WC2H 6LS, UK.
Evrim, Ozel Evrim Yabanci, Dil Kurasi, Cengiz Topel Caddesi 8/2, Camlibel, Mersin. Tel: 74121893.
International School, Eser Apt.A Blok Kasap, Sokak 1617, Esentepe, Istanbul.
Istanbul Turco-British Association, Suleyman Nazif Sokak 68, Nisantasi, 80220 Istanbul. Tel: 1 132 8200.
Istanbul University, Rektorlugu Beyarzit, Istanbul. Tel: 1 522 1489.
Kumlu Dersanerleri, Bursa Merkez, Basak Caddesi, Bursa. Tel: 241 20465.
Kent English, Mithatpasa Cad. 46/3, Kizilay, Ankara.
New Kent English, 1472 sok. No: 32 , Alsancak, Izmir. Tel: (232) 463 2737. Prestigious school, shared flat, social security, health care, guaranteed salary (60 hours a month), paid holiday, travel expenses.

North Africa And The Middle East

With English as the language of the oil business, there are many lucrative jobs available but the region is not without its cultural challenges and can be dangerous.

The situation in the Middle Eastern oil-rich countries can be extremely lucrative, but don't expect to have the time of your life. The cultural differences between the Middle East and most other regions, combined with increasing civil unrest in some areas, mean that it is really only an option for the self-disciplined or the married.

The standard package includes flights to and from the country. English teachers often head off for Bangkok at the end of their contracts.

In some states, such as Qatar and Syria, the most common work is for the spouses of those working in other fields to take private classes, often children.

There has been a great deal of civil unrest in Algeria recently with the rise of Islamic fundamentalism and several foreigners have been murdered. Other countries in the area can also be hazardous. Check our list of countries that the Foreign Office advises against visiting (page163) and consult your Foreign Affairs department before taking a post in the region.

Although the British Council advises teachers to 'proceed with caution' before looking for work in Libya, oil and private companies occasionally recruit teachers. Contact AFMENCO (UK) Ltd, 39 Marsh Green Road, Exeter EX2 8PN.

Bahrain

It is possible to work in Bahrain if you set something up before you leave by contacting the list of schools below. The only opportunities are for qualified teachers. You will have better prospects if you have some experience or the diploma.

Visas and work permits: Visas are not required for British nationals born in the UK. Nationals of other countries might have to get their employers to obtain a No Objection Certificate before entry, although usually they can get a three or five day visa on arrival and the employer can then sort out the arrangements. Work permits are required. The employer must get it soon after the teacher's arrival. New employees must have a medical check-up.

Cost of living: Higher than in neighbouring states in the Gulf, but salaries are not as high.

Salaries and taxes: Salaries range between BD520 and 580 for those with the certificate and between BD580 and BD700 for those with the diploma. The rate for part-time work is between BD6 and 8 per hour. No tax is charged.

Accommodation: A flat with one or two bedrooms will cost between BD180 and 300 per month. There is no deposit but three months' rent is required upfront.

Health insurance: Essential. Health cover can be obtained locally fairly cheaply.

English language newspapers: Gulf Daily News.

Other information: Bahrain is one of the most pro-westen Gulf states.

List of schools in Bahrain

ACCESS, Tel: 722898.
The British Council, Tel: 26555.
IPE, Tel: 290028.
Polyglot Schools Ltd., Tel: 271722.

Egypt

Demand for English is growing all the time as companies put pressure on their employees to learn it. It's not easy for new teachers to find work in reputable schools, although many organisations have minimal requirements.

Apart from company classes, one of the largest markets is for young learners. There are English Medium Schools and private schools teaching International GCSEs.

The recruitment season is in April and May for a September start. One way to avoid waiting for term to start would be to take a certificate course in Cairo: it is cheaper than elsewhere, you make some useful contacts and the cost of living is low.

Visas and work permits: A tourist visa is valid for one month which should be long enough to find a job. The school will apply for a work permit which will take around two weeks.

Cost of living: Cheap.

Salaries and taxes: Expect to earn between UK£5 and £9 per hour in a school, UK£13 to £20 privately. Tax rate is between 20% and

30% though teachers currently don't pay local tax.

Accommodation: Don't expect western standards of accommodation, but it's cheap and easy to find. A decent room in Cairo will cost around UK£100 per month, less elsewhere.

Health insurance: Essential.

Inoculations: Hepatitis A, Polio, Typhoid, Malaria, Yellow Fever.

English language newspapers: The Egyptian Gazette, Middle East Times.

Important cultural differences: Maintain respectful dress and personal relations. It can be difficult to get things done.

Other information: Egypt is less liberal than the west but less conservative than the Gulf states. Women will have far fewer problems than in neighbouring countries.

List of schools in Egypt

The American University in Cairo, CACE, ESD P.O. Box 2511, Cairo. Tel: (202) 357 6870. The English Studies Division, CACE, American University in Cairo offers RSA/Cambrisge CTEFLA and COTE courses.
he British Broadcast College, Dokki.
El Kawmeya International School, Horreya Avenue, Bab Sharki.
El Manar School, Amin Fikry Street, Ramleh Station, Cairo.
El Pharaana School, El Pharaana Street, Bab Sharki.
ILI, 2 Muhammad Bayoumi Street, Heliopolis, Cairo Tel: (202) 2291 9295. Fax: (202) 291 2218.
International Centre for Idioms, (behind Wimpy Bar), Dokki.
International Language Institute Soafeyeen (ILI), 3 Mahmoud Azmi Street, Madinet El Sohafayeen, Embaba, Cairo.
International Language Learning Institute, Pyramids Road, Guiza.
October Language Schools, 13, Saad El Ali Street, Mohandesssin.
Port Said School, 7, Taha Hussein Street, Zamalek 3403435.
Schutz American School, Cairo. Tel: 5701435/5712205.

Israel

If you want to teach English, your only real solution is to emigrate. And emigration is only really possible if you are Jewish. It's very difficult to get casual work in Israel and it's even harder to arrange a work permit. There is already a large English-speaking community in Israel, most of whom emigrated from the States.

There is a burgeoning EFL industry, with a British Council and Berlitz, but it is unlikely to become important until Israel has sorted out its problems with its neighbours. Immigrants would be able to teach in state schools but most posts aren't advertised.

Immigration: Jews from all over the world are encouraged to come to Israel. There is a generous set of perks, including buying a car without paying tax and help with a mortgage. New immigrants spend three to six months in a government-funded orientation centre, called Ulpan, finding their feet and learning Hebrew.

Cost of living: High

Salaries and taxes: English teachers can earn between US$7 per hour and US$33. Tax is paid at around 25 per cent.

Accommodation: Expensive in Tel Aviv, cheaper in the suburbs.

Health insurance: National insurance contributions are low, but non-Jews have to arrange their own health insurance.

Inoculations: Hepatitis A, Polio, Typhoid.

English language newspapers: Jerusalem Post.

Jordan

With an extremely young population, the state schools cannot keep up with the demand for English classes. Liberalization means that there will be increasing numbers of private schools. In the meantime, the British Council employs qualified native speakers on a part-time basis to teach Jordanian children and teenagers. Most part-time teachers are married to locals. To get a full-time contract, apply from your home country.

Visas and work permits: With a full-time contract obtained at home, your employer will sort out the necessary paperwork. Otherwise, part-time teachers pay an index-linked amount each year for a work permit. Expect to pay around UK£300 per year.

Cost of living: High, but basic necessities and transport are cheap.

Salaries and taxes: A full-time teacher at the British Council can expect to earn around UK£900 per month. The hourly rate is £10. Expect to learn less if you find work in a private language school.

Accommodation: One year's rent is often demanded in advance, with the landlord living off the interest. At £300 per month, this is a huge sum. To avoid paying so much, you can share, sub-let or simply try to persuade the landlord to let you pay by the month. The flood of refugees that followed the Gulf War has made it difficult to find cheap accommodation.

Health insurance: Essential.

Inoculations: Hepatitis A, Typhoid, Polio, Yellow Fever.

English language newspapers: Jordan Times, The Star.

Other information: Peace in the Middle East means Jordan is an excellent location for teachers wishing to visit to Israel or Lebanon.

List of schools in Jordan

Amman Baccalaureate School, Amman, Tel: 624872.
The Ahliyyeh School for Girls, Amman. Tel: 624872.
American Language Center, Amman. Tel: 659859.
British Council, First Circle, Jebel Amman, P.O. Box 634, Amman 11118.
The National Orthodox School, Amman. Tel: 685393.
New English School, Amman. Tel: 827154.
Yarmouk Cultural Centre, Amman. Tel: 671447

Kuwait

It is still just possible for unqualified and non-native teachers to find work in Kuwait because English is in such demand. To get a decent standard of living, it is essential to get qualified.

Jobs are advertised abroad, which makes it easier to arrange the papers, and in the local English language papers. Once in Kuwait, there are opportunities for private lessons, but they are still technically illegal.

Visas and work permits: All nationalities need entry visas and work permits. HIV and TB tests must be taken locally before a work permit can be issued.

Salaries and taxes: The usual salary range is between UK£12,000 and UK£15,000 pa. There is no income tax.

Accommodation: Most schools find and pay for flats. Average rent is between UK£420 and £520. Usual deposit is one month's rent.

Health insurance: Advisable.

English language newspapers: Arab Times, Kuwait Times.

Important cultural differences: Sometimes difficult for single women, although, unlike certain neighbouring countries, women are allowed to drive.

List of schools in Kuwait

American International School, Tel: 5318175.
British Council, 2 Al Arabi Street, Block 2, PO Box 345, 13004, Safat, Mansourrija.
ELU, The Kuwait Institute of Banking Studies, PO Box 1080, Safat 13011 (ESP teachers only).
Fahaheel English School, Tel: 3711070.
Gulf English School, Tel: 5629215.
Kuwait English School, Tel: 5629356.
Institute For Private Education, P.O. Box 6320, 32038 Hawalli Tel: 574 3469. Kuwait's leading private sector provider of governmental, corporate and general public training in English Language and English for Specific Purposes.
Language Centre, Kuwait University, PO Box 2575, Safat. Tel: 484 1741
Pitman Secretarial and Business Studies Centre, Tel: 2544840.

Morocco

Moroccan Arabic, Classical Arabic, French, various Berber languages, German, Spanish ... The Moroccans are genuine polyglots, so it comes as little surprise that English is popular. The main markets are in teaching young learners and general English tuition for company-sponsored students.

It's easy to get work with a certificate and experience; possible to get something with just a certificate; and generally not possible without any qualifications. It's best not to come on spec. The British Council will provide a list of schools on request.

Visas and work permits: After you have been offered a contract, the school applies for a residence permit; in theory this should happen before arrival in Morocco but this is not usually the case. It can take up to three months for your papers to come through. You will need original copies of our birth certificate, degree and teaching qualification.

Cost of living: Cheap.

Salaries and taxes: Expect low rates of pay, from 80 to 120 dirhams per hour. Taxation is complicated and rises sharply as salary increases, but it tends to be between 17 and 30 per cent.

Accommodation: Flats vary greatly from area to area. In Rabat, an apartment will cost 2-3,000 dirhams a month; more in Casablanca

Health insurance: Essential.

Inoculations: Hepatitis A, Polio, Typhoid.

Important cultural differences: Morocco takes some adjusting to, but it's manageable. It can be difficult for Europeans, especially women, although some say there is no more hassle than in Milan.

Other information: A knowledge of French is useful.

List of schools in Morocco

American Language Center, 4 zankat Tanja, Rabat.Tel: 76 61 21 9 other centers
The British Centre, 3, rue Nolly, Casablanca. Tel: 27 31 90
The British Council Language Centre, 36 rue de Tanger, B.P. 427, Rabat. Tel: 76 08 36
Business and Professional English Centre, 74 rue Jean Jaures, Casablanca.
The London School of English, 10 ave des FAR, Casablanca.Tel: 26 89 32

Oman

A popular destination, but less well paid than its neighbours. Most jobs are in Muscat. More liberal than some of its neighbours, conditions are relatively good for women and buying alcohol is permitted. Contact CFBT or the English Language Teaching Dept., Ministry of Education, PO Box 3, Ruwi.

Minimum salary: 600-700 rials per month.

Tax: Tax-free.

Visa requirements: Employer's sponsorship required for a permit, which can take some time.

Accommodation: Often provided; if not, 250 rials per month.

English Newspapers: Oman Daily Observer, Times of Oman.

Saudi Arabia

English is the acknowledged second language of Saudi Arabia. It is widely used in commerce and - with an expatriate labour force outnumbering the domestic population - it is the country's lingua franca.

Most of the opportunities are in Business English. Companies with training departments for their Saudi staff recruit most English teachers, whether for EFL or ESL. To find work, look in the ELGazette, Tuesday's Guardian and the Times Education Supplement. Most contracts are for full-time teaching for 12 months and there are few vacancies for women.

There are opportunities for unqualified teachers who are doing something else in Saudi Arabia. Moonlighting is common and spouses often take private classes. Parents like their children to study English with native speakers.

A contract in Saudi Arabia can be an excellent way of saving money, but it's not for everybody: look at the restrictions in the 'cultural difference' section and see if you would be able to cope.

Saudi bureaucracy is very slow, so don't leave your job, let alone book a flight, until you have a signed contract and a visa sorted out.

Visas and work permits: All nationalities need work permits and visas. Teachers must be sponsored by a company in Saudi Arabia which makes all the applications on behalf of the teacher. It is impossible to work on a tourist visa.

Cost of living: High salaries and all-in packages make it easy for foreign nationals to save money.

Salaries and taxes: Most teachers earn between SR7,000 and SR11,000 per month. There is no tax.

Accommodation: It's not too difficult to find accommodation. Local knowledge can take most of the hassle out of the process and employers generally help. Expect to pay SR18,000 per annum for a modest unfurnished two-bedroom apartment. Basic furnishings will cost around SR12,000. One month's deposit is usually expected.

Health insurance: Essential. It is usually part of the contract.

Inoculations: Hepatitis A, Polio, Typhoid, Malaria, Yellow Fever, Meningitis.

English language newspapers: Arab New, Saudi Gazette, Riyadh Daily.

Important cultural differences: There is a strict dress code and many things the west takes for granted - alcohol, women driving, men and women intermingling - are prohibited.

Other useful information: For a single person, the right contract in Saudi Arabia can offer an excellent opportunity to make substantial financial savings. However, it is rarely a career move, unless you work with a global organisation. For a family with children, it is essential to get adequate accommodation and funding for school fees.

List of schools in Saudi Arabia

The British Council, Al Moajil Building, 5th Floor Dhahran Street, Mohamed Street, PO Box 8387 Daman. Tel: 834 3484
English Language Centre, King Adulaziz University, PO Box 1540, Jeddah 21441.
Girls' College of Arts - General Presidency for Female Institute for Languages and Translation, c/o King Saud University, PO Box 2465, Riyadh 11451.
King Fahd University of Petroleum and Minerals, English Language Centre, Dhahran 31261.
Riyadh Military Hospital-Training Division, PO Box 7897, Riyadh 11159.
Saudi Airlines - Saudia cc:452, PO Box 167, Jeddah 21231.
Saudi Language Institute, PO Box 6760, Riyadh 11575.
SCECO-East Central Training Inst., PO Box 5190, Damman 31422.
Yanbu Industrial College, PO Box 30436, Yanbu Al Sinaiyah 21477.

Syria

Although there is a substantial demand for English, the opportunities for teachers are not vast. Unqualified teachers will find it particularly difficult with only the American Language Centre willing to employ unqualified native speakers. It is also advisable to sort out a job before heading out to Syria as the ALC is generally the only centre which ever takes on teachers who have turned up on spec. - most of these are students of Arabic. The British Council demands at least a Preparatory Certificate and doesn't usually arrange residence for part-time teachers.

Visas and work permits: You will need a visa and a work permit.

These are best applied for in your home country.

Salaries and taxes: For private lessons expect around $10 per hour.

Accommodation: Flats are expensive. To rent a room with a family in the old city you could pay around $100 per month.

Health insurance: Advisable.

English language newspapers: Syrian Times

Important cultural differences: The usual differences associated with an Arab/Islamic culture

List of Schools in Syria

Al Razi, Damascus. Tel: 457301.
American Language Center, Damascus. Tel: 2247236.
Dimashk al Lughawi, Damascus. Tel: 454615.

Tunisia

Tunisia remains a Francophone country which means English teachers are not in huge demand. English seems to be slowly replacing French as the language of business, so expect prospects for teachers to improve. It is best to apply to the ELT institutions in the region before leaving home.

Visas and work permits: It can take three months or longer to arrange a working visa, but you should receive a temporary work permit or a letter from your employer allowing you to work in the meantime. Original degree and birth certificates are required.

Cost of living: Tourism has driven up the cost of living.

Salaries and taxes: At 10 to 14 dinar per hour, teachers are paid more than local rates. Tax is around 20 per cent.

Accommodation: It's easy to find somewhere to live. Expect to pay 3-400 dinar per person a month, with one month or more deposit.

Health insurance: Advisable.

Inoculations: Hepatitis A, Polio, Typhoid, Yellow Fever.

Important cultural differences: It's more open and cosmopolitan than its neighbours.

List of schools in Tunisia

English Language Training Centre, British Council, 47 Avenue Habib Bourguiba, Tunis.
IBLV, 47 Avenue de la Liberte, Tunis.

United Arab Emirates

Minimum salary: 5-10,000 dirhams per month.

Tax and health insurance: Tax-free. Health card: 300 dirhams.

Accommodation: Usually provided, otherwise expensive. A single flat costs 20-35,000 dirhams, a double 35-50,000.

Visa requirements: Tourist visa issued readily. You need a sponsor to be able to live and work in the UAE. Rules about visas change at short notice, so contact your local UAE embassy before departure.

English language newspapers: Emirates News, Gulf News, Khaleej Times (D).

Other information: With the growth of tourism, there is a growing demand for both male and female EFL teachers. Both Abu Dhabi and Dubai are cosmopolitan, relaxed cities, without the restrictions normally associated with the Gulf.

Try contacting:

The Abu Dhabi National Oil Co, PO Box 898, Abu Dhabi.
Al-Worood School, P.O. Box 46673, Abu Dhabi. Tel: 9712 447 655. MSA accredited, English-medium, K-12, Private international school with 930 pupils offering IGCSE, AS & A levels, plus High School Diploma.

Yemen

There is a reasonable demand for English and it is quite easy for non-qualified native speakers and non-native speakers to find teaching work. Most of the work is in teaching EFL but English medium schools are growing in the private sector. Parts of the North can be dangerous and foreigners have been kidnapped.

The main markets are in General English and English for special purposes in the oil and gas industries. Most work is part-time or paid at an hourly rate. Most job information can be found in the local chamber of commerce or through the grapevine.

Visas and work permits: Necessary for all nationalities. People do work on tourist visas, but, strictly speaking, it's illegal. It's best to apply for permits at home.

Cost of living: Very cheap.

Salaries and taxes: Tax-free. The going rate for teaching is around US$8 per hour.

Accommodation: It's very easy to find accommodation since the market is depressed. The average rent is US$125 per month, with two or three months' rent as a deposit.

Health insurance: Essential.

Inoculations: Hepatitis A and B, TB, Typhoid, Meningitis, Polio, Rabies.

English language newspapers: Yemen Times, Daily Chew.

Important cultural differences: No alcohol, women must wear long-dresses; and you must not offer things with your left hand.

Other useful information: Although Yemen is a poor and underdeveloped country, it is close to finalising agreement with the World Bank and the International Monetary Fund, which will lead to increased international support.

List of schools in Yemen

Al Farouq Institute, PO Box 16927 Tel: 209 721 Fax: 209 721
The British Council, Po Box 2157 Tel: 244 121 Fax: 244 120
English Language Centre, Po Box 8984 Tel: 248 090
Faculty of Art, English Department, Po Box 6-14) Tel: 32 350
Faculty of Art, English Department Tel: 200 515/6
Faculty of Education, English Department Tel: 250 513
French Culture Centre, Po Box 1286 Tel: 271 666 Fax: 276 124
Madina Institute of Technology (MIT) Tel: 251 453
Modern Yemen School, Po Box 13335 Tel: 206 548
Mohammed Ali Othman School, Po Box 5713 Tel: 211 248/9
Pakistani School Tel: 247 830 and 247 838
Sabaa University, Po Box 14400 Tel/Fax: 205 749
Sana'a International School, Po Box 2002 Tel: 234 437
Spectra Institute, Po Box 16101 Tel: 414 623 Fax: 414 739
University of Science Technology, Po Box 15201 Tel: 207 026 Fax: 207 027
Yemen Language Centre, Po Box 1691 Tel: 285 125

Sub-Saharan Africa

The large number of Anglophone countries and the high level of poverty means that much of the teaching work in this region is limited to voluntary organisations.

Teaching English in sub-Saharan Africa is certainly an experience to be remembered. If you are in search of adventure or are in Africa for some other reason - studies, work or marriage - there are a limited number of opportunities. As a general rule, there is very little work in countries where English is already the official language since teachers can be recruited. But elsewhere, English is associated with liberation and modernism and your skills are in demand.

Since the fall of apartheid, there have been increasing numbers of opportunites for English teachers in South Africa. At the moment, most of the work is for volunteers teaching English as a second language or English as a medium of instruction. Expect more work in years to come.

There are many African countries where there is only a volunteer presence. To work in one of the following countries, contact a volunteer organisation: Benin, Burkina Faso, Cape Verde, Central African Republic, Chad, Comoros, Congo, Cote d'Ivoire, Ethiopia, Gabon, Gambia, Ghana, Guinea, Guinea Bissau, Madagascar, Malawi, Mali, Niger, Nigeria, Sao Tome, Senegal, Seychelles, Tanzania, Togo, Zambia.

Please note that voluntary groups cannot normally guarantee to place successful applicants in the country of their choice.

There is practically no work in Sierra Leone, Kenya, Eritrea or Lesotho. Contact the relevant British Council to see if there are any vacancies if you are set on working in one of these countries.

Botswana

Demand for English language teachers is fairly low as English is the official language and is used in schools. Employers have to give preference to Botswana nationals so work permits can be hard to come by.

Most foreign teachers are recruited through the Teachers for Botswana Recruitmen Scheme, administered by the British Council in Manchester and the Department of Teaching Service Management in Botswana.

Qualified teachers are recruited throughout Botswana twice a year.

Visas and work permits: An entry permit is required to visit. Visitors can usually get a 30-day permit on production of a return ticket and evidence of sufficient finance.

Non-nationals in the private sector require work permits from the Department of Labour, valid for a limited period and renewable.

Cost of living: Cheap.

Salaries and taxes: For a qualified, graduate teacher, salaries begin at around 22,000 Botswana pula per annum, varying according to qualifications and experience.

Accommodation: Subsidised by most state schools. They normally charge a fee of 15 per cent.

There is an accute shortage of housing, particularly in Gaborone, and teachers can expect to spend the first few months in a hotel.

A government two-bedroom flat could cost P400-650 per month while a similar private flat could cost P1,5000-2,500.

Health insurance: Essential.

Inoculations: You are advised to protect yourself against; Diptheria, Hepatitis A and B, Malaria, Polio, Tetanus and Typhoid.

Mozambique

Qualified teachers should be able to find work in Mozambique. Most job information is through the local grapevine. The main teaching areas are secondary, tertiary and general English for adults. Full-time short-term contracts are available from the British Council.

Visas and work permits: Apply for a visa in the Mozambican embassy and a work permit in Mozambique.

Cost of living: Cheap.

Salaries and taxes: Negotiable. No tax is payable.

Accommodation: The average rent is between US$300 and $500 per month. One month's rent is expected as a deposit.

Health insurance: Essential.

Inoculations: Hepatitis A, Polio, Typhoid, Malaria, Yellow Fever.

Important cultural differences: There are many cultural differences: do some research before you leave.

Sudan

English is in great demand in this giant African country. Native speakers - whether or not they are qualified - should be able to find work, if they can sort out a visa.

Most of the teaching involves part-time contracts teaching remedial English but there is plenty of scope for private work. To work in Sudan, first contact the British Council.

Visas and work permits: Everybody except nationals of Arab countries needs an entry visa and a work permit. It is not possible to work on a tourist visa and you should sort out the paperwork before coming to Sudan.

Cost of living: Cheap, but inflation is rampant.

Salaries and taxes: All salaries are negotiable. The going rate for private work is UK£5-10 per hour. Tax is 20 per cent.

Accommodation: It's fairly easy to find somewhere to live and schools often help teachers find accommodation The average rent is only UK£40 per month, but deposits of up to six months are often required.

Health insurance: Advisable. Arrange long-term travel insurance before you leave.

Inoculations: Yellow Fever, Hepatitis A, Typhoid, Tetanus, Cholera, Meningitis, Polio.

English language newspapers: New Horizon and Sudanow. Newsweek is widely available.

Important cultural differences: Friday is the only non-working day and term dates vary for a number of reasons.

Islamic laws are strictly enforced and there are restrictions for women and on alcohol consumption. Westerners find there's a lack of punctuality, privacy and organisation.

Other useful information: Despite the poor resources and facilities, the people are generally very warm, hospitable and responsive.

Swaziland

English is the official language of this small rural country, which means that most of the opportunities are in government-run schools. There are a few expatriate contracts which are mainly taken by qualified teachers from other African countries.

Opportunities occasionally come up in the small number of private schools. It might be possible for unqualified teachers to find work in the private sector. Qualified non-native teachers can find work in Swaziland. The main market is in teaching English as a second language. Jobs are usually advertised in the local press.

Visas and work permits: A visa is not required for Commonwealth citizens, but all nationalities need work permits. It is illegal to work on a tourist visa and far better to apply for paperwork from home.

Cost of living: Cheap. The economy is stronger than most in sub-Saharan Africa.

Salaries and taxes: It varies according to your qualifications and employer. A secondary school teacher in a government school would earn about UK£200-250 per month plus accommodation. In private schools this would be higher. The highest rates are for expatriate contracts, where you stay in the country for more than two years.

You are only taxed if your salary exceeds £220 per month. The maximum rate is 33 per cent.

Accommodation: Cheap rented accommodation is scarce. It is easy to come by flats at the higher end of the scale. A reasonable house with three bedrooms will cost a minimum of £200 per month. One month's rent is expected as deposit.

Government schools generally provide adequate accommodation, especially for teachers on expatriate contracts.

Health insurance: Advisable.

Inoculations: Regulations change regularly. Check before you go.

English language newspapers: The Times of Swaziland and The Observer.

Important cultural differences: Swaziland has a traditional male-dominated culture.

The Far East

An increasingly popular destination for teachers, whether in search of holiday money in Thailand or big earnings in Japan.

 nglish is in huge demand in the Far East. Japan, Korea, Taiwan, Thailand and Hong Kong all need English teachers. Pay is good and teachers can save a great deal, but expect to spend a lot of your time dealing with bureaucracy and paperwork problems.

Though work is available in most other countries if you want to work in Laos, the only option at the moment is to join an aid agency. Please note that volunteer groups cannot normally guarantee successful candidates a place in the country of their choice. At the moment, there is no English language teaching in North Korea, but the Australia Center is rumoured to be moving in.

Brunei

If you want to work in this rich, Muslim country in South-East Asia, you must have a degree and two years' teaching experience and apply for work in the state sector from your home country. It is not difficult for teachers who have established themselves in Brunei to move into private education. Since there is very little public transport and fuel is cheap, a driving licence is essential. Schools usually offer a car loan scheme. CfBt is a major recruiter for the Sultanate.

Visas and work permits: The Brunei High Commission will supply a visa on proof of a job offer, so you need to do your job hunting before leaving your home country. Your passport is stamped on arrival for a period at the discretion of the immigration officer. Once in the country, your employer must apply for a labour licence if you are working in the private sector, followed by a work permit.

Cost of living: Similar to Northern Europe.

Salaries and taxes: Salaries vary enormously in the state sector: it is obviously far less profitable to teach primary school children than post-graduate degree students. You should earn between B$2,400 and B$7,000 a month. Normally there is no personal income tax.

Accommodation: Flats are usually provided or are subsidised as part of the job package, if not, then at B$1,5000 per month, they are prohibitively expensive, as there is often a three-month deposit.

Health insurance: Advisable, but sometimes offered by employers. Have medical and dental check-ups before you go.

Inoculations: Hepatitis A, Polio, Typhoid, Yellow Fever.

English language newspapers: Borneo Bulletin.

Important cultural differences: Dress modestly.

Other useful information: Take enough shoes since they are difficult to buy in larger sizes.

Cambodia

English has been in huge demand in Cambodia since the United Nations started running the country. It is still popular now that it has pulled out, especially Business English.

Most jobs for English teachers and teacher-trainers are with aid agencies such as The Australia Centre, CfBT and VSO. Regents College and the Pacific Technical School also recruit teachers and many small, private Cambodian schools look for foreign teachers. Most schools employ teachers on a casual basis, but the Australia Centre has some contract teachers.

Visas and work permits: Visas will be arranged by the employer if you have a full-time contract.

Cost of living: Cheap.

Salaries and taxes: The minimum pay is about US$7 per hour for unqualified teachers. With a certificate you can earn more than three times that amount, with the usual range being between US$12 and US$25 per hour.

Accommodation: The rates have risen dramatically since the United Nation stopped running the country in 1994. Rates range from US$400 up for a two-bedroomed house or flat.

Health insurance: Essential. Make sure your policy covers evacuation from the country in case of serious illness.

Inoculations: Hepatitis A, Polio, Typhoid, Malaria, Yellow Fever.

Other useful information: There is now a coalition government in place but there are still travel restrictions in parts of the country.

China

Although English is in demand in this vast country, your only chance of finding work is to come in with a voluntary organisation. There are no private language schools - for obvious reasons - so most employment is with universities or colleges. Unqualified and non-native speakers will find it relatively easy to find work. The Chinese government also recruits teachers: apply to your local embassy.

The key areas are General and Business English and there's plenty of scope for private classes. Most jobs offer full-time contracts.

The Chinese authorities distinguish between foreign teachers and foreign experts. The former are normally under 25 and only need a degree; the latter are highly qualified, experienced teachers. Try the education section of your local Chinese embassy as well as the addresses given below.

Visas and work permits: All nationalities have to apply for visas/work permits in their home country. You will need your employer to sponsor you. People do not work on tourist visas.

Cost of living: Cheap.

Salaries and taxes: The usual salary range is between Y800 and Y1,200 per month for a foreign teacher. For a foreign expert, it is between Y2,000 and Y3,500. No tax is paid. Accommodation and flights are usually provided.

Accommodation: It is usually provided by the employer; otherwise it is extremely difficult to find.

Health insurance: Essential.

Inoculations: Hepatitis A/B, Rabies in countryside.

English language newspapers: China Daily, Shanghai Daily Star.

Important cultural differences: There are many differences, do some research before you decide whether to go.

List of employers in China

Chinese Education Association for International Exchange, 37 Damucang Hutong, Beijing Tel: 1-602-0731 Fax: 1-601 6156
Yunnan Institute of the Nationalities, Foreign Affairs Office, Kunming 650031, Yunnan, China Tel: 871-515 4308
British Council, Overseas Educational Appointments Department, 15 Medlock Street, Manchester M15 4AA

China Teaching Program, Western Washington University, Old Main 530, Bellingham, WA 98225-9047, USA Tel: +1-206-650 3753 Fax: +1-206-650 6818

Hong Kong

The market for English language teaching seems to have reached its peak in the early 90s. Since then, many schools have closed down. There is still a huge demand for ELT, though, with English Medium Schools, conversation clubs, universities, the British Council and small private schools all employing teachers.

It is possible to find work even if you are unqualified and prepared to work for low wages. Teachers are often poached by other schools or decide to leave, creating sudden vacancies. Members of the large transient population often pick up casual teaching work in September at the beginning of the academic year. Most schools seem to recruit locally through the ex-patriate grapevine. Expect to work for a number of different employers. It would be difficult to get set up in Hong Kong without any savings or contacts, but teachers can save a great deal of money.

Visas and work permits: British citizens can get a work permit very easily. Other nationalities need to be sponsored by an employer who can guarantee them full-time work.

Cost of living: High.

Salaries and taxes: Unqualified teachers earn around UK£5 per hour in the private sector. This rises to UK£25 per hour for a teacher with a certificate and a year's experience and up to UK£30 per hour for a diploma-qualified teacher. Tax is around 15 per cent.

Accommodation: You will pay around UK£900 per month for a flat, £500 for a room. Two to three months' rent is payable as a deposit. Many teachers stay in hostels.

Health insurance: Advisable.

Inoculations: Hepatitis A, Polio, Typhoid, Malaria.

English language newspapers: Hong Kong Standard, International Herald Tribune, South China Post.

Important cultural differences: Hong Kong seems to be one of the busiest places on the planet. It is hot, humid, crowded, bustling and fast, but transport is good and the countryside is accessible.

Other information: When Hong Kong reverts to Chinese rule in June 1997, English language teaching could go either way. On the one hand, Hong Kong could become China's education centre, attracting students from all over the country. On the other, there could be an anti-English backlash. Only time will tell.

List of schools in Hong Kong

First Class Language Centre, 22a Bank Tower, 351-353 King's Road, North Point. Tel: (5) 887 7555.
Hong Kong English Club, Ground floor, 176b Nathan Road, Tsimshatsui, Kowloon. Tel: (3) 722 1300.
Josiah's Institute of English, 2nd and 3rd floors, 88 Lockhard Road, Wanchai.

Indonesia

To find work in Indonesia, qualified English teachers need to go out there on spec. All recruitment tends to be done locally on an ad-hoc basis. It's very easy to find work in Jakarta, less so in Bandung, which is very popular with teachers.

The market is dominated by North American and Australian teachers. As Indonesia's economy grows, Business English becomes increasingly important. Indonesia is an excellent destination for qualified and experienced teachers who have already saved money elsewhere in the Far East. It can be very expensive to get set up because of the delays in getting your paperwork sorted out.

Visas and work permits: A tourist visa allows you to stay in Indonesia for two months, which should be long enough to find a job. The school will arrange a work visa, which takes a few weeks. You need to take a trip to Singapore to pick it up. You need to submit your passport for a long time to renew your visa. At the British Institute, hourly-paid teachers have to fund their own trip to Singapore, while teachers on a part-time contract get half their expenses paid and those on a full-time contract get them all.

Cost of living: Cheap, but consumer durables are expensive.

Salaries and taxes: The going rate is 25,000 rupee per hour or 2,160,000 rupee per month.

Accommodation: Flats tend to be reasonably priced in Bandung, more expensive in Jakarta. Schools normally help teachers find somewhere to live, which is just as well, considering that one year's rent is payable in advance. They normally arrange a loan.

Health insurance: Advisable. Most teachers fly to Singapore when they get ill.

Inoculations: Hepatitis A, Polio, Typhoid, Malaria, Yellow Fever.

English language newspapers: Indonesian Times, Indonesian Observer and the Jakarta Post.

List of schools in Indonesia

ALT (American Language Training), Jalan R.S. Fatmawati 42a, Keb Baru, Jakarta Selatan. Tel: 769 1001. Five schools.
EEC (English Education Centre), Jalan Let Jen S.Parman 66, Slipi, Jakarta Barat. Tel: 567 1144.
EEP (Executive English Programs), Jalan Wijaya VIII 4, Kebayoran Baru, Jakarta Selatan. Tel: 722 0812. Branch in Bandung.
ELS International, Jalan Tanjung Karang 7 c-d, Jakarta Pusat. Tel: 323211.
ELTI (English Language Training International), Complex Wijaya Grand Centre, Blok f83, 84a &b, Jalan Wijaya II, Keb Baru, Jakarta Selatan. Tel: 720 2957. Branches in Yogyakarta, Semarang and Solo.
IALF (Indonesia-Australia Language Foundation), Wisma Budi, Suite 503, Jalan HR Rasuna Said Kav c-6, Kuningan, Jakarta Selatan 12940. Tel: 521 3350. Branch in Bali.
ILP (International Language Programs), Jalan Panglima Polin IX/2, Kebayoran Baru, Jakarta Sealtan. Tel: 722 2408. Branch in Surabaya.
SIT (School for International Training), Jalan Hayam Wuruk 120c-d, Jakarta Pusat. Tel: 629 3340.
TBI (The British Institute), Setiabudi Building 2, Jalan HR Rasuna Said, Kuningan, Jakarta Selatan. Tel: 512 044. Branch in Bandung.
Triad English Centre, Purnawarman 7b Bandune - 40116. Tel: 62 22 431309. One of the senior and qualified English courses in Indonesia which provides international English teaching.

Japan

Each year, there are fewer school-age children in Japan, which means that the market is shrinking. It's still possible to find work, however, especially if you know people out there.

Unqualified teachers can find work in private schools giving conversation classes or through Japan's Exchange and Teaching (JET) programme. There are also chains of schools, such as GEOS, employing unqualified teachers. A degree is nearly always necessary.

The best time to look for work is from December to February, for an April start. Many jobs are advertised abroad, in the ELGazette and Tuesday's Guardian, and you can apply to the head office of large chains. One trick is to join the Japanese Association for Language Teaching - fax: +81-899 23 5532 - whose newsletter has details of vacancies.

If you decide to go out on spec, you will need quite substantial savings to survive while you look for work and wait for your papers to come through. You will be able to save a great deal in a year or two in Japan, so if you have the money, it is a good investment. If nothing comes up in Tokyo, it's better to go to smaller towns which have yet to be saturated with teachers.

Visas and work permits: You can only get a work visa if you are sponsored by an employer and have a degree. Since it can take up to three months to come through and working on a tourist visa is illegal (even if the papers are being processed), it's best to find work before you go to Japan. It is possible to job-hunt on a tourist visa.

If you do go out on spec, you will have to leave the country and re-enter with sponsorship from your employer, who must guarantee you a minimum salary. You cannot change your status without leaving Japan.

Your school will need a certified copy of your degree, a full CV, a contract in Japanese, details of previous visits to Japan and four photos. Once your permit has arrived, you will need to leave your passport at the embassy for about a week to get a visa.

Cost of living: Expensive, but salaries are much higher. It is possible to save large amounts of money, especially outside Tokyo.

Salaries and taxes: In a state college, you can expect to earn around US$40,000. If you are paid by the hour, you'll get US$20-30 in a private language school or US$40-60 for private classes. Income tax is around 10 per cent, local tax 5 per cent.

Accommodation: Prices vary enormously. A small flat which can be shared can cost anywhere between US$400 and US$1,000 per month. Japanese landlords can be reluctant to rent to foreigners, so it's worth getting somebody to help you. You might have to pay up to US$2,000 as a deposit. Many of the schools which advertise for teachers abroad include accommodation as part of their employment package.

Health insurance: Advisable. It can be purchased locally. Larger schools often have a private scheme for their employees.

English language newspapers: There are four daily English language papers in Japan, all of which carry adverts for teaching jobs. Monday's Japan Times has the best jobs, but The Daily Yomiuri, The Daily Mainichi, The Asahi Evening News also have recruitment adverts.

Important cultural differences: It can take up to six months to get acclimatised to Japan. Prepare yourself before you go. The Japanese school year runs from April to March, with various small breaks.

List of schools in Japan

Aeon Institute of Foreign Languages, 7f Nihonseimei Building, 7f 1-1 3 Shimoishii Okayama-shi 700.
Attorney Foreign Language Institute, Osaka Ekimae Daiichi Building, 1-3-1 Umeda Kita-ku, Osaka.
American Academy, 4-1-3 Kudan Kita Chiyoda-Ku, Tokyo 102.
American School of Business, 1-17-4 Higashi Ikebukuro Toshima-Ku,Tokyo 170.
Azabu Academy, 401 Shuwa-Roppongi Building, 3-14-12 Roppongi Minato-ku, Tokyo 106.
Berkley House Gogaku Centre, 4-2 Go-bancho Chiyoda-ku, Tokyo 102.
Berlitz Schools of Languages (Japan) Inc., Kowa Bldg. 1,5f, 11-41, Alasaka 1-chrome, Minato-ku, Tokyo 107. Bernard Group, 2-8-11 Takezono, Tsukuba City, Ibaraki-Ken, 305 (recruit for British-owned schools).
Cambridge English School, Dogenzaka 225 Building, 2-23-14 Dogenzaka Shibuya-ku,Tokyo 150.
Cambridge School of English, Kikumura 91 Building1-41-20 Higashi, Ikebukuro Toshima-ku, Tokyo 170.
Cosmopolitan Language Institute, Yashima B Building, 4f 1-8-9 Yesu Chuo-ku,Tokyo 104.
CIC English Schools, Kawamoto Building, Imadegawaagaru Nishigawa Karasuma-dori, Kamigyo-ku, Kyoto.
DEH, 7-5 Nakamachi, Naka-ku, Hiroshima 730.
David English House, 2-3f Nakano Building 1-5-17 Kamiyacho Naka-ku, Hiroshima 730.
EEC Foreign Languages Institute, Shikata Building, 2f 4-43 Nakazald-Nishi 2-chrome, Kita-ku, Osaka 530.
ELEC Eigo Kenkyujo (The English Language Education Council), 3-8 Kanda Jimbo-cho Chiyoda-ku,Tokyo 101. Executive Gogaku Centre (Executive Language Centre), 1 Kasumigaseki Building, 12F 3-2-5 Kasumigaseki, Chiyoda-ku,Tokyo 100.

English Circles/EC Inc., President Building 3rd Floor, South-1, Chuo-Ku, Sapporo 060. Tel: (011) 221 0279. Japan's leading language school and conference services company seeks full-time English teachers in Sapporo, Japan's most livable city.

FCC (Fukuoka Communication Centre), Dai Roku Okabe Building, 5f Hakata Eki Higashi, 2-4-17 Hakata-ku, Fukuoka 812.

F L Centre (Foreign Language Centre), 1 Iwasaki Building, 3f 2-19-20 Shibuya-ku,Tokyo 150.

Gateway Gakuin Rokko, Atelier House, 3-1-15 Yamada-cho Nada-ku, Kobe.

ICA Kokusai Kaiwa Gakuin (International Conversation Academy), l Mikasa 2 Building, 1-16-10 Nishi Ikebukuro Toshima-ku, Tokyo 171.

IF Foreign Language Institute, 7f Shin Nakashima Building, 1-9-20 Nishi Nakashima Yodogawa-ku, Osaka.

Kains English School in Gakko, 1-5-2 Ohtemon Chuo-ku ,Fukuoka 810.

Kyoto English Centre, Sumitomo Seimei Building, Shijo-Karasuma Nishi-iru Shimogyo-ku, Kyoto

Kobe Language Centre, 3-18 Wakinoharnacho, 1-chome, Chuo-ku, Kobe 651.Tel: (78) 2614316.

Language Education Centre, 7-32 chome Ohtemachi Nakaku, Hiroshima-shi 730.

Matty's School of English, 3-15-9 Shonan-takatori, Yokosuka 234. Tel: (468) 658717.

Mobara English Institute, 618-1 Takashi, Mobara-shi Chiba-ken 297. Tel: (475) 224785.

Plus Alpha, (Agency) 2-25-20 Denenchofu, Ota-Ku, Tokyo 145.

Queens School of English, 3f Yuzuki Bldg, 4-7-14 Minamiyawata, Ichikawa 272.

Pegasus Language Services, Sankei Building 1-7-2 Otemachi Chiyoda-k, Tokyo 100.

REC School of Foreign Language, Nijojo-mae Ebisugawasagaru Higashihorikawa-dori Nakagyo-ku, Kyoto.

Royal English Language Centre, 4-31-3-2 Chyo Hakata-ku, Fukuoka 8l2.

Seido Language Institute, 12-6 Funado-cho Ashiya-shi, Kyoto.

Sun Eikaiwa School, 6f Cherisu Hachoubori Building, 6-7 Hachoubori Naka-ku, Hiroshima-shi 730.

Shane Corporation, 4f Kimura Building, 4-14-12 Nishi Funa Funabashi Shi Chiba, Ken 273.

Shane Corporation, Yutaka Dai-2 Building, 4f Higashi Kasai 6-2-8 Edogawa-Ku, Tokyo.

Shane English Schools (Head Offices):
Fujisawa, 251 Fujisawa Homon Building, 6f , Fujisawa 484-25, Fujisawa-shi, Kanagawa-ken 251.
Kimura Building, 4f, Nishifuna 4-14-12. Funabashi-shi, Chiba-ken 273.
Maehara Building, Sakuragi-cho, 2-455-2, Omiya-shi, Saitama-ken 331.

Stanton School of English, 12 Gobancho Chiyoda-ku, Tokyo 102.

Chunichi Bunka Centre, 4-5f Chunichi Building 4-4-1 Sakae Naka-ku, Nagoya 460.

Smith Ohokayama Eikaiwa School, 2-4-9 Ohokayama Meguro-ku, Tokyo 152.

Ten'noji Academy of Business and Languages, 2-9-36 Matsuzaki- cho Abeno-ku, Osaka.

Tokyo YMCA College of English, 7 Kanda Mitoshiro-Cho Chiyoda-ku, Tokyo T-101.

Tokyo Language Centre, Tatsunama Building, 1-2-19 Yaesu, Chuo-Ku, Tokyo 103.

Tokyo English Centre, (TEC) 7-9 Uguisudai-cho Shibuyaku, Tokyo 150.

Toefl Academy, 1-12-4 Kundankita, Chiyoda-ku, Tokyo 102. Tel: (3) 2303500.

World Language School Inc., Tokiwa Soga Ginko Building, 4f 1-22-8 Jinnan Shibuya-ku, Tokyo 171.

Yoko Ishikawa, 480 GO, Takaatano, Anjo, 730.

Malaysia

English is in such demand in Malaysia that even unqualified and non-native teachers should be able to pick up work fairly easily. There are opportunities in all markets, including Business English, young learners and ESL, although most work is on a part-time basis. It's quite easy to pick up private classes. Most jobs can be found through the Malay Mail and word of mouth in the huge expatriate community in Kuala Lumpur.

Visas and work permits: Apply for a visa in your home country, go to Malaysia to job-hunt and apply for a work permit once you have found something. Many teachers work on tourist visas as they wait for their papers to come through. The bureaucracy is unwieldy, slow and unpredictable.

Cost of living: Cheap, with excellent shops and street markets.

Salaries and taxes: Full-time teachers earn between RM2,000 and RM4,000 per month. The going rate for an hour-long class is between RM40 and RM50.

Non-residents pay 30 per cent tax. Once your papers are in order and you have lived in Malaysia for a certain length of time - the rules change - you become a resident and pay 15 per cent.

Accommodation: It's quite easy to find accommodation. Teachers who share normally pay around RM800. You'll need to pay a one-month deposit, a smaller deposit for the utilities bill and two months' rent up front.

Health insurance: Advisable.

Inoculations: No requirement but inoculations against Hepatitus B, Polio and Malaria may be desirable.

English language newspapers: The Malay Mail, The Star, The Sun, The New Straits Times

Important cultural differences: Malaysia is a Muslim country and students come from a very teacher-centred, non-communicative background.

Other information: Malaysia is an excellent base if you want to explore south-east Asia. It has a hot, humid climate.

List of schools in Malaysia

The English Language Centre, 1st Floor, Lot 2067, Block 10, K.C.L.D., Jalan Keretapi, PO Box 253, 93150 Kuching, Sarawak.
The Kinabulu Commercial College, 3rd & 4th Floors, Wisma Sabah, Kota Kinabulu, Sabah.

Myanmar (Formerly known as Burma)

English is essential in Myanmar and is taught in state schools from an early age. Most private language schools can't afford to pay native teachers, but with a teaching certificate and a sense of adventure it should be possible to find work. Look for adverts in the press in Singapore.

The situation is complicated by the fact that private education is not yet legal, although it is tolerated because English is in such demand. Without qualifications, it is extremely difficult to find work and there are limited opportunities for private classes. At present, there are very few English teachers in Myanmar, but the numbers are increasing every year. Schools tend to offer full-time contracts, but don't expect too many facilities.

Visas and work permits: Arrange a one-month tourist visa in your own country and then extend it when you are out there. Schools

have to apply for work permits for their foreign staff.

Cost of living: Very cheap.

Salaries and taxes: The usual salary range is from UK£4,000 per annum with accommodation to UK£12,000 for extremely well qualified teachers. The tax rate is 10 per cent.

Accommodation: There isn't much choice, but acceptable accommodation is widely available. Schools often help teachers find somewhere to live. The average rent is from US$300 to $500 per month (when quoting prices, people in Myanmar tend to jump between different hard currencies). The refundable deposits tend to be very large. They can cost between US$1,000 and 2,000.

Health insurance: Essential.

Inoculations: Hepatitis A, Malaria, Polio, Typhoid, Tetanus. Check with a doctor before planning your trip.

English language newspapers: New Light of Myanamar.

Important cultural differences: Consult guides to Myanmar, especially Culture Shock in Burma.

Singapore

English as a second language is extremely popular in Malaysia's tiny neighbour. Most of the opportunities are for qualified native speakers and Singaporeans, teaching everybody from young learners to businessmen. There is also a booming market in teaching EFL.

Not many schools offer full-time contracts but there are some private classes available. To find work, it's necessary to do the round of schools or apply from home.

Visas and work permits: Visas are not necessary for a tourist visit to Singapore, but all nationalities need work permits. You can apply for a work permit while you are in Singapore but it is not possible to work without it.

Cost of living: Singapore is wealthy and westernised.

Salaries and taxes: S$30 per hour or S$80,000 per annum on a full-time contract. Teachers usually pay around 10 per cent tax.

Accommodation: Accommodation is relatively easy to find, so schools rarely help formally, although they may lend a hand. The average rent for an apartment which can be shared is S$1,500. Three months deposit is usually expected.

Health insurance: Essential.

English language newspapers: Straits Times.

South Korea

Although not many people go to teach English in Korea at the moment, numbers seem to be increasing. Koreans are keen to learn English and it is often compared to Japan 10 years ago. In fact, Korea rivals Japan and Taiwan as a destination for teachers.

Backpackers can take casual teaching shifts on a tourist visa quite easily without any qualifications. If you want to work legally, you should find a job before you leave the country by writing to schools, registering with recruitment agencies and - if you are near a Korean community in the States - looking in the Korea Times.

You should be aware that any list of schools in Korea will be incomplete since small language schools open and close all the time. It also helps to learn a little Korean before you leave.

Often, young Koreans supplement their years of study with conversation classes to help them get into American universities. The university vacations, in July, August, January and February, see a huge increase in the number of students studying at private language schools.

Visas and work permits: It is fantastically complicated to get a visa and work permit. You will need to send a copy of your contract, a completed form from the embassy, photocopies of your qualifications, your CV, eight photos, a family statement and a photocopy of your passport to the school. You should then leave your passport and a telex fee at the embassy for three weeks.

Cost of living: Don't pack too much: it is possible to buy many things far cheaper than in the west.

Salaries and taxes: Although all teachers get paid in won, there's an enormous variation between different schools. Most teachers will need to take private classes to supplement their incomes.

Accommodation: Traditionally in the Far East, people pay a year's rent upfront and the landlord lives off the interest. Korea is no

exception, but there are ways of avoiding paying UK£8,000 for a flat. Most schools will pay the 'key money' and deduct it from salaries at source. By sharing, teachers can cut the amount needed and foreigners can sometimes negotiate a deal involving a combination of rent and a deposit. Other ways of avoiding key money include living with a family - an excellent way of learning Korean - or sleeping on a mattress on the floor in a cheap hotel.

Health insurance: Essential.

Inoculations: Hepatitis A, Polio, Typhoid.

English language newspapers: Korea Times.

Other information: Getting official information is difficult.

Taiwan

Gone are the days when anybody could pick up a little teaching work in Taiwan: in 1992 the Taiwanese government clamped down on teachers working illegally. Many schools were visited by the police and some teachers were deported.

This means that nowadays schools must get a work permit, so, according to the regulations, teachers must have a degree. There is a sharp distinction between reputable schools which will sponsor teachers and cowboy outfits which expect people to work illegally.

With low unemployment and a healthy economy, there is plenty of in-company teaching. There is plenty of demand for teachers of children. Many schools prefer American teachers.

Visas and work permits: Taiwan has some of the most complicated visa regulations in the world. There are two types of working visa available: the single entry visitor visa and the residency visa. The former is simpler since you can teach while judgement is pending and pick it up in Hong Kong. Teachers must have sponsorship and a degree to obtain a work permit. If you enter on a tourist visa and find work, you must leave the country to apply for a work permit. You need a health certificate, including the results of an AIDS test. It costs NT$1680 and it is down to the teacher to pay it.

Cost of living: High, especially in Taipei.

Salaries and taxes: Any decent school should pay about NT$400 per hour. In Taipei, schools should guarantee a minimum salary of at least NT$35,000 per month. Expect lower rates in the provinces or without qualifications.

Tax is 20 per cent for the first 183 days in Taiwan during a calendar year. After that, it's 6 per cent and you can claim back any tax paid over the previous six months which exceeded 6 per cent.

Accommodation: A room in a shared flat in Taipei costs NT$7,500 per month, less in the provinces. Most landlords will want three months' rent in advance.

Health insurance: Foreigners are entitled to join the Taiwanese government health insurance scheme for about NT$700 per month which guarantees very cheap medical cover. Reputable schools will offer a private scheme to protect teachers who fall seriously ill and require hospital treatment or need to be flown home.

Inoculations: Hepatitis A, Polio, Typhoid, Yellow Fever.

English language newspapers: China Post, China News, China Daily News.

List of schools in Taiwan:

ELS, 12 Kilung St, Taipei. Tel: 397 2304
Gram English Institute, 7th Floor, 216 Tun Hwa South Road, Sec 1, Taipei. TelL: 741 0970
Hess Language School, 83 Po Al Road, 2f Taipei. Tel: 382 5442.
Kang Ning English School, P.O. Box 95, Chutung 310. Tel: 035 952 332.

Thailand

It is getting harder and harder to find work without any qualifications and it is extremely badly paid.

Teachers considering working in Thailand should get qualified and get some experience first. They should also visit the country to see if they can cope with the culture and the climate. Avoid Bangkok if you don't like stress, pollution and noise.

There is enormous demand for English, which means that there are limitless opportunities for private classes. Previously, it was hard to find teaching work outside Bangkok but that seems to be changing.

Most recruitment is done locally, through local papers and the grapevine. It is relatively easy to find a full-time contract. You

could end up teaching anybody from children to executives, housewives to academics.

Visas and work permits: Although all nationalities require work permits, New Zealanders do not need an entry visa. All other nationalities do, but many people work on tourist visas. It's not legal and you have to leave the country every three months, but work permits can only be obtained if you work at a recognised educational institution. If you get a letter of invitation from a company, it is easier to enter the country.

Cost of living: Cheap, especially outside Bangkok.

Salaries and taxes: Qualified teachers earn between 15,000B and 20,000B per month. The tax rate is 7 per cent.

Accommodation: It's not too easy finding somewhere to live: you need a Thai speaker to help and schools don't normally give you a hand. Most accommodation tends to be too expensive or too far away.

A bedsit could cost from 5,000B per month and a two-bedroom flat is between 15,000B and 20,000B per month. Three months' rent is payable as a deposit.

Health insurance: Essential.

Inoculations: Typhoid, Hepatitus and Tetanus are advised.

English language newspapers: Bangkok Post and The Nation.

Important cultural differences: Do some research before you go to Thailand: it has a completely different culture and there are too many differences to list here.

List of schools in Thailand

American University Language Centre, 179 Rajadarmi Road, Bankok 10330. Tel: 252 8170/3
ECC, 430/19-20 Chula 64, Siam Square, Bangkok 10330. Tel: 2551856.
The English Language Schools, 26/3, 26/9 Chonphol Lane 15, Bangkok 10900. Tel: 25110439.
Training Creativity Development in Languages, 28 Soi Kasem (24) Suhkumvit Road, Bangkok 10110. Tel: 2587036.
LCC Language Institute, 8/64-67 Ratchadapisek-Larprao Road, Bangkhaen, Bangkok 10900.

The Rest Of Asia

There are some private teaching opportunities but most work available is with voluntary or aid organisations.

 nglish teachers are in less demand than in the Far East, but it should be possible to work in Asia as a volunteer. Since English is one of India's official languages, there is very little demand for foreigners to teach: there are many qualified and competent Indian teachers. It is extremely difficult to arrange a work permit.

Opportunities are also extremely restricted in Mauritius since foreign nationals are rarely granted work permits. Projects in Bhutan, Mongolia and Pakistan are generally organised through aid agencies such as VSO, the United Nations, CfBT, the Peace Corps plus the British Council and the Bell Educational Trust.

If you want to work in Kazakhstan, Kyrghystan, Turkmenistan and Uzbekistan, contact the Peace Corps.

Please note that aid agencies cannot normally guarantee volunteers work in the country of their choice.

Bangladesh

English is in great demand in Bangladesh, both as a foreign and as a second language, but the British Council runs the only school, in the western sense of the word. Most opportunities tend to be in part-time private work.

There are opportunities for unqualified teachers, especially the spouses of those working in Dhaka. Qualified teachers often end up in teacher training.

Visas and work permits: All nationalities need entry permits and work permits. Some people do work on tourist visas although it is not legal. It can take months for the correct papers to come through.

Cost of living: Cheap.

Salaries and taxes: Paid on an hourly basis. Foreigners do not usually pay tax.

Accommodation: It's fairly easy to find accommodation since a lot of new flats are being built. However, the drawback is that a year's rent is generally expected in advance. Flats cost around UK£300 per month, so, even if you share, it is expensive.

The British Council finds accommodation for its teaching staff.

Health insurance: Essential.

Inoculations: Hepatitis, Rabies.

English language newspapers: The Daily Star, The Bangladesh Observer, The Independent.

Other information: Dhaka is very crowded and noisy with poor sanitation.

Nepal

Kathmandu offers the best prospects for English language teachers. Visitors should be able to pick up some work, but for a long-term stay, only the British Council and the American Language Center will be able to get you a visa. Apply for work before you leave your home country.

Voluntary Services Overseas, the Peace Corps and other voluntary organisations all operate in Nepal. Apply to their relevent headquarters well in advance - the process can take more than a year. If you apply to VSO, there's no guarantee that you will end up in Nepal.

Visas and work permits: A two-week tourist visa is available on entry. Residency visas and work permits have to be arranged by the employer. People do work unofficially on tourist visas, but be careful with the date stamps.

Cost of living: Extremely cheap.

Salaries and taxes: Salaries are low. At US$10 per hour, the highest rates are paid by the British Council and the American Language Center.

Accommodation: Agents will find you a flat for a small fee. A two-bedroom flat will cost around US$100-150 per month. Deposits aren't usual for informal agreements, but if your company finds the flat, you can pay anything between US$300 and more than US$5,000.

Health insurance: Essential.

Inoculations: Hepatitis; Rabies; Tetanus; Japanese Encephatitus.

English language newspapers: The Rising Nepal and The Kathmandu Post.

Important cultural differences: Nepal is a culturally diverse and challenging place. The Hindu/Buddhist/Christian/Moslem faiths and traditions are all here.

Papua New Guinea

English is an official language in Papua New Guinea - education is all in English. However, with over 800 language groups, English is only loosely the second language. Jobs exist mainly in the secondary sector, and few are purely EFL posts. Teacher training is fairly advanced. Salaries are not high, although taxes are.

Visa requirements: Teachers must secure a job before applying for a working visa. The employer has to lodge an application with the authorities in Papua New Guinea and the prospective employee must apply to the immigration department of any Papua New Guinea High Commission.

Other information: The locals are excellent linguists. Although a beautiful country, their High Commission in London say it is not a suitable destination for "those of nervous disposition", and some areas are controlled by bandits.

VSO and the UN also recruit volunteers to work in Papua New Guinea.

Addresses:

University of Papua New Guinea, Allude, for teacher training.
Papua New Guinea University of Technology, Lae, for tertiary EFL.

Sri Lanka

The civil war between the Tamils and Sinhalese is confined to the North and East of the country but it is worth checking the exact situation before you leave: at the time of going to press, violence was escalating. English is in demand and it is encouraged by the government as a way of bridging the gap between the two sides of the civil war.

There aren't many language schools. VSO and the British Council have a presence and there are a number of international or British schools. It is impossible to find work on spec.

Visas and work permits: The employer gets the work permit; the employee gets the visa.

Cost of living: Cheap.

Salaries and taxes: Most teachers earn UK£2,000 per annum, which is a good local salary. British Council employees who have the diploma could earn between UK£11,000 and £13,000, half of which is paid in sterling and half of which is paid in rupees. There is no tax in the first year.

Accommodation: A three-bedroom flat will cost UK£250 per month. A year's rent is paid upfront. It is advisable to share and go with some savings.

Health insurance: Advisable.

Inoculations: Hepatitis A, Polio, Typhoid, Malaria, Yellow Fever.

English language newspapers: The Island, Daily News.

Important cultural differences: There are extremes of riches and poverty. Many people have domestic servants.

List of Schools in Sri Lanka

International English Language Services (PVT) Ltd., 292/1 Galle Road, Colombo 4. Tel: (94) 1 590 707.

A WORD OF WARNING

The cultural, economic or political troubles in some countries mean it is advised that you proceed with great care should you decide to work in them. Conditions change and you should always check with your embassy before taking up employment in a volatile area. At the time of going to press the UK Foreign Office advised its nationals against visiting:

Afghanistan, Algeria, Angola, Boznia/Herzovagina, Burundi, Iraq, Kashmir, Liberia and Western Sahara.

It also advised that only visits on essential business should be made to:

The Congo, Ruanda and Zaire.

Latin America and the Caribbean

Despite the political and economic volatility of some of the countries in this regions there is still a demand for English teachers.

There are opportunities for teachers in the bigger Latin American countries - Mexico, Argentina, Brazil, Chile - but economic problems seem always to come and go. Opportunities sometimes arise in Bolivia, one of Latin America's poorest countries. Positions are usually in English medium-secondary schools or with voluntary organisations.

The opportunities in Belize, Dominican Republic, the eastern Caribbean, Guatemala, Guyana, Honduras, Nicaragua and Panama are mainly for volunteers or people working illegally on tourist visas. Economic problems mean that Cuba is not a destination for English language teachers.

Teachers sometimes work illegally or semi-legally in private schools or bilingual schools in Costa Rica, one of the richest countries in central America. For further information contact The Instituto Britanico, Apd. 8184, San Jose 1000.

Teaching in El Salvador is not to be recommended unless it is arranged by an aid agency.

Argentina

Gone are the days when backpackers could pick up a little teaching work in Argentina as they travelled around Latin America: nowadays there is plenty of competition from English language graduates and English-speaking immigrants. English is big business and there are increasing numbers of schools.

There are always vacancies for qualified teachers and Argentina seems to have a huge turnover of teachers. Private classes are not difficult to find.

It is best to start writing application letters in October. This gives employers enough time to arrange a work-permit for a March start. If you want to go out to look for work on spec, the best time is in late January.

Visas and work permits: It is not possible to find anything other than private classes without any papers. No special entry visa is required because employers can arrange a work permit, but the process is lengthy and bureaucratic, taking up to eight months. It is best to look for work months before you intend to leave.

The government welcomes qualified immigrants. You can apply for a residency permit after two years in the country.

Cost of living: Fairly high. The Argentinian economy is relatively healthy and inflation is low by Latin American standards.

Salaries and taxes: Pay depends on qualifications and experience. It is common practice to pay teachers per course - usually 10-12 hours per month for each course - and earnings vary between US$100-300 per month for this work. Expect to earn the equivalent of about US$1,500-1,800 per month for 25 hours, teaching work.

The going rate for private classes in Buenos Aires is US$30-35 per hour, and around $25 per hour elsewhere.

Return flights are often included in contracts if you find your job while you are overseas.

Accommodation: A one-bedroomed flat could cost around US$400, with a two-month deposit. Teachers often live in family-owned pensiones until they have saved enough money for a flat.

Health insurance: Local medical care is expensive. Private medical insurance is recommended.

Inoculations: Cholera, Hepatitis A, Polio, Typhoid, Malaria.

Important cultural differences: The academic year is from March to December.

List of schools in Argentina

British Councul, Marcalo T De Alvera 590 (4th Floor), 1058 Buenos Aires. Tel: 54 1 311 9814
Colegio Peralta Ramos, Maipu y Salta, 7600 mar de Plata, Buenos Aries.
The Franklin Institute, Vicente Lopez 54, Salta 4400.
IELI, Alberti 6444, San Jose de la Esquina, Santa Fe 2185.
Instituto Cultural Argentino-Britanico, Calle 12, No 1900, La Plata.
Instituto Rush, La Prida 820, Tucman.
International House, IH Belgrano, Arcos 1830, 1428 Capital Federal, Buenos Aires. Tel: 541 785 4425
Liceo Superior de Cultura Inglesa, Italia 830, Tandil, 7000 Pica de Buenos Aries.
St John's School, Recta Martinoli 3452, V Belgrano 5417 Cordoba, Pica de Cordoba.

Brazil

English is in demand in Brazil, but things are complicated by the red tape involved in getting a visa. Teachers can either go out to Brazil on spec or apply for jobs from home in February or July.

If you do decide to go out on spec, there are intensive courses which start all year. Otherwise, it is best to contact the national headquarters of chains which have schools in Brazil.

Poor teaching in the state sector means that parents are keen to get native speakers to teach their children. There is increasing competition from Brazilian teachers with excellent levels of English.

Visas and work permits: It is the individual's responsibility to arrange a working visa, which takes at least two months. You need to be qualified and have at least two year's experience to be eligible.

It is possible to come to Brazil, find a job, apply for a visa and pick it up in a neighbouring country, but it is not popular with the beareaucrats. It is worth checking with the Brazilian embassy before you leave since the rules might be changed. Visitors can work illegally without papers, but it is not recommended.

Cost of living: Basic items such as food are very cheap but consumer products are more expensive than in the UK or USA. The currency is still very unstable.

Salaries and taxes: Teachers are paid for 13 months but the levels depend very much on the region. Don't expect to save a great deal, but incomes can be supplemented with private classes. Teachers with the diploma can expect to earn nine times as much as unqualified teachers.

Tax is 25 per cent and includes a contribution to the national medical scheme.

Accommodation: Some schools provide it free, others subsidise it. Expect to pay between a third and a half of your salary.

Health insurance: Can be taken out locally.

Inoculations: Cholera, Hepatitis A, Polio, Typhoid, Malaria.

English language newspapers: Brazil Herald.

Important cultural differences: The two semesters start after carnival - normally in February - and in August.

Other useful information: Internal flights are expensive, but many airlines offer special deals on air passes which you can only get outside Brazil.

Brazil is an enormous country, so it is worth doing more research into the areas you are interested in.

List of schools in Brazil

Britannia Schools, Rua Garcia D'Avila 58, Ipanema, Rio De Janeiro RJ, 22421-010. Tel: (55 21) 511-0940. Fax: (55 21) 511-0893.

Britannia Special English Studies, Rua Dr Timoteo, 752 Moinhos De Vent, Porto Alegre Rs.

Britannia Special English Studies - Juniors, Rua. Barao da Torre 599 - Rio de Janeiro, CEP 22411-003, Rj. Tel: 55 21 239-8044. Fax: 55 21 286-0861. .

Britannia Executive School, Rua Barao De Lucena 61, Botofogo, Rio de Janeiro 22260.

Britannic English Course, Rua Joao Ivo Da Silva 125, Recife Pe.

Cambridge Sociedade Brasileira do Cultura Inglesa, Rua Piaui 1234, Londrina 86020 320 Pr. Tel: 043 324 -1092.Fax: 324-8391

Casa Branca, Rua Machado De Assis 372 Boqueirao, Santos Sp.

Ccli, Rua Dr Silvio Henrique Braune 15, Nova Friburgo Rj.

Cel-Lep, Av. Cidade Jardin 625, Sao Paulo - Sp.

Centro de Enseñanza P.L.I., Rua de Octubro, 1234 Conj 4, Porto Alegre, RS 90000.C

Centro De Cultura Inglesa, Av Guapore 2.236, Cacoal - RO, CEP 78 975-000. Tel: 55 (69) 441-2833. Fax: 441-5346.

Centro De Cultura Inglesa, Rua 12 De Outubro 227, Cuiaba Mt.

Cultura Inglesa, Rua Mamanguape 411, Boa Vigem, Recife Pe.

Cultura Inglesa, Rua Goias 1507, Londrina Pr, School House, Rua 4, No. 80 Esq. Rua 3, Goiania Go.

Cultura Inglesa, Av Bernardo Vieira De Melo 2101, Jaboatao Pe.

Cultura Inglesa, Rua Natal 553 V. Municipal, Arianopolis, Manaus -Am.

Cultura Inglesa, Visinde De Alburquerque 205, Madalena, Recife Pe.

Cultura Inglesa, Goiana, Rua 86 No.7 - Setor 74083-330 Goiana - Go. Tel: 55 62 241-4516, Fax: 241-2582.

Cultura Inglesa, Rua Ponta Grossa 1565, Dourados Ms.

Cultura Inglesa, Av. Barao De Maruim 761, Aracaju, Sergipe 49015-040. Tel: 55 97 224-7360/4637. Fax: 221-1195.

Cultura Inglesa, Av Ouze 1281, Ituiutaba Mg.

Cultura Inglesa, Rua Eduardo De Moraes 147, Bairro Novo

Olinda Pe.

Cultura Inglesa, Av Tiradentes 670, 36300 Sao Joao Del Rei MG. Tel: (032) 371-4377, Fax: (032) 371-4377.

English Forever, Rua. Rio Grande Do Sul, 356, Pituba, Salvador-Ba.

Ibi, Sep Sul Entrequadra 710/910, Brasilia Df.

Inst Academico De Cultura Inglesa, RuaConde De Porto Alegre 59, Duque De Caxias Rj.

Instituto Britanico, R Dep Carvalho Deda 640, 49025-070 Salgado Filho, Aracaju SE. Tel: 079-23-2791. Fax: 079-27-2645.

International House-Matriz, The School House, Rua 4, 80 Se Goiania 74110-140, Goais.

Liberty English Centre, R Amintas De Barros 1059, Curitiba Pr.

Sbci, Casa Forte, Av 17 De Agosto 223, Recife Pe.

Sbci, Av Dos Andradas, 536 Juiz De Fora Mg.

Sbci, Rua Antonio De Alburquerque 746, Belo Horizonte Hg.

Sbci, Rua Do Progresso 239, Recife Pe.

Sbci, Rua Raul Pompeia 231, Rio De Janeiro Rj.

Sbci, Ponta Verde, R Eng Marion De Gusmao 603, Maceio Al.

Sbci, Rua Marechal Deodoro 1326, Franca Sp.

Sbci, Rua Visc De Inhauma 980, Ribeirao Preto Sp.

Sbci, Rua Julia Da Costa 1500, Curitiba Pr.

Sbci, Rua Humberto De Campos, Campo Grande Ms.

Sbci, Pca Rosalco Ribeiro 10, Maceio Al.

Sbci, Rua Joao Pinheiro 808, Uberlandia Mg.

Sbci, Av Rio Grande Do Sul 1411, Joao Possoa Pb.

Sbci, Av Guilherme Ferreira 650, Uberaba Mg,

Sbci, Rua Maranhao 416, Sao Paulo Sp.

Sbci, Rua Acu 495, Petropolis, Natal Rn.

Sbci, Rua Plinio Moscoso 945, Jardim Apopema, Salvador Ba.

Sbci, Rua Ana Bilmar 171, Aldeota, Fortaleza Ce.

Sbci, Rua Jeronimo Coelho 233, Joinville Sc.

Sbci, Av Simoa Gomes 400, Garanhuns Pe,

Sbci, Seps 709/908 Conjunto B, Brasilia Df.

Sbci, Rua. Sao Sebastiao 1530, Sao Carlos - Sp.

Sbci, Rua Mal Floriano Peixoto 433, Blumenau Sc.

Sbci, Av Rio Branco 17, Haringa Pr.

Sbci, R Paula Xavier 501, Ponta Grossa Pr.

Sbci, Praca Mauricio Cardoso 49, Porto Alegre Rs.

Sbci, Av. Gov. Jose Malcher 1094, Belem Pa.

Seven Language & Culture, R. Bela Cintra 898, 01415-000, Sao Paulo - Sao Paolo.

Soc. Bras. de Cultura Inglesa, R. Fernandes Tourinho, 538 - Savassi BH-MG 30112.000 Tel: 031 221 6770

St. Peter's English School, Rua Berilo Guimaraes, 182 Centro Itabuna, Bahia.

Universitas, R Gongalves Dias 858, Belo Horizonte Mg.

Chile

English is in demand in Chile. Although there is a slim possibility of finding work without a qualification, it is advisable to get a recognised teaching certificate: this means your employer can apply for a one-year permit.

All the main markets are covered in Chile, from business learners to children. Most jobs tend to be part-time, but there is the possibility of private classes.

Visas and work permits: You should apply for a visa and a work permit at home. You are not allowed to work on a tourist visa.

Cost of living: Cheap.

Salaries and taxes: Teachers' salaries vary from UK£5 to UK£10 per hour.

Accommodation: Schools don't help teachers find accommodation, but it's easy to stay in hostals which offer long-term accommodation with good facilities. A room costs around UK£100 per month, a flat costs about UK£220 per month. Landlords expect one month's deposit with one month upfront.

Health insurance: Essential.

Inoculations: Hepatitis A, Polio, Typhoid.

English language newspapers: News Review.

Important cultural differences: The academic year runs from March to December.

List of schools in Chile

British Council, Eliodora Yanez 832, Casilla 115 Correo 55, Santiago. Tel: 56 2 236 1199

Craighouse, Casilla 20007, Correo 20, Santiago. Tel: 242 4011

Instituto Chileno-Britanico De Cultura, Mondea 1467, Santiago. Tel: 696 3215

Colombia

Not surprisingly, it is quite easy to find work in Colombia since many teachers are scared off by its violent reputation. In fact, foreigners are unlikely to get involved in any trouble.

Fe

Teachers have the best prospects in the big cities. North Americans are in great demand, with American English being the first choice for most Colombians. Many of the private schools are American-owned. There are also English Medium International Schools, Centros Americanos and British Council centres in Bogota and Cali.

It is possible for unqualified teachers to find work, but don't expect to earn enough to live on. As a stop-gap while travelling, it's fine, but if you want to stay more than a few months, get qualified first.

Visas and work permits: All non-Colombian teachers must have a permit. It is only possible for well-qualifed teachers to get a permit.

Red tape is a problem and delays in issuing visas and work permits should be expected. Any reputable institution will get the permit and visa for its employees; reluctance to do so means the schools should be treated with caution.

Cost of living: Low, but inflation is currently around 20 per cent. Teachers have a good standard of living despite low salaries.

Salaries and taxes: The average monthly salary ranges from between 825,000 and 1,120,000 pesos per month. Many institutions pay teachers 14 times in a 12-month period. With a normal work visa, teachers will pay anything from 8 per cent tax. Unqualified teachers getting paid by the hour can expect to earn as little as 1,600 pesos.

Accommodation: In Bogota and most other cities, expect to pay about 250,000 pesos for a one-bedroom flat in a reasonably exclusive area.

Health insurance: Essential.

List of schools in Colombia

Bogata
Academia Ingles Para Niños, Calle 106 No 16-26, Bogota.
Advanced Learning Service, Transversal 20 No 120-15, Bogota.
Aprender Ltda, Calle 17 No 4-68 Ql. 501, Bogota.
Aspect, Calle 79a No 8-26, Bogota.
BBC De Londres, Calle 59 No 6-21, Bogota.
Babel, Avenida 15 No 124-49 Cf. 205, Bogota.
Bi Cultural Institute, Avenida 7 No 123-97 Of. 202, Bogota.
Britanico Americano De Idiomas, Avenida 13 No 103-62, Bogota.

The British Council, Calle 87 No 12-79, Bogota
Carol Keeney, Carrera 4 No 69-06, Bogota.
Centro Audiovisual De Ingles Chelga, Calle 137 No 25-26, Bogota.
Centro Colombo Andino, Calle 19 No 3-16 Of. 203, Bogota.
Centro De Ingles Lincoln, Calle 49 No 9-37, Bogota.
Centro De Idiomas Winston Salem, Calle 45 No 13-75, Bogota.
Centro De Lengua Inglesa, Calle 61 No 13-44 Of. 402, Bogota.
Coningles, Calle 63 No 13-24 Of. 502, Bogota.
English For Infants (John Dewey), Diagonal 110 No 40-85, Bogota.
English Language & Culture Institute (Elci), Calle 90 No 10-51, Bogota.
Escuela De Idiomas Berlitz, Calle 83 No 19-24, Bogota.
Genelor International, Avenida 78 No 20-49 Piso 20, Bogota.
I.C.L., Calle 119 No 9a-25, Bogota.
Ingles Cantando Y Jugando, Calle 106 No 16-26, Bogota.
Instituto Anglo Americano De Idiomas, Carrera 16a No 85-34 Of. 204, Bogota.
Instituto Electronico De Idiomas, Carrera 6 No 12-64 Piso, Bogota.
Instituto Meyer, Calle 17 No 10-16 Piso 80, Bogota.
Interlingua Ltda., Carrera 18 No 90-38, Bogota.
International Language Institute Ltda, Carrera 11 No. 65-28 Piso 3, Bogota, Tel: 571 235-8152/72. Fax: 310-2892.
International System, Transversal 6 No 51 A 33, Bogota.
K.O.E De Columbia, Calle 101 A No 31-02, Bogota.
Life Ltda., Transversal 19 No 100-52, Bogota.
.Oxford Centre, A.A. 102420, Santate de Bogota.
Way's English School, Calle 101 No 13 A 17, Bogota.

Barranquilla
Boston School of English Ltda, Carrera 43 No 44-02, Barranquilla.
California Institute Of English, Carrera 51 No 80-130, Barranquilla.
Centro De Lenguas Modernas, Carrera 38 No 69 C 65, Barranquilla.
Esquela De Ingles, Calle 53 No 38-25, Barranquilla.
Idiomas-Munera-Cros Ltda, Carrera 58 No 72-105, A.A. 52032, Barranquilla.
Instituto De Lenguas Modernas, Carrera 41 No 52-05, Baranquilla.
Instituto Experimental De Atlantico, "jos Celestino Mutis", Calle 70 No 38-08, Barranquilla.
Instituto De Ingles Thelma Tyzon, Carrera 59 No 74-73, Barranquilla.

Cali/Cartegina
Ave, Carrera 45 El Palo 52-59, Cali.
Centro De Idiomas Winston Salem, Avenida La Ceste No 10-27, Santa Teresita, Cali.
Instituto Bridge Centro De Idiomas, Carrera 65 No 49 A 09, Cali.
Centro De Idiomas Y Turismo De Cartagena, Popa Calle 30 No 20- 177, Cartagena.
Ceico, Calle Siete Infantes, San Diego, Cartagena.
International Language Institute Ltda, Carrera 13 No 5-79 Castillogrande, Cartagena.
Medellin
Business Language Centre Ltda., Carrera 49 No 15-85, Medellin.
Centro De Idiomas Winston Salem, Transversal 74 No C2-33 Laureies, Medellin.
Easy English, Carrera 45 A No 34 Sur 29 Torre No 4, Portal Del Cerro , A. A. 80511, Envigado, Medellin.
El Centro Ingles, El Poblado Carrera 10 A.No 36-39, Medellin.

Neiva
Centro Anglo Frances, Carrera 11 No 6-12, Neiva.
International Language Institute, Carrera 5a No 21-35, Neiva.

Costa Rica

One of the safest but most expensive Latin American countries. There are many private language schools, but often with huge classes of mixed ability and poor facilities. Qualified teachers who speak Spanish could work in the private bilingual schools. Qualified teachers can enjoy a reasonable standard of living in a beautiful, friendly and diverse country.

Salary and taxes: The equivalent of $300 per month.

Visa requirements: Rarely a problem.

Accommodation: $100-200 a month for a shared flat.

For further information contact:
The Instituto Britanico, Apdo. 8184 San Jose 1000
Tel: 25 0256.

Cuba

Cuba is facing economic difficulties now that Russia no longer helps its economy. However, the growing tourism market may cause growth in the demand for English

Minimum salary: The state system has a set wage. The private sector pays a small salary in dollars which is convertible on the black market.

Tax and health insurance: No tax, free health insurance, but private cover is advisable.

Visa requirements: There is a restricted immigration policy, so it is hard to get a work permit. Apply to the local Cuban embassy, or contact the British Council in Havana.

Accommodation: Difficult to find.

List of schools in Cuba

Universidad de Cienfuegos, Departamento de Inglés, Carretera a Rodas, Km 4, Cuatro Cam. Cienfuegos 55100.

Ecuador

There is a plethora of language schools in Ecuador, making it very easy for English teachers to find work, whether they are qualified or not. In fact, it is one country where unqualified teachers might be at an advantage since it is difficult for career teachers to get ahead.

Many ex-British Council teachers have set up their own reputable schools, but it's important to have personal contacts to work in them. Other private language schools tend to be less fussy.

The demand for business and general English and young learner classes is enormous, especially in the cities. Conditions vary a great deal from the smallest operations imaginable to the British Council.

Most recruitment is done locally, except at the British Council which hires teachers through its own network.

Visas and work permits: It is illegal to work on a tourist visa, but, of course, some teachers do. It is only valid for three months; you have to prove you have an independent income to have it extended.

You are only entitled to spend six months of any year in Ecuador if you are on a tourist visa, so if you arrive in July and leave at Christmas you could spend 12 months there.

If you intend to work legally, there is a rule which says that a tourist visa cannot be swapped for any other kind of visa. Effectively, this means that you have to come in on a tourist visa, find a job and leave the country to pick up the working visa which your new employer should sponsor.

Cost of living: Cheap.

Salaries and taxes: The monthly rates for unqualified teachers is UK£150, rising to £250 in more reputable schools. The British Council pays £600 and only looks at teachers with certificates. Everyone is taxed at 7 per cent, regardless of legality.

Accommodation: It's very easy to find a full range of accommodation, from bedsits to flats and shared houses. Expect to pay around £40 per month for a room in a shared flat or £100 for a place of your own. The usual deposit is two months' rent.

Health insurance: Essential. Buy it before you come.

Inoculations: Hepatitis A, Polio, Typhoid, Malaria, Yellow Fever.

English language newspapers: Q Magazine has job adverts in it. Inside Ecuador is the other local EL paper.

Important cultural differences: Passing exams is considered more important than actually learning.

Other information: Check the rate of inflation before you go. It can be anywhere between 20 and 300 per cent.

List of language schools in Ecuador

Benedict, 9 De Octubre 1515, Y Orellana, Quito.
Lingua Franca, Edificio Jerico, 12 De Octubre 2449 y Orellana, Casilla 17-2-68, Quito. Tel: 546075. Fax: 593-2-568664.
Quito Language And Culture Centre, Republica De El Salvador, 639 Y Portugal, Quito.

Jamaica

Although Jamaica's first language is English there is some work available teaching EFL to new Jamaican residents plus some Business and Remedial English.

Visas and work permits: There is no need for an entry visa but you will need a work permit which are best applied for in Jamaica.

Salaries and taxes: Income tax is 25%. There is also a 15% General Consumption Tax. Working in a school you could expect

to earn in the region of J$140 an hour. For private lessons you may earn in the region of J$200-J$500

Accommodation: Rents vary widely ((J$7,000 - J$20,000 for a studio or 1 Bedroom flat). Deposits are usually one or two months' rent. Affordable accommodation is very hard to find..

Health insurance: Advisable.

List of schools in Jamaica

Language Training Centre Ltd, 24 Parkington Plaza, Kingston 10. Tel (809) 926 03756
Target English Associates, 9a Duquesnam Ave., Kingston 10, Tel: (809) 929 2473

Mexico

Mexico's proximity to the US means that English will always be in demand. At the moment it's relatively easy to find teaching jobs on spec, even though the economy is still troubled.

Teachers are mainly recruited locally because schools can no longer afford to pay for a flight. As always, you will stand a better chance of finding something if you give the impression that you want to stay in the country for a couple of years. A certificate will help greatly to find work. Most contracts are full-time for 12 months.

The main market is for company classes. English is becoming increasinglty important for Mexican business with the economic union with the States and Canada.

Visas and work permits: It usually takes a couple of months for visas and work permits to come through once you have found a job. Even if you initially come on a tourist visa, you must get your documents certified by a lawyer who will confirm that your qualifications are valid. Your nearest Mexican consulate will then stamp them.

When you are looking for work in Mexico, ask employers if they will get the relevent papers for you. If not, it is extremely difficult. If you have the right papers, you can do casual work on a three-month tourist visa while you wait for them to be processed.

Cost of living: In Mexico City much higher than most people expect. Elsewhere it is still cheap, but rising steadily. Expect a lower income in the provinces.

Peru

Salaries and taxes: Teachers are paid a Mexican salary of around UK£400 per month. This is enough to live on, but don't expect to save a great deal unless you take lots of private classes. As a rule, Mexican companies have not been giving pay rises to keep up with inflation, but occasionally employees are compensated. Taxation is around 25-35 per cent.

Accommodation: There are cheap places to live if you look outside city centres. A small flat will cost around UK£90-100 per month for two people. Most people spend between a quarter and a third of their salary on accommodation. Furnished accommodation is rare.

Health insurance: Essential. It is expensive in Mexico.

Inoculations: Hepatitis A, Polio, Typhoid, Malaria, Yellow Fever.

English language newspapers: There are jobs in The Mexico City Times and The News.

Other information: Check the rate of inflation before setting out.

List of schools in Mexico

Univ. Autonoma De Aguascalientes, Rio Tamesis 438, 20100 Aguascalientes, Ags.
Universidad Autonoma De Baja California Sur, Carr. Al Sur. Km. 5.5, 23080 La Paz, Bcs.
Univ. Aut Del Carmen, Fac. De Ciencias Educativas, 24170 Cd. Del Carmen , Camp Alabama 2401, Quintas Del Sol, 31250 Chiuahua, Chih.
Universidad Autonoma De Chiapas, Apdo. Postal No. 933, 29000 Tuxtla Gutierrez, Chis Cipresses No. 12, Fracc. Los Laureles, 30780 Tapachula, Chis.
Univ Aut De Coahuila, Depto. De Idiomas, Hidalgo Y Gonzalez Lobo, Col. Republica De Oriente, 25280 Saltillo, Coah.
Universidad De Colima, Escuela De Lenguas Extranjeras, Josefa Ortiz De Dominguez S/N, 28950 Villa De Alvarez, Col.
Univ. Aut. De Guerrero, Av. Lazaro Cardenas 86, 39000 Chilpancingo, Gro.
Universidad De Guanajuato, Centro De Idiomas, Lascurian De Retana 5, 36000 Guanajuato , Gto.
Universidad Autonoma De Hidalgo, Centro De Lenguas, Carr. Pachuca/Tulancingo S/N, 42000 Pachuca, Hgo.
Universidad De Guadalajara, Esc Superior De Lenguas Modernas, Apdo. Postal 2-416, 44280 Guadalajara, Jal.
Univ Autonoma Del Edo De Mexico, Centro De Ensenanza De Lenguas, Rafael M. Hidalgo No. 401 Pte., 50130 Toluca, Edo De

Mexico.
Universidad Autonoma Del Edo De Morelos, Centro De Lenguas, Rayon 7b- Centro, 62000 Cuernavaca, Mor.
Universidad Autonoma De Neuvo Leon, Fac. Filosofia Y Letras, Apdo. Postal 3024, 64000 Monterrey, Nl, Mil Cumbres No. 4853, Col. Villa Mitras, 64170 Monterrey, Nl
Univ Aut Benito Juarez De Oaxaca, Centro De Idiomas, Armenta Y Lopez 700, Centro, 68000 Oaxaca De Juarez, Oax.
Universidad Autonoma De Puebla, Dpto Lenguas, 4 Sur 104, 72000 Puebla, Pue.
Universidad Autonoma De Queretaro, Escuela De Idiomas, Cerro De Las Campanas, 76010 Queretaro, Qro.
Universidad Autonoma De San Luis Potosi, Centro De Idiomas, Zaragoza No. 410, 78200 San Luis Potosi, S.L.P.
Universidad De Sonora, Idiomas, Rosales Y Blvd. Luis Encinas, 83000 Hermosillo, Son,.
Universidad Autonoma De Tlaxcala, Depto De Filosofia Y Letras, Carretera A San Gabriel S/N, 90000 Tlaxcala , Tlax.
Universidad Veracruzana Udih, Fac. De Idiomas, Fco Moreno Esq Ezequiel Alatriste, 91020 Xalapa, Ver.
Universidad Autonoma De Yucatan, Fac. De Educacion, Calle 61 No 525 (Entre 66 Y 68), 97000 Merida, Yuc.
Universidad Autonoma De Zacatecas, Centro De Idiomas, Alameda 422, 98000 Zacatecas, Zac.

Peru

English is becoming more commonly studied. Unqualified teachers can work in volunteer agencies and it is possible to take private classes.. A full-time contract is a prerequisite for a work permit.

The main markets are for general English and ESP, especially for business, a big growth area. It's best to find a job before you leave the country in order to sort out a work permit.

Visas and work permits: It's illegal to work on a tourist visa, but a few people do. The immigration authorities are weeding them out. To work in Peru, you must have a work permit issued in Peru. It takes two to three months to come through.

Cost of living: Cheap.

Salaries and taxes: Teachers tend to earn between UK£3,000 and £5,000 pa in private schools, more in the British Council. The tax rate is 16 per cent.

Accommodation: The average rent is between UK£150 and £200 per month, with two months' rent paid in advance as a deposit. Schools generally help teachers find somewhere to live.

Health insurance: Essential.

Inoculations: Hepatitis A, Polio, Typhoid, Malaria, Yellow Fever.

List of schools in Peru

Interaction In English, Manco Capac 649, Miraflores, Lima 18.
Newton College, Av Ricardo Elias, Aparic, Urb Las Lagunas De La Molina, Miraflores, Lima 12. Tel: 363 211
William Shakespere Instituto De Inglese, Avenida Dos Mayo 1105, San Isidro, Lima. Tel: 221 313.

Uruguay

Qualified English teachers should find work quite easily. English is in demand, but most of the teaching is done by Uruguayans, giving native speakers rarity value. Even so, unqualified teachers will probably only be able to find private classes.

It is relatively easy to find private classes but most of the work is in bilingual schools for children. Most recruitment is done locally.

Visas and work permits: Expect a wait and a trip across the border to pick up your documents.

Cost of living: The standard of living has more in common with Argentina and Chile than its poorer neighbours.

Salaries and taxes: Schools pay around 90 pesos per hour, with 20 per cent tax. Teachers earn more from private classes.

Accommodation: Expensive. In hard currency, you will probably pay between US$300 and 400 a month, with two months' deposit.

Health insurance: Essential.

Inoculations: Hepatitis A, Polio, Typhoid.

List of schools in Uruguay

British Schools, Maximo Tajes esq Havre, Carrasco, Montevideo.
Dickens Institute, 21 De Setiembre 3090, Cp 11300 Montevideo.
English Studio Centre, Obligado 1221, Montevideo.
Instituto Cultural Anglo-Uruguayo, Casilla de Correo 5087

Sec.1, San Jose 1426, Montevideo.
London Institute School of Languages, Caramaru 5609, Montevideo.Tel: 61 33 83.We teach English, Spanish and Portuguese for English and French speaking people. Summer courses too.
St Patrick's College, Av J.M. Ferrari 1307, Montevideo.

Venezuela

Economic difficulties have made Venezuala a less attractive destination. Inflation is very high and most schools do not renegotiate their salaries. You should either apply directly to the British Council or the American Bi-National Centres from your own country or save money first.There are small private schools which will take on backpackers - qualified or not - but the pay is not good. Most recruitment is done locally.

Visas and work permits: A lot of paperwork is involved. Teachers can job-hunt on a tourist visa, but it means leaving the country while the working visa is being arranged. It is possible to work on a tourist visa, but the authorities are cracking down.

Cost of living: Extremely high if you are paid at local rates.

Salaries and taxes: Not linked to inflation.

Accommodation: Expensive. Check inflation rates before you go or try to persuade your employer to include it in the package.

Health insurance: Essential.

Inoculations: Hepatitis A, Polio, Typhoid, Malaria, Yellow Fever.

English language newspapers: The Daily Journal.

Other Information: Check state of economy before heading out.

List of schools in Venezuela

Berlitz Escuela de Idiomas, Av. Madrid, Urb. Las Mercedes, Caracas 1060.
The British Council, Torre La Noria, Piso 6, Paseo Enrique Eraso, Urb. Las Mercedes, Aptdo. 65131, Caracas 1065.
Centro Venezolano-Americano, Av. Principal Jose Marti, Urb. Las Mercedes, Caracas 1060.
English Lab, Quinta Penalba, Av. Venezuela, Urb. El Rosal, Caracas 1060.

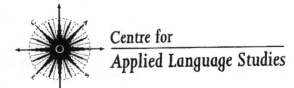

Business English

As the world becomes smaller, it is more important than ever for companies to be able to communicate with customers in every country. With English being globally recognised as the language of business, this means it's more important than ever for a company to invest in language training. The following pages contain information for training/personnel managers on the different approaches to language training which they can consider.

174 What Is Business English?

175 What Kind Of Business English?

178 Assessing The Language Needs Of Your Company

179 The Training Option

181 Business English Courses

189 The Technology Option

192 Recruiting English Speakers

What Is Business English?

It is one of the growth areas of English Language Teaching but what exactly is Business English and how can it benefit your company?

Business English is, essentially, a condensed version of the language focussed on the grammar, vocabulary and skills needed to conduct business in English

 nglish is the Lingua Franca not only of science and technology but also of most international trading: half of all the world's business is done in English. Indeed, most of the estimated 300 million people currently learning English are doing so to improve their job prospects. But people learning English for business are not necessarily learning Business English. To understand why, we need to understand the nature of Business English.

Business English is, essentially, a condensed version of the language focussed on the grammar, vocabulary and skills needed to conduct business in English. It offers a short cut to communicative competence by concentrating only on areas the student needs to communicate in. The more specialised and specific the business need, the more specialised and specific the material and teaching techniques. Courses which require a high level of specialist input generally come under the label of ESP or English for Specific Purposes.

Business English and an ESP clearly require skilled and experienced trainers often with business expertise. Good Business English teachers should have at least an initial teaching certificate and 3 years' teaching experience, though if they come from a business background they may have spent less time in the classroom. In many ways they are not teachers but professional trainers specialising in language just as others may specialise in management techniques. Many trainers will have further qualifications, perhaps a specialist course in the field, a diploma or an MA. Such trainers can earn considerably more than an inexperienced unqualified teacher, though exact rates vary from country to country and in many cases are still less than for other professional trainers. Add to that the fact that a true Business English course generally requires extra preparation time and will have fewer students than its general English equivalent and we can see that it is likely to be more expensive than a normal language course. Compared to the cost of other professional training, however, and given the impact it can have on company performance, it still offers excellent value.

The most frequent 2,000 words in English account for over 70% of all the language used, regardless of subject

For the consumer, the advantage of Business English and ESP is that it saves time. By finding out a student's actual language needs, a process called needs analysis, and devising or adapting material and teaching techniques to suit it, Business English courses can reduce the time it takes learners to work effectively in their job areas. What Business English and ESP cannot do is provide an instant way to learn a language or dramatically reduce the learning time for every learner whatever their job needs.

The main way Business English aims to short-cut the language learning process is by leaving out language which is unnecessary for the job. Some jobs, however, require an employee to use the whole range of the language. Moreover, a certain amount of basic language is essential and cannot be left out. Research on the British National Corpus shows that the most frequent 2,000 words in English account for over 70% of all the language used, regardless of subject. Until learners have mastered these words and the basic grammatical structures that accompany them, there is little point trying to teach them specialist language. There is some disagreement about the exact level students need to attain before they can really benefit from Business English but few schools would recommend such a course before elementary level which generally means a student should have had 100-150 hours of English.

Even then, elementary students will still need a fair amount of general language input in any Business English course. This is also true of people who have studied English in the past but forgotten it. For such students general Business English courses, which teach general English within a business context, are an increasingly popular alternative. Confusingly such courses are marketed under a wide variety of different names. Indeed some of the less scrupulous schools sell " ESP courses" which are little more than general Business English.

True Business English courses do not suit everybody. However, once students are at pre-intermediate level or above (have completed 200-300 hours of English) they will truly benefit from a high-cost, high-quality Business English course.

What Kind Of Business English ?

Having recognised the need for Business English training in your company, it is important to identify exactly what kind of Business English is needed.

Even quite low-level jobs can require operational English

The traditional way of dividing Business English is vertically in job areas. This can range from general industry areas such as English for Banking to more specialised ESP. It is possible though to divide language needs in different ways. Companies, for example, often need a way of assessing language needs across job areas. They need to prioritise their language training and, especially in times of recession, concentrate most of the training spend on the employees who need it most.

A company may call in an outside consultant to do such work for them in a Language Audit (see page 178). But on a smaller scale they may simply look for a simple framework to help them sort out their language training priorities.

One such framework , devised by publishers Ruth Gates and Melanie Butler at Addison Wesley Longman divides learners into 4 categories:
a) Operational learners who work in English all or most of the time and are high priority learners.
b) Instrumental learners who need English to do certain specific tasks and, depending on the importance of those tasks, may also have a high priority need.
c) Informational learners who access professional information through English and who need a completely different set of skills.
d) Aspirational learners who do not need English immediately and want it for career advancement or even for reasons of status. These may be the lowest priority in terms of training budget, at least in the short term. In the long term, though, the investment in language training may pay dividends.

Why employ an English speaking sales force if your customers can't contact them because they can't communicate with your telephonist

For reasons made clear on page 174, whatever the type of learner, they will need at least 150 hours of general English before they can take advantage of any kind of specialist course.

Operational Learners

When employees must use English 40% of their working time or more it is their operational language. Operational work areas range from air traffic communications to international money dealers. Even quite low-level jobs can require operational English: research suggests that hotel telephonists, for example, spend 80% of their working time operating in English.

Some jobs which do not normally require operational English may suddenly do so in the future. Military personnel, for example, do not operate in English in their own country but may have to do so when they join a multinational force.

What this means for employers: If you need employees to operate in English, you should only employ people for those positions who already have a good level of general English. For most operational jobs this is a minimum of pre-intermediate level or 200-300 hours of English.

Organisations who do not follow this rule, and there are a surprising number, often waste a lot of time and money. Research by the EL Gazette some years ago found a major French bank which placed dealers in the UK money market on the basis of their experience in France and did not check their level of English. Two of the dealers spoke no English and as a result did not make a single deal in 6 months.

It is most often in low-level jobs that employers ignore the need for operational English. Yet why employ an English-speaking sales force if your customers can't contact them because they can't communicate with your telephonist?

Simply recruiting people with good English does not solve all the training needs in this area. Even when operational employees do have a good level of general English, they will often need a course which focuses on the specific English they need for their job. Even employees who have done a specialist English course as part of their professional training may need to use different skills in a work context.

What kind of course: Of all employees, operational learners are the most likely to benefit from job-specific Business English or ESP course. As a rule of

The more the success of the task depends on it being done effectively in English by the employee, the more urgent the need for language training

thumb, however, the more specialised the job, the more specialised the course. Our telephonist may benefit most from a general English course, our money dealer will need a job specific one.

Since operational employees often can't work effectively until they have the specialised English they need, and since they should have a reasonable level of English to start with, these are the most likely to benefit from an intensive course when they first start their job. If they are new to the field, this may also need to include some training in the job area itself, a combination that is often called English Plus. As mentioned earlier operational learners are the employees most likely to benefit most from job-specific Business English and ESP courses. Operational learners do not, however, usually require more than one course of study unless they change job area.

Instrumental Learners.

Instrumental learners do not operate most of the time in English. For them the language is a tool that they need to accomplish certain specific parts of their jobs: making sales presentations to overseas clients, for example, or negotiating particular contracts. They are often at a relatively high level in an organisation. In a hotel context, for example, Food and Beverage managers may need English for tasks such as dealing with guest complaints or liaising with head office. Waiters on the other hand need to operate in English all the time. Indeed the majority of learners at a managerial level need instrumental rather than operational English.

In deciding the training priority, it helps to focus on the task, not the employee.

What this means for employers: It is often not possible to employ someone who already has a sufficient standard of English in a job where they only need to use it for specific tasks. Other skills and job experience in the field may be equally or more important. Instrumental learners, therefore, generally need language training after they are in post.

In deciding the training priority, it helps to focus on the task, not the employee. How important is it? Does it really need to be done in English? Does the

employee's level of English prevent him from doing it effectively? Does it really need to be done by this employee, rather than, say, using an interpreter? The more the success of the task depends on it being done effectively in English by the employee, the more urgent the need for language training.

What kind of course: If they are pre-intermediate level or above, instrumental learners should be able to concentrate on the language they need to perform their tasks. Probably the best way is to have a short specially designed course although there is an increasing number of business skills courses concentrating on areas such as negotiation or presentations which can also be very effective.

Instrumental learners with an elementary level of English may be able to learn the English to deal with less complex tasks - the combination courses, which offer general business English supplemented by one-to-one tutorials can be useful at this level.

Whatever their level, instrumental learners will generally require language maintenance because the nature of their work means that they do not get constant opportunity to practise their skills. Language, like any practical skill, needs constant practice. As a general rule, students need two hours a week to keep up their English. This can be provided by a teacher, telephone teaching works well for this purpose, or - for more motivated students self-study.

Informational Learners

An increasing number of professionals receive all or most of their professional information through the medium of English. This is particularly true in the areas of science and technology as in the case of a doctor reading medical journals or a bioengineer attending an international conference.

What this means for the company: Informational learners are in a way instrumental learners but the tasks they perform require a completely different set of skills, in particular reading and listening.

Most people with a scientific or technical

background will have a good grasp of the specialist vocabulary of their area and will have done at least some of their studies in the medium of English. Someone new to the technical field, perhaps a librarian moving into pharmaceuticals, however, will need an ESP course in the specialist area often combined with general teaching on the subject, a combination often known as English Plus.

The major mistake made in this field is that employees are classified as informational but at least some of their work is actually instrumental. They may need to present papers at the conference, or discuss things with their English-speaking colleagues. In this case they are also instrumental learners and need the kind of language provision suggested above.

What kind of course: Informational learners with a good basic command of English and some experience of studying in the English medium are the ideal candidates for a self-study course. Self study is most effective in the areas of listening and reading and this kind of student is usually able to make the most of high-tech distance-learning platforms such as CD Rom and the internet. The main problem here is the lack of material in some of the more specialised fields.

Learners without the experience of studying in English will benefit most from a course which includes a lot of study skills, while people new to the field will need an ESP course. In either case the choice of teacher is critical. Unless the teacher knows the field well, they are unlikely to be able to provide the kind of English such learners need.

Aspirational Learners

Aspirational learners do not need to use English in their jobs, although many of them will find it useful for travelling, socialising, etc. This kind of learner wants to learn English, perhaps to improve his or her job prospects or simply because knowledge of English confers social status. They are generally highly motivated and learn well.

What this means for the company. In purely

economic terms, aspirational learners should be the lowest priority for a company - after all they can do their jobs perfectly well without it. However, these are highly motivated learners and, in the longer term, investment in English training can reap benefits in terms of employee satisfaction and in increasing career mobility.

Another consideration for any training manager is what is the status of the individual. Very often it is high-level executives, whose actual job areas require little or no English, who make up a large proportion of the company's aspirational learners. As the principal of one of the UK's foremost ESP centres admits: "up to 20% of our students are high-ranking executives, often at director's level, who do not need English at all. Certainly they do not need the kind of highly specialised, tailor-made, individualised courses that we offer and which are, of course, very expensive. We do try and tell the companies this, but they send them anyway."

The critical decision with aspirational learners, then, is to choose the appropriate course.

Choosing the right course: Business English and ESP courses are rarely appropriate for aspirational learners because they work by analysing the students, needs and in this case those needs are rarely clear or immediate. For most aspirational learners a general English course or a General Business English course (see page174) are much more suitable.

In most cases an extensive course of two to four hours a week is the most suitable for an aspirational learner who in any case will need language maintenance as they do not use the language regularly. Self-study or guided self-study (where there is a tutor on hand to help out) can be very effective for the more motivated, although motivation can tend to slip as time goes on. One way to maintain motivation, whether for self-study or face-to-face teaching, is to ask employees to pay a small contribution towards language learning costs. One Italian company which introduced this system found the drop out rate in its language classes fell from 40% to under 10%.

Assessing The Language Needs Of Your Company

Having recognised the need for language training, it is important to make sure the right education goes to the right employees.

ompanies are experts on their own products and markets and usually have quite a clear idea of the kind and level of English they need at what level. But what are the precise needs of each type of employee? Who should you train, and how? Is your company making the most effective use of the English-speaking staff which it already has? And how can you choose from among the plethora of courses and methods of learning which are now available? For companies who want to assess their language needs on a companywide basis the best way to answer these questions is to carry out a language audit with a professional auditor from outside the company.

The Language Auditor

A good business language auditor has language expertise and understands commercial needs. The auditor will want to get to know your company in order to assess existing language competence and discover present and future requirements. He or she will conduct research into which specific tasks and in which specific situations English is needed.

The auditor will assess whether employees must speak, write, read or listen to English, and decide on the level of fluency and accuracy they require. He or she will then recommend training to close the gap between the existing skills and abilities of employees and their goals.

The auditor should suggest various training options and methods within your budget and other constraints such as working conditions and availability of employees. Other options such as translation and interpreting, may also be considered.

There is a growing number of independent specialist language consultancies who carry out audits. Some of the private language schools with branches, affiliates, or franchises in many countries, can also offer this service.

The British Council may be able to help you find a language auditor and in some locations will undertake the task itself for a fee. Two British Councils, in Quito, Ecuador and Dhaka, Bangladesh, carry out regular language audits, and those in Singapore and Hong Kong have strong links with industry.

The precise methods which each auditing company employs are often guarded as 'secret'. Most audits will generally follow the principles outlined here, which draw on the model developed by the London-based Centre for Information on Language Teaching and Research (CILT).

You are more likely to benefit from an auditor's services if you do some preliminary research on your company's needs, have a clear idea of what you want to achieve, and begin to develop a language policy which fits into your company policy as a whole.

Language training can be viewed in two ways. Firstly you might see it as a way of satisfying short-term and operational requirements, with limited objectives, such as the need for receptionists to handle calls in English and welcome English-speaking visitors. Secondly you can look at it in terms of your company's medium to long-term strategy - when you expect to be in a market long-term or are planning to enter a new market.

You should concentrate on who needs to use English. To help decide this you should consider all the tasks which involve using the language, such as:
meetings: formal, informal and social, both with customers and colleagues
sales: presentations, describing the product, seminars, conferences, exhibitions
telephone calls: telemarketing, answering enquiries, technical support, customer feedback
Even before an audit takes place, you can promote English in your company by giving status to language skills and making them prominent in recruitment. Ideally, you should adopt a long-term policy towards language training to cover the updating of existing skills, new training, the recruitment of English-speaking staff, and the forecasting of future requirements.

The Training Option

If you decide to use a teacher to train your staff, there are numerous variations available to suit your company's requirements.

Individual or 'one-to-one' tuition is usually the fastest way to learn

 When choosing employees for language training you must assess a number of interrelated factors such as company needs, employees' roles, each individual's aptitude for learning a language, and his or her willingness to do so.

Company needs and employees' roles can be assessed during a language audit. Aptitude may be measured either by an auditor or a training provider. Experts say that aptitude tests are not entirely reliable, but the following factors are generally recognised as affecting the rate at which individuals learn: the level of existing knowledge of a language or languages, motivation to learn the language and interest in the country or people where the language is spoken, ability to overcome fear of making mistakes in public, the personal relationship between tutor and student, the student's perception of the relevance of the course and incentives.

Grouping trainees

If you choose group training, you should consider their size and make-up very carefully. For non-language training it may be most cost-effective to train as many employees as possible in one class. For language training it is most effective to group students according to needs and level. This will not always coincide with your company's hierarchy. You may have to make compromises when a group with the same needs does not have the same language level and vice-versa. Some schools may be able to group all those students with the same level together for some lessons and bring all those with the same needs together for others. A student who misses a lesson may fall behind and lose motivation. If this happens with many different students over a number of weeks, the group is likely to break down.

For language training it is most effective to group students according to needs and level

Training Options

Face-to-face: Classroom or workplace learning with a tutor, 'one-to-one' or in small groups. This is usually regarded as essential. Students get the chance to practise their English with a teacher.

Distance learning, open or self-study: Students work on their own with self-study materials, including books, cassettes, videos or computer programmes. See page189 for more details.

One-to-one tuition: Individual or "one-to-one" tuition is usually the fastest way to learn. Once a student has a basic command of English (100-150 hours) the trainer is able to take full account of the student's needs, language level, and objectives. But the student has no contact with other students and it may be difficult to carry out role plays which need three or more participants, such as seminars or negotiations.

What kind of course?

Intensive: Up to 30 hours a week, six hours each day (including self-study time) over 2-3 weeks. Such courses can be extended but a one-week break is recommended. This is good for employees who are imminently going abroad, as a kick-start for non-intensive courses, or as a refresher. Too many companies though, think that employees will learn twice as much in 6 hours as they will in 3. Effective learning requires full concentration and research suggests that that the amount of language you learn starts to fall after 3 hours. For beginners, periods of more than 3 hours a day are not recommended.

Non-intensive: usually 1-2 hours per session, twice a week. The problem with such courses is that motivation can be difficult to maintain (progress may be slow for beginners who may feel they are getting nowhere), but they are ideal for an on-site programme at the end of the working day with a group of 5-8 employees. Maximum benefit can be derived if lesson time is matched by self-study time.

Choosing A Training Provider

An in-house teacher: Getting a teacher to come to your premises saves the time and cost of travelling to a language school, which can detract from students' ability to learn, especially after a tiring day at work. Whether you choose a teacher from a language school or a freelancer, you should ask to see a list of

The Training Option

Recruitment agencies may be able to help you find a suitable trainer

his or her former clients and check qualifications, experience and business background.

If the trainer is freelance, check that he or she can provide continuity should you decide to renew the training contract. Will they disappear once the contract ends? The British Council in many countries can offer appropriately qualified and experienced in-company trainers.

The disadvantages of in-company courses compared to those at language schools include the risk of interruptions to classes, when, for example, students have to take urgent telephone calls. You also need to ensure that you have an appropriate room available and the necessary equipment.

Recruitment agencies may be able to help you find a suitable trainer. Check that the agency has experience in your field of business, and compare their rates with local schools. An agency's commission might seem high, but using one can save a lot of time and expense.

Language schools: Some employees may feel that, compared to the workplace, the atmosphere of a school is 'unnatural'. Those whose compulsory education ended many years ago may react badly to being 'back in school'. But others may find they can study better in a place dedicated to learning. A school may have equipment which would be expensive to install at a company.

Some employees may feel that, compared to the workplace, the atmosphere of a school is 'unnatural'

Make sure that a prospective school can give a demonstration lesson; test the aptitude of students to learn languages; group students by level/ability; map a training plan against learning goals; adapt your company's materials into the proposed language course; select a method in line with individuals' learning style; provide self-study facilities; allow your company to discuss selection of tutors; monitor quality of training; offer public tests or exams; and provide end-of-course tests, and reports.

Check that the school has a history of teaching Business English, that teachers are qualified and that they have business experience, preferably with knowledge of the business culture of the English-speaking country you work with. Ask about class sizes and request references from former clients.

Local schools are likely to have classes of students who all speak the same native language, which means they are not forced to communicate with each other in English and may feel uncomfortable doing so. There is no opportunity to learn about the culture of an English-speaking country first-hand.

Schools in an English-speaking country: There are schools specialising in Business English in the UK, the USA, Canada, Australia, New Zealand and Malta. Their main advantages over local schools are experience and expertise in running Business English courses, the chance to learn about a country's culture first-hand, and opportunities to practise and learn English outside the classroom, perhaps with a host family. Students in groups may be of several different nationalities which creates a natural need and desire to communicate in English.

Check that schools are members of the recognition system operating in their country. In Europe, they may also be members of Europe-wide organisations which ensure high quality.

Homestay in an English-speaking country: This offers a learning environment that can be intensive but relaxing. Students live in the trainer's home and so benefit from his or her hospitality, speaking English in non-teaching situations as well as during lessons. There is an opportunity to 'live' the language, not just study it.

Cultural training: All good schools should have a component of this in their courses. But some employees may need additional cultural training. Farnham Castle Centre for International Briefing, Farnham, Surrey, is the UK's leading centre in this field. In the USA, The Society of International English Cultural Training and Research (SIETAR) in Washington runs teaching courses in crosscultural training. The Society can also provide advice and recommendations on other training organisations which may be more suitable for you.

Business English Courses

College	Course title	Course length	FT/PT	Fees	Start dates	Entry requirements	Contact	Comments
Anglo-Continental Educational Group, Bournemouth, UK	English For Business/ Legal Practice/ Finance/Medical Practice/ Hotels and Restaurants	2 to 4 weeks	Full-time	2 weeks £610 3 weeks £865 4 weeks £112	Monthly (with additional dates in June, July, August)	Min age 18 Min. language level Lower Intermediate	Robin Sanders	30 lessons per week, 20 of Gen. Eng. 10 in the Language/ Background of Specialisation
	Executive Programme	1 to 6 weeks	Full-time	From £740	Fortnightly. Weekly in Jan, June, July and August	Min age 20. Language level Beginner to Advanced	Robin Sanders	Group sessions plus 10 sessions of individual tuition. Indiv. course also available
Berlitz, Geneva, Switzerland	Doing Business in English	Varied	Both	On application	All year round	None	Suzanne Lhemery	Marketing, banking presentations, engineering - Test of English for International Comm.
Bournemouth Business School, UK	Business Management Diploma	11to 33 weeks	Full-time	£150 per week	26/2, 9/4, 6, 28/5, 1, 29/7, 19/8, 30/9, 28/10, 18/11	Intermediate English, finished secondary education	Shane Wilkinson	Preparation for work or further study. Exams provided. Computer skills can be studied simultaneously
	Tourism and Travel Diploma	11 to 33 weeks	Full-time	£150 per week	26/2, 9/4, 6/5, 28/5, 1/7, 29/4, 19/8, 30/9, 28/10, 18/11	Intermediate English, finished secondary education	Shane Wilkinson	Tourism exams provided
Collingham, Brown + Brown, Oxford, UK	English for Business and/or Commerce	From 1 week to 1 year as required	Both	From £2,250 per term or £250 per week depending on course.	Throughout year	An elementary level must be achieved beforehand. Courses are available to support this	A. J. Shepherd	English required for Bus. + Comm. from Prelim to Adv. Exam Bds LCCI + Oxford
Derwent Executive Language, Via Calver, UK	Budget/ Executive/ Business English	Min 1 week, no max.	Full-time	Budget £497 Executive £1200-£1400 Business £995-£1145 All residential	Any Monday throughout year	None	Jo Shaw	Tuition and Business visits + Executive Host family
	Ladies Course	Min 1 week, no max	Full-time	£1,200 - £1,400 Residential	Any Monday throughout year	None	Jo Shaw	For ladies who for religious or cultural reasons prefer single sex courses
Ecole de Langue Anglaise, Lausanne, Switzerland	English for Executives	Various	Both	Dependent on course	8 January, 15 March, 2 September + additional dates	—	Trevor P. Bent	Tailored to students' requirements
ELT Banbury, UK	Executive English	2 weeks	Full-time	From £385 per week	Mondays throughout year	—	Dr T. T. Gerighty	Tailor made, often one to one special part of course

Business English Courses

College	Course title	Course length	FT/PT	Fees	Start dates	Entry requirements	Contact	Comments
English Home Tuition Scheme, London, UK	English For Business + Commerce	Week-end/1 week to 4 weeks	10, 15, 20 or 25 hours. One to one tuition weekly	Available on request	Any day of year	None	Nadia Cole	Nationwide throughout GB and Ireland. Individually designed courses
English Language Centre, Dublin, Ireland	Business English/ Management English	2 weeks + time-saver w/e and telephone courses	Both	£500 per week	Any Monday	None	The English Language Centre	Course tailor made, lvls include Beg., Inter., Adv.
Gateshead College, Gateshead, UK	English In Northumbria English For Specific Purposes/Business English	As required	Full-time	Available on request	Any Monday	None	Patricia Lauret	ESP course tailor made and includes Marketing and Telecoms training
Gateway Language, Dunning, UK	English For Business	Min. 1 week. Max 2 weeks	Full-time	Min of £230 per student pw. Incs full board and use of campus facilities	All year round	Prefer Upper Int. but testing will be done on entry.	Gateway Language	Covers all aspects of business - from running existing bus. to setting up.
Harrogate Language Academy, Harrogate, UK	Various	Various	Both	On request	On request	—	Charlie Martineau	Courses normally one to one
House of English, Brighton, UK	Business English Course Group 5	Min. 2 weeks	30 lessons per week	2 weeks £845 3 weeks £1,195 4 weeks £1,545	2 or 3 times a month (on Mondays)	Intermediate level of English	Mrs S. Camilleri	Also offer Executive English course + specialised one to one courses
Kingsway English Centre, Worcester, UK	Professional English	1+ weeks	Full-time (31 or 35 hrs p/w)	£495 (31 hours) £600 (35 hours)	Every Monday	Min Lower Intermediate	Rick Johns	Mix of group and one to one lessons. Also offer Prof. Flexicourse
Language Centre, University of Aberdeen, UK	Various	Various	Both	On request	On request	—	Mrs Christine Burgess	Courses designed to client requirements
LTS Training & Consulting, Bath	English for Business /Effective Int. Communication/ Practical Communication /Individual Tuition	1-2 weeks	Full-time	£680-£1,325 per week	Throughout year	Lower intermediate, business/ professional background	A. Pilbeam, M. Ellis	Tailored, professional courses
Lydbury English Centre, Manchester, UK	Intensive Combined Programme	Min 2 week Max 3 weeks	Full-time	£1,395 p/w fully inclusive	Every Monday	—	Duncan Baker	Also offer One week intensive combined and Reduced Intensive
	One to One Programme	By arrangement	Full-time	Usually around £1,845 p/w	Every Monday	—	Duncan Baker	Up to 27 hours one-to-one private tuition
	Beginners Programme	4 weeks	Full-time	£3,750 fully inclusive	Every Monday	—	Duncan Baker	Includes 18 hours one-to-one tuition

Business English Courses

College	Course title	Course length	FT/PT	Fees	Start dates	Entry requirements	Contact	Comments
Lynda Hazelwood Language Services, Bristol, UK	Intensive Course in Business English	1 week upwards	Full-time	£1,775 p/w (homestay inclusive) (£1,975 p/w hotel inclusive)	Any Sunday	Not suitable for beginners	Lynda Hazelwood	Includes business lunches and visits to industry
	Course in Business English	1 week upwards	Full-time	£995 p/w (homestay inclusive) £1,295 p/w (hotel inclusive)	Any Sunday	Not suitable for beginners	Lynda Hazelwood	One to one tuition for 25 hours inc. business lunches
Multi Lingua, Guildford, UK	English Language and Business	5 weeks	Full-time	£5,190 including full acomm., materials, social and cultural events	Any Monday	None, skills individually assessed	Julienne Eve	Qualifications awarded include LCCI certificate and Multi Lingua English Language Cert.
	Intensive English Language and Business	4 week examination course. 2 week minimum study period	Full-time	Per four weeks one to one £6,180 Per four weeks two to one £8,185	Any Sunday	Not suitable for beginners	Lynda Hazelwood	One to one tuition for 25 hours inc. business lunches
New College, Durham, UK	English For Professional People	As required and recommended	Both	Vary depending on course - approx £45 per hour	As required	—	Mary Pearson	Course adapted to linguistic and prof. needs of clients
Newnham Language Centre, Cambridge, UK	Intensive English/ Business English	4 weeks	Full-time	£710-£760	All year round	Intermediate/ Advanced	Marie-Louise Banning	Combined with intensive English in morning
Open Doors, Paris, France	Business English and Commercial English	30 hrs (1 wk or 10 wks in evening)	Both	5250F HT/30 hrs	Intermediate: 3/96, 8/96, 11/96 High Lvl: 2/96, 3/96, 4/96, 7/96, 10/96	Evaluation of the level	Mrs Le Roy	Special training method
Oxford House College, London, UK	Business English & Commun- ication Studies	8 weeks	Full-time	£456 plus £25 Exam fee £60	Any Monday	Upper Intermediate level of English	Oxford House College	Oxford Int. Bus. Eng. Certificate (First lvl) held at school. 97% rate of success
Oxford School of Intensive English, Oxford, UK	English For Professional Purposes	Min 1 week No max	Both	From £750	To suit	—	Angela Radford	Can cater for specific exam requirements and specialised areas
Pendragon School of English, Guildford, UK	English for Business Purposes	Varied	Both	Varies according to course	Any	None. Beginners accepted	The Principal	Can offer work experience and company visits
Reading University, UK	Business English	2 -6 weeks	Both	On application	Any	—	Pauline Robinson	Course completely tailor made to fit client

Business English Courses

College	Course title	Course length	FT/PT	Fees	Start dates	Entry requirements	Contact	Comments
Regent Oxford, UK	Business Communication Course	1 or 2 weeks	Full-time (30 hours intensive)	One week £600 Two weeks £1,100	Every 2 weeks from 2/1 to 2/12	Pre-course test and needs analysis	Katherine Tustain	Courses in very small groups tailored to needs of participants
Saint George International, London, UK	Executive Programme	Min. 1 week 45 hrs per week	Full-time	1 week £1,575 2 weeks £3,150 Extra wk £1,500	Any Monday, with one week's notice	Min age 16 completion of needs analysis questionnaire	Stephen Barnes	Student continually watched by team of experienced teachers from morn. to eve.
	In-Company Corporate Programme	Can vary from 2-3 hours weekly to more intensive blocks	Part-time	Contact St George Int. for details	All year flexible	—	Stephen Barnes	Usually taught on company's premises to small groups
	Crash Course Programme	Min 1 week 30 hrs per week	Full-time	1 week £360 2 weeks £1,920 Extra wk £910	Any Monday	Min age 16 completion of needs analysis questionnaire	Stephen Barnes	Intensive one to one programme
Schiller English Language Institute, Wickham, UK	Customised Course	Min. 1 week	As required	On demand	Mondays	According to course content	Louise Cody	Course designed to suit individual client. Includes company visits
Sels College of London, UK	Varied	Daily or twice a week	—	£44 per hour	To suit	—	Y Rouss	One to one courses
Shane School of English, London, UK	English for Executives	2 weeks min.	Full-time	£550 for 2 weeks	Any Monday	Intermediate level	David Wilkins	20 hrs p/w group work on Gen Eng. 5 hrs p/w one to one
West Sussex School of English, Steyning, UK	Business Intensive Course	1 - 2 weeks	Full-time	£970 per week	Any September - June	18+	Charles Deane	One to one, includes business consultancy
Worldwide Teachers Development Institue, Boston, USA	Intensive Executive English/American English Communication Practices/ Executive Individual Courses	2 weeks, 4 weeks, individually designed courses	Both	Depends on course	Monthly	Individual assessment	David Dr Thomas A Kane	Consultation to companies on location; available for Business American English Audits
York Associates, York, UK	Personnel Communication	1 week	Full time	£600 per week	8 July	Intermediate level English	Trish Stott	Communication skills, inc. presentation + interviewing
	Secretarial Communication	1 week	Full-time	£600 per week	4 March, 17 June	Intermediate level English	Trish Stott	Includes handling visitors, telephoning, fax and letter writing

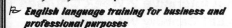

The Technology Option

Instead of, or in addition to, formalised lessons technology can offer a more flexible teaching option.

For language learning, most trainers advise that technology should be used as a backup or supplement to face-to-face training

With foreign language learning becoming an urgent management priority for many companies, firms are increasingly looking towards technology to meet their training needs. Multimedia is the buzz word of the moment and features strongly at educational trade fairs. But how useful is technology in language learning? Do new computer applications packages satisfy your training needs, and what issues should you address before investing in expensive hardware?

Educational consultants have noted two common scenarios to avoid when choosing training technology. Perhaps an enthusiastic training manager is given a free hand to choose whichever training media he or she prefers. He or she has stores full of expensive, unused equipment and runs out of money or company support before an efficient training programme can be set up. Or a company decides to plump for one training technology throughout the company using the latest hi-tech systems even if this is not the most appropriate or cost-effective solution.

It is likely that cheaper computer-based digital video systems, and CD-ROM drives will become the dominant training platform of the future

For language learning, most trainers advise that technology should be used as a backup or supplement to face-to-face training. It can be used before residential courses abroad, and by employees wishing to maintain or refresh their language skills. Perhaps most effectively of all, it can be used concurrently with language school or in-company courses. The advantages for companies are plain: expensive face-to-face training is extended and reinforced by employees who may be motivated to use technology at self-access learning facilities in their own time. So which technology and which platforms is it best to employ?

Audio and Video Cassette

The audio cassette has long been a mainstay of language teaching. It allows the student to hear complex business situations with different voices and accents. The student can work at his or her own pace, rewinding a tape as often as necessary.

Although many language schools (and even some companies) may have sophisticated language labs, the other advantage of audio tape is its portability. Employees can listen to the tapes in their cars or on personal stereos.

Although the video tape may be less portable, it has many of the advantages of audio. Since it is much used in teaching business skills, it is also a medium that employees will be familiar with in a study context. There are two approaches to using video in language study. Either a specialised language training video, of which there are many high-quality examples available. Alternatively more advanced students may watch videos targeted at native speakers as a means of widening their linguistic or cultural knowledge. However, the full benefit of this form of study would definitely require interaction with a teacher.

CD-ROM and CD-I

A Keynote market review predicted that analogue video and LaserDisc systems will still remain significant within the training industry due to the considerable investment which some companies have already made. But it is likely that cheaper computer-based digital video systems, and CD-ROM drives, whether stand-alone CD-I or as part of a PC or network, will become the dominant training platform of the future.

It is claimed that multimedia has certain benefits over traditional methods of learning. Since it is a new and increasingly fashionable medium, students are more enthusiastic about using it and less likely to regard it as work - many CD-ROM programs emphasise this positive approach to computer learning which in the United States is referred to as Edutainment. It responds quickly to students, giving them further information and correcting them more quickly than a teacher. This is vital since it allows each learner to learn at his or her own pace. In addition, it can instantly replay sounds (unlike a tape which has to be rewound), which is useful for pronunciation practice, and it can be highly involving and motivating. Language teachers,

Full-motion video and voice recognition are the keys to the future of language learning hi-technology

however, warn that no computer programme - however sophisticated - can replace the unpredictable interaction which takes place in a student group and the exposition and problem-solving skills of a human teacher.

Full-motion video and voice recognition are the keys to the future of language learning hi-technology. It may be a long time before the latter becomes widely available, but full-motion video is already here. Low-cost platforms such as CD-ROM and Philips CD-I are capable of replaying video (in combination with Indeo, MPEG or other compression technology), although it takes up a large amount of memory. LaserDisc has the greatest capabilities in this area, but has not gained widespread currency as a language training medium.

As yet voice-recognition technology is not refined enough to meet learners' pronunciation training needs. Most CD-ROMS are only capable of a 'parrot' function which allows the student to listen to a recording of a native speaker (the model), then record his or her own effort to copy the model, and finally compare the two. However, one company has now developed a programme which compares the student's pronunciation efforts on a scale of 1 to 10 with an electronically-stored model.

The Internet

Managers should be wary of wanting to use technology for technology's sake when traditional methods may be more suitable

Although ELT resources on the Internet are growing at a rapid rate, most of them are directed at the general learner rather than a learner interested in English for specific purposes such as business..

Considering that the Internet has been dominated by native English speakers, this is not surprising. However, with the development of the Internet throughout Europe, Latin and Central America and Asia, the need for the production and provision of more directed and professionally produced EFL materials is beginning to be felt. As the corporate sector is the fastest-growing sector on the Internet the market for English language materials and resources directed at this vast market presents itself as one of the major growth areas for ELT over the

next decade.

At the moment very few resources exist for the Business English market. IATEFL's Business English Special Interest Group (BESIG) recently opened a web site (http://www.compulink.co.uk/~lydbury/besig.html) and Edunet has a nascent Business English section on its site (http://www.edunet.com/english/business/index.html).

For the imaginative teacher there are countless ways to employ the business resources found on the Internet in class situations. The Internet abounds with business articles, financial reports, company information, CV's and news articles relevant to business. These can be downloaded into wordprocessors and used to create exercises or used on-line in 'search and report back' type exercises.

Over the next year you can also expect to see a sharp increase in the number of sites with dedicated sections for Business English as the demand increases and materials are produced.

Making The Choice

Managers should be wary of wanting to use technology for technology's sake when traditional methods may be more suitable. As is often pointed out, the humble book is a random-access, highly portable piece of technology. Audio cassettes too, have advantages over other media: they can be used by trainees in their cars. Dr A.W. Bates, professor of educational media research at the UK's Open University, warns in a paper dealing with the issue: 'In educational and cost terms, there is no 'super-medium'; different media have different strengths and weaknesses. This means that a combination of media is usually the most appropriate decision.'

Provided it is part of a well thought-out language policy, hi-technology can be an efficient training solution. Take time to analyse its costs and benefits compared to lowtech and non-technical solutions and it may become an important element in your company's training strategy.

Recruiting English Speakers

New employees may have a variety of language qualifications, but what do they mean?

Key to Coverage

W	Writing
R	Reading
L	Listening
S	Speaking

Key to Levels

1	Beginner
2	Elementary
3	Pre-Intermediate
4	Lower-intermediate (waystage)
5	Intermediate (threshold)
6	Upper-intermediate
7	Post-intermediate Proficiency
8	Advanced
9	Bilingual

Notes

These indicate aims and status. For more details, see English Language Entrance Requirements in British Educational Institutions. (HMSO 1991)

Having established that your organisation would benefit from an improved level of English, you may decide to recruit staff with language skills. However, in addition to the standard difficulties recruitment presents to most organisations, assessment of language capability must also be taken into account. Depending on your budget and the importance of the position, you may choose to engage a specialist agency with the capability to determine candidates' language level, or trust in your own selection procedure. In either case, there are a number of key questions which will influence your recruitment decision.

The Position

The level and type of language ability required are dependent upon the role that the prospective employee will play in your organisation. It is essential to keep this in mind throughout the recruitment process. A receptionist must be able to answer telephone queries in another language, it is of little significance to you they can translate Shakespeare. Remember that linguistic ability is a tool with which someone can improve the way in which they do a job; it is no substitute for the ability to do the job in the first place.

Qualifications

Unless your own English is impeccable, the most reliable way of judging a candidate's skills is by their qualifications and matching those qualifications to your needs. A Master's degree in English Literature may look very impressive on paper, but it is no proof of its owner's ability to sell your latest product to a Swedish chain-store.

There is now a selection of internationally recognised English qualifications (and many confusing acronyms) so a guide to what the qualifications actually mean is essential. The following table gives a brief summary of the main examinations. It is not intended to be a comprehensive list of all EFL examinations available and the amount of information is naturally restricted. New specialist qualifications, such as LCCI's English for Tourism and Cambridge's CEIBT. are always being developed, so you can be quite specific in your demands.

Interpreting Qualifications

Board	Examination	Coverage	Level (on a scale of 1-9)		Notes
ARELS	Diploma	General LS	Pass	8	Spoken English exams conducted in a language lab or with radio equipment. Oral counterparts of the Oxford EFL exams.
	Higher Certificate	General LS	Pass	6	
	Preliminary Certificate	General LS	Pass	4	
Educational Testing Service	TOEFL	General LR	550	5/6	TOEFL 550 accepted by most US universities. UK institutions may demand evidence of writing and speaking skills. EuroCert =TOEFL+TSE+TWE.
	TSE	General S	550	5/6	
	TWE	General W	550	5/6	
	TOEIC	Business LR	Level 5	5	Widely used in commerce/industry.
International Baccalaureate	English as aSecond Language	General RWS	Not available		Higher: college entrance exam for English majors. Subsidiary: for non-English majors.
International Certificate Conference	Language Certificate System- English	General + ESP R(W)LS	Not available		German-based exams available in Europe. Business, Hotel & Catering, Technical English exams also available.

Interpreting Qualifications

Board	Examination	Coverage	Level (on a scale of 1-9)		Notes
London Chamber Of commerce	English for Commerce	Business RWS	1st 2nd 3rd	3 5 7	Traditional business English exam
	English for Business	Business RWS			More recent Business English exam
	SEFIC	Business LS	Threshold Intermediate Advanced	5 6 7	Spoken English for Industry & Commerce. Available in combination with EfB and EfC (above)
	English for Tourism	Tourism LS	1st 2nd	3 5	Language exam for tourism industry
Michigan	MELAB	General RWL (S)	75	5/6	Accepted by most US universities
NEAB (JMB)	University Entrance Testing ESOL	Academic RWLS	Pass	6	Widely accepted by UK universities
Pitman	ESOL & spoken ESOL	General LRW & LS	Intermediate Higher Intermediate Advanced	5 6 7	Five stage exams available on demand. Higher intermediate accepted by some UK universities
	English for Business Communication	Business LRW	Elementary Intermediate Advanced	5 6 7	Three-stage business exams available
Trinity College London	Spoken English Grades	General LS+RW at higher levels	Initial (1-3) Elementary (4-6) Intermediate (7-9) Advanced (10-12)	1/2 3/4 4/5 6/8	A series of 12 graded tests in spoken English with examiners from the UK
University of Cambridge (UCLES)	Proficiency (CPE)	General RWLS	Pass	7	Established exam accepted by most UK universities
	Cert in Advanced English (CAE)	General RWLS	Pass	6	Newer exam accepted by most UK universities
	1st Certificate (FCE)	General RWLS	Pass	6	Established exam widely accepted by employers
	Preliminary English Test (PET)	General RWLS	Pass	4	Elementary test to encourage further learning
	Key English Test (KET)	General RWLS	Pass	3	Lower level exam introduced in 1994
	Cert in Communicative Skills in English (CCSE)	General RWLS	I II III IV	4 5 6 7	Formerly RSA CUEFL
	IELTS	Academic RWLS	Bands 1-9 = bands 1-9 on scale		Bands 6/7 accepted by UK universities
	CEIBT	Business RWLS	Pass	7	Cert in English for International Business & Trade
University of London (ULEAC)	GCE O Level (syllabus B)	General RW	pass	6	Grade C accepted by most UK universities
	Certificates of Attainment	General RWL (S)	1 2 3 4 5 6	3 4 5 6 7 8	Six stage graded tests with optional speaking tests
University of Oxford	EFL Certificates	General RW	Higher Preliminary	6 3	Higher (credit) + ARELS Higher accepted by some universities
	International Business English Certificate	Business RWLS	First Executive	4/5 6/7	Business and Tourism exams based on authentic situations
	International Business English Certificate	nbvnbvnbv	First	4/5	

Reference Section

For the new or the experienced teacher this section is full of information - addresses of language schools and universities throughout the world, a guide to the key themes in teaching and a beginners' introduction to the world of the Internet and how it can benefit teachers in the classroom and in the search for jobs.

196 Recognition Schemes

197 An Insider's Guide: Methodology

199 An Insider's Guide: The Internet

203 ELT Book Suppliers

205 Conference Calendar

206 RSA/Cambridge And Trinity College Centres

207 Addresses

215 Index Of Advertisers

216 Index

Recognition Schemes

A quick guide to the major recognition bodies and the related associations.

Non-membership of an organisation does not mean the school is necessarily inadequate

 umerous organisations have been set up to monitor the standards of teaching and student welfare throughout the world. Unfortunately recognition schemes can be confusing. Non-membership of an organisation does not mean the school is necessarily inadequate. However, it is worth contacting one of the major recognition organisations if you want information on a school or college.

Australia

The ELICOS (English Language Intensive Courses for Overseas Students) Association represents English language colleges. It established the National ELICOS Accreditation Scheme (NEAS) to approve schools and colleges meeting its required standards.

Canada

English teaching is largely confined to the state sector. The University and College Intensive English Programs aim to advance standards in intensive English courses at universities and colleges.

Ireland

Eighty percent of accredited schools also join ARELS

Standards in private language schools are maintained by the Advisory Council for English Language Schools (ACELS) under the aegis of the Department of Education. ACELS has representation from The Recognised English Language Schools Association (RELSA) and NATEFLI (National Association of TEFL in Ireland). The Association for Teacher Training in TEFL (ATT) has been set up to ensure Irish qualifications are of international standard.

New Zealand

FIELSNZ (the Federation of Independent English Language Schools) and CRELS (Combined Registered English Language Schools) represent the interests of private language schools, and member schools have been approved by the New Zealand Qualifications Authority (NZQA). NZEIL (New Zealand Education International Limited) aims to support private and state schools in providing educational services to international students.

United Kingdom

The situation is complicated. The British Council run an accreditation scheme for private language schools. The seven categories that are checked for recognition of these schools are : management and administration, premises, resources, professional qualifications, academic management, teaching and welfare. However, some schools are not eligible for accreditation - if they've been running for less than two years, for example. Eighty percent of the accredited schools also join ARELS, the trade organisation for recognised private language schools which has 195 members. However, smaller schools may not be able to afford to join ARELS.

Another group of language schools decided to set up their own association, FIRST. Standards are upheld by a system of Initial and Mutual Audit - FIRST's members are audited by fellow member institutions.

There is also a British Council validation scheme for state colleges and polytechnics - which requires colleges to be members of BASELT (the British Association of State English Language Teaching).

United States

There is no accreditation agency specifically for English as a Second Language (ESL) programs, although some states set particular requirements. In Florida, private schools are accredited by ACCET (Accreditation Council for Continuing Education and Training). The American Association of Intensive English Programs (AAIEP) is open to organisations offering intensive courses, and aims to promote professional standards for English language study in the USA.

TESOL has developed a program of self-study for adult training courses based on a 'Statement of Core Standards for Language and Professional Training Programs'. The TESOL statement is generally accepted as the standard by the profession.

An Insider's Guide: Methodology

The world of language teaching is a very dynamic one with new theories constantly challenging old orthodoxies. This is a summary of some of the key fashion changes.

Grammar and translation is alive and well and living in a large number of classrooms

In the beginning there was grammar and translation. Language learners studied a text and learned the grammar with analysis of parts of speech, and then translated it. The classroom language was overwhelmingly the mother tongue, not the language being learned, and the aim was the imparting of content (knowledge of the language) rather than teaching a skill (ability to use the language). In the cyclical way of things, grammar is back with a bang, but translation has never quite recovered its hold on the classroom.

Louis Alexander, the distinguished coursebook author, once said that a coursebook had three lives. First, its life in the methodologically advanced, affluent native speaker teacher-oriented metropolitan schools of the UK, the USA, and Western Europe, Latin America, and parts of the Far East. Then its life in schools in less affluent markets. Thirdly came its life in new markets but non-existent at the time the course was launched. In this way, said Alexander, a coursebook might have a life of up to 15-20 years and different methods used by different generations of coursebooks might co-exist at different locations in the world. As with coursebooks, so with methodology. Grammar and translation is alive and well and living in a large number of classrooms, but is not a recommended approach for new teachers.

Audio-lingual/direct method

The use of the mother tongue became frowned upon in the classroom, as emphasis was firmly placed on breaking down the language into small structural units

In the Fifties and Sixties the audio-lingual method was adopted by language schools in the UK and US, influenced by behavioural psychology. This method was characterised by a shift from teaching about language to teaching a language skill. Stress was placed on students speaking rather than listening to the teacher and on language practice rather than on translation. The use of the mother tongue became frowned upon in the classroom, as emphasis was firmly placed on breaking down the language into small structural units easily presented in simple English or through drawings and actions.

The Direct Method, as the application of the audio-lingual method was called, was highly structural. Students were taken up the verbal ladder from present continuous to present simple to present perfect. Ingenious, but rigid, drills were developed to practise the new patterns learned in the classroom. Often the practice took place through language laboratories, with students sitting in booths listening to recordings, repeating and altering pattern sentences according to instructions.

This method has left its mark on teaching today with its insistence on structured progression; in systematic lesson progression from presentation to practice to free expression; in the demand that teachers talk less and learners talk more; and in the use of English wherever possible. The rigid practice of structural patterns has fallen out of favour, as to some extent has the use of language laboratories.

Situational teaching

The rigid structural progression and learning of language patterns was tempered by the incorporation of new patterns in situations - meeting a friend, losing and finding things and so on. Situational teaching bridged the gap between the structural approach and the functional approach that followed.

The functional/notional approach

At the end of the Sixties, a major shift occurred in the way teachers understood language, influenced by the research of Professor Noam Chomsky into language learning and the existence of a Language Learning Device (LLD), which is the ability of the brain to automatically make sense of the language it absorbs. In the mid-seventies David Wilkins at Reading University formulated the functional and notional approach to language description, which categorised language not into a structural framework, but into how it was used. This meant that instead of teaching tenses, teachers focused first on functions, greeting, apologising etc. They then taught the appropriate structures in relation to the function being presented. The aim was to get learners using the language in a meaningful way as

soon as possible. This format was enshrined in the
Council of Europe Threshold Level Specification for
English in 1974. Functional approaches to languages
then caused a shift in emphasis from presentation of
new structures in situations to the development of
communication skills among learners. The
functional approach is still central to the way we
look at language analysis today.

The communicative approach

The communicative approach describes a way of
applying a functional analysis of language to the
classroom. Functionalism stresses the teaching of
language as it is used in real life, so the stress is on
the development of communicative skills - listening,
speaking, reading and writing. Skills work in the
classroom is not new, but the development of
functional analysis meant that language could be
taught in a different way. Take listening and
reading, for example - a listening comprehension
once had a text with a series of questions (mainly
multiple choice). With a communicative approach
stress was placed on problem solving - listening for
gist, retrieving specific information, identifying
locations and characters. The aim became to make
the learner conscious of the automatic processes that
go on in them as native speakers.

Alongside this approach came greater emphasis on
authentic materials - materials not especially
developed for learning English. Bus tickets and train
timetables became the raw materials of reading and
listening. At the same time, in developing speaking
and writing skills, learners were asked to carry out
roleplays and simulations, write letters to newspapers
and answer job advertisements.

Communicative teaching is enormously influential
today. It has given learners a greater sense of
relevance in the language they are learning and
teachers have gained greater opportunities for
creativity both in the classroom and in the
development of their own materials.

But there has been a downside. With a clear eye on
structural progression and informed teaching of

lexis, communicative teachers have had great success.
But the approach has inevitably favoured native or
near-native speakers of English over the non-native
speaker (most English teachers) and, in
unprofessional hands, could lead to an unstructured,
'phrase book' type of instruction in which little
systematic knowledge of the grammatical framework
or the pronunciation system was imparted.

Where are we now?

The pendulum has swung back, with the recognition
of the importance of the grammatical framework,
but teachers and writers have adopted a 'multi-
syllabus' approach, in which a teaching programme
includes not just a grammatical and lexical syllabus,
but also pronunciation, study skills and crosscultural awareness. There's also a growing focus on
autonomous and independent learning to support
the classroom teacher. This is reflected in the growth
of self-access learning centres in schools as a
supplement to classwork. What makes learning
centres different from libraries is that these materials
are accompanied by graded worksheets and
monitored by a qualified teacher so that students can
read authentic materials appropriate to their level.

The name of the game now is 'eclecticism'. This
doesn't mean, 'Do what you like', but rather
'develop your own teaching style using the principles
of good teaching and good classroom management
that have been developed over the last 30-40 years'.

Alternatives

A couple of fringe developments have been and are
now very influential in language teaching and
learning. Professor Stephen Krashen of the
University of Southern California developed 'the
natural approach' to learning language. Instead of
strictly graded texts at a presupposed level, Krashen
proposed the idea of 'Comprehensible Input' -
comprehension material that was slightly above the
level of the student. Although controversial on their
introduction, many of Krashen's ideas have been
quietly absorbed into language teaching materials
and methods.

An Insider's Guide: The Internet

Although on-line classrooms may be viewed warily by some teachers, the Internet is not a threat but a vast resource with much to offer teachers and students alike.

By now the only way that you wouldn't have at least heard of the Internet is if you are buried deep in the Amazonian jungle or langouring on a small island in the South Pacific - even then, someone could flip open a laptop any minute and start muttering strange incantatory words such as - 'telnet', 'ftp', 'email', 'World Wide Web', 'POP'. So what is all the fuss about and what do these words mean?

What is it ?

It is a global system of connected computers that allows computers to 'talk' to each other. Because the system allows data to take a number of different paths between one computer and another, there is no danger of the whole system collapsing if one computer in any chain was inoperative - the communication would just choose another route. The 'highway' analogy, now a cliché, is quite a useful way to imagine the movement of data. You set out from A to go to B. If there are computers which are out of order then the data will choose another route, much as you would take a detour.

Contrary to some of the wilder fantasies about the Internet, it is very unlikely that using it will make your teeth whiter, improve your marriage or lead you to Cyber-Heaven. Or, for that matter, ruin your children's lives and introduce Satan into your living room. It is a global communications system that can greatly improve the way we communicate information between each other. When it becomes a part of our daily lives as the telephone and fax have before it, the hype will fade and it will take its place alongside other methods of communication.

To make the Internet (the system that moves the data) useful, a number of distinct 'tools' have been developed . The key 'tools' are email, ftp, the World Wide Web, and Telnet. Each has a specific function:

Email

The electronic mail system which allows you to send messages to other email addresses on the Internet.

This is a rapid and very cost-effective way to communicate internationally and nationally. Messages can be sent in groups (like a bulk mailing) and they are far cheaper than fax.

World Wide Web

The most rapidly growing sector of the Internet. Its graphic interface means that you can present your information (courses, brochures, newsletters etc.) in full colour. Information can be accessed any time, anywhere by anyone with an Internet connection and WWW software running on their computer. As it is also a 'tool' which is in very rapid development, new possibilities for the WWW are opening up on almost a weekly basis. Very soon it will be a realistic proposition to include sound files, multimedia files and animation files in WWW documents.

The opportunities offered by the WWW are vast and range from the presentation of simple information pages to the presentation of whole brochures, database searching, on-line enrolments, on-line courses, on-line methods, etc. You can see how the WWW is currently being used for EFL by visiting some of the sites listed below.

Telnet

Telnet is the tool used for communicating directly with another remote computer. One use, for example, is for an organisation with a school in France and another in the UK and another in Germany to use Telnet to enable directors of those schools to access a central computer and open a specific software package, for instance, to get or enter financial data, student data, teaching resources etc. Although widely used by the Internet community, the general user would be far more likely to use email, the World Wide Web and ftp

File Transfer Protocol (FTP)

FTP allows you to send or get packages of data (files). The files are held on ftp sites and are usually organised into library systems so that you can search the site and find what you are after.

Apart from Internet specific software you will find software available for EFL teaching, languages, administration

This is a very useful tool on the Internet and one that is often underused by newcomers. It allows you to transfer to your computer whole software programs that can then be installed and run. This is particularly useful as most of the developers writing software for the Internet make freeware (no cost) or shareware (minimal payment after a trial period) programs available on ftp sites. Apart from Internet specific software you will find software available for EFL teaching, languages, administration ... almost any area that you could have an interest in. A word of caution! Viruses can be downloaded in a software file. Run a virus scan on any software you download.

How do I get onto the Internet?

Firstly, you need to have the basic equipment - telephone line, computer, modem. Then you need to find yourself an ISP (Internet Service Provider) in your country. There will be several. Find out how much each one costs and what they offer. The minimum you are likely to want is email and WWW services. Make sure the provider has a POP (Point of Presence - the telephone number you dial to log onto the Internet from your computer) near to you - if not, you may have steep telephone bills. The ISP should provide you with all of the software that you need to get going. Install the software and away you go!

There is a growing number of sites offering EFL resources for teachers and students

What can the Internet do for English Language Teachers?

The Internet is already doing a lot for English Language Teachers. There is a growing number of sites offering EFL resources for teachers and students, there are newsgroups and listserves (you subscribe to a listserve and information is automatically emailed to you), job recruitment sections, c.v. posting sections, directories of English language schools, qualification courses, English language resources such as dictionaries, cobuilds, grammars and even lesson plans.

If you are more adventurous and want to experiment with the potential of the Internet for ELT you could get hold of an HTML (Hypertext Markup

Language - the language used on the WWW) editor and create your own resource section for teachers or learners. One step on from that is to provide courses - although this requires a lot of thought, a lot of time and commitment and skills beyond those required for the basic creation of Web pages. The best way to get your feet wet is to leap in ! Have a look at some of these sites or subscribe to a listserve to give you an idea of what is available.

ESL Virtual Catalogue:
http://wwwpvp.com/esl.htm
Index of resources for students and teachers
Edunet English For Speakers of Other Languages (ESOL) Index: http://www.edunet.com/esol-idx.html The home page of a multi-sectioned site with information for teachers, students and administrators in EFL.
Weekly Idiom Page: http://www.interport.net/~comenius/idiom.html Idioms and sample dialogues.
Edunet On-Line English Grammar: http://www.edunet.com/english/grammar/index. html An English grammar aimed at EFL students but heavily used by teachers and students alike.
Yahoo Searchable Index: http://www.yahoo.com/ Education /Languages/English_as_a_ Second_ Language A good place to start your wandering. One of the largest indexes on the Internet covering hundreds of categories.
The Virtual English Language Center: http:// www.comenius.com/ESOL / EFL sections for both teachers and students
EFL Web Home Page : http://www.u-net.com/eflweb/A variety of resources and information sections for teachers and students. The site hosts a CV section where teachers can send up their CV's to be viewed by prospective employers.
Heinemann's ELT site http://www.heinemann.co .uk/ heinemann/elt/elt.html Growing fast and with a lot more on it than the titles of their publications.
CELSE :Centre for English Language Studies in Education, University of Manchester http://www. mcc.ac.uk/CELSE/
Collins' Cobuild http://titania. cobuild.collins.co. uk/ (ESL/EFL) A subscription service with concordances and a weekly competition.

English Express™ - now on CD-ROM

Make the most of Multimedia ...

Interactive Language Teaching Ltd. is the publisher of English Express, a series of three EFL multimedia CD-ROM courses, directed at absolute beginner, pre-intermediate and intermediate levels. English Express contains over 1,000 graduated exercises, 36 progress tests with diagnostics, 8 hours of audio and, importantly, over 3 hours of broadcast quality full screen full motion video. Other facilities include sub-titles, dictionary, help and voice record/playback. The courses in business and social English are based on the highly practical and effective 'functional' approach of the Council of Europe's Threshold Level.

Begin at the Beginning
(Absolute Beginner)

Over 80 hours of training on 6 CD-ROM's with workbook and answer keys, course content book, user guide and quick start guide; with mother tongue voice support and bi-lingual dictionary, as well as an online 'tutorial' to orient both student and teacher.

Putting it into Practice
(Pre-Intermediate)

Over 120 hours of training on 6 CD-ROM's with workbook and answer keys, course content book, user guide and quick start guide. This course is built around a compelling storyline with native and non-native speakers which continues through the next course.

Practice makes Perfect
(Intermediate/Advanced)

Over 120 hours of training on 6 CD-ROM's with workbook and answer keys, course content book, user guide and quick start guide. In this course language skills, fluency and confidence building are further advanced and consolidated.

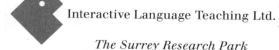

ELT Book Suppliers

Where to buy that crucial text book.

ABU DHABI
Al Mutanabbi Bookshop
PO Box 71946

ARGENTINA
Libreria Rodriguez,
Sarmiento 835,Buenos Aires.

AUSTRALIA
AEE, PO Box 455, Cammeray,
NSW 2062
The Bridge Bookshop, 10
Grafton Street, Chippendale
NSW 2008
Language Book Centre, 555
Beaufort Street, Mnt Lawley,
Western Australia 6050.

The Language People, 207
Boundary Street, West End,
Queensland, 4101.

BRAZIL
Sodilvro, Rua Sa Freire 40,
CP 3655, 20930 Rio, RJ.
Livraria Nobel SA, Rua de
Balsa 559, 02910 Sao Paulo
SBS, Alameda Barros, 75/83
01232-001 Sao Paulo

CANADA
Dominie Press, 1316
Huntingwood Drive, Unit 7,
Agincourt, Ontario, M1S 3JI.

CYPRUS
Bridgehouse Bookshop, PO
Box, 4527 Bridgehouse
Building, Nicosia.

DENMARK
**Atheneum International
Booksellers**, 6 Norregade,
1165 Kobenhavn.

ECUADOR
The English Book Centre,
Acacias 613, y Avenida Las
Monjas, Guayaquil.

EGYPT
International Language

Bookshop, Mahmoud Asmy
ST, PO Box 13, Imbaba,
Cairo.

FINLAND
Akateeminin Kirjakauppa,
Keskuskatu 1 SF-00100
Helsinki.

FRANCE
Attica, 64 Rue De La Folie,
Mericourt, 75011, Paris
Bradleys Bookshop, 32 Pl
Gambetta, 3300 Bordeaux.
W.H. Smith
La Librarie Anglaise
248, rue de Rivoli 75001 Pans,

France
Just Books, 1 Rue de la Paix, Grenoble.
Decitre, 29 Pl Bellecour, 69002 Lyon.
English Books, 8 Rue Doree, 30000 Nimes.
Librairie des Facultes, 2 Rue de Rome,Strasbourg.

GREECE
Kosmos, 59 Panepistimiou St, 105 64 Athens.
Efstathiadis Group, Olympou 34, 546 30 Thessaloniki.

HONG KONG
Commercial Press, 9-15 Yee Wo Street, Causeway Bay, Hong Kong.

ICELAND
Bokabud Malsog Menningar, Laugavegi 18, 101 Reykjavik.

INDONESIA
Triad Book Centre, Jl Purnawarman 76, Bandung, 40116.
PT Bhratara Niaga Media, Jalan Cipinang, Bali No. 5A, Jakarta Timur.

IRELAND
International Books, 18 South Frederick Street, Dublin
Modern Languages Ltd., 39 Westland Row, Dublin 2

ISRAEL
Eric Cohen Books, 5 Hanakin St, Ra'anana 43 464.

University Publishing Projects, 28 Hanatziv St. Tel Aviv 67015, Israel

JAPAN
Biblos, Fl Bldg 1-26-5 Takadanobaba, Shinjuku-ku, Tokyo 160.

JORDAN
Jordan Book Centre, PO Box 301, (Al Jubeiha) Amman.

KENYA
Book Distributors Limited, PO Box 47610, Weruga Lane, Nairobi.

KUWAIT
Kuwait Bookshops, Thunayan Al Ghanem Bldg, PO Box 2942, Safat.

MALAYSIA
STP Distributors, SDN BHD 31 Green Hall, 10200 Penang.

MEXICO
Libreria Britannica SA, Serapio Rendon 125, Col San Rafael, 06470 DF.

MOROCCO
Librairie Nationale, 2 Avenue Mers Sultan, Casablanca
American Bookstore, 4 Zankat Tanja, Rabat.

NEW ZEALAND
University Bookshop, 34 Princes Street, Auckland.

NORWAY
Norsk Bokirnport, Postboks 784 S Ovre Vollgate 15, 0106 Oslo.**Olaf Norlis Bokhandel**, Universitetsgt 18, 0162 Oslo.

SPAIN
Turner, C/ Génova 3 y 5,

28004 Madrid.
Booksellers S.A. Liberia Inglesa, 48 28003 Madrid.

SWEDEN
The English Book Centre, Surbrunnsgatan 51,102 34 Stockholm.

SWITZERLAND
Librairie Francke, Neuengasse 43\Von Werdt Passage, 3001 Bem.
Elm Video and Books, 5 rue Versonnes, 1207 Geneva.

TAIWAN
Caves Books, 103 Chung Shan N Road, Sec 2 Taipei.

TURKEY
Haset Kitabevi A.S. Sair Nevres Bulvari No 3/B, Alsancak, Izmir
ABC Kitabevi, 461 Istiklal Cad, Istanbul.
Baris Kitabevi, Koca M Pasa Cad, No5914, Cerrahoasa, Istanbul.

UNITED KINGDOM
Hudsons Bookshop, 116 New Street, Birmingham, B2 4JJ
The English Language Bookshop, 31 George Street, Brighton, East Sussex, BN2
Cambridge International Book Centre, 42 Hills Road, Cambridge, CB2 1LA
Albion Bookshop, 13 Mercery Lane, Canterbury, Kent.
James Thin Ltd, Buccleuch Street, Edinburgh.
John Smith & Son Ltd, 578 St Vincent Street, Glasgow.
International Bookshop, White Rock, Hastings East

Sussex, TN34 1JY.
BEBC London, 106 Piccadilly, London W1
European Bookshop, 4 Regent Place, London W1R 6BH
KELTIC, 25 Chepstow Comer, Chepstow Place, London W2 4TT.
LCL Benedict Ltd, 104 Judd Road, London WC1.
Skola Books, 27 Delaney Street, London NW1 7RX.
Haigh and Hockland Ltd, The Precinct Centre, Oxford Road, Manchester.
Thornes Bookshop, Grand Hotel Percy Street, Newcastle Upon Tyne, NE1 7RS.
Blackwells, 50 Broad Street, Oxford OXI 2BQ.
The English Book Centre, 24 Middleway, Oxford OX2 7LG.
Bournemouth English Book Centre, 15 Albion Close, Parkstone, Poole, Dorset BH12 3LL
Sherrat and Hughes, 94 Above Bar,Southampton SO9.**Cactus Bookshop**, 104 College Road, Stoke on Trent
Thomas C Godfrey Limited, 32 Stonegate, York, North Yorkshire Y01.

USA
Alta Book Center, 14 Adrian Court, Burlingame CA 94010.
Lado Institute Bookstore, 2233 Wisconsin Avenue, Washington DC 20007
Delta Systems Co, 1400 Miller Pkwy, McHenry IL
Worldwide Teachers Development Institute, 266 Beacon St Boston MA 02116

Conference Calendar

Some of the worldwide conferences and seminars to look out for in 1996.

9-10 March
17th Annual TESOL Greece Convention
"Focus on the Teacher: Changing
Direction."
Place: Divania-Caravel Hotel, Athens,
Greece
Contact: Mrs Eleni Giannopoulou
Tel: 30 74 88 459

14 March
4th Annual Professional BATQI
Conference: "Towards a British Institute of
Language Teaching: Issues and Options."
Place: London University Institute of
Education, England
Contact: Charles Lowe Fax: 44 171 495
0689

26 March-30 March
TESOL Annual Conference
Place: Chicago, Illinois, USA
Contact: TESOL, 1600 Cameron St.,
Suite 300, Alexandria, Virginia 22314-
2751, USA. Tel: 703 836 0774

29 March-1 April
Association for Language Learning (ALL)
Language World
Place: Exeter, England
Contact: ALL, C. Wilding, 16 Regent
Place, Rugby, England, CV2 2PN

1-4 April
13th Annual Conference on Language,
Literature and Transliteration
Place: Yarmouk University, Irbid, Jordan
Contact: Muhammed R Zughoul Fax: 962
2 274 4725

April (Date Tba)
Annual Meeting of TESOL
Place: Anaheim, California
Contact: TESOL (see above)

9-12 April
30th IATEFL International Conference
Place: Keele, Stoke on Trent, England

Contact: IATEFL, 3 Kingsdown
Chambers, Kingsdown Park, Whitstable,
CT5 2DJ. Tel: 010 44 1227 276 528

10-13 April
2nd Teachers of English in Austria
Conference: "Literature for Language
Learners"
Place: University of Vienna, Austria
Contact: TEA Tel/Fax: 43 587 50 47

10-22 April
2nd International Maastricht-Lodz
Colloquium on Translation and Meaning
Place: Maastricht, The Netherlands

20-23 April
Languages and Cultures International
Language Festival
Place: Moscow, Russia
Contact: International Consultants for
Education and Fairs, Am Hofgarten 18, D-
53113 Bonn, Germany

20-22 May
The Malaysian International Conference
on English Language Teaching
Place: Rasa Sayang Resort, Penang,
Malaysia

27 May-1 June
13th Annual Symposium of the Computer
Assisted Language Learning Instruction
Consortium:"Distance Learning"
Place: Sheraton Old Town, Albuquerque
and The University of New Mexico
Contact: Duke University. Tel: 919 660
3180

June
1st Joint BETA/BESIG/ESPIG
Conference: "Managing Change in English
for Business and in English for Special
Purposes - Challenges and Opportunities"
Place: Romania
Contact: Zoia Manolescu Tel/Fax: 40 1
311 13 47

15-19 July
Twenty Third International Systemic
Functional Congress
Place: University of Technology, Sydney,
Australia
Contact: Diane Slade, Faculty of
Education, University of Technology,
Sydney, PO Box 123, Broadway 20007,
NSW, Australia

19-24 July
International Systemic Functional Congress
Place: Peking, China
Contact: Hu Zhuang-lin, Peking
University, Department of English, Beijing
100871, People's Republic of China

4-9 August
AILA 96: 11th World Congress of Applied
Linguistics
Place: Jyvaskyla, Finland
Contact: Ms Taru-Maija Heilala (Ms)
Jyvaskyla Congresses, PO Box 35, SF-
40351, Jyvaskyla, Finland.
Tel: 010 358 41 603 663

18-21 September
5th National Conference on Community
Languages and English for Speakers of
Other Languages
Place: Hamilton, New Zealand
Contact: Jill Hobden, Conference
Convenor, The University of Waikato
Language Institute, The University of
Waikato, Private Bag 3105, Hamilton,
New Zealand Tel: 64 7838 4193

26-28 September
British Council/IATEFL Special Interest
Group Symposium
Place: University of Vienna, Austria
Contact: IATEFL (see above) or Andrea
Eschner, The British Council,
Schenkenstrasse 4, 1010 Vienna, Austria,
Tel: 43 1533 261 676

The following centres offer RSA/Cambridge courses. Check pages 207-214 for full contact details and the relevant Table for further information on many of these courses.

Argentina: International House Buenos Aires (D)
Australia: Australian Centre for Languages (C), Australian TESOL Training Centre (C&D), Insearch Language Centre (C), International House Queensland (C), Centre for Applied Linguistics (C), The South Australian College of English (C), Holmesglen College of TAFE (C), ITTC (C), La Trobe University (C), Royal Melbourne Institute of Technology (C), Milner International College of English (C), St Mark's International College (C& D).
Austria: International House (C)
Canada: International Language Institute (C), Concordia University (C).
Czech Republic: International Language Centres (C&D)
Egypt: American University in Cairo (C), British Council Cairo (C&D), International Language Institute (C).
France: British Institute Paris (D), International Language Centre (C), Universite Lyon II (D).
Greece: Centre for English Language and Training (D)
Hong Kong: British Council (C & D)
Hungary: International House Language School (C & D)
Indonesia: The British Institute (C)
Ireland: University College Cork (C), Language Centre of Ireland (C & D).
Italy: British Institute Florence (C & D), British Council Milan (C &D), British School Milan (C &D), British Council Naples (C), International House - Accademia Britannica (C), The British School of Udine (C), Cambridge School Verona (C&D)
Japan: International Language Centre (D), Language Resources Kobe (C), The British Council - Cambridge English School (C).
Kuwait: British Council Kuwait (C)
Malaysia: The British Council Langauge Centre (C)
Malta: NSTS English Language Institute (C)
Netherlands: The British School ELC (C)
New Zealand: Auckland Language Centre (C), Dominion English School (C), Languages International Limited (C&D), ILA South Pacific Limited (C), Language Institute University of Waikato (C), Capital Language Academy (C)
Oman: British Council Muscat (C), Polyglot Institute Oman LLC (C)
Poland: International House (C&D), British Council (D)
Portugal: The British Council DTO (C & D), Cambridge School of English (C), International House Lisbon (C)
Qatar: The British Council (C)
Saudi Arabia: The Britsh Council (C)
Spain: International House Barcelona (C&D), York House English Language Centre (C), British Language Centre (C&D), International House Madrid (C), International House Palma (C), Campbell College Teacher Training Centre (C)
Switzerland: ELCRA Bell s.a. (C), The Bell Language School (C), Volkshochschule des Kantons Zurich (C), Department of Applied Linguistics (C)
Thailand: EEC (Thailand) (C)

Turkey: Bilkent University School of English (D), The British Council Istanbul (C), British Council Teachers Centre Istanbul (C&D), British Council Teachers Centre Izmir (D)
United Arab Emirates: Basic University Education Centre (D), The British Council Abu Dhabi (C), Higher College of Technology (C)
United Kingdom: Amersham & Wycombe College (C), Anglia Polytechnic University (C), Anglo Continental (C), Angloschool (C), Barnet College (C),) Basil Paterson/Edinburgh Language Foundation (C), Bedford College (C), The Bell Language School Bath (C), The Bell Language School Cambridge (C&D), The Bell Language School Norwich (C & D), The Bell Language School Saffron Walden (D), Bournemouth & Poole College of FE (C), Bromley School of English (C), Brooklands College (C), Brunel College of Arts & Technology (C), Cheltenham International Language Centre (C), Chichester College of Arts & Technology (C&D), City of Bath College (C), Clarendon College (C), Colchester Institute (D), Concorde International Study Centre (C), Devon School of English (C), Eastbourne College of Arts & Technology (C&D), Eastbourne School of English (C & D), ELT Banbury (C), Filton College (C), Frances King Teacher Training Centre (C), GEOS English Academy Brighton & Hove (C), GLOSCAT (C&D), Godmer House Teacher Training (C), Greenhill College (C), Hammersmith & West London College (C&D), Handsworth College (C), Harrow House (C), Hendon College (C), Hilderstone College (C&D), Huddersfield Technical College (C), International House Hastings (C&D), International House London (C&D), International House Newcastle-upon-Tyne (C), International Language Institute Leeds (C), International Teaching and Training Centre (C&D), King's College London (D), Leeds Metropolitan University (C), Lexis Language Learning (C), Loughborough College (C), Marble Arch Teacher Training (D), Mid-Cheshire College of Further Education (C), Newnham Language Centre (C), North Trafford College (C), Oxford Brookes University (C), Oxford College of Further Education (C&D), Pilgrims English Language Courses (C), Regent Language Training (C), St Giles College (C), School of Oriental & African Studies (SOAS) (C), Skola Teacher Training (C), Solihull College (C), South Devon College (C), South Thames College (C), Stanton Teacher Training (C), Stevenson College (C), Stoke-on-Trent College (C), The Studio School of English (C), Thames Valley University (C), University of Central England in Birmingham (D), University of East Anglia (C), University of Edinburgh, Institute for Applied Linguistics (D), University of Glamorgan (C), University of Glasgow (C), University of Hull (C) University of Northumbria at Newcastle (C) University of Strathclyde (C), University of Wales Centre for Applied Language Studies (D), UTS, Oxford Centre (D), Waltham Forest College (D), Westminster College (C) Wigan & Leigh College (C&D), Wigston College of Further Education (C),
United States of America: The Centre for English Studies (C), Coast Language Academy (C), English International San Francisco (C), Georgetown University (C), St Giles Language Teaching Centre (C).
UK And Overseas: International House London Distance Training Programme

The following centres offer Trinity College courses. Check pages 207-214 for full contact details and the relevant Table for further information on many of these courses.

United Kingdom: Aberdeen College (C&D), Abon Language School (C), Basingstoke College of Technology (C), Blackpool & The Fylde College (C), Bracknell College of FE (C), Bradford and Ilkley Community College (C), Bury College (C), Cicero Languages International (C), City College Manchester (C), Colchester Institute (C), Continuing Education & Training Services (C), Coventry TESOL Centre (C), Darlington College of Technology (C), East Berkshire College, Langley (C), Edinburgh Tutorial College (C), E.T.C. (C), Farnborough College of Technology (C&D), Golders Green College (C), Grimsby College of Technology (C), Grove House Language Centre (C), Hart Villages Centre (C), Hopwood Hall College (C), The Hull College (C), inlingua Teacher Training & Recruitment (C), Institute of Language Studies (D), International Language Institute (D), International Training Network (D), ITS English School (C), Joseph Priestly College (C), King Street College (C), Kingsway College (C), Language Link Training (C), Leeds Metropolitan University (C), London Study Centre (C), Medway Adult Education Centre (C), Middlesborough College of FE (C), North Lindsey College (C), Oaklands College (C), Oxford House College (C&D), Park Lane College (C), Plymouth College of Further Education (C), Northbrook College (C), Polyglot Language Services (C), The Regency School of English (C&D), Richmond Adult & Community College (C), St Brelade's College (C), St George's School of English (C&D), Sandwell College of F & HE (C), Scot-Ed Courses (C), S. E. Essex College of Arts and Technology (C&D), The Sheffield College (C&D), Sidmouth International School (C), South Nottingham College (C), Southwark College (C), Sheffield Hallam University (C&D), Stafford House School of English (D), Surrey Language Centre (C), Surrey Youth & Adult Education Services (C&D), Students International Ltd. (C), Surrey Youth & Adult Education Services (Elmbridge) (C&D), Sutton College of Liberal Arts (C), Thurrock College (C), Universal Language Training (C), University of Luton (C&D), University of Wales (C), University of the West of England (C), University of Wolverhampton (C), Waltham Forest College (C), Windsor Schools TEFL (C)
Ireland: Grafton Tuition Centre (C)
Japan: Saxoncourt Teacher Training (C)
New Zealand: International Academy of Languages, International Pacific College (C), Seafield School of English (C),
Paraguay: Stael Ruffinelli De Ortiz - English (C),
Spain: The Language Institute (C), Novalingua/Oxford House College (C), Universal Language Training (C)

UNITED KINGDOM

Aberdeen College of Further Education, Dept of English & Communication, Holburn Street, Aberdeen AB9 2YT

Aberdeen College, Gallowgate Centre, Gallowgate Aberdeen AB9 IDN Tel: (01224) 640 366

Abbey College, The, Wells Road, Malvern, Worcs. WR14

Abon Language School, 25 St. Johns Road, Clifton, Bristol BS8 2HD Tel: (0117) 973 0354

Anglia Polytechnic University, East Road, Cambridge CB1 1PT Tel: (01223) 363 271

Anglo-Continental School of English, 33 Wimbourne Road, Bournemouth BH2 6NA Tel: (01202) 557 414

Anglo European Study Tours, 8 Colesbridge Mews, Porchester Road, London W2 6EU

Anglo Lang, 20 Avenue Road, Scarborough, North Yorkshire YO12

Anglo School, 146 Church Road, London SE19 2NT Tel: (0181) 653 7285

Anglo-World, Cambridge,75 Barton Road, Cambridge CB3 9LJ

Anglo-World Oxford, 108 Banbury Road, Oxford OX2 6JU

ARA, 26 Hay's Mews, London W1X

ARELS (Association of Recognised English Language Schools) 2 Pontypool Place, Valentine Place,London SE1

BALEAP (British Association of Lecturers in English for Academic Purposes),English Language Unit, Huw Owen Building, OCW, Penglais, Aberyswyth, Dyfed, Wales

BASELT (Association of UK State Colleges),Cheltenham and Gloucester College of Higher Education, Francis Close Hall, Swindon Road, Cheltenham, Glos

Basil Paterson College, 22-23 Abercromby Place Edinburgh EH3

BEBC, 9 Albion Close, Parkstone, Poole, Dorset, BH12 3LL

BEBC London, International House, 106 Piccadilly, London W1V

Bedford College of Higher Education, School of Humanities Mander Buildings, Cauldwell Street, Bedford MK42 9AH

Bedford College, 13 The Crescent, Bedford MK40 2RT Tel: (01234) 271 492

Bedford Study Centre, 94-96 Midland Road, Bedford MK40 1QE

Beet Language Centre, Nortoft Road, Charminster, Bournemouth

Bell Language School Bath, Henley Lodge, Western Road, Bath BA1 2XT

Bell Language School, Cambridge, Red Cross Lane, Cambridge CB2 2QX Tel: (01223) 247 242

Bell Language School, London, 34 Fitzroy Square, London W1P 6BP

Bell Language School, Norwich Bowthorpe Hall, Norwich Bowthorpe, Norwich NR5 9AA Tel: (01603) 745 615

Bell Language School, The Old House, Norwich, Church Lane, Eaton, Norwich NR4 6NW

Bell Language School, Saffron Walden, South Road, Saffron Walden Essex CB1 3DP Tel: (01799) 522 918

Berlitz Publishing Co Ltd, Berlitz House, Peterley Road, Oxford OX4 2TX

Berlitz School of Languages Ltd, Wells House, 79 Wells Street, London W1

Bidbury House, Bidbury Lane, Havant Hants PO9 3JA Tel: (01705) 483 217

Birmingham UCF,Faculty of Education, Westbourne Road, Birmingham

Blackpool and The Flyde College, Ashfield Road, Bispham, Blackpool SY2

Bournemouth Business School, 4 Yelverton Road, Bournemouth BH1 1DF Tel: (01202) 780 776

Bournemouth & Poole College of Further Education, Landsdowne Centre, Bournemouth BH1

Bone & Company (International Ltd), Les Brehauts St Peter, Guernsey CI

Bradford and Ilkley Community College, English Language Centre, 8E Westbook Building Great Horton Road, Bradford West Yorkshire BD7 1AY Tel: (01274) 753 207

Brasshouse Centre, 50 Sheepcote Street Birmingham B16 8AJ Tel: (0121) 643 0114

Brighton University, The Language Centre, University of Brighton, Falmer, Brighton BN 9PH

Bristol University, School of Education, 35 Berkeley Square, Bristol BS8 ITA

British Council, 10 Spring Gardens, London SW1A 2BN

British Council, Medlock Street, Manchester M15 4AA

Bromley School of English, 2 Park Road Bromley Kent BR1 1HP Tel: (0181) 313 0308

Brooklands Technical College, Heather Road, Weybridge, Surrey KT13 8TT

Brudenell School of English, Larnerton House, 27 High Street London W5

Business Language School, Old Library Building, Newcastle University, Newcastle Upon Tyne NE1 7RU Tel: (0191) 222 7098

Cambridge Centre for Languages, Sawston Hall, Cambridge CB2 4JR

Cambridge School of Languages, 119 Mill Road, Cambridge CB1 2AZ Tel: (01223) 312 333

Canterbury Christ Church College, North Holmes Road, Canterbury,Kent CT1 1QU Tel: (01227) 458 459

Canterbury Language Training, 73 Castle Street,Canterbury, Kent CT1 2QD Tel: (01227) 760 000

Central Bureau for Exchange, Seymour Mews House,Seymour Mews, London W1H 9TE

Central Manchester College, St Johns Centre, Lower Hardman Street Manchester

CfBT Education Services, Quality House, Gyosei Campus,London Road, Reading RW1 5AQ

Cheltenham International Language Centre Fulwood Park, Suffolk Square,Cheltenham, Glos Gl60 2EB Tel: 01242 532 925

Chichester College of Arts, Science and Technology, International Department, Westgate Fields, Chichester, W Sussex PO19 1SB Tel: (01243) 536 294

Chichester School of English, Tutorial College, 45 East Street, Chichester, W Sussex PO19 1HX

Chichester Institute of Higher Education, The Dome, Upper Bognor Road, West Sussex PO21 1HR Tel: (01243) 865 053

Chippenham Technical College, Commercial & Media Studies Department, Cocklebury Road, Chippenham SN15

Christ Church College, Language Studies, North Hulmes Road, Canterbury CT1 1QU

Christians Abroad, 1 Stockwell Green, London SW9 9HP

Chrysalis Language Courses, PO Box 193, Exeter, Devon EX2 8YR Tel: (01392) 431 521

Cicero Languages International, 42 Upper Grosvenor Road, Tunbridge Wells, Kent TN1 2ET Tel: (01892) 547 077

City of Bath College, Avon St., Bath BA1 1UP. Tel: 01225 312 191

Clarendon College of Further Education, The Berridge Centre, Stanley Road, Fimest Fields, Nottingham NG7 6HW

Colchester English Study Centre, 19 Lexden Road, Colchester, Essex CO3 3PW Tel: (01206) 44422

Colchester Institute, Dept of Humanities, Sheepen Road, Colchester, Essex CO3 3IL Tel: 01206 718 000

College of Ripon and York, St John College Road, Ripon HG4 2QX

College of St Mark & St John, International Education Centre, Derriford Road, Plymouth PL6 8BH Tel: (01752) 636 821

College of St Paul & St Mary, TEFL Unit, Francis Close Hall, Swindon Road, Cheltenham GL50 4AZ

Collingham Brown + Brown, 31 St Giles Oxford OX1 3LF Tel: (01865) 728 280

Concorde International, Radnor Chambers, Cheriton Place, Folkestone, Kent CT20 2BB

Coombe Cliff Centre, Coombe Road, Croydon CRO 5SP

Coventry International English Studies Centre 9 Priory Row, Coventry, CV1 5EX Tel: (01293) 223 379

Coventry Technical College, Meridian, Tesol Centre, Butts Coventry CV1 3GD

Croydon College of Continuing Education, Fairfield, College Road, Croydon CR9 1DX

Davies School of English, 56 Ecclestone Place, London SW1V 1PO

Devon School of English, The Old Vicarage 1 Lower Polsham Road, Paignton, Devon TQ3 3HF

DSS (Overseas Branch), Newcastle upon Tyne NE 98 1YX.

East Berkshire College, Station Road, Langley, Slough SL3 8BY

Eastbourne College of Art and Technology, St Annes Road, Eastbourne BN2 2HS Tel: (01323) 644 711

Eastbourne School of English, 8 Trinity Trees, Eastbourne BN21 3LD Tel: (01323) 721 759

East European Partnership, 15 Princeton Court, 53-55 Felsham Road, London SW16

Eaton Hall International, Retford, Nottinghamshire DN22 OPT2

Ebury Executive English, 132 Ebury Street London SW1W 9QQ Tel: 44 171 730 3991

Edinburgh Tutorial College, 29 Chester Street, Edinburgh EH3 76N

Edinburgh Language Foundation, Dugdale-McAdam House, 22-23 Abercromby Place, Edinburgh

Edinburgh School of English, 271 Canongate, The Royal Mile, Edinburgh EH8 8BQ Tel: (0131) 557 9200

Edinburgh Tutorial College, 29 Chester Street, Edinburgh EH3 7EN Tel: (0131) 225 9888

The Education Policy Information Centre, The Mere, Upton Park, Slough, Berks SL1 2DQ

EF Institute, 74 Roupell Street, London SE1 8SS Tel: (0171) 795 6685
EF International, 1/2 Sussex Square, Brighton BN2 1FJ
EF Schools, 74-80 Warrior Square, St Leonards-on-Sea, Hastings
EL Gazette, 10 Wright's Lane, London, W8 6TA
ELC Norwich, 46 Unthank Road, Norwich NR2 2RB
Elmbridge Institute of Adult Education, The Day Centre, 19 The Green,Esher, Surrey
ELT Banbury, 49 Oxford Road Banbury, Oxon OX16 9AH Tel: (01295) 263 502
ELT School of English, 32 North End Road, Golders Green, London NW11 Tel: (0181) 455 2999
Embassy Language and Training Centre, 5/7 Willbury Villas, Hove Tel: (01273) 721 135
English Home Tuition Scheme, 21 Dobell Road, London SE9 1HE Tel: (0181) 850 9459
English Language Centre Bournemouth, 163-169 Old Christchurch Road, Bournemouth BH1
English Language Teaching Division, Dept of Morden Languages, Livington Tower, 24 Richmond Street, Glasgow
English Language Unit, School of Oriental and African Studies, 4 Gower Street, London WC1E 6HA Tel: (0171) 580 8272
English and Spanish Studies, London House, High Street Kensington London
English Teaching Information Centre, The British Council, 10 Spring Gardens, London SW1A 2BN
Eurocentre, Bournemouth, 26 Dean Pk Road, Bournemouth BH1 1HA
Eurocentre, Lee Green, 21 Meadowcourt Road, London SE3 8EU
Eurolink, 3 Abbeydale Road South, Millhouses, Sheffield S7 2QL Tel: 0114 262 1522
European Council of International Schools, 21b Lavant Street, Petersfield, Hampshire GU32 3EL
European Training & Communications, 83-85 Ferensway, Hull, North Humberside HU2 8LD
Executive Training Centre, 8 St. Peter's Grove, York YO3 6AQ
Farnborough College of Technology, Manor Park Centre, Manor Walk, Aldershot, Hampshire GN12
Filton Technical College, EFL Dept, Filton Avenue, Bristol BS12 7AT (0117) 931 2121
Frances King Business English, 195 Knightsbridge, London SW7 1RE (0171) 838 0400
Frances King School of English, 5 Grosvenor Gardens, Victoria, London SW1W 0BB Tel: (0171) 584 6411
Gateshead College, Durham Road, Gateshead, Tyne and Wear NE9 5BN Tel: 0191 490 2261
Gateshead Training Consultancy, Durham Road, Gateshead, Tyne and Wear NE9 5BN Tel: 0191 490 2261
Gateway Language, Cairnie View, Dunning, Perthshire PH2 02Q Tel: (01764) 684 528
GEOS, 55-61 Portland Road, Hove,Sussex BN3 5DQ
Globe English Centre, 71 Holloway Street, Exeter, Devon EX2 4JD

Gloscat, Dept of Management & Business, The Park Campus, 73 The Park, Cheltenham Glos GL50 2RR Tel: (01242) 532 144
Godmer House, 90 Banbury Road, Oxford OX2 6JT
Goldsmith's College, Lewisham Way, London SE14
Greenhill College, Lowlands, Harrow, Middx HA1 3AQ
Grove House Language Centre, Carlton Avenue, Horns Cross, Dartford Kent DA9 9DR Tel: (01322) 386 526
Hammersmith & West London College Dept of English Studies, Gliddon Road, Barons Court, London W14 9BL Tel: (0181) 741 1688
Harrogate Language Academy, 8a Royal Parade, Harrogate, N Yorks H61 2SZ
Harrow House International College, Harrow Drive, Swanage,Dorset BH19 1LE Tel: (01929) 424 421
Hart Villages Centre (Basingstoke) Robert Mays School, West Street, Oldham, Basingstoke RG25 1NA
Hendon College of FE, Montague Road Centre, Hendon, London NW4 3ES (0181) 200 8300
Highland Language Centre, 12 Marine Terrace, Rosemarkie, Ross-shire IV10 8UL Tel: (01381) 620 598
Hilderstone College, English Study Centre, St Peters Road, Broadstairs, Kent CT10 2AQ Tel: (01843) 869 171
Hopwood Hall College, St Mary's Gate, Rochdale OL12 6RY
House of English, 24 Portland Place, Brighton BN21DG Tel: (01273) 694 618
Huddersfield Technical College, New North Road, Huddersfield HD1 5NN Hull College, Queen's Gardens, Hull HU1 3DG
IATEFL, 3 Kingsdown Chambers, Tankerton, Whitstable, Kent CT5 2DJ
ICELS, Oxford Brookes University, Headington, Oxford OX3 6BP
ILC Recruitment, 1 Riding House Street, London W1A 3AS
inlingua Teacher Training & Recruitment, Rodney Lodge, Rodney Road, Cheltenham Gl50 1JF Tel: (01242) 253 171
Institute of Education, University of London, TESOL Dept., 20 Bedford Way, London WC1 0AL
Institute for International Communication, 56 Eccleston Square, London SW1V 1PQ Tel: (0171) 233 9888
International House, Hastings, White Rock, Hastings, E Sussex TN34 1JY Tel: (01424) 720 100
International House, London, 106 Piccadilly, London W1V Tel: (0171) 491 2958
International House, 14-18 Stowell Street, Newcastle upon Tyne NE1 4XQ
International Language Academy, 12-13 Regent Terrace, Cambridge CB2 1AA
International Language Academy, Hinton Chambers, Hinton Road, Bournemouth BH1 2EN Tel: (01202) 557 522
International Language Academy, 4 Russell Gardens, London W14 8EY
International Language Academy, 7 Norham Gardens, Oxford OX2 6PS
International Language Academy, Castle Circus, Union Street, Torquay TQ1 3DE Tel: (01803) 297 166

International Language Centre, 24 Polworth Gardens, Edinburgh EH11
International Language Institute, County House, Vicar Lane, Leeds LS1
International Language Services, 36 Fowlers Road, Salisbury Wilts SP1
International Teaching and Training Centre, 674 Wimbourne Road, Bournemouth BH9 2EG Tel: (01202) 531 355
International Training Network, 28 Howard Road, Bournemouth, Dorset BH8 9EA
ITS English School, Hastings, 43-46 Cambridge Gardens,Hastings, E. Sussex TN34 1EN Tel: (01424) 438 025
Intuition Languages, 109 Shepperton Road, London N1
James Thin Ltd, Buccleuch Street, Edinburgh
Japan Information and Cultural Centre, Embassy of Japan, 104 Piccadilly,London W1V 9FN
JET Programme Officer, Japan Information Centre,Embassy of Japan, 9 Grosvenor Square, London W1H
JKM Language and Education Centre, Westbrooke House, 76 High Street Alton Hants GU34 1EN Tel: (01420) 543 679
KELTIC Bookshop, 25 Chepstow Corner, Chepstow Place, London W2
King Alfred College of Higher Education Sparkford Road, Winchester Tel: (01962) 827 387
Kings College London, The English Language Unit, Kensington Campus, Camden Hill Road, London W8 7AH
Kingsway College, EFL Unit, Vernon Square Centre, Penton Rise, London WC1X 9El
Kingsway English Centre, Northwall House, 11 The Butts, Worcester WR1 2PA Tel: 44 1905 27511
Kirkby College of F.E., Oman Road, Linthorpe, Middlesborough, Cleveland TS5 5PJ
Language Matters, 4 Blenheim Road, Moseley,Birmingham B13 9TY
Language Project, The, 78-80 Colston Street, Bristol BS1 5BB(0117) 927 3993
Language Service Ltd, The Riverview Suite, Christine House, Sorbonne Close, Thornaby Stockton on Tees, Cleveland TS17 6DA Tel: (01642) 673 608
Language Training Services, 5 Belevedere, Lansdowne Road, Bath, BA1
LCCI, Marlow House, Station Road, Sidcup, Kent, DA15
LCL Benedict Ltd, 104 Judd Road, London WC1
Language 2 Associates, 25 Woodway Crescent, Harrow HA1 2NH Tel: 0181 907 2618
Linguarama Ltd, 53 Pall Mall, London SW1Y 5JH/Oceanic House, 89 High Street, Alton, Hants GU34
Liverpool Community College, Bankfield Road, Liverpool L13 0BQ
Living Language Centre, Highcliffe House, Clifton Gardens, Folkstone, Kent CT20 2EF
London Guildhall University, Old Castle Street, London E1 7NT Tel: (0171) 320 1251
London Montessori Centre, 18 Balderton Street, London W1Y 1TG
London School of English, 15 Holland Park Gardens, London W14 8DZ Tel: (0171) 603 1656

London Study Centre, Munster House, 676 Fulham Road,London SW6
Loughborough College, Radmore, Loughborough Leics., LE11 3BTTel: (01509) 215 831
Luton College of HE, Park Square, Luton, Bedfordshire LU1 3JU
LTS Training & Consulting, 5 Belvedere, Landsdown Road, Bath, Avon BAI SED
Lydbury English Centre, The Old Vicarage, Lydbury North, Shropshire
Lynda Hazelwood Language Services, 38 Charlton Park, Keynsham, Bristol BS18 2ND Tel: 01179 860 688
Mancatz, Lower Hardman Street, Manchester M3 3ER
Manchester Business School, Language Centre, Booth Street West, Manchester M15 6PB
Manchester Central College, Lower Hardman Street,Manchester M3 3FP
Manchester City College, Fielden Centre, Barlow Moor Didsbury, Manchester M20 2PQ
Manchester Metropolitan University, Faculty of Community Studies, 799 Wilmslow Road, Manchester M20 8RR
Marble Arch Teacher Training, 21 Star Street, London W2 1QB
Mid-Cheshire College FE, Management Dept, Chester Road, Hertford Campus, Northwich CW8 1LJ Tel: (01606) 74444
Millbrook College, TEFL, Bankfield Site, Bankfield Road,Liverpool, Lancs L13 0BR
Moray House College of Education, Holyrood Road, Edinburgh EH8 8AQ Tel: (0131) 558 6337
Multilingua, St Michaels House, 53 Woolbridge Road, Guildford GU1 4RF Tel: 44 1483 35118
NATFHE (National Association of Teachers in Further and Higher Education) 27 Britannia Street, London WC1X 9JP
National Extension College, 18 Brooklands Avenue, Cambridge CB2
NEATEFL, Newcastle College, Rye Hill Newcastle on Tyne
Netherhall International College, Nutley Terrace, Hampstead London NW3 5SA Tel: (01710 794 1122
Newnham Language Centre, 8 Grange Road, Cambridge CB3 9DV
Nord Anglia International Ltd, 10 Eden Place, Cheadle, Stockport, Cheshire SK8 1AT
North East Surrey College of Technology, Reigate Road, Ewell Fosom, Surrey KT17 3DS
North Trafford College, Talbot Road, Stretford, Manchester M32 0XH Tel: (0161) 872 3731
Northumbria House, 22 Summerhill Stella, Blaydon-on-Tyne NE21 4JS Tel: (0191) 414 3646
Norwich Institute For Language Education (NILE), PO Box 2000, Norwich NR2 2EY Tel: 44 1603 451
NUT (National Union of Teachers), Hamilton House, Mabledon Place, London WC1
Oaklands College, Borehamwood Campus Elstree Way, Borehamwood, WD6 1JZ Tel: (0181) 953 6024
OCTAB (The Overseas Contract Teachers and Advisors Branch of the IPS) The Secretary, 24 Ashford Road, Manchester
Oxford Academy, The, 18 Bardwell Road Oxford OX2 6SP Tel: (01865) 53751

Oxford Brookes University, Gypsy Lane Campus, Headington, Oxford OX3
Oxford College, Oxpens Road, Oxford OX1 1SA
Oxford House College, 28 Market Place, London Tel: (0171) 580 9785
Oxford Study Centre, 17 Sunderland Avenue, Oxford OX2 8DT Tel: (01235) 554 747
Park Lane College, Park Lane, Leeds LS3 1AA Tel: (0113) 244 3011
Pilgrims Language Courses, 8 Vernon Place, Canterbury ,Kent CT1 3NG
Pitman School of English, 154 Southampton Row,London WC1B
Polyglot, 214 Trinity Road, London SW17 7HP Tel: (0181) 767 9113
Practical TEFL Training, PO Box 191, London SW1Z
Primary House, 300 Gloucester Road, Bristol BS7 8PD
Queen's University of Belfast TEFL Centre Belfast BT7 1NN Tel: (01273) 335 373
Regency School of English, Royal Crescent, Ramsgate, Kent
Regent Capital Centre, 5 Percy Street, London W1P9FB Tel: (0171) 580 6552
Regent Oxford, Godmer House Group, 90 Banbury Road, Oxford OX2 6JT Tel: (01685) 515 566
Regent School of English, Teacher Training, 4 Percy Street,London W1P
Returned Volunteer Action, 1 Amwell Street, London EC1R 1UL
Richard Language College, 43-45 Wimborne Road, Bournemouth, Dorset
Richmond Adult Community College, Clifden Road, Twickenham TW1 4LT Tel: (0181) 891 5907
ROBACO, Box 479, Admiral House 66 East Smithfield, London E1 9XY
Royal Holloway University of London English Dept, Egham Hill, Egham, Surrey TW20 0EX Tel: (01784 44 3214
Salisbury School of English, 36 Fowlers Road,Salisbury, Wiltshire SP1 Tel: (01722) 331 011
Sandwell College, Pound Road, Oldbury, W. Midland B68 8HA
Saxoncourt (UK) Ltd, 59 South Molton Street,London W1Y Tel: (0171) 499 8533
Scarborough International School, Cheswold Hall, 37 Stepney Road, Scarborough, W Yorks YO12 5BN Tel: (01723) 362 879
Schiller English Language Institute, Wickham Court, Layhams Road, West Wickham, Kent BR4 9HW Tel: (0181) 777 8069
Scot-Ed, 1-3 St Colme Street, Edingburgh EH3 6AA
Severnvale, Central Language Academy, Shrewsbury SY1 1ES
Shane English School (see Saxoncourt)
Sheffield College, The, Stradbroke Centre Spinkhill Drive, Sheffield S1B
Sheffield Hallam University, The TESOL Centre, Totley Hall Lane, Sheffield S17 4AB
Skill Share Africa, 3 Belvoir, Leicester LE1 6SL
Skola Teacher Training, 21 Star Street, London W2 1QB
SLS York, Cromwell House, 13 Ogleforth, York YO1 2JG
SOAS, University of London, Thorhaugh Street, Russell Square London WC1H OXG

South Devon College of Arts & Technology, Newton Road, Torquay,Devon TQ2 5BY
South East Essex College of Arts and Technology, Carnarvon Road, Southend-on-Sea, Essex SS2 6LS Tel: 01702 220 400
South London College, Knights Hill, West Norwood,London SE27 0TX
South Thames College, 50-52 Putney Hill, London SW 15 6QX Tel: (0181) 918 7367
Southampton Institute of Higher Education, East Park Terrace, Southampton, Hants SO9 4WW
Southend College of Technology, Dept of Gen Education & Science Carnarvon Road, Southend-on-Sea, Essex SS2 6LS
Southwark College, 209-215 Blackfriars Road,London SE1 8NL Tel: (0171) 815 2109
St Brelade's College, Mont Lex Vaux, St Brelade, Jersey JE3 8AF Tel: 01534 41305
St George's International, 4 Duke Street London, W1M 5AA Tel: (0171) 486 5481
St George's School of English, 37 Manchester St, London W1M 5PE Tel: (0171) 935 6959
St Giles, Brighton, 69 Marine Parade, Brighton, E Sussex BN2 1AD Tel: (01273) 682 747
St Giles' College, London, 51 Shepherds Hill, Highgate, London N6
St Mary's University College, Strawberry Hill, Waldegrave Road, Twickenham TW1
Stanton Teacher Training,167 Queensway, London N2 4SB Tel: (0171) 221 7259
Stevenson College, Bankhead Avenue Sighthill, Edinburgh EH11 4DE
Studio School of English, 6 Salisbury Villas, Station Road, Cambridge CB1
Stoke on Trent College, Stoke on Trent S14 2DG Tel: (01782) 208 208
Studio School, 6 Salisbury Villas, Station Road, Cambridge CB1 2JF Tel: (01223) 369 701
Students International Ltd, Melton Mowbray, Leics.
The Sudan Embassy, The Recruiting Officer, Cultural Section, 31 Rutland Gate, London W7 1PG
Surrey Language Centres, Sandford House, 39 West Street Farnham, Surrey GU9 7DR Tel: (01252) 23494
Surrey Youth and Adult Continuing Education Centre, Danesfield Centre, Grange Road, Woking, Surrey
Surrey Youth and Adult Education Area, Henriatta Parker Centre, Ray Road West Molesley, Surrey KT8 2LG
Sutton College of Liberal Arts, St Nicholas Way, Sutton, Surrey SM1
Swan School of English, 11 Guild Street, Stratford-upon-Avon CV37 6RE Tel: (01789) 269 161
Swan School of English (Oxford) 11 Banbury Road, Oxford OX2 6JX
Trebinshun Group, Brecon, Powys, Wales LD3 7PX
TEFL Training, Friends Close, Stonesfield, Witney, Oxon OX8 8PX Tel: 01993 891 686
Thames Valley University, St. Mary's Road, Ealing, London W5 3RE
Thomas C Godfrey 32 Stonegate, York, North Yorkshire YO1
Thurrock College, Love Lane, Aveley Essex RM15 4HT Tel: (01708) 863 011

Thurrock Technical College, Woodview, Grays, Essex ILM16 4YR

Trinity College, London, 11-13 Mandeville Place,, London W1M 6AQ

UCLES (University of Cambridge Local Examinations Syndicate), 1 Hills Road, Cambridge CB1

UNIPAL, 12 Helen Road, Oxford OX2

United Nations Association, UNA International Service, 3 Whitehall Court, London SW1A 2EL

UTS Oxford Centre, Wolsey Hall, 66 Banbury Road, Oxford OX2 6PR Tel: (01865) 516 162

United Nations Volunteers, c/o VSO, 317 Putney Bridge Road London SW15

Universal Language Training The Old Forge, Ockland Lane, Ockham, Surrey GU23 6NP Tel: (01483) 210083

University College Of Wales, Bangor Dept of Education, Deinol Road, Bangor LL57 2UW

University College of Wales, Cardiff P.O. Box 78, Cardiff CF1 1XL

University College of Wales, Aberyswyth, Dept of Education, Old College, King Street, Aberystwyth, Dyfed S723 2AX

University of Aberdeen, Dept of English, Aberdeen AB9 1FX

University of Aston, Language Studies Unit, Aston Triangle, Birmingham B4

University of Birmingham, Dept of English, P.O. Box 363 Birmingham B15 2TT

University of Brighton, Language Centre, Falmer, Brighton,Sussex BN1 9PH Tel: (01273) 643 344

University of Bristol, School of Education, 35 Berkley Square, Bristol BS8 1JA Tel: (0117) 928 7046

University of Central England, Perry Bar, Edgebaston, Birmingham B42 2SU

University of Durham, Elvet Riverside, 11 New Elvet, Durham DH1 3JT

University of East Anglia, School of Modern Languages, Norwich

University of Edinburgh, Applied Ling & Lang Studies 21 Hill Place, Edinburgh EH8 9DP

University of Essex, Wivenhoe Park, Colchester CO4 3SQ

University of Exeter, School of Education,St Lukes, Heavitree Road, Exeter EX1 2LV

University of Glasgow, English Lang Dept, Glasgow G12 8QQ

University of Hertfordshire Watford Campus, Aldenham, Watford Herts WD2 8AT

University of Hull, Language Centre, Cottingham Road Hull HU6 7RX

University of Kent, Inst. Lang & Ling, Cornwallis Building, Canterbury, Kent CT2 7NF

University of Lancaster, Dept of Lings & Mod Eng Lang, Lancaster LA1 L7T

University of Leeds, Overseas Education Unit School of Education, Leeds LS2

Leeds Metropolitan University Centre For Language Study, Beckett Park Campus, Leeds LS6 3QS Tel: (0113) 233 2600

University of Leicester, School of Education, 21 University Road, Leicester LE1 7RF

University of Liverpool, E L Unit, Mod Langs Building P.O. Box 147, Liverpool L69 3BX

University of London, Birbeck College, Applied Linguistics, 20 Bedford Way,London WC1H 0AL

University of London, Birbeck College, Malet St,London WC1E 7HX

University of Luton, Faculty of Humanities, 75 Castle St Luton, Beds LUI 3AJ

University of Manchester, CELSE, School of Education, Oxford Road, Manchester M13 9PL

University of Newcastle-upon-Tyne St Thomas Street, Newcastle-upon-Tyne NE1

University of Northumbria at Newcastle, Lipman Building, Newcastle-upon-Tyne NE1 8ST

University of Nottingham, Dept of English Studies University Park, Nottingham NG7 2RD

University of Oxford Delegacy of Local Examinations Ewert House, Summertown, Oxford OX2 7BZ

University of Portsmouth, Wiltshire Building, Hampshire Terrace, Portsmouth PO1 2BU

University of Reading, Centre for Applied Lang Studies, Whitenights, PO Box218 Reading, Berks RG6 2AD

University of St Andrews Buffs Wynd, St Andrews Fife KY16 9AL Tel: (01334) 462 255

University of Sheffield, ELT Centre, Arts Tower, Sheffield S10 2TN

University of Southampton, Faculty of Educational Studies, Southampton SP9 5NH Tel: (01703) 594 671

University of Stirling, Centre for ELT, Stirling FK9 4LA

University of Strathclyde, Livingstone Tower, Richmond Street,Glasgow G1

University of Surrey, English Language Institute, Guilford, Surrey Tel: (01483) 259 910

University of Sussex, Language Centre, Arts A,Falmer, Brighton BN1 9QN Tel: (01273) 678 006

University College Swansea Centre for Applied Lang Studies Swansea SA2 8PP

University of Ulster at Coleraine, Education Faculty Cromore Road, Coleraine Co. Londonderry NI BT52

University of Wales, Education Dept, Old College,King Street, Aberyswyth SY23 2AX Tel: (01970) 622 104

University of Warwick, Centre for English Lang Teaching, Westwood, Coventry CV4 Tel: (01203 523 200

University of Woverhampton Stafford St, Wolverhampton WV1 1 SB

University of Westminster School of Languages, Peter Street, London W1V

University of York, Dept of Linguistic Science & Lang Teaching Centre, Heslington, York YO1 5OD

Voluntary Services Overseas, 317 Putney Bridge Road, London SW15 Tel: 0181 780 1331

Waltham Forest College, Gen. Ed. Dept, Forest Road, Walthamstow, London E17

Waverley Adult Ed. Institute Bridge Road, Godalming, Surrey GU7 3DU

West Sussex School of English 7 High St. Steyning West Sussex BN44 3QQ Tel: (01903) 814 512

Western Language Centre Ltd Forge House, Kemble, Glos GL7 6AD

Wigston College of F.E., Station Road, Wigston Magna, Leicester LE8 2DW Tel: (0116) 288 5051

Windsor Schools, 89 Arthur Road, Windsor, Berks SL4 1RU Tel: (01753) 858 995

Woking & Chertsey Adult Ed. Institute, Danesfield Centre, Grange Road Woking, Surrey GU21 4DA

Women in TEFL, 42 Northolme Road, London N5 2UX

York Associates, 116 Micklegate York YO1 1JY Tel: 01904 624 246

AUSTRALIA

ATESOL, P O Box 296, Rozelle, NSW 2039

Australian Centre for Languages, Teacher Education Institute, 420 Liverpool Road, South Stratfield, Sydney NSW 2136 Tel: (612) 7425277

Australian College of English (C/D), P O Box 82, Bondi Junction, NSW 2022

Australian TESOL Training Centre, PO Box 82, Bondi Junction, NSW 2022 Tel: (612) 389 0249

Bond University English language Institute, Gold Coast, Queensland 4229 Tel: +61 75 595 2659

CALUSA, GPO Box 2471 Adelaide, South Australia 5001 Tel: 618 3021555

Camosun College, 3100 Fowl Bay Road, Victoria, British Columbia V8P 5J2

Canberra College of Advanced Education, P O Box 1, Canberra 2616

Centre for English Language Learning, PO Box 12058, A Beckett St., Melbourne 3001 Tel: (61) 3 963 90 300

ELICOS Association, 3 Union Street, Ayrmont, NSW 2009

Holmesglen Institute of TAFE, PO Box 42, Chadstone Victoria 3148 Tel: 61 3 9564 1819

Insearch Language Centre, University of Technology, PO Box K1206, Haymarket, NSW 2000 Tel: 612 281 4544

Institute of Technical and Adult Teacher Education (D), 62 Kameruka Road, Northbridge, 2063

International College of English, 230 Flinders Lane, Melbourne, Victoria 3000

International House Queensland, 130 Mcleod St., Cairns, Queensland 4870 Tel: (070) 313 466

International TESOL Training Centre, 185 Spring Street, Melbourne 3000

La Trobe University, Kingsbury Drive, Bundoora 3083, Victoria

Macquarie University, Sydney, N.S.W. 2109. Tel: 61 2 850 7673

Milner International College of English 1st Floor, 195 Adelaide Terrace Perth WA 6004 Tel: 61 9 325 5444

National Curriculum Resource Centre 5th Floor, 197 Rundal Mall Adelaide 5000

Overseas Service Bureau P O Box 350, 71 Argyle Street Fitroy, 3065 Victoria

Phoenix English Language Academy 223 Vicent Street North Perth 6006 Western Australia Tel: 61 227 5538

RMIT, Technisearch Centre for English Language Learning 480 Elizabeth Street, Melbourne , Victoria 3000

St Mark's International College 375 Stirling St, Highgate, Perth Western Australia Tel: (09) 227 9888

South Australian College of English 254 North Terrace, Adelaide, S. Australia 5080

Sydney College of Advanced Education Office of the Principal, Secretary & Admin, 53-57 Renwick Street, Redfern 2016, P O Box 375, Waterloo, New South Wales

University of Canberra Tesol Centre, PO box 1 Bellonen ACT University of New South Wales P O Box 1, Kensington, NSW 2033
University of Melbourne Parkville, Victoria 3052 Tel: 61 3 344 4919
University of South Australia (see CALUSA)
University of Southern Queensland Toowoomba Queensland 4350 Tel: 61 76 311 804
University of Sydney, NSW 2006
University of Tasmania at Launceston PO Box 1214 Launceston Tasmania 7250 Tel: (61 03) 243 509
University of Wollongong Northfield Av, Keiraville, NSW 2522 Tel: +42 214 678
Western Australian College of Advanced Education Rensen Street, Churchlands 6018 P O Box 217, Western Australia

AUSTRIA
International House Schwedenplatz 2/6/55, Alolo, Vienna

BRAZIL
Britannia Association for Teacher Education, Rua Nascimento Silva 154, Ipanema Rio De Janeiro
British Association for Teacher Education Brasil (Bate) Rua Vinicius De Moraes 179 Ipanema 22411, Rio
Braztesol Rua Julia da Costa 1500, 80430 Curitba PR
International House Rua 4, No 80, Setor Oeste, Goiana
LAURELS (Latin American Association of Registered English Language Schools) c/o Liberty English Centre, Rua Aminta de Barros 1, 05980 Curitiba Paran
Sociedad Cultura Brasiliera da Cultura Inglese Av Graca Aranha, 327-7CP Caixa Postal 821 Rio de Janeiro

CANADA
Canadian Council of Second Languages 151 Slater Street, Ottawa, Ontario T1P
Canadian University Services Overseas 135 Rideau Street, Ottawa
Columbia College 6037 Marlborough Ave Vancouver V6A3J3, British Columbia
Ontario Institute for Studies in Education 252 Bloor St. West, Toronto M5S 1V6
University of Alberta Edmonton AB, T6G 2G5
University of British Columbia, 2125 Main Mall, Vancouver V6T 125
University of Calgary, 2500 University Drive NW Calgary AB, T2N 1N4
Concordia University, 1455 de Maisonneuve Blvd, Montreal QC, H3G 1M8
University College of the Cariboo, Box 3010 Kamloops, British Columbia Tel: 604 828 5277
Universite Laval, Cite Universitaire, 3250 Pavillon De Koninck, Quebec, G1K 7PX Tel: 418 656 7673
McGill University 3700 McTavish Street, Montreal QC H3A 1Y2
Saint Mary's University, 923 Robie Street, Halifax, Nova Scotia, B3H 3CC Tel: 902 420 5276
University of Saskatchewan, 326 Kirk Hall, 117 Science Place, Saskatoon SK, S7N 5C8 Tel: 306 966 5563

Simon Fraser University, Burnaby BC, V5A 1S6
University of Victoria PO Box 170, Victoria BC, V8W
University of Western Ontario, Room 23, Stevenson-Lawson Building, London, Ontario N6A 5B8 Tel: 519 661 3633
University of Winnipeg, 515 Portage Avenue, Winnipeg, Manitoba, R3B 2E4

CHILE
Instituto Chileno- Britanico de Cultura Casilla 3900, Santiago

COLOMBIA
Association Colombiana de Profesores de Lenguas, Centro Oxford, Apartado Aereo 102420, Unicentro, Bogota

CYPRUS
Bridge House Bookshop, PO Box 4527, Bridgehouse Bldg, Nicosia
The English Institute, c/o The English School, Nicosia

CZECH REPUBLIC
The Bell School, Nedvezska 29, 100 00 Praha 10
International House Prague, Lupacova 1, 130 00 Praha 3 Tel:42 22 75 789

DENMARK
Association of English Teachers in Adult Education, EETAE, Toftegardsvej, 24 DK 3500 Vaerlose

ECUADOR
Ecuadorian English Teachers Society, PO Box 10935, Guayaquil.

EGYPT
American University of Cairo, Centre for Adult and Continuing Education, English Studies Division Room 407, PO Box 2511, Cairo
British Council 192 Sharia El Nil, Agouza, Cairo
International Language Institute American University El Sahafeyeen, PO Box 13, Embaba, Cairo
International Language Institute 2 Mohamed Bayoumi Street, Heliopolis, Cairo

FINLAND
Association of Teachers of English in Finland, Rautatielaisenkatu 6A 00520, Helsinki

FRANCE
Accord Ecole de Langues, 52 rue Montmartre 75002 Paris Tel: 33 1 42 21 17 44
American University of Paris 34 Ave de New-York 75116 Paris Tel: (33) 1 47 20 44 99
The British Institute, 11 Rue de Constantine, 75007 Paris
ESIEE Cite Descartes, 2Bd Blaise Pascal - BP99, 93162 Noisy-le-Grand Cedex
Executive Language Service 20 Rue Sainte-Croix-De-La-Bretonnerie 75004 Paris Tel: 44 54 58 88
International House Paris 20 Passage

Dauphine 75006 Paris Tel: 00 33 1 44 41 80 20
International Language Centre 20 Passage Dauphine, 75006 Paris
Open Doors, 130 rue de Rivoli 75001 Paris Tel: 40 28 07 84
TESOL France, 71 rue St. Denis, 75002 Paris
University Lyon 11-Formation 86 Rue Pasteur, 69007 Lyon

GERMANY
Munich English Language Teachers Association Maistrasse 21, 8000 Muenchen 2.

GREECE
British Council Plateia Philikis Etairias 17, Kolonaki Square, PO Box 3488, Athens 10216
British Council 9 Ethnikis Amynis, P O Box 10289 541013 Thessaloniki
CELT Athens, 77 Academias Str. 106 78 Athens Tel: 01 33 02406
Efstathiadis Group Olympu 34, 546 30 Thessaloniki
PROFILE A Frantzi & Kallirois St., 11745, Athens Tel: 9222 065 9241 543
Study Space, Pavlou Mela 19, Thessalonika 54622 Tel: 3031 269 697
TESOL Greece 87 Academis Street, Athens

HONG KONG
The British Council English Language Institute Easey Commercial Building 255 Hennessy Road

HUNGARY
International House PO Box 95, Budapest 1364 Tel: (361) 212 4219
BELL Iskolak Kft Tulipan u. 8. 1022 Budapest II
Kecskemet Association for Teachers of English Akademia Korut , 20.1.31 Kecsemet 6000.

INDONESIA
The British Institute, Setiabudi Building 2, Jalan HR Rasuna Said, Jakarta 1292
The British Institute, Jalan RE Martadinata 63 40115 Bandung
TBI, Setiabudi Building 2, Jalan HR Rasuhna Said, Jakarta Tel: 525 6750

IRELAND
Academy of Education, 44 Lower Leeson Street, Dublin 2
Alpha College of English, 4 North Great George St, Dublin 2
Bluefeather School of Languages, Montpelier House, Montpelier Parade, Monkstown, Dublin Tel: 280 6288
Centre of English Studies, 31 Dame Street, Dublin 2
Cork Language Centre International, Wellington House, St Patrick's Place, Wellington Road, Cork
Dublin School of English, 11 West Moreland Street, Dublin 2
Emerald Cultural Institute, 10 Palmerston Park, Rathgar, Dublin 6
English Language Education Institute, 30 The Mall, Tralee, Co. Kerry

English Language Studies Institute, 99 St. Stephen's Green, Dublin 2
Excel International College of Languages, IDA Enterprise Centre, North Mall, Cork City Tel: 353 21 304 770
Foyle Language Centre, 73 Clarendon Street, Derry, BT48 7ER Tel: 01504 371 535
Galway Language Centre, The Bridge Mills, Galway
Grafton International, Dublin, Tel: 353 1 494 6576
Grafton Tuition, Grafton Buildings, 34 Grafton Street, Dublin 2
International Study Centre, 67 Harcourt Street, Dublin 2
Irish College of English, 6 Church Road, Malahide, Dublin Tel: 353 1 845 3744
Irish Tourist Board, Baggot Street Bridge, Dublin 2
Langtrain International, Torquay Road, Foxrock, Dublin 18
Language Centre of Ireland, 9-11 Grafton Street, Dublin 2
NATEFLI National Association of Teachers of English as a Foreign Language in Ireland PO Box 1917, Dublin 2
Shannonside Language Centre Coolbawn Nenagh Co. Tipperary Tel: 353 67 28062
TEFL Training Institute of Ireland, 38 Harrington Street, Dublin 8 Tel: 353 1 478 4035
Trinity College, Centre for Language and Communication Studies, Dublin 2
University College of Dublin, Belfield, Dublin 4
Words Language Sevices, 109 Lower Baggot Street, Dublin 2 Tel: 661 0240
Westlingua Language School, Cathedral Blds, Middle Steet, Galway Tel: 353 91 568 188

ITALY
Academia Brittanica, International House, Viale Manzoni 57, 00185 Rome
AISLI, British Institute, via Quattro Fontane 109, Rome
BMC-Bell School of English Viale dei Mille, 2, 42100 Reggio Emilia
British Council Milan Via Manzoni 38, 20121 Milan Tel: 00 39 2 7722 2216
British Council Naples, Via Dei Mille 48, 80121 Naples Tel: (0039 81) 421 321
British Institute , Via S Stefano 11, 40125 Bologna
British Institute of Florence, Via Tornabuoni 2, 50123 Firenze
British School of Friuli- Venezia Giulia, Via Torrebianca 18, 34-132 Trieste
British School of Milan, Via Montenapoleone 5, 20121 Milan.
British Schools, Viale Liegi 14, Rome
Cambridge School Verona Via San Rocchetto 3, 37121 Verona Tel: 045 800 3154
CLM-Bell, Via Pozzo 30, 38100 Trento
CLM-Bell, Via Canella 14, 38066 Riva del Garda
International House Rome, Viale Manzoni 22, 00185 Rome Tel: 704 76894
Regent School of Rome, Via Monterone 4, 00185 Rome
The British School, Via Montenapoleone 5, 20121 Milan
The Milan Training Centre , Via Fabio Filzi 27, 20131 Milano

JAPAN
The British Council, 2 Kagurazaka 1, Chome Shinjuku-Ku, Tokyo 164
International Education Service, Shin Taiso Building, 2-10-7 Dogensaka, Shibuya-ku, Tokyo 150
International Language Centre, Iwanami Jimbocho Building 9F, 2-1 Kanda Jimbocho Chiyoda-Ku, Tokyo 101 Tel: (03) 3264 7464
International Language Centre, Shirakabe Building 7F, Shibata 114-7, Kita-Ku, Osaka
JALT (The Japan Association of Language Teachers) Lions Mansion Kawaramachi 111, Kawaramachi Matsubara-Agaru Shimogyo-ku, Kyoto 600
Language Resources Ltd, Tayo Bldg 6F, 1-2 Kitanagasa-Dori, 5-Chome, Chuo-Ku, Kobe-Shi, F650 Tel: 81 78 382 0394
Saxoncourt Teacher Training, Horiki Bldg 2F, 2-18-3 Gyotoku Ekimae, Ichikawa shi, Chiba ken, Japan 272-01. Tel: 0473 565 256
Stanton School of English, Ikebukuro School (Academic Division) 5F West Building, Higashi Ikebukoro, Toshima-Ku, Tokyo 170

KOREA
TESOL Korea, Kangnung University San-1, Chi byon-dong, Kangnung, Kang-won-do 210-702

KUWAIT
The British Council, P O Box 345, Safat
International Language Centre Military Language Institute P O Box 3310, Salmiya 22034

LUXEMBOURG
Association Luxembourgeoise des Ensiegnants d'Anglais BP 346, L-2013 Luxembourg
English Language Centre 65 Avenue Gaston Diderich, 1420

MALAYSIA
British Council Language Centre, P O Box 595, 10770 Penang
British Council Language Centre, 3rd Floor, Wisma Hangsam Box20, 1 Jalan Hang Lekir 5000 K.L.

MALTA
NSTS English Language Institute 220 St Paul Street, Valletta VLT 07 Tel: (356) 244 983

MEXICO
Anglo Mexican Cultural Institutes Antonio Caso 127, Mexico 4, D.F.
Institute Anglo-Mexicano de Cultura AC, Felipe Villanueva No 52, Colonia Guadalupe Inn, 01020 DF
Institute Anglo-Mexicano de Cultura AC APDO 12755, Guadalajara, Jalisco
Institute Anglo-Mexicano de Cultura Plaza Crystal 9-12A Blvd Valsequilo y Cir. Int., Puebla Pve, CP 72440

NEW ZEALAND
Auckland Language Centre, 1-11 Short Sreet, PO Box 1652, Auckland, Tel: (649) 303 1962
Auckland Institute of Technology, School of Languages, 450 Queen Street, Private Bag 92006, Auckland
Capital Language Academy PO Box 1100, Wellington Tel: 64 4 472 7997
Dominion English Schools, 47 Customs St. East Auckland Tel: 64 0 9377 3280
FIELSNZ, PO Box 2577,Auckland,
International Language Academy South Pacific Ltd, 21 Kilmore Street, PO Box 25170, Christchurch Tel: 3 379 5452
Languages International, Po Box 5293, Wellesley St, Auckland Tel: 64 9 309 0615
Massey University, Dept of Linguistics and Second Language Teaching, Palmerston North
NZEIL, PO Box 10500, Wellington,
Seafield School of English, 99 Seaview Road, New Brighton, PO Box 18516, Christchurch Tel: 03 388 3850
University of Waikato Language Institute, PO Box 1317, Waikato Mail Centre, Hamilton. Tel 64 7 838 4193
Victoria University of Wellington, PO Box 600, Wellington Tel: 64 4 471 5316

NORWAY
LMS Modern Language Association of Norway, Jonas Liesvei, 1B 1412 Sofiemyr.

OMAN
Polyglot Institute Oman, PO Box 221 Ruwi - Code 112 Tel: (968) 701261
British Council Muscat, PO Box 73 Postal Code 115 Medinet Qaboos Tel: 00 968 600 548

PAKISTAN
SPELT, F 25 D, Block 9, Clifton, Karachi 75600

PARAGUAY
Centro Anglo Paraguay, Artigas 356, Asuncion

PERU
Asociacion Cultural Peruano Britanica, Av Arequipa 3495, San Isidro, Lima 27 Tel: (5114) 468 787
Newton College, Apartado 18-0873, Miraflores, Lima 18

POLAND
The British Council, AL. Jerocolimskie 59, 00-697, Warsaw
Gama-Bell School of English, ul Smolensk 29, 31-112 Krakow

PORTUGAL
APPI, Associaco Portuguese de Professores de Ingles Apartado 2885, 1122 Lisbon
Cambridge School, Avenida da Liberdade, 173, 1250 Lisbon Tel: 352 7474
Institute Britanico Em Portugal, Rua Cecilio de Sousa 65, 1294 Lisbon Codex
International House, Rua Marques Sa Da Bandiera 16, 1000 Lisbon

QATAR
British Council, PO Box 2992, Doha,

SINGAPORE
Art Language Centre, 7th & 8th Floors, Tanglin Shopping Centre, Tanglin, 1024

SOUTH AFRICA
English Language Educational Trust, 74 Aliwal Street, Durban 40

SPAIN
Academia de Idiomas Lacunza, Urbieta 14-1, San Sebastian 20006
APAC Associaco de Professors D'Angles de Catalunya Apartado 2287, 08080 Barcelona
Association de Professors de Ingles de Galicia, Apartado de Correo 1078 Santiago de Compostela
British Council, Calle Almagro 5, 28010 Madrid
British Council, Teacher Development Unit, General Martinez Campos 31, 28010 Madrid
British Language Centre, Bravo Murillo 377/2, 28020 Madrid Tel: (010341) 733 0739
Campbell College Teacher Training Centre, Calle Pascual y Genis 11-3 46002 Valencia Tel: (34) 6 352 4217
International House, Zurbano 8, 28010 Madrid
International House Barcelona, Trafalgar 14 Entlo, Barcelona 08010, Tel: (343) 268 4511
International House, Escuela Industrial 12, 08201 Sabadell,Barcelona
International House, Pascual y Genis 16, 46002 Valencia
International House, Paseo de Mallorca 36, Palma de Mallorca 07012
International House Madrid C/Zurbano 8, 28010 Madrid Tel: 010 34 1 310 1314
Novalingua/Oxford House College, Traversa de Gracia 15, Barcelona Tel: 93 209 7730
Stanton School of English, Montera 24 2 Piso, 28013 Madrid
TESOL Spain, Universidad de Cordoba, Departmento de Ingles, Cordoba 10678
York House Language Centre, Mutaner 479, 08021 Barcelona

SRI LANKA
Colombo International School, 28 Gregory's Road, Colombo 7

SWEDEN
Kursverksamheten Vid, Lunds Universitet, Regementsgatan 4, 21142 Malmo
Kursverksamheten Vid, Stockholms Universitet, P O Box 7845, 10398 Stockholm
LMS Lars Ake Kall, Wallingaten 12, S111 60 Stockholm

SWITZERLAND
ASC Langues, 72 Rue de Lausanne, 1202 Geneva Tel: 41 22 731 8520
Bell Language School Geneva, ELCRA-Bell, 12 Chemin Des Colombettes 12-2 Geneva Tel: 740 2022
Bell Language School Zurich, Genferstrabe 23, 8002 Zurich Tel: 01 281 0781
Benedict - Schools, P O Box 300, CH1000 Lausanne 9 Berlitz, 1 Carrefour de Rive1207 Geneva Tel: (022) 786 1476
Castle's English Institute Baarerstr 63, 6300 Zug Tel: (041) 710 55 70
Ecole Lemania, 3 Chemin de Preville, 1001 Lausanne
Ecole de Langue Anglaise, Ch. de Mornex 11, Ch - 1003, Lausanne Tel: 021 323 23 30
ETAS (English Teachers' Association Switzerland) Bolsternstrasse 22, 8483 Kollbrun
inlingua, Weisenhuasplatz 28, 3011 Berne
Klubschule Migros, Oberer Graben 35, 9000 St Gallen
Volkshochschule Zurich Limmatquai 62, CH 8001 Zurich Tel: 01 261 28 32

TAIWAN
Saxoncourt, 4F, 271 Hsin Yi Rd, Section 2, Taipei, Taiwan, R.O.C. Tel: 886 2351 7755

TURKEY
Bilkent University School of English Language PO Box 40, 06660 Kucukesat Ankara
British Council Ankara, 9 Kirlangic Sokak, Gaziosmanpasa 06700 Ankara
British Council Istanbul, Ors Turistik Is Merkezi Istiklal Caddesi 251-253, Kat 2,3,5, Beyoglu Istanbul 80060 Tel: (212) 252 7474
British Council Izmir, Ismet Kaptan Mahallesi, 1374 Sokak, Selvili Is Merkezi No: 18 K: 3 D: 301-306 Cankaya 35210 Izmir Tel: (0232) 446 01 3132
English Preparatory School, Eastern Mediterranean UniversityPO Box 95, Gazi Magusa Mersin 70 Tel: 392 366 6588
Istanbul Turco-British Association Suleyman Nazif Sokak 10 Nisantasi, 80220 Istanbul
METU, DBE, Dept of Basic English, Ankara 06531
School of Languages, Bogazici University, PK2 Bebek, Istanbul

THAILAND
St John's-Bell Language Centre, St John's College, Ladprao Bangkok 10900
Assumption Thonburi-Bell Language Centre, Bangphai, Pasicharoen, Bangkok 10160

UNITED ARAB EMIRATES
The British Council, P O Box 6523, Abu Dhabi
Abu Baker Cultural & Scientific Institute, PO Box 81199, North Al Yahir, Al Ain. Tel: 971 3 827 227
ECS Ltd, PO Box 25018, Abu Dhabi

UNITED STATES OF AMERICA
American Language Academy, 2105 Grove Street, Berkeley California 94704
Berlitz International Inc Research Park, 2923 Wall Street, Princeton NJ 08540
Coast Language Academy, 200 S.W. Market Street, Suite 111, Portland, Oregon, 97201 Tel: 1503 224 1960
ELS,5761-6 Buckingham Parkway,Culver City CA 90230
English International, 655 Sutter Street (Suite 500), San Francisco Ca 94102
ERIC, Centre for Applied Linguistics, 118 22nd Street NL, Washington DC
Eastern Mennonite University 1200 Park Road, Harrisonburg VA 22801
Eurocentres 101 North Union Street, Suite 3000 Alexandria, Virginia VA 22314
Goshen College, 1700 S-Main St, Goshen IN 46526
International Language Institute, 1601 Connecticut Avenue NW, Washington DC 20009
International Educator (The) International Educators Institute, PO Box 103 West Bridgewater MA 02379
inlingua School of Languages 551 Fifth Avenue, New York NY 10176
International School of Languages, P O Box 6188, 958 W Pico Boulevard 90212 Beverley Hills, CA
Monterey Institute of International Studies, 425 Van Buren Street, Monterey California 93940
Old Dominion University, Dept. of English Norfolk, VA 23529-0078
Peace Corps, 1990 K St NW, Washington DC 20526
St Giles College Educational Trust, 2280 Powell Street, 94133 San Francisco CA
School For International Training, Brattleboro, Vermont 05301
School of Teaching EFL, 2601 NW 56th St, Seatle WA 98107
TESOL, 1600 Cameron Street, Suite 300, Alexandria, Virginia 22314-2705
Adelphi University, Harvey Hall, Room 130, Garden City, New York 11530
University of Alabama Department of English, Morgan Hall PO Box 870244, Tuscaloosa Alabama 35487-0244
The American University, Asbury Building, Room 326, 4400 Massachusetts Avenue NW, Washington DC 20016-8045
University of Arizona, Department of English, Modern Languages Room 458 Tucson, Arizona 85721
Arizona State University Language and Literature BuildingRoom B504, Tempe Arizona 85287-0302
Azusa Pacific University, 901 East Alosta Avenue, Azusa California 91702-7000
Ball State University, Department of English, Muncie, Indiana 47306
Biola University, Marshburn Hall, 13800 Biola Avenue, La Mirada, California 90639-0001
Boston University, TESOL Program, School of Education 605 Commonwealth Avenue Boston, Mass 02215
University of California at Davis, Titus Hall, Room 130, Davis, California 95616
University of California at Los Angeles, Dept of TESL and Applied Linguistics, 3300 Rolfe Hall, 405 Hilgard Avenue, Los Angeles, California 90024
California State University, Dominguez Hills, Carson, California 90747
California State University, Fresno, Leon S Peters Building Room 383, 5245 North Backer Avenue, Fresno, California 93740
California State University, Fullerton, Humanities Building Room 835C Fullerton, California 92634
California State University, Long Beach 1250 Bellflower Boulevard Long Beach,

California 90840-2403
California State University, Northridge, Sierra North 318, Northridge, California 91330
California State University, Sacramento, 6000 J Street, Sacramento California 95819-2694
University of Colorado, Admissions Committee Chair, Linguistics-Box 295, Boulder, Colorado 80309-0295
University of Delaware Department of Educational Studies 206 Willard Hall, Newark, Delaware 19716
East Carolina University, GCB 2201 Greenville, North Carolina 27858-4353
Eastern Michigan University Foreign Languages and Bilingual Studies, 219 Alexander, Ypsilanti, Michigan 48197
Eastern Washington University, Mailstop #34, Dept. of Modern languages, Cheny, WA99004 Tel: 509 359 2259
University of Florida, 112 Anderson Hall,Gainesville, Florida 32611
Florida International University School of Education DM 291Tamiami Trail Miami Florida 33199
Fordham University at Lincoln Center Room 1025, 113 West 60th Street, New York NY 10023
George Mason University, Department of English, Fairfax, Virginia 22030
Georgetown University, School of Languages and Linguistics, Washington DC 20057
University of Georgia, Aderhold 125, Athens, Georgia 30602
Georgia State University, Atlanta, Georgia 30302-4018
Harvard University, 54 Dunster Street, Cambridge, Mass 02138
University of Hawaii at Manoa, Moore Hall 570, 1890 East-West Road, Honolulu, Hawaii 96822
Hofstra University, 236 Gallon Wing, Mason Hall, Hempstead, New York 11550
University of Houston, University Park, Department of English, Houston, Texas 77004
Hunter College of the CUNY, Department of Curriculum and Teaching, West Building Room 1025, 695 Park Avenue Box 568, New York 10021
University of Idaho, Dept of English, Moscow, Idaho 83843
University of Illinois at Chicago Department of Linguistics Box 4348, Chicago, Illinois 60680
Illinois State University, Normal, Illinois 61761
Indiana University, Department of Linguistics, Lindley Hall 401, Bloomington,Indiana 47405
Inter American University of Puerto Rico, San German Campus, Call Box 5100, San German, Puerto Rico 00683
Inter American University of Puerto Rico, Metropolitan Campus, PO Box 1293, San Juan, Puerto Rico 00919-1293
University of Iowa, Iowa City, Iowa 52242
Iowa State University, Department of English, 203 Ross Hall, Ames, Iowa 50011
University of Kansas, 427 Blake Hall Lawrence, Kansas 66045-2140
University of Miami, 222 Merrick Building, PO Box 248065, Coral Gables, Florida 33124
Michigan State University, Center for International Programs, East Lansing,

Michigan 48824-1035
University of Minnesota, 1425 University Avenue Southeast, Minneapolis, Minnesota 55455
University of Mississippi, School of Education, Room 152b, University of Mississippi 38677
Monterey Institute of International Studies, 425 Van Buren Street, Monterey, California 93940
Nazareth College, 4245 East Avenue, Rochester, New York 14618, University of Nevada, Reno, Reno, Nevada 89557-0031
University of New Mexico, Mesa Visa Hall 3090, Albuquerque, New Mexico 87131
College of New Rochelle, Chidwick 103, Castle Place, New Rochelle, New York 10805-2308
New York University, TESOL, 829 Shrimkin Hall, 50 West 4th Street, New York NY 10003
State University of New York at Albany, TESOL Program, Albany, New York 12222
State University of New York at Buffalo, Dept of Learning & Instruction, 593 Christopher Baldy Hall Buffalo, New York 14260
State University of New York at Stony Brook, Dept of Linguistics, Stony Brook, New York 11794-4376
Northern Illinois University, Dekalb, Illinois 60115 Tel: 815 753 6625
Northern Arizona University, Box 6032, Flagstaff, Arizona 86011-6032
University of Northern Iowa, Baker Hall 155, Cedar Falls, Iowa 50614-0502
Notre Dame College, 2321 Elm Street, Manchester, New Hampshire 03104
Nova University, 3301 College Avenue, Fort Lauderdale, Florida 33314
Old Dominion University, Norfolk, Virginia 23529-0078
University of the Pacific, School of Education, 3601 Pacific Avenue, Stockton, California 95211
Pennsylvania State University, 305 Sparks Building University Park, Pennsylvania 16802
University of Pittsburgh, 2816 Cathedral of Learning, Pittsburgh, Pennsylvania, 15260 Tel: 412 624 5900
Portland State University, PO Box 751, Portland, Oregon 97207-0751
University of Puerto Rico, Rio Pedras, Puerto Rico 00931
Rhode Island College, Mann 043, 600 Mount Pleasant Avenue, Providence, Rhode Island 02908
St Giles' Language Teaching Centre, 1 Hallidie Plaza (Suite 350), San Francisco, CA 94102. Tel: (1415) 788 3552
Saint Michael's College, Center for International Programs, Winooski Park, Colchester, Vermont 05439
Sam Houston State University, Teacher Education Centre, Huntsville, Texas Tel: 409 294 1104
University of San Francisco, School of Education, 2130 Fulton San Francisco, California 94117
San Francisco State University, Department of English, 1600 Holloway Avenue, San Francisco, California 94132
San Jose State University, San Jose, California 95192
Seton Hall University, 400 South Orange Avenue, South Orange, New Jersey 07079

University of South Carolina, Linguistics Program, Tampa, Florida 33620
Southeast Missouri State University, Grauel Language Arts Building, Room 208B, Cape Girardeau, Missouri 63701
University of Southern California, Dept of Linguistics, Los Angeles, California 90089-1693
Southern Illinois University at Carbondale, Faner 3236, Carbondale, Illinois 62901
University of Southern Maine, 400 Bailey Hall, Gorham, Maine 04038
University of Southern Mississippi, George Hurst Building, Room 110, Southern Station Box 5038, Hattiesburg, Mississippi 39406
Syracuse University, 316 HB Crouse, Syracuse NY13244-9489,
Teachers College of Columbia University, 525 West 120 Street , New York NY10027
Temple University, Ritter Hall, Broad and Montgomery, Philadelphia, Pennsylvania 19122
University of Texas at Arlington, Box 19559, Arlington, Texas 76019
University of Texas at Austin, Education Building 528, Austin, Texas 78712
University of Texas at San Antonio, 6900 North Loop 1604W, San Antonio, Texas 78259
University of Texas Pan American, Edinburg Texas 78539
Texas Womens University, Box 23029, Denton, Texas, 76204 Tel: 817 898 2040
University of Toledo, University Hall 5040, Toledo, Ohio 43606-3390
United States International University, Daley Hall of Science, Room 307, 10455 Pomerado Road, Poway, California 92131
University of Utah OSH 341, Salt Lake City Utah 84112
University of Washington, English Graduate Office GN-30, Seattle, Washington 98195
Washington State University, Pullman, Washington 99164-5020
West Chester University, Main Hall 550, West Chester, Pennsylvania 19383
Western Kentucky University, Bowling Green, Kentucky 42101
University of Wisconsin-Madison, Department of English, 5134 Helen C White Hall, 600 North Park Street, Madison, Wisconsin 5370
University of Wisconsin-Milwaukee, Enderis Hall, Room 355, PO Box 413, Milwaukee, Wisconsin 53201
USIA Information Agency, English Language Teaching Division, 301 4th Street South WestWashington DC 20547
Worldteach, Phillips Brooks House, Harvard University, Cambridge, Mass 02138
Worldwide Teachers Development Institute, 266 Beacon St., Boston, MA 02116, Tel: 617 262 5722
Wright State University, 438 Millet Hall, Colonel Glenn Highway, Dayton, Ohio

URUGUAY
Dickens Institute, 21 de Setiembre 244, CP 11300, Montevideo Tel: 5982 707 555
Instituto Cultural Anglo-Uruguayo, San Jose 1426, Montevideo Tel: 92 3773

Index Of Advertisers

Aberdeen College	42	International House, London	37, 91, 96, IFC
ACTDEC	35	International House, Portugal	46
Anglo Continental	172	International House, Rome	46
Aston University	95	International House, USA	49
ATT	49	Intuition Languages	104
Australian Centre for Languages	49	ITS English School, Hastings	39
Basil Paterson College	42	ITTC	39
BBC English	190	Kingsway	36
BEBC	203	Language Project, The	95
Bell Language Schools	36	Linguarama	96
Bradford & Ilkley College	42	Lloyds Bank	122
British Council	44	London Guildhall University	38
British Council, Naples	46	Lydbury English Centre	188
British Language Centre, Madrid	46	Lynda Hazlewood Language Services	35, 187
Buckswood International	104	Lyon Pilcher	121
Cambridge School	44	Merit Audio Visual	202
Cambridge University Press	186	Moray House	90
Campbell College, Spain	46	Multi Lingua	41
Canterbury Christ Church College	94	New College Durham	187
CELT Athens	47	NSTS, Malta	44
Central European Training Program	98	OISE	187
CfBT	96	Oxford House College	OBC
Chichester Institute	93	P J Hayman	119
City of Bath College	40	Pendragon	188
CMDT	114	Personal English Tutors,	104
Colchester Institute	36	Pitman	73
College of Preceptors	35	Redcliff English Study Centre	104
Collingham Brown & Brown	185	Regency School of English	40
Concorde International	41	Robaco	35
Derwent Executive Language	188	Saudi Development and Training Company	98
Devon School of English	41	Saxoncourt Recruitment	98
Dyned International	202	Sels College	186
Eagle Star	120	Shane English School	188
Eastbourne School of English	38	Sheffield Hallam University	42, 94
ECC(Thailand)	46	Southwark College	42
Ecole de Langue Anglaise	185	St George	172
Ecole Lemania	187	St Giles	36
Edinburgh Tutorial College	41	St Mary's University College	95
EF	96	St. Brelades	42
ELT Banbury	40, 187	St. Georges	91
Embassy Study Tours	104	Stanton Teacher Training	38
English Express	201	Students International Ltd	41
English Home Tuition Scheme	187	Studio School	42
English International	48	TEFL Training	35
English Language Centre Dublin	185	The English Language Centre	185
English Worldwide	98	TOEFL	4
Eurolink	35	Trinity College London	37
Eurotunnel	186	UCLES	6
Excel International	47	University College Cork	49
Executive Language Services	98	University of Aberdeen	188
Extrasure	119	University of California, Riverside	48
Foyle Language Centre	47	University of Edinburgh	91
Frances King Teacher Training	42	University of Essex	90
Gateshead College	185	University of Hertfordshire	95
Gateway Language	188	University of Leeds	94
GEOS English Academy	39	University of Liverpool	93
Grafton International	35	University of Manchester	92
Hammersmith & West London College	39	University of Oxford	194
HarperCollins Electronic Reference	202	University of Portsmouth	41
Harrogate Language Academy	188	University of Reading	92, 172
Harrow House	39	University of Sheffield	95
Hawaii Pacific University	45	University of Southhampton	95
Hilderstone College	38	University of Southern Queensland	43
Hospital for Tropical Diseases	119	University of Stirling	94
House of English	185	University of Surrey	50
IATEFL	194	University of Waikato	47
ILI, Leeds	39	University of Wales	93
Insearch Language Centre	49	University of Warwick	91
International Business Images	190	Westminster College	40
International House Madrid	43	Windsor Schools TEFL	40
International House, Barcelona	44	Worldwide Teachers Development Institute	48, 185
International House, Budapest	46	Worldwide Travel Insurance	118
International House, Hastings-Paris-Prague	45		

Index

ACTDEC	33	ESP (English for		Peace Corps	108
Agents	105, 111	Specific Purposes)	76, 80	Peru	170
Argentina	164	Estonia	139	PhD	58, 67
ATT	18			Poland	141
Audio Lingual	198	Financial Planning	121	Portugal	131
Australia	20, 53, 73, 107, 108,	Finding Work	100, 101, 106, 107, 113	Publishing	111
Austria	123	Finland	125	Recruitment Agencies	113
		France	126	RELSA	18
Bahrain	146	Functional Approach	197	Returned Volunteer Action	108
Bangladesh	162			Romania	142
Belgium	124	Georgia	140	RSA/Cambridge Certificate	11, 13
Bookshops	203	Germany	127	RSA/Cambridge Diploma	53, 55
Botswana	152	Greece	128	Russia	143
Brazil	165	Homestay	105		
British Council	11, 32, 53, 105	Hong Kong	155	Saudi Arabia	149
Brunei	154	Hungary	140	Self Employment	105, 109
Bulgaria	137			Serbia and Montenegro	144
Business English	80, 175, 176, 178	In-House Training	31	Singapore	159
		Indonesia	156	Situational Teaching	197
Cambodia	154	Insurance	121	Slovakia	144
Canada	19, 62, 106	Internet	199	Slovenia	144
Careers	100, 111, 113	Israel	147	South Korea	160
		Italy	129	Spain	133
CD-ROM	189,			Specialising	76
CEELT	87	Jamaica	169	Sri Lanka	163
Certificates	11,	Japan	156	Sudan	153
Chile	166	Jobshops	113	Summer Schools	101
China	154	Jordan	147	Swaziland	153
College of Preceptors	33			Sweden	136
Colombia	166	Kuwait	148	Switzerland	136
Communicative Approach	197			Syria	150
Costa Rica	168	Language Audit	178		
COTE	12, 26	Loans	9	Taiwan	160
Croatia	137	Lithuania	141	TESOL	19, 62, 106
Cuba	168			Thailand	161
Cultural Studies	76	Malaysia	158	Translation	111
Cyprus	138	Masters Degrees	62, 67, 73	Trinity College Certificate	11, 16
Czech Republic	139	Medical Cover	117	Trinity College Licentiate	
		Methodology	197	Diploma	53, 56
Denmark	125	Mexico	169	Tunisia	150
Diplomas	53, 58, 63, 74	Morocco	148	Turkey	145
		Mozambique	152		
Distance Learning	32	Multimedia	189, 199	United Arab Emirates	151
DOTE	12, 55	Myanmar (Burma)	159	United Nations Volunteers	108
				University Courses	58, 62, 73
EAP	76	Nepal	162	Uruguay	171
East European Partnership	108	Netherlands	130	USA	19, 62, 106
Ecuador	168	New Zealand	20, 73, 107		
EL Gazette	113	Newspapers	113	Venezuala	171
Egypt	146			Volunteer Services Abroad	108
ELICOS	20	Oman	149	VSO	108
ESL (English as a		Overseas Service Bureau	108		
Second Language)	79			World Teach	108
		Papua New Guinea	163	Young Learners	11, 77, 101